The Evolution
of Grammar

· · ·

•   •   •

The Evolution of Grammar

TENSE, ASPECT, AND MODALITY IN THE
LANGUAGES OF THE WORLD

• • •

Joan Bybee
Revere Perkins and
William Pagliuca

The University of Chicago Press
• Chicago and London •

Joan Bybee is professor of linguistics at the University of New Mexico. She is the author of *Morphology: A Study in the Relation between Meaning and Form*. Revere Perkins is the author of *Deixis, Grammar, and Culture*. William Pagliuca is a researcher in the Department of Linguistics at the University of Illinois at Urbana-Champaign.

The University of Chicago Press, Chicago 60637
The University of Chicago Press, Ltd., London
© 1994 by The University of Chicago
All rights reserved. Published 1994
Printed in the United States of America

03 02 01 00 99 98 97 96 95 94   1 2 3 4 5

ISBN: 0-226-08663-1 (cloth)
      0-226-08665-8 (paper)

Library of Congress Cataloging-in-Publication Data

Bybee, Joan L.
   The evolution of grammar : tense, aspect, and modality in the languages of the world / Joan Bybee, Revere Perkins, and William Pagliuca.
      p.   cm.
   Includes bibliographical references and index.
   1. Grammar, Comparative and general—Grammaticalization.
2. Linguistic change. 3. Grammar, Comparative and general—Tense. 4. Grammar, Comparative and general—Aspect. 5. Modality (Linguistics). I. Perkins, Revere D. (Revere Dale) II. Pagliuca, William. III. Title.
P299.G73B93 1994
415—dc20   93-43517
                                            CIP

Contents

• • •

Figures and Tables

• • •

Preface and Acknowledgments

This book is the primary report on the GRAMCATS project, originally funded by the National Science Foundation as "A Cross-Linguistic Study of Grammatical Categories" (BNS 83–18262). Other shorter reports appeared in 1990 in "On the Asymmetries in the Affixation of Grammatical Material" and in 1991 in "Back to the Future." It was a long-term and complex project to which a number of funding agencies and a number of individuals contributed. In order to give the reader an idea of how such a project is organized and implemented, in this preface we sketch the stages of development of the project and the contributions of the various individuals and agencies at each stage.

The initial formulation of the theory and method for the project in 1983 was inspired by the research that Joan Bybee was conducting for her book that was published in 1985. On the one hand she was verifying that one could study grammatical categories in a large number of languages with reference grammars, and on the other, she saw that insight into grammaticization could be gained by the cross-linguistic comparison of unrelated languages. The seminal idea was based on the finding (reported in Bybee 1985) that deontic or agent-oriented modalities usually have periphrastic expression while subordinating and epistemic moods are usually inflectional. The diachronic interpretation of this finding is that the former develop into the latter via grammaticization. Her hope was that if categories in other semantic domains with periphrastic and inflectional expression were considered, similar diachronic correspondences would emerge.

The methodology of the project was based on the method Bybee was already employing in her work on morphology, which in turn had been based on the work that Revere Perkins reported on in his dissertation (Perkins 1980). Perkins had already made a strong case for rigorous and appropriate sampling techniques in his work, and he had extracted relevant grammatical information from reference grammars in the search for statistical tendencies. Diachronic avenues of explanation had always been prominent in Bybee's work, as in the work of others, such as Greenberg and Givón, and the notion of grammaticization played a clear, though not yet prominent, role in functional and typological linguistics. The topics to be explored, form-meaning parallels in grammaticization and the nature of semantic change in grammaticization, which at that point appeared to be largely reductive, suggested interesting correspondences with phonological change, which also appears to be largely reductive, a topic researched in William Pagliuca's dissertation (Pagliuca 1982). Also explored there was the conception of phonological change in terms of evolutionary pathways and the retention of earlier detail, and the potential of these concepts in addressing problems of reconstruction. Thus Bybee asked Perkins and Pagliuca to join the project as research associates, if funding could be obtained to pay their salaries. In the summer of 1983, Bybee wrote a grant proposal and submitted it to NSF.

The project was funded by NSF, but not in the full amount requested. Additional support was sought from Joan Bybee's parents, Robert and Elizabeth Bybee of Houston, Texas, whose generous contributions were matched by funds from the Exxon Foundation. By the time this book was finished, the contributions of the Bybees and the Exxon Foundation had exceeded the amounts of the original and supplemental grants from NSF. We are extremely grateful for their support. Other essential support, in the form of research assistants and space, was contributed by the Department of Linguistics at the State University of New York at Buffalo under the chairmanship of Wolfgang Wölck.

Early in 1984, Perkins designed the language sample (see chap. 2 and app. A) and implemented the design by making the original selection of languages. The languages were selected randomly without prior knowledge of the availability of reference material. Thus one of the major efforts early in the project was the search for reference material on the selected languages. This process was begun in the summer of 1984 by Bybee and Pagliuca and continued in the fall primarily by Pagliuca, with the help of Perkins. When it became evident that no adequate material existed on a selected language, Perkins selected replacement languages. Pagliuca had primary responsibility for securing the reference material once the bibliographic data were available, and he was aided in this task by Tom Willett and Soon Ae Chun.

The hardware and software was selected and installed by Perkins, who also designed the database and implemented it in R:BASE and wrote the data input and output programs.

In weekly meetings over the five years in Buffalo, theory and method underwent considerable elaboration, refinement, and evaluation. From the outset, our intention was to come as close as possible to establishing a set of hypotheses that would be both comprehensive in scope and testable on the database we were building. All three of us contributed to the development of the theory and method as represented in the results reported here, with Bybee and Pagliuca more often proposing and exploring specific hypotheses and Perkins more often evaluating how we might best insure that their formulation allow for rigorous testing.

The final aspect of the project set-up was the design of a coding procedure—a procedure for extracting the information we needed from the reference material. This process was led by Bybee, based on her previous experience with coding morphological data, and benefited from the input of Pagliuca and Perkins.

The most time-consuming, difficult, and tedious task of the project was the actual coding of the reference material. For each language we answered approximately thirty-five questions about each grammatical morpheme associated with the verb, including giving three examples of use in sentences for each sense. The number of forms coded for each language ranged from as few as fifteen to over a hundred for some languages. Countless decisions had to be made in the coding process. To try to make codings by different individuals as similar to one another as possible, we all coded the same languages (individually, then compared codings) until our inter-coder reliability approached ninety percent. Thus three languages were coded by the three of us as a group. After reaching reliability, we coded individually, but we brought our most difficult questions to a weekly coding meeting. About halfway through the process, we again checked our reliability by coding another language jointly and found that we were maintaining our reliability.

Perkins was the most productive coder, conquering thirty languages (including the prolific and exhaustively suffixing Inuit with 112 forms and the fusionally creative Abkhaz with 126 forms). Bybee coded twenty of the languages and Pagliuca, fifteen languages. Seven languages were coded jointly (including the four mentioned above) by the whole group or by two members. We are also grateful to Martin Haspelmath for coding Latin and Uigur, Roula Svorou for coding her native Modern Greek, Nancy Woodworth for coding Krongo, and Dan Devitt for help in coding Kanakuru. Bybee subsequently recoded four languages after better information on them became available. Special thanks also go to Keren Rice of the University of Toronto, who, prior to the publication of her grammar of Slave, spent two days in Buffalo with Bybee and Pagliuca, answering our coding questions about Slave in person. We began coding early in 1984 and finished in the spring of 1989.

While we coded, the data were input into the computer by Tom Willett, Zi-Yu Lin, Roula Svorou, Nancy Woodworth, and Dan Devitt, all of whom also performed countless important tasks for the work of the project, attended weekly meetings, and contributed to both theory and method. Their work was overseen primarily by Perkins and Pagliuca.

When two thirds of the languages were coded and entered in the database, as contained in chapters 3, 5, 6 and 7 of this book, analysis was begun. Futures were analyzed by Bybee and Pagliuca first for the paper "Back to the Future," which applied the analyses they introduced in "The Evolution of Future Meaning." Release time to begin this work was available thanks to a fellowship awarded to Bybee by the Guggenheim Foundation. The qualitative analysis involved going back to the reference material to check each form, to make sure that the assignment of meaning labels was consistent, and also to find what other tidbits of information might be contained in the grammatical description. Naturally some codings were changed after this procedure. Using the coded information and additional information found in the reference material, as well as information about languages outside the sample, the task was to postulate paths of development and mechanisms of change for each meaning considered. How best to conceive of pathways, what to predict for the developments along a particular pathway, and how to reconstruct probable histories for gram-types (§ 1.2) from evidence which was not always as complete as we would like were matters on which we all made substantial contributions. While we were all still in Buffalo, Bybee did the qualitative analysis for perfectives and for perfectives and related senses (chap. 3), with input from the other two authors. Subsequently, Bybee analyzed imperfectives and related senses (chap. 5) and mood and modality (chap. 6), and Pagliuca reanalyzed the future material for chapter 7 with input from Bybee.

The quantitative analysis, as contained in chapter 4, involved designing the three measures of formal grammaticization, which was contributed to equally by the three authors, and was reported on earlier in "Back to the Future." For the present work, Bybee conducted the qualitative analysis of chapter 3, which yielded the five perfages (§ 3.17), while Perkins conducted the statistical analyses and wrote portions of chapter 4.

Writing the current book has taken about four years, interspersed with other academic responsibilities, and was done primarily by Bybee. Chapter 1, the introduction, was co-authored with Pagliuca. Chapter 2, which reports on methods—the design and implementation of Perkins's sampling procedure and the procedures for coding form and meaning—was written by Bybee and revised by Pagliuca. Chapter 3 was written by Bybee, with some revisions by Pagliuca. Chapter 4 was written by Bybee and Perkins. Chapters 5 and 6 were written solely by Bybee and chapter 7 was written by Pagliuca, with revisions by Bybee. Chapter 8, the conclusion, was written by Bybee.

We are grateful to Dan Devitt, Greg Thomson, and Valerie Daniel for preparing the appendixes and for formatting and printing the manuscript at various stages. Greg Thomson and Pagliuca were responsible for preparing the indexes.

Besides the people who participated formally in the project, we are grateful to those whose interest in grammaticization and willingness to exchange ideas with us has contributed to the conceptual development of this project: Ulrike Claudi, Östen Dahl, Martin Haspelmath, Bernd Heine, Friederike Hünnemeyer, Sandra Thompson, and Elizabeth Traugott.

• • •

Abbreviations

ABL	ablative	DIF	direct information flow
ABS	absolutive		
ACC	accusative	EMP	emphatic
AFF	affirmative	ERG	ergative
AG	agentive	EX DUR	excessive duration
ALL	allative	EXCL	exclusive
ANT	anterior	EXPER	experiential
ANT CONT	anterior continuing	F	feminine
		FAM	familiar
AP	absolutive pluralizer	FREQ	frequentative
		FUT	future
ART	article	GEN	genitive
AUX	auxiliary	GER	gerund
AUX-I	auxiliary-inflected	GNOM	gnomic
AUX-U	auxiliary-uninflected	GOAL	goal
		HAB	habitual
CAUS	causative	HOD	hodiernal
CERT	certain	HYPO	hypothetical
CF	counterfactual	IFUT	indefinite future
CIF	contrary information flow	INFL	inflectional
		IMM	immediate
CNJ	conjunction	IMP	imperative
COMP	completive	IMPF	imperfective
CONC	concessive	IMPRS	impersonal
COND	conditional	INCHO	inchoative
CONJ	conjunctive	IND	indicative
CONT	continuative	INDF	indefinite
D	dual	INF	infinitive
DAT	dative	INFER	inferential
DEF	definite	INTEN	intentional
DERIV	derivational	INTR	intransitive

IRR	irrealis		REDUP	reduplication
LOC	locative		REFL	reflexive
M	masculine		REL	relative
MOD	modal		REM	remote
NCL	noun class		RESULT	resultative
NEG	negative		S	singular
NI	non-identical		SBJ	subject
NM	nominalizer		SIM ACT	simultaneous action
NOM	nominative			
NONPAST	non-past		SP	sentence particle
OBJ	object		STAT	stative
OBL	obligation		STCH	stem change
OPT	optative		SUB	subordinate
P	plural (noun)		SUBJ	subjunctive
PART	participle		SUFF	suffix
PARTCL	particle		TEMP	temporal
PASS	passive		TNCH	tone change
PAST	past		TR	transitive
PERF	perfective		VN	verbal noun
P-HOD	pre-hodiernal		I	first person
PL	plural (verb)		IE	first person exclusive
POSS	possessive			
POT	potential		2	second person
PRE	prefix		3	third person
PREP	preposition		:	in glosses separates two morphemes
PRES	present			
PROB	probability		.	in glosses joins two meanings of one morpheme
PROG	progressive			
PROH	prohibitive			
PROT	protasis		-	marks morpheme boundary in form and gloss
PURP	purposive			
REAL	reality			
REC	reciprocal			

Theoretical Background

1.1. Introduction

In its broadest interpretation, the goal of linguistics is to discover how human languages are alike and how they differ, and to propose and test theories that explain the similarities and differences. There are many alternative paths to this goal, for there is much to explain. The particular approach taken here seeks to investigate the substance of linguistic categories using a world-wide database of languages. It follows the tradition established by Joseph H. Greenberg in numerous works (Greenberg 1963, 1966, etc.) in three ways: It is broadly cross-linguistic, using seventy-six languages of a genetically stratified probability sample; it focuses on the semantic substance of grammatical categories and on the phonological substance of their expression; and it approaches theory with a diachronic perspective, by taking into account the origin and development of linguistic elements in order to explain their similarities and differences across languages.

We do not take the structuralist position that each language represents a tidy system in which units are defined by the oppositions they enter into and the object of study is the internal system the units are supposed to create. Rather, we consider it more profitable to view languages as composed of substance—both semantic substance and phonetic substance. Structure or system, the traditional focus of linguistic inquiry, is the product of, rather than the creator of, substance. Substance is potentially universal, but languages differ as to how it is shaped because it is constantly undergoing change as language is used. One of the consequences of this ongoing evolution is that, cross-linguistically and within a given language, we can expect to find grammatical material at different stages of development. In our view, then, language-internal systems, whether tidy or not, are epiphenomenal, and the clues to understanding the logic of grammar are to be found in the rich particulars of form and meaning and the dynamics of their

coevolution. Thus we take as our goal the study of the substance
of linguistic elements and the processes of change that mold these
elements. This substantive approach is not unique to the present
study, but is rather part of a growing literature that takes a similar
perspective, by which linguistic categories such as "subject," "topic,"
"passive," "causative," "verb," "noun," "aspect," and "tense" are universal phenomena with language-specific manifestations (cf. the work
of such researchers as Givón, Hopper and Thompson, Comrie, and
others). Among the particular precursors to the present work are
Friedrich 1974 and Comrie 1976, which have shown that verbal categories, and in particular aspect, the seemingly least tractable of verbal
categories, can profitably be studied in a cross-linguistic perspective,
and that certain semantic properties tend to recur in the verbal categories of unrelated languages. This work was followed up by Bybee
1985 and Dahl 1985, two studies which used much larger language
samples and achieved very similar results: the finding that certain
semantic ranges occur very commonly with grammatical expression
in genetically and areally unrelated languages. In addition, both these
latter studies identified certain correspondences between the meanings of grammatical morphemes and the form of expression they
take, namely, whether they are bound as affixes or have periphrastic
expressions. The success of these two studies motivates the current
one, which is both broader in scope, in the sense that it uses more
languages and investigates a wider range of categories, and more detailed, as it is based on more information about each linguistic form
and each language included in the study.

1.2. Goals of the present work

The present work focuses on a formally defined set of linguistic
elements—the grammatical morphemes associated with verbs. Unlike the large open lexical classes of nouns and verbs, grammatical
morphemes are closed-class elements whose class membership is
determined by some unique grammatical behavior, such as position of occurrence, co-occurrence restrictions, or other distinctive
interactions with other linguistic elements. Formally, grammatical
morphemes may be affixes, stem changes, reduplication, auxiliaries,
particles, or complex constructions such as English *be going to*. We
refer to all of these types equally as grammatical morphemes and for
convenience shorten this term to "gram".[1] Our study examines only
those grams which have a fixed position with respect to the verb.
Given a set of linguistic elements identified formally in this way, we

1. The term "gram" was coined by Bill Pagliuca and first used in Bybee 1986.

ask whether there are any regularities or commonalities across languages in the meanings expressed by these elements.

In particular our analysis focuses on some of the semantic domains most often marked morphologically on verbs—tense, aspect, and modality. Rather than taking these domains to have structural status and studying the contrasts made within them, we take a diachronic approach and study the way the semantic substance of these domains is molded into grammatical meaning. Thus our chapter headings reflect major paths of diachronic development as identified in Bybee and Dahl 1989: anterior, perfective, and related senses (chap. 3); progressive, imperfective, present, and related senses (chap. 5); future (chap. 7). Only chapter 6 is headed by category names—mood and modality—but here the goal is also the identification of major paths of development and mechanisms of change. As argued in Bybee 1985, the functions united under mood labels consist of diachronic chains more than synchronic realities.

Like Dahl 1985, we take the universal categories at the level of future, past, perfective, imperfective (for example) to be the atoms of our theory and refer to them as cross-linguistic gram-types. We neither try to break their semantic foci down into smaller features, nor do we try to group grams into higher categories such as tense, aspect, or mood. The latter represent for us cognitively significant semantic domains, but not structurally significant categories (Bybee 1986).

A diachronic approach is desirable for several reasons. First, a diachronic dimension greatly increases the explanatory power of linguistic theory. Demonstrating that a given form or construction has a certain function does not constitute an explanation for the existence of the form or construction; it must also be shown how that form or construction came to have that function (Clark and Malt 1984; Bybee 1988a). For instance, it is not enough to say that future morphemes tend to have modality senses because modality has to do with degrees of certainty and the future is uncertain (Chung and Timberlake 1985:243); in fact, when one investigates why modality senses are associated with future morphemes, it becomes clear that it has nothing whatever to do with uncertainty, but rather has to do with the specific lexical sources out of which future grams develop and the inferences available in the contexts in which they are used (Bybee and Pagliuca 1987; Bybee 1988b; chap. 7).

Second, the cognitive and communicative factors which underlie grammatical meaning are often more clearly revealed as change occurs, or, generally, in variable as opposed to static situations. Linguistic elements are largely conventionalized and used unconsciously, and linguists may propose a variety of descriptions and interpretations, but often the nature of change points to the interpretation that is correct (Kiparsky 1968; Slobin 1977).

Third, language does not provide a static organization of meaning. Grammatical meaning is changing constantly. Studying only a thin synchronic slice does not allow us to understand and explain the range of meanings covered by particular grams. Viewing the synchronic slice as simply one stage in a long series of developments helps us explain the nature of grammar at any particular moment.

The final and most important reason for taking a diachronic approach is that the similarities among languages are more easily seen from a diachronic perspective. That is, as we will show, generalizations are more effectively formulated as generalizations about paths of development than as generalizations about synchronic states. While it is possible to make synchronic generalizations about the grammatical meanings most often expressed by languages in the domain of tense and aspect (Dahl 1985), diachrony provides more meaningful and more revealing accounts of the form/meaning correlations, as well as of the differences among languages in the meanings expressed, such as the difference between the Slavic perfective and other perfectives (Bybee and Pagliuca 1985; Bybee and Dahl 1989). The recurring regularities of development, which in effect form the basis of a theory of universals of semantic change, thus provide us with a level at which otherwise non-comparable languages become comparable.

1.3. Grammaticization

Reduced to its essentials, grammaticization theory begins with the observation that grammatical morphemes develop gradually out of lexical morphemes or combinations of lexical morphemes with lexical or grammatical morphemes.[2] The process by which this occurs exhibits a number of characteristics that are regular over independent instances of grammaticization.[3]

Like many other researchers, we do not restrict our interest in

2. Since the recent revival of interest in grammaticization in the early 1970s, two terms—grammaticalization and grammaticization—have been used, usually interchangeably. When we began the current work in 1983, both terms were in use and we settled on the shorter, more elegant of the two: grammaticization. Since that time the longer term has appeared in print more frequently than the shorter one. We nonetheless adhere to our original choice, without, however, feeling that an issue needs to be made of this choice between two perfectly adequate terms.

3. Lehmann 1982 and Heine, Claudi, and Hünnemeyer 1991b review the history of grammaticization theory from its beginnings in the work of Condillac and Horne Tooke in the eighteenth and early nineteenth centuries to the present, citing as important milestones the contributions of Humboldt, Gabelentz, Meillet, Whitney, and Kuryłowicz, among others. Recent general works besides Lehmann 1982 and Heine, Claudi, and Hünnemeyer 1991b include Heine and Reh 1984 and Bybee 1985.

grammaticization to the transition between lexical and grammatical status, but rather recognize the same diachronic processes at work in a long chain of developments. Included are changes in lexical morphemes by which some few of them become more frequent and general in meaning, gradually shifting to grammatical status, and developing further after grammatical status has been attained. The events that occur during this process may be discussed under the rubrics of semantic, functional, grammatical, and phonological changes, though we will argue that these processes are intimately connected with one another.

Lexical morphemes belong to large, open classes and typically have very rich and specific meanings that restrict their contexts of use more or less narrowly. For instance, English movement verbs such as *walk, stroll, saunter, swim, roll, slide* each contain considerable detail about the nature of the movement and thus are appropriate only with certain types of subjects. The more generalized movement verbs *go* and *come*, however, lack specifics concerning the nature of the movement and are thus appropriate in a much wider range of contexts. It follows that the latter two verbs are the most frequent of the movement verbs in English: appropriate in more contexts, they are used more often. It is lexical items of this degree of generality that are used in constructions that enter into grammaticization.

A similar difference exists between the meanings borne by grammatical as opposed to lexical morphemes. As descendants of lexical items, grams have lost most if not all of the specificities of lexical meaning they formerly had; the meaning that remains is very general and is often characterized as abstract or relational. For instance, the verb *go* in the grammaticized phrase *be going to* or *gonna* at one time had its full semantic value of movement in space, and the construction meant '[the subject] is on a path moving toward a goal'. In current usage, however, the restriction that the subject be moving in space toward a goal is no longer in effect, that is, has been eroded or lost, and the meaning of the construction is more general, namely, that the subject is in any sense (spatial or otherwise) on a course toward a particular endpoint in the future. With human or animate subjects (agents capable of willful behavior), the course may have been set by the subject's having decided to do something or by his or her being a participant in a process which has already begun, as in (1) and (2).

(1) I'm gonna be a pilot when I grow up.
(2) She's gonna have a baby.

The more generalized meaning also allows subjects which are not capable of physical movement and events which do not involve movement in space, as in (3) and (4).

(3)   That tree is gonna lose its leaves.
(4)   That milk is gonna spoil if you leave it out.

In fact, a form in the late stages of grammaticization has no selectional restrictions of its own (e.g. for choosing the subject); whatever selectional restrictions are in force are those of the lexical item upon which it is dependent.

The correlation of greater generality of meaning with increased appropriateness and therefore use in a wider range of contexts thus appears to hold on three levels: for lexical items within a given domain; for grammatical as opposed to lexical morphemes in general; and across earlier and later stages of already grammaticized material. Since at all levels we see increasing generality or loss of specificities leading to wider applicability of use, the evolution of grammatical material is best viewed as a single continuum along which the same processes are operative.

One type of semantic change in grammaticization is **semantic generalization,** so called because it correlates with a generalization of the contexts in which the gram can be used (Bybee and Pagliuca 1985). Certain components of meaning are lost in this process and so it can also be called **semantic reduction,** in explicit parallel to the phonological reduction which grammaticizing material undergoes. Other terms used for this process are **bleaching** (Givón 1975) and **erosion** (Lehmann 1982; Heine and Reh 1984). (Of course, as we will see later, there is also infusion of new meaning from the context.)

Parallel to semantic reduction, **phonological reduction** continues to take place throughout the life of a gram. With the loss of stress or independent tone that accompanies the loss of lexical status, the consonants and vowels of grams undergo reduction processes, which often result in the reduction or loss of segmental material and a reduction in the length of the gram. Thus the first vowel of *gonna* is a shwa reduced from a full [ow], and the medial consonant, a nasalized flap, is the coarticulated remnant of the nasal consonant of the progressive participle and the [t] of *to*. Note that this reduction is both **substantive** (the actual articulatory gestures are reduced) and **temporal** (the articulations are compressed so that the temporal duration of the sequence is decreased) (Pagliuca and Mowrey 1987). That is, fusion or compression within the formerly three-morpheme phrase (*go + ing to*) renders it unsegmentable.[4]

As the gram reduces phonologically and semantically, it becomes more dependent on surrounding material and begins to fuse with other grammatical or lexical morphemes in its environment. Even if

---

4. The forms of *be* accompanying *gonna* reduce in the same way in all their auxiliary functions, contracting with the subject.

such fusion does not eventually lead to affixation, it may lead to phonological changes in the gram conditioned by adjacent material; and where the adjacent material varies, allomorphy is created. Thus, the English indefinite article *a/an,* although not a prefix, has two allomorphs depending on whether the following word begins with a consonant or a vowel. The creation of allomorphy continues throughout the life of a gram, with both the gram itself and the lexical material to which it attaches being susceptible to phonological variation, which eventually becomes morphophonemic.

Parallel to the growing phonological dependence on surrounding material is a growing semantic dependence on surrounding material. As the gram loses more and more of its original semantic content, its interpretation is more and more dependent on the meaning contained in the context, and it eventually is affected by this context.

With semantic and phonological reduction and dependence comes an increasing rigidification of the syntactic position of the gram and its scope relations with other elements. That is, most languages allow at least some manipulation of the ordering of lexical morphemes for semantic and pragmatic purposes, but grams are typically not modifiable by lexical items and not permutable for the purposes of changing their modifying scope. For instance, the Past Tense suffix of English *-ed* cannot be stressed for emphasis, nor can it be modified; if we wish to stress or modify the Past Tense portion of a sentence, we must use the periphrasis with *do.*

(5)   I certainly **did** wash the car.
(6)   *I certainly wash**ed** the car.

Related to this fixing of scope is the development of mutual exclusivity among members of a class. For instance, it was formerly possible to use certain of the modal auxiliaries together, as in (7). In fact, in some dialects, this is still possible for certain combinations, as in (8).

(7)   I shall cunne come. (Cf. I shall be able to come.)
(8)   You might should go now.

These combinations are not semantically anomalous, but their lack of use nowadays relates to the tendency of each of these auxiliaries to develop propositional scope while at the same time losing the intrinsic semantic content which made them part of the proposition and thus modifiable. Thus, although these older uses (such as weak and strong obligation) are still viable on their own, as in (9) and (10),

(9)   You shouldn't leave those meetings so early.
(10)   You must go now.

they are not possible if another modal is present. In such cases, obligation is now expressed by the more recently evolved *have to,* which, with its more specific meaning, freely nestles under the propositional scope of the older modals; compare (11) through (13).

(11) He may have to go to the hospital.
(12) No one should have to pay such outrageous prices.
(13) In the Pentagon, even a brigadier general must have to do a lot of saluting.

The fixing of scope and rigidification of positioning creates a situation in which a gram tends to fuse with other elements in its environment.

It is also typical of grammatical or closed classes to reduce further in size. Individual members are lost, usually by one member generalizing to take over the functions of other members. Such reduction in size is especially evident in classifier systems in which one member tends to increase in productivity and displace other smaller classes. It is also observable in other cases, such as in the competition between *will* and *shall* in English, which belong to the same class and serve similar functions. In American English, *will* has largely replaced *shall*. Such developments would seem to be the consequence of semantic generalization. As a gram generalizes in meaning, it becomes appropriate in the contexts in which another gram might have been used previously.

We have already mentioned the extreme frequency differences between lexical and grammatical morphemes. One phenomenon associated with grammaticization is frequency increase, which, as we suggested above, continues well after grammatical status has been reached. The high frequency of grams is in part due to their semantic generality, which allows them to occur in a wide range of contexts, but it is also due to the use of grams in environments where their contribution is actually redundant. That is, grams come to be used not just where the meanings they supply are strictly necessary, but also any time that meaning is compatible with the general context and the speaker's intentions. Thus English Past Tense is used not only where it is supplying the new information that the situation took place in past time, but also where this information has already been supplied, either explicitly or by the context. Once a gram or class of grams has come to be used in all appropriate contexts, redundantly or not, the lack of a gram of that class in the appropriate context becomes meaningful. Thus if a past tense gram develops and comes to be used in both redundant and non-redundant situations, the cases where it does not appear will be interpreted as signaling meaning other than past. The tense category in that language will have become obligatory, with an overt gram for past and a zero marking for present (Bybee 1990b).

This short sketch of the grammaticization process is intended only to orient the reader to the types of phenomena that are being studied in this book. The bulk of this work is devoted to illustrating and examining instances of grammaticization from the point of view of a set of hypotheses we have formulated about how grammaticization takes place. In the next section we introduce the reader to these hypotheses and some of the considerations which animated them.

1.4. Toward a set of hypotheses for a theory of grammaticization

1.4.1. Source determination

In the preceding section we characterized the semantic changes which lead to grammaticization and continue during grammaticization as changes that increase the generality of the meaning of grams. The particular mechanisms of semantic change that produce generalization of meaning are discussed in connection with particular examples throughout the book and brought together in a summary discussion in chapter 8. A preview of these mechanisms is found in § 1.6. In the present section we discuss the hypothesis that the actual meaning of the construction that enters into grammaticization uniquely determines the path that grammaticization follows and, consequently, the resulting grammatical meanings. To examine this hypothesis we must consider the meanings that serve as sources for grammaticization.

We pointed out above that the lexical units that enter into grammaticization have already undergone considerable generalization of meaning and usually represent, in the purest fashion, the basic semantic features of their domains. Thus 'come' and 'go' are the motion verbs chosen most often for grammaticization, 'do' is the dynamic transitive verb, and 'have' and 'be' are the stative verbs. However, two additional factors need to be considered: the first concerns lexical sources that cannot be characterized as semantically general, and the other concerns the grammatical elements that sometimes participate in the source construction.

When we consider the full range of lexical sources for grams, we find that they do not all evince generality of meaning in the same way. A sampling of the lexical sources of tense, aspect, and modality markers would yield, in addition to the maximally general 'go', 'come', 'do', 'be', and 'have', other verbs of less general meaning, such as anteriors arising from 'finish', 'throw away', and 'pass by'; futures from 'want' or 'desire'; and obligation markers from 'be proper or fitting' and 'owe'. Especially with 'finish', 'throw away', 'want', 'desire', 'owe', and the like, the actions and relations described are not "general" in the same sense, even though it is possible, for instance in English, to invoke items which convey more specific (or at least more affectively charged) kinds of 'throwing away'—*discard, jettison, dump, flick away*—or 'desire'—*crave, hanker for, lust after.*

Unlike 'go', 'be', and 'have', which describe general spatial movement, location, existence, or possession, 'finish', in referring to a particular phase of an event (its closure), and 'desire' and 'owe', in referring to internal and social states respectively, encode what appear to be more complex properties and relations of the world in which humans find themselves. But since this is the world that human commentary concerns itself with, their specificity relative to verbs which describe generalized physical events is not of concern. Rather, what is relevant is that they encode major orientation points in human experience. They are thus equivalent in status to the most generalized verbs of existence, possession, physical location, or attitude and movement in space. It appears then that rather than generality, it is the reference plane of basic, irreducible notions—whether they concern existence or movement in space or psychological or social states, perspectives, and events—which serves as the basis for grammatical meaning in human languages.

Others have come to a similar conclusion: Traugott (1982: 246) refers to source notions as fundamental to the speech situation; Heine, Claudi, and Hünnemeyer (1991b: 33) make the interesting observation that the source concepts that enter into grammaticization are basic to human experience and thus largely culturally independent in that "they tend to be conceived of in a similar way across linguistic and ethnic boundaries." The latter observation would partially account for the great similarities in grammaticization paths across genetically and areally unrelated languages (see § 1.4.3).

One problem in identifying the properties of lexical items that are candidates for grammaticization is the problem of determining at exactly what point we can say that grammaticization has begun. Perhaps 'finish', 'throw away', and even 'want' and 'owe' have generalized well beyond their lexical meaning and become abstract in content before grammaticization has actually begun. A case to consider in this regard is the use of body part terms in grammatical constructions signaling spatial relations. Svorou 1986, 1993 and Heine, Claudi, and Hünnemeyer 1991b document phenomena such as the use of the word for 'face' in a construction meaning 'in front of' in a large number of unrelated languages. Certainly 'face' must be considered quite specific in its meaning, referring as it does to a very specific and complex part of the human body. But note that it is not 'face' with its specific body part meaning that enters into grammatical constructions. Rather 'face' generalizes perhaps by metaphorical extension to mean 'front', as in English *the face of the cliff,* and only after it has taken on the sense of a general spatial relation does it enter into the grammaticization path by which it can become a spatial adposition.

In addition to lexical items, constructions undergoing grammaticization usually incorporate certain units that are already grammatical, such as tense or aspect markers and adpositions or case markers, all of which contribute meaning to the construction. The position of units entering into a grammaticizing construction either with regard to one another or with regard to the lexical or phrasal unit they are modifying may also contribute meaning to the construction. For this reason, in tracing the origin of grammatical meaning, we must attend to the syntax and morphology of the source construction and not simply to the referential meaning of its lexical items.

Constructions involving movement verbs, for example, are found to be the sources of markers not only of future, but also of pasts and progressives. Were we to limit our attention to the lexical stem, we would be able to offer nothing beyond an unenlightening list of the possible grams which verbs such as 'go' and 'come' could evolve into. But movement futures generally (cf. our discussion of *be going to* in English) evolve from constructions which signal spatial movement toward a goal, which requires that the verb stem bears appropriate tense/aspect and directional marking. In the ideal case, this means that, as in *be going to*, we should expect to see imperfective (here, progressive) and not perfective or past marking, and the allative component, encoded in this case with a preposition (Bybee, Pagliuca, and Perkins 1991).

What we would not expect to find (and do not find) are past-marked and/or ablative-marked movement verbs evolving into future grams. Rather, constructions with movement verbs and ablative marking evolve into anterior and perfective grams (e.g. French *venir de*). By the same token, progressives from movement verbs have neither allative nor ablative components, but rather indicate 'movement while verbing', as in Spanish *ir* + Present Participle.

Thus we disagree with Heine, Claudi, and Hünnemeyer (1991b: 338) that "one source concept can give rise to more than one grammatical category." It is the entire construction, and not simply the lexical meaning of the stem, which is the precursor, and hence the source, of the grammatical meaning. Even the case Heine et al. cite in support of their claim shows one lexical unit entering into two very different grammatical constructions. In So (a Kuliak language of northeastern Uganda) the verb *ac* 'to come' has developed into a derivational suffix indicating 'movement toward the speaker or deictic center'. It also enters into another construction in which it was an auxiliary verb and then a proclitic indicating future. In the two cases, the ordering of verb and gram are different: a suffix gives rises to a derivational

venitive in one case, while in the other case, a pre-verbal auxiliary
gives rise to a future. The two grammatical constructions yielded different meanings and hence different grammatical categories.

In other cases where it might appear that multiple grammatical
senses develop from the same source, it is often the case that these
grammatical senses are different stages along the same grammaticization path. Thus in some languages we find *have* or *be* plus a past
participle giving rise to a resultative (Latin and Old English), in others
an anterior (English and Spanish), and in still others a perfective
(French) or past (German). All these grammatical meanings are positioned on the same grammaticization path. Thus our claim is not that
the source meaning gives a unique grammatical meaning, but rather
that the source meaning uniquely determines the grammaticization
path that the gram will travel in its semantic development.

When we take into consideration the meaningful units that comprise a grammatical construction, we find that the meaning present in
the source construction bears a definable relation to the grammatical
meanings that later arise and that these earlier meanings prefigure
the grammatical meaning. Givón 1973 has claimed that the core of
the grammatical meaning is contained in the lexical meaning. The
view of semantic change as generalization or the loss of specificities of
meaning depends on this view to some extent. However, generalization is not the only type of change that occurs in grammaticization
(see § 1.6), so a fully predictive account of the relation between source
and path will require the examination of a large number of cases and
a complete understanding of all the mechanisms involved. The application of the source determination hypothesis to a number of diverse
cases of grammaticization in the domains of tense, aspect, and modality is presented in the chapters to follow as a contribution to the
enterprise of determining the exact nature of the relation between
sources and paths.

1.4.2. Unidirectionality

Implicit in much of our discussion so far, the unidirectionality hypothesis is fundamentally an assertion about the orderliness and trac-
tability of semantic change. Our conception of grammaticization in
terms of the evolution of semantic and phonetic substance is the result
of repeated observations about what does and does not seem to occur
in languages throughout the world.

Resultative constructions generalize to anteriors, which may then
evolve into perfectives or pasts (Harris 1982; Bybee and Dahl 1989;
chap. 3), but the reverse direction is unknown. Futures may arise
from movement constructions, desideratives, and obligation markers

(Bybee and Pagliuca 1987; Bybee, Pagliuca, and Perkins 1991) but do not later re-evolve into markers of desire, obligation, or movement in space. Nor does a future from one source—movement, say—later acquire desire or obligation uses (Bybee and Pagliuca 1985, 1987; Bybee, Pagliuca, and Perkins 1991). The cross-linguistic consistency of such results encourages us to see the creation of grammatical material as evolution of substance from the more specific to the more general and abstract. In later chapters we will see examples of seemingly specific meanings arising as branches along grammaticization paths (for instance, the development of evidentials from resultatives in chap. 3). Even such changes arising by inferential mechanisms are predictable to a large extent and not reversible. Change by inference as well as by generalization appears to be unidirectional. To the extent that metaphorical change enters into grammaticization (an issue that is taken up in chaps. 6 and 8), it also produces predictable, unidirectional semantic change (Heine, Claudi, and Hünnemeyer 1991a, 1991b).

In addition to the unidirectionality of semantic change in grammaticization, there is abundant evidence for unidirectionality in the grammatical and phonological change that accompanies grammaticization (see Heine and Reh 1984: 74–76; also Givón 1979a and Lehmann 1982). Once phonological segments are reduced or deleted from grams, the grams do not again assume their fuller form unless that fuller form has also been preserved in the language and replaces the reduced form. Thus, for instance, if the compound element *like* in English *godlike* replaced the nominal suffix *-ly* in *godly*, which was earlier derived from the ancestor of *like*, it would not be *ly* resuming its older, fuller form, but actually its replacement by a different unreduced form.

Once affixation has occurred, grams do not ordinarily detach themselves and assume a free form again, so that growing dependence on surrounding lexical material is not usually reversed. The few examples adduced in support of the reverse process are either reconstructed and thus hypothetical cases (Jeffers and Zwicky 1980) or cases where an element cliticizing to material on one side of it seems to be reanalyzed as belonging with the material on the other side of it (Matsumoto 1988). Only one example of affixed material that has become free has come to our attention, and in this Irish case there is strong paradigmatic pressure for the reanalysis of a person/number suffix as a free pronoun.

In most Modern Irish dialects, the person/number agreement suffixes on the verb have been lost and replaced by obligatory subject pronouns that directly follow the verb (since the language has VSO word order). However, the first person plural suffix, *-mid/-muid*, the only one of the suffixes that was a complete syllable, has not been lost.

It occurred in the paradigm in the same position as the free subject pronouns.

mol 'praise' Present Tense

1s	*molann mé*	1p	*molaimid*
2s	*molann tú*	2p	*molann sibh*
3s	*molann sé, sí*	3p	*molann siad*

Now the suffix in its non-palatalized form *-muid* can occur as an independent pronoun, replacing the earlier first plural pronoun *sinn*, as shown in examples (14)–(15) where the emphatic suffix *-e* is added to it.[5]

(14) Osclaíonn tusa   an geata agus imríonn muide cluifí.
open.PRES 2S.EMP the gate and play.PRES 1P.EMP game.PL
'**You** open the gate and **we** play games.'
(15) Is muide a   rinne   é.
be 1P.EMP who do.PAST it
'It's we who did it.'

Thus under very special circumstances, an affix can become free again. Note that in this case, the meaning of 'first person plural' can remain the same despite a shift from verbal affix to free pronoun. We suspect that the semantics of this suffix is important to the special conditions under which this very rare type of change can occur.

For the evolution of grammatical material in general, then, we posit a direction characterizable as involving a series of developments by which the originally concrete and specific meanings associated with lexical material are gradually eroded, with the resulting grams displaying increasingly abstract and general meaning. At the same time, reduction of form takes place along with a growing dependence of the gram on material in its environment (see § 1.4.5).

1.4.3. Universal paths

The source determination and unidirectionality hypotheses together predict that there will be some cross-linguistically similar paths for the development of grammatical meaning. Any grammaticizations that begin with the same or similar source meaning can be expected to follow the same course of change. This prediction does not disallow

---

5. Further evidence of the reanalysis of *muid* is the fact that it is now used with the same verb form as the other person/numbers, i.e. *molann* in this case, and it is always used in its non-palatalized variant no matter what the phonological shape of the verb. We are grateful to Alan Hudson for discussing this case with us and providing examples.

language-specific or even unique instances of grammaticization which can arise by the idiosyncratic selection of source material, but given that the source material that enters into grammaticization is similar cross-linguistically, it predicts cross-linguistic similarity in paths of development.

The degree of cross-linguistic similarity that recent studies have uncovered suggests that forces in language are pushing toward the selection of particular source material and movement along particular paths propelled by certain common mechanisms of change. The empirical studies contained in this book have turned up good evidence for certain well-traveled paths of change, as has previous research by Heine and Reh 1984; Bybee and Dahl 1989; and Heine, Claudi, and Hünnemeyer 1991b. We attribute the fact that certain grammaticization paths are common in diverse genetic and areal groups to the existence of common cognitive and communicative patterns underlying the use of language.

Not only are paths similar cross-linguistically, but paths from different sources tend to converge as grammatical meaning grows more general and abstract in later stages of grammaticization. Thus the most general of grammatical meanings are very common cross-linguistically and very similar even if they developed from different sources; that is, many languages have a general past, perfective, present, imperfective, or future whose functions are very similar (Dahl 1985; Bybee and Dahl 1989). The further study of these very common cross-linguistic gram-types and how they develop will help us identify the important cognitive and discourse factors that shape language.

In the following chapters of this book we replicate the findings of Dahl 1985, who showed that at least one of the two closely related gram-types, past and perfective, occurs nearly universally. In addition we show that there is considerable evidence that these gram-types develop in very similar ways across languages (chap. 3). Unlike Dahl, who treats present as a default category, we also study the paths leading to the development of the major gram-types imperfective and present, which are also nearly universal in distribution (chap. 5). We also treat future, supplementing our previous studies with cross-linguistic detail (chap. 7). Finally, we launch a new investigation of the paths of development for mood and modality in chapter 6, finding once again strong cross-linguistic similarity in the grammaticization of mood.

1.4.4. Retention of earlier meaning

Since we are claiming that semantic substance evolves in grammaticization and that the meaning of the source construction determines the subsequent grammatical meaning, we are not surprised to find that certain more specific semantic nuances of the source construction can be retained in certain contexts long after grammaticization has begun. In Bybee and Pagliuca 1987 we argued that some of the nuances of meaning inherent in English *will*, *shall*, and *be going to* result directly from the meaning of their source constructions. Thus, although *will* has largely displaced *shall* as a future, contexts remain in which only *shall* and not *will* may occur (contrast [16] with [17]).

(16) Shall I call you a cab?
(17) Will I call you a cab?

Shall is more appropriate in first person questions because its obligation sense implies external imposition of duties; thus the question can be construed as asking for confirmation from the addressee concerning the speaker's adoption of this particular responsibility. The same question with *will* sounds odd because the older 'desire' sense of *will* seems to come through, suggesting that the speaker is quite inappropriately asking whether s/he wants to call a cab. The flavor of willingness is also present, but appropriate, when the subject is other than the questioner.

(18) Will you call me a cab?
(19) Will he call me a cab?

Such examples show that remnants of earlier meanings of *will* as well as *shall* survived their evolution into markers of future and are detectable in certain contexts. Thus, despite the highly generalized meaning achieved by these two grams and the ongoing displacement of *shall* by *will*, there remain definable conditions under which one and not the other is appropriate.

The example of *will* and *shall* shows that grams may retain some of their original territory for quite some time, even after they have otherwise been largely displaced as the dominant marker. This semantic survival in extremis is reminiscent both of the formal and semantic survival of older markers in certain kinds of allomorphy (e.g. umlauted plurals in Germanic languages or ablaut pasts in Indo-European generally) and of the fate of once-robust lexical items which, following displacement, survive in specialized niches. As examples we might cite the survival of morphophonemically irregular forms such as *brethren* and *wrought* with very specific meaning, while their regularized counterparts, *brothers* and *worked*, have been put to general use. In addition we find instances of the earlier 'desire' meaning of the now-grammaticized *will*, as in (20), and of the earlier 'lack' or 'need' readings of the semi-grammaticized *want*, which replaced *will* (and may someday follow it into marking future).

(20)   Do what you will, I won't betray my comrades.
(21)   Since they've never wanted for anything, it's hard for them to
       comprehend what life under such circumstances is like.

Another case which demonstrates the effect of the source meaning
on the exact nature of later grammatical meanings arises in the comparison of perfectives derived from anterior constructions, such as
the French *Passé Composé*, with perfectives derived from locative prefixes, as in the Slavic languages. Dahl (1985: 74–75) argues that the
former type of perfective views the situation as a single whole, while
in the Slavic type, the perfective implies that some limit has been attained. The Slavic perfective prefixes originally signaled locative notions which made the verb telic (just as *go out, go through,* and *eat up*
are telic in English). Despite considerable generalization of meaning
so that the French perfective and the Slavic one are used in many
comparable discourse situations, and despite loss of some of the specific locative semantics, the Slavic perfective retains the sense of attainment of a limit. (See Bybee and Dahl 1989 and § 3.12 for further
discussion.)

1.4.5. Consequences of semantic retention

The notion that grammatical meaning consists of semantic substance
that has evolved in a predictable way from lexical meaning and that
grams often retain traces of this lexical meaning has consequences for
synchronic analysis, for comparative studies (such as this one), and
for internal reconstruction.

First, observe that the examples discussed in the previous section
where highly grammaticized morphemes are shown to retain lexical-
like richness of meaning are at odds with the traditional conception
of grammatical markers as pure relational elements. Of course, their
most important semantic property is their pure relational function,
but the characteristic that makes this relational function so difficult to
describe is precisely the presence of traces of older, more specific
meanings, such as 'obligation' for *shall,* 'willingness' for *will,* and 'attainment of a limit' for the Slavic perfective. The evidence from grammaticization suggests that it is not worthwhile to search for the one
abstract meaning of each gram, the least common denominator that
underlies all its uses, but rather it is better to study the different uses
of grams as though they were links on a chain, one having given rise
to another. Our understanding of the nature of grammatical meaning
then would arise from an understanding of the mechanisms that lead
a gram from one context of use to another.

In our cross-linguistic analysis we regard multiple uses of a single
gram as stages on a grammaticization path and, applying the hypothe-

sis that semantic development is predictable, postulate earlier versus later uses of a single gram that allow us to categorize the gram itself as being located at some point or range of points along a grammaticization path. Multiple uses, then, are not randomly distributed: given uses are associated only with certain others, sometimes uniquely, and from these associations we can construct diachronic developments.

Moreover, certain uses are associated only with particular lexical origins. For example, anterior grams ("perfects"), which are used to indicate past actions which are relevant to the current situation, may evolve by generalization from either resultatives, which indicate that a present state exists as the result of an action in the past, or from completives, which indicate that an action has been performed thoroughly or to completion. Because resultatives and completives have different sources—resultatives descending from constructions built on stative verbs like 'be' and 'have' (as in Germanic and Romance perfects) and completives from dynamic verbs like 'finish'—the earlier history of any given anterior can often be reconstructed by examining its non-anterior readings or uses. Thus, even in the absence of direct attestation of the source of an anterior gram, that source can with confidence be reconstructed as having been built on a stative verb if the gram has resultative as an alternate use, and on a dynamic verb if the gram has completive as an alternative use. (See §§ 3.4 and 3.5 for evidence and discussion.)

Thus we find that multiple uses and the retention of lexical specificities can be employed as diagnostics of the earlier history of grammatical material, even in languages for which historical attestation is sparse or nonexistent. A future with a remnant flavor of obligation or willingness, for example, is a cross-linguistically reliable indicator of the nature of the lexical source from which the future descends (Bybee and Pagliuca 1987; Bybee, Pagliuca, and Perkins 1991; chap. 7). When enough cross-linguistic evidence has been accumulated to establish possible sequences of developments, the notion "possible grammaticization path" may be applied in reconstruction to distinguish retentions from source meanings from later developments on grammaticization paths. Then, as a parallel to the use of the notion "possible sound change" in phonological reconstruction, we will in effect have a methodology for the reconstruction of grammatical meaning.

Like retained specificities, then, patterns of multiple uses in effect constitute fossil evidence and can thus serve as a diagnostic of earlier history. Just as full and reduced phonetic forms of individual lexemes or grams constitute a synchronic record of earlier history, patterns of multiple uses encapsulate part of the semantic history of a grammatical marker, with older versions surviving even as reduction proceeds in vanguard environments and contexts of use. It is thus possible to recover and reconstruct not simply information about the source lexical constructions of grams, but also the stages along their developmental pathways.

This method is applied throughout the book as a means of constructing paths and reconstructing sources of synchronic constructions. For purposes of cross-linguistic comparison we have chosen seventy-six maximally unrelated languages and gleaned all the information we could about them from published synchronic descriptions (see chap. 2). However, just as phonological reconstruction is aided and informed by knowledge of documented changes, our understanding of grammaticization paths is aided significantly by the study of documented changes. Thus we use what is known about the development of Indo-European and other well-documented languages alongside what we have found in the controlled sample. While it makes sense to use every possible piece of evidence and methodology at one's disposal, the danger is the introduction of a bias from the better known languages.

1.4.6. Semantic reduction and phonological reduction

We asserted above that semantic history can to some extent be read or reconstructed from the pattern of multiple uses which a gram displays much as some of the phonetic history of a lexeme or gram can be read from its full and reduced phonetic variants. The relation between phonetic and semantic development is much more intimate than such a parallel suggests, however. We have already argued that the semantic evolution of grams, from their lexical sources through the developmental stages leading to full maturity, is characterizable in terms of successive instances of generalization or semantic reduction. What remains is for us to provide some justification for the hypothesis we proposed earlier—that this semantic reduction is paralleled by phonetic reduction.

It is non-controversial that in terms of segmental length, the grams of a language in general tend to be shorter than the lexical items. More systematic observation (e.g. Zipf 1935) informs us that the most frequently used forms of a language are also among the shortest. Since grams form small closed classes which are often obligatory, we should therefore expect, within a given language, the incidence of use of any individual viable gram to be significantly higher than that of the typical individual lexical item. Moreover, since the more generalized a gram is, the wider its domain of applicability, we should expect that the more generalized a gram is, the higher its incidence of use. On the basis of these observations we can draw the following conclusions.

> 1) There is a link between frequency of use and phonetic bulk such that more frequently used material, whether grammatical or lexical, tends to be shorter (phonetically reduced) relative to less often used material.
> 2) Grams are phonetically reduced relative to generalized lexical items, which in turn are reduced relative to more specific lexemes.

These conclusions suggest a phonetic continuum that is directly parallel to the continuum for semantic reduction which we have already established. It therefore seems natural to look for a direct, and even causal, link between semantic and phonetic reduction in the evolution of grammatical material, beginning with the earliest stages of development from lexical sources and continuing throughout the subsequent developments grams undergo. Our hypothesis is that the development of grammatical material is characterized by the dynamic coevolution of meaning and form.

The question at this point is how precise this dynamic relation between meaning and form is. How closely can the continued semantic reduction which grams undergo as they evolve toward full maturity be correlated with continued phonetic reduction?

Some indications of the closeness of the relation are already available. We know, for instance, that there is a strong correlation between the generality of aspectual meanings and their usual modes of expression. Habitual and progressive grams, for example, typically have periphrastic expression, whereas imperfective and perfective grams are more often inflectional affixes (Bybee 1985; Dahl 1985; Bybee and Dahl 1989). Since periphrastic expression is typically phonetically less reduced than bound expression, and since progressives, for instance, are known to evolve into imperfectives, in cases such as these we see precisely the sort of close relation between semantic and phonetic reduction predicted by the hypothesis.

In "Back to the Future" (Bybee, Pagliuca, and Perkins 1991) and in chapter 4 of this book, we test the hypothesis that form and meaning covary in grammaticization on a large body of data, using multiple measures of formal reduction and fusion. In the research underlying the current work we have recorded both the semantic and formal properties of over two thousand grammatical morphemes. The formal properties that we use in testing the parallel reduction hypothesis include the number of consonants and vowels in the gram, the number of allomorphs, the type of conditioning of allomorphs, the presence of stress or non-neutral tone on the gram, its position with respect to the verb, and whether it is written bound to the verb. Our method is to group these properties into three scalar measures—dependence, fusion with the verb, and shortness—each of which can be compared to the degree of semantic development for grams on particular paths. (See chap. 4 for further details.)

Clustered measures provide us with a more detailed view of the sometimes subtle differences in the extent to which grams are substantively reduced, thereby allowing us to extend our reach beyond such useful but limited measures as whether a gram is expressed periphrastically or by an affix or whether one gram contains more or fewer segments than the next. Moreover, in the context of cross-linguistic research, an elaborated set of metrics is necessary in order to be able to control for the potential influence of typological factors. With statistical methods for detecting the effects such factors have on our results, we can more confidently engage in direct comparison of heavily affixing languages with isolating ones, or of languages with radically different morphophonological properties.

Our results, reported in Bybee, Pagliuca, and Perkins 1991 and chapter 4, strongly support the hypothesis that form and meaning covary in grammaticization. Our results also show a strong effect of language typology on the degree of dependence and fusion with the verb that grams attain.

1.4.7. Layering

The data we report on here clearly show that a language may have more than one gram as the exponent of a gram-type, such as future. English with its three futures, *will, shall,* and *be going to,* is typical rather than atypical in this regard. The situation with respect to future marking in English also makes clear that the rise of a new marker is not contingent on the loss or dysfunction of its predecessors, as traditional views of change have sometimes suggested. In fact, especially in domains such as the expression of future and modality, it is not unusual to find an array of grammaticized and grammaticizing constructions of different ages and sources sharing or competing for overlapping territories (Hopper 1991). Such richness of alternatives is akin to the way in which referential space may be shared by clusters of lexical items in a given domain, by alternative phrasal idioms, and even by alternative syntactic structures.

Nor does the existence of multiple grams depend on the grams' having developed from distinct sources. The presence of one marker of a given origin does not prevent the rise of another along the same pathway. Verbs of possession, for instance, often derive from verbs whose earlier meanings were more like 'take' or 'obtain', which readily evolve into 'have', the stative result of the act of taking. Thus, in English *got* and *have got* may be viewed as having now evolved into equivalents of *have* not only lexically but also in the grammatical use of *('ve)gotta* alongside *have to* (and the older *must*); cf. (22)–(24).

(22)   You must respond to this IRS notice immediately.
(23)   You have to respond to this IRS notice immediately.
(24)   You('ve) gotta respond to this IRS notice immediately.

The existence of multiple grammaticizations along the same path and the retention of lexical substance from earlier stages are two of the reasons we regard "system" or "structure" to be epiphenomenal rather than basic to the nature of grammatical substance and exponence. Successive layers of grammaticization along similar paths produce grams with similar meanings rather than grams participating in maximal contrasts (see e.g. §§ 5.6.1–2). It should be clear now that rather than studying the "structure" of grammatical expression in a language, we advocate the study of the way that grammatical meaning and expression are attained across languages as a way of understanding the inherent properties of natural language.

1.4.8. Relevance

In related work, Bybee 1985 argued that there were two major determinants of inflectional expression, relevance and generality. Relevance is the extent to which the meaning of a grammatical category affects the inherent meaning of the lexical stem with which it is associated. The degree of relevance predicts the likelihood of lexical or derivational expression of the grammatical category, the order of affixes with respect to the stem, and the degree of morphophonological fusion between the gram and the stem. In terms of grammaticization, relevance helps to predict the likelihood that affixation will take place, since affixation is more likely where the stem and gram form a coherent semantic unit (see also Bybee, Pagliuca, and Perkins 1990).

Relevance applies to categories of all kinds—lexical, derivational, inflectional, and periphrastic. However, generality distinguishes inflectional from all the rest. Inflectional categories are more general—have a wider range of applicability with predictable meaning—than lexical, derivational, or periphrastic categories. Thus generality is a necessary defining feature of inflection. Derivational categories tend to be lexically specific and to develop idiosyncrasies of meaning. Periphrastic categories tend to have more specific meaning and often lexical restrictions as well. Only inflection is necessarily completely general. One way of viewing the present study is to say that it concerns the way that generality is achieved in the development of grammatical morphemes.

1.5. Testing the hypotheses

Multiple hypotheses are necessary to make up a coherent theory, but they cannot all be tested in the same way nor in a single study. The current study intertwines the cross-linguistic with the diachronic. It is both exploratory and hypothesis-oriented. While we wanted to test the hypothesis that grammaticization paths are similar across languages, we also wanted to discover what those paths are and formulate specific hypotheses about those paths. To ensure that the study was broadly cross-linguistic, we took care to select a sample of languages (see Table A.4 in appendix A) that is representative of all the major genetic groups in the world. On the other hand, in formulating our hypotheses, we made use of not just the languages of the sample but also languages whose history is known or reconstructed through the comparative method. Thus in constructing some paths and hypothesizing some mechanisms of change, we use historical evidence from Germanic, Romance, Celtic, Dravidian, and Bantu languages. The paths hypothesized in this way are then tested for cross-linguistic validity on the languages of the sample. Of course, a certain bias toward the better-studied languages is inevitable here—since we know more about them, our theoretical constructs tend to be based on them. However, since we used a broad sample of languages, certain developments are attested in our material that do not occur in European languages.

Not all the hypotheses outlined above are tested in the same way in this study. A rigorous statistical test of some of the hypotheses is possible with our data, but other hypotheses are tested in the looser way that linguists usually use to test hypotheses—by showing that the hypothesis yields an interesting analysis that provides new insights into the linguistic data.

The quantitative analysis reported in chapter 4 tests the universal paths, parallel reduction, and unidirectionality hypotheses; if any of these hypotheses were false, we could not have obtained the statistical relations reported there. In order to complete a statistical analysis, it was important that we use a stratified probability sample of languages.

The other hypotheses are tested in the looser sense. Source determination, semantic retention, layering, and relevance are invoked in the examination of specific cases where they yield significant insights. However, no serious attempt has been made to find counterexamples to these hypotheses or to apply them rigorously in every case.

1.6. Mechanisms of semantic change

The study of grammaticization as applied here and in other recent works, such as Heine, Claudi, and Hünnemeyer 1991b, provides a new approach to the understanding of grammar: by studying the

pathways and mechanisms of the creation of grammatical morphemes, we hope to get closer to an understanding of why human
language has grammar at all and why grammar takes the particular
form and meaning that it does. Compared to structuralist frameworks
which separate synchrony and diachrony, the current approach raises
a whole new set of questions, questions about the psychological and
communicative processes that lead to the creation of grammar. Thus
our ultimate goal is not just to study pathways of change and make
predictions about them; it is rather to uncover the actual mechanisms
of change that operate in everyday language use that eventually give
rise to grammatical categories.

Grammaticization takes place very slowly and proceeds very gradually; for instance, the grammatical development of *will* in English
spans the entire documented period of approximately one thousand
years. The mechanisms of change that we wish to study are revealed
in the small and subtle changes that take place during the give and
take of language use. They cannot always be illuminated just by comparing lexical sources to resulting grammatical category. Rather, to
understand how particular changes proceed and the mechanisms that
drive them, it is often necessary to look at the use of grams in text at
periods in which they are undergoing particular changes. Thus at
times our broadly cross-linguistic study does not yield sufficient detail
to answer the how and why questions that the cross-linguistic patterns
raise and must be supplemented with language-specific detail.

Using a combination of documented language-specific change and
cross-linguistically established general patterns, we seek to catalogue
the mechanisms of change that are necessary to explain grammaticization. Our examination of a large number of cases in the domains of
tense, aspect, and modality suggests that there is no one simple
mechanism of change that produces grammatical meaning, but rather
that there are several mechanisms or types of change. These different
mechanisms that lead to semantic change and eventually grammatical
meaning may be associated with different points along grammaticization paths and thus with different semantic substance.

Some of the changes found in grammaticization seem to be describable as motivated by metaphorical extension from one domain to another. Indeed, some authors argue that the major motivation for
semantic change in grammaticization is the problem-solving tech-
nique of using an old concrete form for the expression of a new abstract concept (Heine, Claudi, and Hünnemeyer 1991a, 1991b; see
also Sweetser 1988). While it is true that when one compares source
concepts to related grammatical concepts one can construct a metaphorical relation between the two in many cases, our evidence suggests that the actual formation of metaphors is not the major

mechanism for semantic change in grammaticization. Rather we see metaphor operating only on the more lexical end of grammaticization paths rather than propelling grams into the more and more abstract domains of grammatical meaning.

For example, the well-known TIME is SPACE metaphor which is operative in lexical innovations (Lakoff and Johnson 1980) could also be invoked to explain why so many locative notions grammaticize as tense or aspect notions. However, a close examination of the semantic content and implications of temporal grammatical notions derived from spatial ones casts doubt on the need for metaphorical extension to explain such changes. For instance, a very common source for progressive aspect is a construction meaning 'the subject is AT verbing', where the element 'AT' actually has locative meaning. At first, such constructions would be appropriate in situations in which the subject is actually located in a certain place involved in an activity. Later, the progressive meaning would simply signal that the subject was involved in an activity without being in a particular location. There seems to be a metaphorical jump from the spatial domain to the temporal.

However, no metaphorical leap from one domain to another has actually taken place. If a subject is located spatially in an activity, it is unavoidable that that subject is also located temporally in that activity. Thus the temporal notion is implied by the spatial one and the temporal meaning is intrinsic to the construction all along. The change that takes place to derive a progressive meaning is the loss of the spatial meaning. Thus the real mechanism of change to be explained is how the spatial meaning gets lost. This would seem to be an instance of semantic generalization—the loss of specificities of meaning. However, the question to consider is whether "generalization" is just a description of the results or an actual mechanism of change itself. Our approach, then, is not to be satisfied with comparing input and output and guessing about the mechanism of change. Even though it is not possible in all cases discussed in this book, our ultimate goal would be to examine in detail the actual mechanisms of change from one meaning to another.

Another commonly cited mechanism that propels semantic change toward greater grammaticization is inference or the conventionalization of implicature (Dahl 1985; Bybee 1988a; König 1988; Traugott 1989; Traugott and König 1991; Faltz 1989; Heine, Claudi, and Hünnemeyer 1991b). In this type of change, a gram that often occurs in an environment in which a certain inference may be made can come to be associated with that inference to such an extent that the inference becomes part of the explicit meaning of the gram. In order to know if inference has produced a change in the meaning of the gram, it is necessary to study texts using the gram before the change took place in order to see if the gram is associated with the inference sufficiently often to absorb its meaning. Faltz 1989 has conducted such a study of the English gram *self*, which formerly was an emphatic pronoun. Faltz found that in certain Old English texts *self* was used most commonly for reflexive reference because it is precisely here that coreference is unexpected and thus needs extra emphasis (see also Haiman 1983). Apparently because of its common occurrence in reflexive environments, the speakers inferred that *self* means reflexive. It is this meaning that survives today as the central meaning, and its emphatic use now has minor importance.

Especially in later stages of grammaticization, the context comes to play a significant role in the interpretation of grams. As a gram loses more and more of its original inherent meaning, it is more susceptible to changes brought about by the contexts in which it occurs. This is especially true in the domain of mood, as we show in chapter 6. For instance, inference appears to be the mechanism behind the development of epistemic meaning (Traugott 1989). Moreover, modal grams enter into subordinate contexts where their meaning harmonizes with the context instead of making an independent contribution. From these cases where they are semantically redundant, modal grams apparently spread to other subordinate contexts. Also, subjunctives can be created by the development of new indicative forms in main clauses. The older indicatives, restricted to subordinate contexts, appear to absorb the modality of their linguistic context, thereby changing from indicative to subjunctive mood (see § 6.11).

This book contains the analysis of numerous cases of grammaticization in the domains of tense, aspect, and modality. In chapter 8 the mechanisms needed for explaining these changes are extracted and compared to one another in order to determine how many independent mechanisms of change must be recognized.

CHAPTER TWO

Method Used in The Study

The choice of a methodology for a study that proposes to test hypotheses concerning the universality of the development of grammatical morphemes must attend to two problems: first, how to achieve universality in selecting languages to study; and second, how to achieve comparability in the information about those languages. Our solution to these problems is based on the methodology employed by Perkins 1980, which is a more rigorous version of the methods used by Greenberg in works such as his famous 1963 article on the "order of meaningful elements." Perkins's method is also informed by the work of Raoul Naroll in cultural anthropology (Naroll and Naroll 1973; Naroll and Cohen 1973; Naroll, Michik and Naroll 1974). The method includes the following four basic steps.

1. Construct a stratified probability sample.
2. Find reference material for the languages of the sample.
3. Construct a coding procedure for extracting comparable information from each reference.
4. Test hypotheses on the coded information.

Our particular implementation of steps 1–3 is explained in this chapter, while the results of step 4 constitute the remainder of the book.

2.1. Sampling procedure

The choice of an appropriate sample depends on the types of hypotheses that one sets out to test. Our study was conceived of as a large-scale study that proposed to discover the semantic range of verbal grams in the languages of the world, as well as to test a number of hypotheses, some restricted to specific types of grams and others covering large numbers of grams of varied types. Given our experience with a sample of fifty languages (Perkins 1980; Bybee 1985), we felt that in order to uncover enough grams of each of the types we wanted to study, we needed between seventy-five and a hundred languages in our sample. Since it is known that one source of similarity among languages is genetic relation, and since we wanted our sample to represent all the languages of the world, we wanted a sample which has languages from each of the known language families. In fact, independent research indicates that the optimal sample would contain between seventy-five and a hundred languages that are all as distantly related to one another as possible.

Consequently, the sample had to be selected from a universe (a list of languages) that is stratified for genetic relations. Such a stratified list of languages is presented in Voegelin and Voegelin 1978, where over four thousand languages are listed with their known genetic classifications. Of course, there are a number of problems inherent in a large-scale classification such as that provided by the Voegelins. First, there are many languages for which genetic classification is unknown, unclear, or under dispute. Second, more is being learned each day about genetic relations, so that some of the information published in 1978 may be incorrect. Third, different criteria were used in establishing the groupings in different parts of the world. In some cases, genetic grouping is based on extensive historical documentation and historical-comparative work (as in the case of Indo-European languages); in other cases, the groupings are based on lexicostatistical surveys; and in still others, it is admittedly only a geographic region that is being identified as a group. Despite these problems, the Voegelin and Voegelin list is appropriate for our research since it provides an objective basis for sampling that was established independently of any hypotheses that we wished to test.

Another source of possible bias in language samples is geographic proximity. That is, genetically unrelated languages may be similar to one another because they are spoken in the same or adjacent regions. It is possible to control for areal bias in much the same way as genetic bias—by selecting languages that are maximally distant from one another geographically (Perkins 1980). However, we have not chosen to stratify our sample, which we call the GRAMCATS sample, in this way. Rather, we have selected languages without regard to their geographic proximity, but we have included in our survey information about the location of the region in which the language is spoken so that we may test our results for the possible influence of areal factors.

The precise sampling algorithms used for selecting the GRAMCATS sample are explained in Appendix A, but here we provide a short

overview so that the reader understands the rationale and the structure of the sample.

2.1.1. Stratification of the sample

The highest level of classification used by the Voegelins is the phylum.
They list some eighty phyla for the world's languages, but these vary
in size from phyla containing one language to a phylum containing
1046 languages. In order to have a representative sample, it was necessary for us to treat the phyla differently according to the number of
languages they contain. In particular, we distinguished the very small
phyla, those containing from one to six languages, which we call **minimal groups,** from the other, larger phyla.

> *55 minimal groups:* 47 isolates (groups containing only one
>   language), 8 groups with 4 to 6 members
> *24 other phyla:* phyla ranging in size from 22 languages to
>   1046 languages

It was our aim to distribute our choices over the entire population
as evenly as possible. Thus we assigned a minor role to the isolates
and minimal groups, selecting only two languages in these groups.
They happened to be Basque, which is an isolate, and Inuit, which
belongs to a phylum with only six members. The disadvantage to
selecting only two languages from the minimal groups is that the diversity of language isolates may be underrepresented. On the other
hand, we wanted to avoid the problem encountered in the Perkins
1980 sample, which was that the inclusion of isolates had the effect of
putting a disproportionate number of North American Indian languages in the sample, and these turned out not to be so diverse in
their morphological characteristics as one would expect of unrelated
languages (cf. Greenberg 1987).

Pidgin and creole languages present another type of sampling
problem. Voegelin and Voegelin list these languages under the language group which contains the language from which most of their
lexicon has been derived. Thus English-based pidgins and creoles are
listed as Germanic, French-based as Romance, and so on. For our purposes, such a classification is inappropriate since the grammatical
characteristics of pidgins and creoles are not based on the language
from which the vocabulary is drawn. As a practical solution to this
problem, we grouped all the pidgin and creole languages together
and selected one from this group. The justification for this solution is
the fact that pidgin and creole languages are very similar to one another with regard to our hypotheses: they have a very shallow time

depth, and it has been argued that they have very similar tense, aspect, and modal systems (see Bickerton 1975).[1]

All the other languages of the sample were selected from the 24 major phyla. Here again, it was necessary to distinguish groups on the basis of size. Phyla with fewer than forty members each contributed one language to the sample. Thus the sample contains one Macro-Algonquian language, one Aztec-Tanoan language, one Caucasian language, one Dravidian language, and so on. Phyla with more than forty languages contributed more than one language each, with the number and affiliation of the selected languages depending on the subgrouping within the phylum.

If the phylum has first-level or primary subgroups with more than twenty member languages, then one language was selected from each of these primary subgroups. If one of these primary subgroups is further divided into secondary subgroups of twenty languages or more, one language is selected from each of these subgroups. For instance, Afro-Asiatic is divided into the following groups, listed here with the numbers of languages in parentheses:

Maximal Group	Primary Subgroup	Secondary Subgroup
Afro-Asiatic (209)	Chadic (108)	East Chadic (32)
		West Chadic (76)
	Berber (24)	
	Cushitic (29)	
	Omotic (23)	
	Semitic (24)	
	Egyptian[a] (1)	

[a] Primary residue.

According to our procedure, we selected one East and one West Chadic language and one language from each of the other primary subgroups.

In some cases, there were primary subgroups with fewer than twenty languages. For instance, in Indo-European, the Italic and Indo-Iranian branches have greater than twenty members (in fact, Indo-Iranian has two subgroups with greater than twenty members each), but the other branches have fewer members: Baltic has seven, Celtic eight, Slavic fourteen, and so on.[2] These smaller groups were

1. Elizabeth Traugott (personal communication) has pointed out that pidgins, as non-native languages, are not appropriately included in the study. Fortunately, our random choice turned out to be Tok Pisin, which is a creole language despite its name.

2. In making up this residual grouping the pidgin and creole languages listed under Indo-European were excluded since they were included in another grouping, as explained above.

put together and languages were selected from them at the rate of one language for every thirty languages in the residual group, but not selecting more than one from any subgroup. In the case of Indo-European, two languages were selected from this residual group— Continental Scandinavian and Modern Greek.

In a few cases, even the secondary subgroups are quite large. For example in the largest phylum, Niger-Kordofanian, with 1046 member languages, the secondary subgroup of Niger-Congo, Benue-Congo, has 700 members. In Austronesian and Indo-Pacific as well, there are secondary subgroups of more than one hundred languages. However, it was decided not to sample more languages from these secondary subgroups for two reasons. First, the Niger-Congo languages, despite their large numbers, are very closely related to one another and would not provide us with the desired diversity. (In fact, our analysis revealed that even the Niger-Congo languages we did include in the sample are very similar morphologically.) Second, in the case of the Pacific languages, the subgroupings below the secondary level are primarily based on regional proximity rather than comparative study which would reveal genetic affiliations. Thus by selecting more languages from these groups, we might be selecting languages that are closely related genetically.

Using this procedure yielded a sample size of ninety-four languages. However, our final sample contains only seventy-six languages because it turned out to be impossible to obtain appropriate reference material on some of the subgroups from which our procedure required us to select languages. The gaps occur primarily in Austronesian and Indo-Pacific, where many of the languages have not yet been described, and in Ge-Pano-Carib, where many of the languages are extinct. A complete listing of the sampling subgroups and the languages selected within them is given in appendix A.

2.1.2. Selection of languages

Within each of the strata or subgroups described above, we randomly selected the prescribed number of languages using a table of random numbers. Random selection was necessary to ensure that the sample was not biased in any way. That is, we did not select languages that were known to have the phenomena we were interested in or that we knew would support our hypotheses. After making our random selections, we began a bibliographic search for material on the selected languages. Since a large portion of the languages listed in Voegelin and Voegelin are not described at all, we often could not use our first, or even our second, random selection and had to proceed down the list until we found a language with an adequate description.

The question of an adequate description was often a difficult one to decide. Given the considerable differences in theoretical orientation, training, interests, and experience of the authors, our reference material presents quite a range of variation. Two minimal requirements for the inclusion of a language were that the reference material purported to give an exhaustive treatment of morphology associated with the verb and that the level of detail given about each form was sufficient to allow us to answer the coding questions. Our material includes reference grammars (written by linguists, missionaries, and lay people), teaching grammars, and journal articles. These materials tend to be very rich in detail about the form of the grams we were interested in, but the level of detail concerning the meaning and use was unfortunately varied—ranging all the way from a mere label and a translated example to an elaborate exposition with many examples embedded in context. The languages with less adequate descriptions were allowed into the sample simply because no better material on languages of that sampling group could be found.

Given the bibliographic difficulties posed by a random selection method, we have been asked why we do not simply choose the best described language in each group. Why, for example, do we use Tigre as a representative of Semitic rather than Arabic or Hebrew? The reason we use the random selection method is to guard against introducing a bias into the sample. If we selected the best described languages of each group, in most cases we would also be selecting the language with the largest number of speakers, perhaps a language spoken in an urban area, often a language with a written tradition and some degree of standardization. Since Perkins 1980 and 1992 has shown that some morphological and syntactic traits of languages correlate with the cultural environment of the speakers, a sample of the best-described languages of the world would not represent the full range of diversity present in the world's languages.

2.2. Consequences of the use of secondary sources

Even the best reference grammar can only give a schematic outline of the morphology and can never substitute for actual exposure to native speakers for understanding the details of usage and analysis. However, our goal is not to produce an analysis of each language nor to understand the details of each language. Rather our goal is to produce a broad survey with quantifiable results that samples the full range of linguistic diversity, isolates principal versus marginal phenomena, and allows us to test certain hypotheses. Such a survey is meant to complement detailed language-specific study by providing a broadly based framework for understanding language in general.

Two methodologies for gathering data for such studies are in use by linguists today—the one which we employ, which extracts information from published reference material; and an alternate, which uses a questionnaire to gather data from native speakers or linguists working with native speakers. These two methods have different strengths and weaknesses, which we discuss below. They also yield slightly different coverage of the phenomena studied. However, results of the two methodologies applied to the same phenomena have been shown to be mutually confirming. In two independent studies, Bybee 1985 and Dahl 1985, the phenomena of grammatically expressed tense and aspect were investigated. While Bybee 1985 is a survey of reference grammars of fifty languages and Dahl 1985 is a questionnaire survey of sixty-four languages, both these studies revealed that the same small set of tense and aspect gram-types were commonly expressed across languages (see Bybee and Dahl 1989). The remarkable similarity in the content of the gram-types revealed by these two studies validates both procedures while at the same time providing strong support for the universality of grammatical categories.

Perhaps the first cross-linguistic questionnaire survey was that conducted by Keenan and Comrie 1977 in their study of noun phrase accessibility. A questionnaire survey was particularly suitable for this study because reference grammars written to that point did not contain the syntactic information necessary for testing their hypotheses. Thus the investigators constructed a number of example sentences and elicited the translations of these sentences from native speakers of approximately fifty languages.

Dahl (1985) used this method for investigating tense and aspect in 64 languages. He constructed a written questionnaire which consisted of more than two hundred sentences and asked native speakers or linguists working with native speakers to translate these sentences into their languages. The sentences were given in English, except that the verb whose tense or aspect was of particular interest was given in a non-inflected form, so as not to bias the choice of tense or aspect. Also in many cases a bit of context was provided to direct the informant to the intended sense of the questionnaire sentence.

The major advantage of the questionnaire method is that it yields highly comparable data: for each language the investigator has precisely the same set of sentences to study. In contrast, a reference grammar survey confronts the difficulty of making divergent information comparable. Each reference grammar author describes the grams of the language in his or her individual way, giving or not giving examples as s/he deems appropriate, making it difficult to ascertain whether a gram in one language is similar or not to a gram in another language. Moreover, there are many gaps in the information. For instance, if we would like to know how common it is for a future gram to be used in a clause introduced by *when,* then such a clause could be included in the questionnaire (as in Dahl's "When I GROW old, I BUY a big house"), and the form of the verb in that clause can be compared across languages. On the other hand, extracting such information from a reference grammar is often difficult because the properties of such clauses are rarely mentioned explicitly in grammars. Thus the advantage of the questionnaire method is that the investigator can construct the questionnaire in such a way as to get at precisely the information s/he is interested in and have access to comparable information on a large number of languages.

The disadvantage of the questionnaire method for studying grammatical categories is that the range of functions that can be studied is limited by what goes into the original questionnaire. Of course, a questionnaire such as Dahl's can be quite thorough since it is based on a careful study of aspectual and temporal phenomena in well-known languages. Still, it cannot disclose grammatical functions that are not anticipated in advance. On the other hand, if one examines reference grammars, one is forced to deal with whatever is reported there. A difference between Dahl's study and the current one is in the distribution of grams that we call **completive.** The sense of these grams is that something is done thoroughly and completely, totally affecting the object. Dahl's questionnaire survey of sixty-four languages turned up two cases of grams with this sense (which he calls CONCLUSIVE, see Dahl 1985: 95), while our reference grammar survey of seventy-six languages turned up more than thirty cases of grams with this sense. Completive grams are not central inflectional grams that are obligatory, nor are they necessarily of high text frequency in the languages in which they occur, but they are not entirely marginal either. Their importance to a general theory of verbal categories is in their diachronic relation to perfective and past grams (as we show in chap. 3), and thus their inclusion in the present study is crucial. To discover these completives with a questionnaire would require many more sentences than it would be practical to use. For our purposes, then, the reference grammar survey provides the appropriate range of data in that it allows us to sample a greater number of grams.

There are two other differences in the range of data obtainable in a questionnaire versus reference grammar survey. One concerns the behavior of semantic classes of lexical verbs. With a limited number of example sentences on a questionnaire, it is not possible to distinguish systematic from idiosyncratic differences in the interaction of grams with lexical verbs. For instance, the GRAMCATS reference grammar survey turned up a significant number of instances of a perfective gram that can be used for present tense with stative verbs (see

§ 3.9). Dahl's questionnaire survey apparently missed this point, either because there were no questionnaire examples that explicitly elicited this information, or because it was not possible to get information on large classes of verbs out of two hundred questionnaire sentences that are devised to cover a wide range of tense and aspect senses.

A second problem with the questionnaire method is that it does not always uncover alternate ways of expressing the same (or similar) meanings. For instance, in some languages the future gram can be used in generic expressions (e.g. *Boys will be boys*). However, most, if not all, languages have another, more usual way of expressing the generic sense, and this is the expression that is most likely to appear on the questionnaire. Without explicitly asking, "Can you use the future in this sentence?" the questionnaire cannot reveal this particular use of the future. On the other hand, reference grammars do sometimes mention such uses, even though they are alternate means of expression.

Given the goals of our particular study, then, we have chosen the reference grammar survey as the method most likely to provide us with the range of data we need. However, this method presents a number of difficulties which should be mentioned.

The first difficulty concerns the comparability of information. As we mentioned above, our reference materials are written in different styles and theoretical frameworks by authors of varied training in linguistics (including untrained missionaries and British colonial officers as well as internationally known linguists). Publication dates span nearly a century, and the works are written in several languages (Dutch, German, English, French, Spanish, Russian). In order to make these data comparable, we had to devise a coding procedure according to which we extracted information from our sources and entered it into a personal computer–based database manager, R:BASE. The coding procedure is a method of interpreting the information found in grammars and restating it in a uniform fashion for later comparison. Our coding procedure is outlined and discussed in sections 4, 5, and 6 of the present chapter.

A number of problems remain in making all the material we worked with comparable. The most pervasive difficulty arises from gaps in the information—crucial pieces of information that are simply not mentioned in the reference material. From our reference materials we extract information about both the form and the meaning of each gram. In materials produced by linguists since approximately 1940 (the majority of our sources), the information about the form of expression of grams is quite complete and largely comparable. The gaps in our information occur primarily in the description of the meanings and uses of these grams.

In the typical case, the information about meaning is given as a label assigned to the gram (e.g. First Singular, or Past Tense), a short description of the meaning in one or two sentences, and an example or two. With a gram used for first person singular, there is usually no problem, since there is little variation in what this means across languages or authors of reference grammars. However, a label such as "Past Tense" is always suspect from our point of view, since it is sometimes the case that such grams also express some aspectual meaning. Thus the author's definition must be studied carefully and compared with the examples provided. If the definition or examples are unclear or contradictory, we often search texts or other sections of the reference grammar for further examples to clarify the meaning and uses of the gram. This information, as scanty as it may seem, does provide a general picture of the function of a gram, and it is, after all, only the general picture that we seek. The purpose of this study is to construct a broad overview of the nature of verbal categories across languages and not to study language-specific details.

There are, however, certain details of function that would be extremely useful but which are often missing from the descriptions. First, statements about the relative frequency of the grams would be useful in determining how generalized the meaning of the gram is. For example, the Dutch progressive construction (as in *Ik ben an het koken*) could be translated with the English progressive (*I am cooking*), but the Dutch progressive is very rarely used compared to the English progressive and, in fact, has a much more specific meaning—the meaning of actually being engaged in an activity at the moment. Since details of meaning and frequency are often not given, we are unable to discover finer distinctions of meaning that might be useful to us. Second, grammars often lack statements about the cooccurrence restriction of grams vis-à-vis lexical verbs. Taking progressives again, our hypotheses suggested to us that as progressives develop diachronically, they are gradually used with more and more semantic classes of verbs. Unfortunately, however, the grammars we used tended not to analyze the use of the progressive in terms of semantic classes of verbs. This means that certain aspects of our hypotheses must be tested on more detailed language-specific studies.

Having worked through seventy-six sets of reference material seeking the information we need for testing our hypotheses, we recognize better than anyone else possibly could how much we are limited by our source material. On the other hand, the reader will see as we proceed that for all their gaps, reference grammars are very rich sources of information and that quite a number of useful and interesting generalizations may be formulated on the basis of what is presented in reference grammars. Because of the differences in quality of our sources, however, some figure more prominently in our discussions than others. Information from all our sources is included in our quantitative results, but for examples and observations that help us understand the meanings and functions of grams as well as their diachronic development, we naturally rely more heavily on the sources that are richer in detail and in whose accuracy we have greater confidence.

2.3. The selection of forms to code

The most general hypothesis to be tested in this book is that grammatical morphemes in the languages of the world have comparable meaning; that is, that grammatical meaning is neither totally language-specific nor is it arbitrary. We assume that identifying the cross-linguistic similarities in grammatical meaning will give us insight into the general cognitive and communicative principles that underlie grammar. The test of this hypothesis requires that we use formal criteria to identify the morphemes to include in the study. That is, our hypothesis is that certain formally identifiable morphemes in the languages of the world have certain semantic properties and are drawn from certain areas of semantic space. Thus it would not be appropriate to use semantic criteria in choosing these morphemes. The only semantic criterion used is (4) below, the criterion that the morpheme have a predictable meaning in all contexts.

While grammatical morphemes of all types are of interest to our general hypothesis, for practical reasons we choose to restrict our study to verbal grams and further to focus our study on inflectional categories, excluding from study any grams whose function is to change the syntactic category of the verb.[3] Inflectional morphemes are at the very core of our study, but since inflection is not discretely separable from other modes of expression (Bybee 1985), and since we are interested in how inflection develops, it was necessary to sample a much wider range of grams than just bound inflectional ones. Our study thus includes the derivational and non-bound grams that we believe to be most closely related synchronically and diachronically to verbal inflection. Our formal criteria for including grams in the study are the following.

(1) *The gram must belong to a closed class.* This criterion distinguishes grammatical morphemes from lexical ones. A class in the sense intended here is a set of forms exhibiting the same grammatical behavior—that is, occurring in the same position or positions, having the same co-occurrence restrictions, and the same morphological marking. The lexical classes of noun, verb, and adjective are usually open

3. Woodworth 1991 has shown, however, that the hypotheses presented here apply equally well to nominalization and verbalization processes.

to receive new members that arise through borrowing or derivation, whereas grammatical classes are generally regarded as being closed and not accepting new members. Of course, in this book we will be discussing the way in which new grammatical morphemes are established in a language, but the establishment of new grams differs from the establishment of new nouns, verbs, or adjectives in two ways. First, grams develop only very gradually over time, changing from lexical to grammatical very slowly. Second, new grams do not usually enter pre-existing closed classes; rather they develop their own peculiarities of position and co-occurrence and thus form new closed classes.[4]

For the most part, our reference material is quite explicit about which classes are closed. Even without explicit statements, short lists of morphemes with behavioral properties in common are easily recognizable as grammatical. Occasionally, however, one encounters a closed class that is quite large. For instance, the category of "modal verb" in Cambodian is described by Huffman 1967 as a closed class, even though it contains some twenty-seven different verbs. This class meets our coding criteria, and we originally hoped to include such large classes in our survey in order to sample the full range of grammatical morphemes, from those that are closer to lexical to those that are clearly inflectional. However, the process of coding was so time-consuming that we had to set an arbitrary limit of twelve on the number of items in a class that would be included in the study.

(2) *The gram must have a fixed position in relation to the verb.* We hypothesize that a certain amount of semantic coherence will result from restricting the grams under study to those that are positioned with respect to the verb, since these grams are very likely to modify the verb and hence have meanings relevant to the verb. Of course, grams that modify verbs cover a very wide range of grammatical functions since the verb is the core relational element in the clause. However, the most common verbal grams tend to be more exclusively relevant to the verb.[5]

We also include items that have more than one position relative to the verb, such as Spanish clitic pronouns, which precede the finite verb in most cases but which follow the non-finite and affirmative im-

---

4. For instance, the currently developing modal auxiliaries of English, e.g. *gonna*, *wanna*, *hafta*, etc., do not develop the behavioral properties of the older set of modals, e.g. *may, might, can, could, will,* etc. which undergo subject inversion and precede the negative, but rather when they are grammaticized will have their own behavioral properties and form their own closed class.

5. On a strictly numerical basis, person/number grams are the most common type in our database. However, this quantitative effect is due to the fact that languages have multiple grams for person/number, if they have any at all. In our database, we have languages with as many as thirty-seven person/number grams.

perative verb. Since both of these positions are grammatically determined, we consider these forms to have a fixed position. On the other hand, quantifiers and adverbs, which sometimes belong to closed classes, are usually moveable within the clause depending on their scope, and these forms are excluded from our study if they do not have their position determined by the position of the verb.

When a form occurs in a fixed position with respect to the verb but also occurs with other lexical classes, such as nouns, we did not include this form in our study unless it was the primary means of negating the verb phrase. Since we know that all languages have verb phrase negation, we thought it useful to include such forms in order to have as complete a set of data about negation as possible.

Languages in which the grams that modify the verb occur in sentence-second position present a problem for our coding criteria. If we excluded second position auxiliary complexes, such as occur in O'odham, we would be excluding many of the tense, aspect, and modality grams that are relevant to our study. Thus we extended our formal criteria to include obligatory grams that occur in sentence-second position.

(3) *The gram must be lexically general.* This criterion is met if the gram occurs with all verbs or with all the members of a large semantic class of verbs, such as stative verbs, motion verbs, transitive verbs, and so on. The intent of this criterion is to exclude derivational morphemes that are not productive and that have lexical idiosyncrasies. Such morphemes are farther from the inflectional core and more likely to have language-specific idiosyncrasies. This criterion also excludes closed class items that only occur in idioms or fixed phrases.

(4) *The gram must have a predictable meaning in most contexts.* Like the preceding criterion, this one serves to exclude grams that occur primarily in unproductive and idiosyncratic lexical derivations, as well as frozen phrases and idioms.

All these criteria leave some room for interpretation, especially as applied to the varied types of reference material utilized in this study. Thus we do not claim to have strictly isolated THE set of grams from the languages of our sample that meet these criteria. Rather, we hope to have included in our study all the grams that fit these criteria best and many grams that meet these criteria to a large degree. That is, the set of grams we analyze in the following chapters is a set with fuzzy and uneven boundaries, but our analysis concentrates on the central core of this set.

As we mentioned above, the focus of our study is inflection, but we consider it germane to also study morpheme-types that border on inflection. Thus it is important to consider the two types of continua that include inflection. One is the grammaticization scale, discussed in

chapter 1, in which inflection is the final stage of diachronic development for lexical phrases and words which develop into auxiliaries or
particles and then eventually into affixes.

Grammaticization scale:

phrases
or
words   non-bound grams   inflection
──▶
                                                      more grammaticized

The second scale is not necessarily a diachronic one, but rather a
scale based on the degree of fusion present between the expression
units for two concepts, in particular a concept that could be grammatical, such as gender or aspect, and a lexical concept, expressed as
a root or stem. In Bybee 1985 it is argued that the degree of fusion
between two linguistic units depends in large part on the degree of
relevance of the meaning of those two units to one another. This scale
ranges from syntactic or periphrastic expression, which is the free
combination of units and thus the lowest degree of fusion, to expression by more dependent units such as particles and auxiliaries,
through inflection and derivation, to lexical expression wherein two
concepts are expressed in the same morpheme.

Degree of fusion:

syntactic   non-bound grams   inflection   derivation   lexical
──▶
                                                        greater fusion

The focus of our study is around the intersection of these two
clines, as illustrated by Figure 2.1.

2.4. Coding form

Another major hypothesis to be tested in this study is the hypothesis
that a non-arbitrary relation exists between the meaning of a gram
and its mode of expression. We are particularly interested in correlations between form and meaning that come about during the grammaticization process. Thus the formal properties of grams that we are
most interested in coding are those that are indicative of degree of
grammaticization.

It is important to note that our goal was not to find the most elegant
analysis of the morphological systems we studied, but rather to record
relevant information about the grams in these systems in such a way
that we could recover this information later and make comparisons

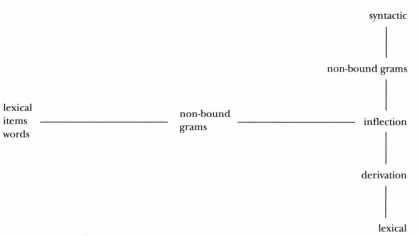

Fig. 2.1. The expression types included in this study.

across grams and across languages. If at all possible, we accepted an
author's analysis of the division of words into morphemes and the
assignment of meaning to morphemes. However, some cases required
some reanalysis on our part in order to render different languages
comparable. Some of the linguistic data in our materials was under-
analyzed and some overanalyzed. We departed from the author's
analysis only in order to have an approximately uniform level of
analysis across all our data.

The following, then, is a brief statement of the type of formal data
we have coded for each gram, with some explanation of the decisions
that had to be made in order to make the information useful for our
later analysis.

> *Form number:* We assigned each form that we coded an ar-
> bitrary number to serve as a convenient way of tracking the
> forms in our data and in the computer. These numbers ap-
> pear in the tables displayed in the following chapters. They
> are of no inherent interest except that they will allow the
> reader to use appendix C to locate the orthographic shape of
> the gram and a reference to the material in which the gram
> was described.
>
> *Orthographic shape:* For future reference we recorded the
> shape of the gram in the orthography used by the author.
> This item and some others which are mentioned below re-
> quired us to choose one prime allomorph if the gram had
> more than one phonological variant. The criteria for choos-
> ing the prime allomorph were:
>
> First, choose the longest allomorph. Since we hypothesize
> that grams reduce in length as they undergo more devel-
> opment, a primary criterion based on length (in terms of

numbers of segments) would make the grams more comparable to one another and eliminate a possible source of bias
in our data. The longest allomorph (e.g. for English Past
Tense, /ɨd/ rather than /d/ or /t/) in most cases is closest to the
original source and further contains the most phonological
information.

However, if the longest allomorph was clearly irregular or
marginal or if all the allomorphs were of the same length,
then we coded the allomorph that the author indicated was
the most basic, the most frequent, or the most important in
some way.

If none of these criteria yielded a unique choice, then we
coded the allomorph that the author mentioned first.

Prime mode of expression records whether the prime allomorph is a prefix, suffix, infix, inflected or uninflected auxiliary, particle, zero, reduplication, stem change, stress change,
or tone change.

Non-bound grams are regarded as either auxiliaries or particles. Inflected auxiliaries are easy enough to identify, since
their inflection is indicative of verb-like behavior. Uninflected
non-bound grams were coded as auxiliaries if they exhibited
any verb-like behavior at all or if they appeared to bear an
etymological relationship to a verb. Other uninflected forms
were coded as particles.

Many of the forms we coded consisted of more than one
morpheme or element. The most common type of complex
form consists of an auxiliary plus a special non-finite form of
the verb (e.g. English *be* + *ing*). Such forms were coded as
consisting of two elements, and a full set of information about
the form of each element was recorded.[6] Further, more specific information about the form of each element was coded
as follows.

Conditions stem change: If the element conditions a stem
change in the verb, then we noted whether this was a change
in the vowels, consonants, tone, or stress. Such changes were
not recorded if they were automatic phonological processes
that occurred in all environments. We recorded only changes
conditioned morphologically, and these even if they occurred
only in a few verbs.

Phonological shape: We recorded the IPA transcription of the
prime allomorph of each element.

Syllable structure: Using the symbols C (consonant) and V
(vowel), a schematic syllable structure for the element was entered, including an indication of vowel length.

6. In this way non-finite forms are included in our data, but only as elements of
other forms. As far as we know, we have coded no forms that are simply non-finite
forms.

Other allomorphs: We recorded the number of (non–phonetically conditioned) allomorphs of the element. This variable has only four values: 1, 2, 3, and >3.

Concerning the allomorphs, we recorded whether they were phonologically conditioned (e.g. by the shape of the stem), morphologically conditioned (by another gram) or lexically conditioned (specific to certain verb classes). Further, we noted whether any of the allomorphs was a reduced version of the prime allomorph or completely irregular.

The information concerning the positioning of the elements and the extent to which they are fused with the verb was recorded as follows: We noted whether or not any open class items intervene between the element and the verb, whether or not the element has independent word stress, whether any purely phonological processes occur in the element conditioned by the stem, and whether the element is written bound to the stem. Finally, we noted the position of the element with respect to the verb stem, taking into account all possible morpheme sequences and determining positions outward from the stem in both directions.

Our coding sheets also included a place to register the form number of any grams conditioning allomorphy in the element in question and also a place to record alternate modes of expression (e.g. in cases in which one allomorph is an affix and another is reduplication, zero, etc.).

2.5. Coding meaning

Since the structural and formal properties of grammatical morphemes have been studied extensively and are generally believed to be comparable across languages, developing the procedure for coding form was primarily a matter of finding convenient ways of recording fairly well understood information. In contrast, grammatical meaning is less well understood and has not been subject to the same extensive cross-language comparison. In the realm of meaning, then, it is more difficult to establish uniform a priori coding categories, and, in general, the research is more exploratory.

2.5.1. Distinguishing uses

In order to compare the meaning of the forms we coded, we had to find a level of analysis that would allow us to make a meaningful comparison across languages, and we had to establish a system of describing the meanings we found expressed by the grams in our study.

Perhaps the most concrete level of comparison would be the comparison of individual sentences, as in a questionnaire survey. How-

ever, a set of comparable sentences for each language was not
available through reference grammars, so a slightly more abstract
level of comparison was necessary. But a very abstract analysis in
which a single abstract meaning is assigned to each morpheme (as in
Kirsner 1969; Waugh 1976) is not useful because this approach assumes that grammatical meaning is determined by language-specific
oppositions which are not directly comparable across languages. We
also do not find it useful at this point to attempt a reduction of grammatical meaning into a small number of semantic primes in the style
of Wierzbicka 1972.

Rather, it is more practical for our purposes to follow Anderson
1982, who treats grammatical morphemes as covering one or more
"uses" or functions. This approach is practical because apparently
both linguists and native speakers find the different uses of a morpheme to be fairly accessible. Opening almost any reference grammar, one finds the author enumerating the "uses" of particular
morphemes. Columbo and Flores D'Arcais 1984 have shown that native speakers can distinguish different uses of Dutch prepositions and
rank them for degree of relatedness. This is not to say that the
boundaries between different uses are always discrete, nor that one
can always decide in every instance which use is illustrated. Since the
uses of a single gram are related, they are very likely to overlap in
certain cases.

Consider an example of an English gram with two uses.

(1)   I must find that article before it's too late.
(2)   It must be under one of these piles of papers.

In the first sentence *must* is used to express **obligation,** while in the
second one *must* expresses **inferred certainty** (see Steele 1975). *Must*
would be coded as having (at least) two uses, and we would characterize these with the "meaning labels" (see below) **obligation** and **inferred certainty.**

Despite our confidence in the ability of authors to distinguish the
uses of a gram, we do not accept their classifications uncritically. At
times too many uses are distinguished, especially in cases where the
context is contributing a difference in sense. At other times, not
enough uses are distinguished. For this reason, all example sentences
are studied carefully, and the following diagnostics are applied to determine the number of uses to code.

> (1) Two uses of a single morpheme are distinguished if
> these uses would be expressed by different grams in another
> language. For instance, English distinguishes **habitual** and
> **continuous** in the past with *used to do* and *was doing*. Other
> languages use a **past imperfective** for both of these mean-

ings. Thus an author might explain the Past Imperfective by saying that it could be used to mean habitual or continuous.

(2) Two distinct uses of a gram will have two different paraphrases. For instance, the English sentence *He may come in* could be paraphrased as "he has permission to come in" or as "he will possibly come in."

(3) A gram might take on a different sense (and thus be coded as having a second use) when it occurs with other grammatical morphemes or with verbs of a specific semantic class. For instance, the Past Tense in English has a **hypothetical** sense when used with the morpheme *if*. Another example is *must* in example (2), which has the epistemic meaning of **inferred certainty** when used with stative predicates.

When it does happen that a distinct use is conditioned by the presence of other elements, we are careful first to determine whether there is in fact a different sense of the gram in question, or whether the difference in meaning is contributed entirely by the presence of the other element. If the other element is entirely responsible for the difference in sense, a distinct use is not coded. However, if the additional element conditions the emergence of a different sense, then a distinct use is coded and the requirement that certain co-occurrence restrictions apply to this use is also noted. For instance in the case of *must* with stative predicates, the stative does not mean "inferred certainty," even though it co-occurs with that sense. Thus a use of *must* would be coded, noting the restriction that this sense occurs only with stative predicates. In the case of *if* with a Past Tense, *if* is contributing the sense of hypotheticality. However, the Past Tense meaning is different in this context, because it does not signal PAST. Thus we code a different use for Past Tense, labeling it HYPOTHETICAL and noting the obligatory presence of *if* in this use.

2.5.2. Assigning meaning labels

Each use is characterized by one or more **meaning labels.** In our framework, meaning labels are names for the conceptual content of the uses. They are not features of a componential analysis: they are designed so that most often a single meaning label will exhaustively characterize a single use, although in some cases it takes two or more meaning labels from different semantic domains to characterize a single use. For instance, one use of a gram might be characterized by both PAST and HABITUAL, another might require three—FIRST PERSON, SINGULAR, and SUBJECT.

We follow Dahl 1985 in assuming that the units we should compare across language are not features of a componential analysis (such as Jakobsonian distinctive features) but the semantic content of each gram, which may be thought of as focal points in conceptual space. For us, grams do not derive their meaning from the oppositions they enter into in a language, but rather have semantic content of their own which contributes to the formation of the conceptual system of the language. This view accords with the diachronic perspective that we have adopted here, since it is the semantic content of grammaticizing lexical units and phrases that evolves into the semantic content of grams. Although grammatical meaning is very generalized and abstract, we still view it as semantic substance. Bybee and Pagliuca 1987 have shown that grams retain traces of their earlier lexical meaning long after acquiring grammatical properties. This could only be the case if grams have actual semantic content.

Thus it is the semantic substance of grams that we wish to compare across languages. The earlier studies by Dahl 1985 and Bybee 1985 have shown that considerable similarity in the meaning of grams in different languages can be established. Theoretically, then, our meaning labels should be able to characterize the semantic substance of the focal points in conceptual space that are encoded by grams. These conceptual focal points can be thought of in functional terms as relating to clusters of uses. Our method is to label these uses uniformly so that we can later identify similarities in the relations among uses across languages.

Ideally, each use should be describable by a single meaning label. However, as we mentioned above, certain semantic domains, such as tense and aspect or person and number, intersect in single grams, so in order to avoid the needless proliferation of meaning labels, we do allow uses to be characterized by more than one label.

A major goal of the current research was the establishment of a list of defined meaning labels that is suitable for characterizing the conceptual content of verbal grams in the languages of the world. To the extent possible, the labels and their definitions were based on the standard terminology in the linguistic literature. Meaning labels for some domains, such as person and number, have long been established in the literature, while others, such as tense and aspect, have more recently been the focus of attention. Our definitions of tense and aspect uses are based on Comrie 1976, 1985b; Dahl 1985; Bybee 1985; and the works cited in these books. Definitions and labels for modality and mood were based on Steele 1975; Bybee 1985; Palmer 1979; Bybee and Pagliuca 1985; and our own unpublished studies of modality in a smaller sample. The meaning labels for evidentiality were developed by Tom Willett, on the basis of the literature, especially Chafe and Nichols 1987, and his own study of evidentials in a smaller sample, which is published in Willett 1988. Of course, the results might have been somewhat different if different definitions had been chosen.

Our list of meaning labels remained open-ended throughout the study. Since the grams to be included in the study were identified by distributional criteria (they had to belong to a closed class and have their position fixed with respect to the verb), we had to establish meaning labels for whatever uses we came upon in the reference material. Thus we added new meaning labels to our list throughout the study. We made little attempt to constrain the number of meaning labels; rather, we added new ones whenever we felt the meaning we were considering was not adequately described by the existing labels. Of course, our hypothesis was that the same meaning labels would be applicable across the languages of our sample, and this was true for a small number of core meaning labels. However, we also discovered an amazing array of diversity in the meanings expressed in individual languages.

The total list of meaning labels grew to include 325 defined labels. This number should be compared to the number of grams we coded in the seventy-six languages, which was 2187. About one third of the meaning labels occur only once in our database; that is, they were used for only one gram in one language, attesting to the variety of language-specific possibilities for grammaticization. So far no attempt has been made to reduce this list by reconfirming that the forms with the unique meaning labels actually meet our coding criteria and that other, more commonly used meaning labels are not appropriate in these cases. Instead our attention has been directed toward the fifty-five meaning labels that occur more than twenty times in our data. Among these we have chosen to analyze the twenty-four meaning labels that express aspect, tense, and modality functions. We have also treated in the current work about twenty other meaning labels that occur less frequently but are expressed by the same grams as express the more frequent meanings we analyzed. (The list of meaning labels used in this book and their definitions may be found in appendix B.)

Before leaving the question of our method for approaching grammatical meaning, some comments on the relation of language-specific grams to universal semantics are in order. We distinguish three levels at which we may talk about grammatical meaning (see Bybee and Dahl 1989).

First, the highest level is that of universal conceptual space, a space created by the interaction of cognition and communicative needs. The universal semantic content is independent of the type of expression that these universal concepts have in particular languages. Second, the lowest level is the language-specific level of the meaning of particular grams in particular languages. The third level is one mediating between the universal concepts and the language-specific grams, a postulated level of universal **gram-types,** which singles out areas of the universal semantic space that are frequently grammaticized across languages. The gram-types are prototypes or idealized categories whose individual realizations—the language-specific grams—may differ from one another in detail while sharing the same focal properties. Gram-types for tense and aspect have been proposed by Dahl 1985 and by Bybee and Dahl 1989. These proposals are further refined in the light of the diachronic and synchronic information contained in our database in the following chapters.

2.6. Lexical sources

Given our diachronic perspective and our hypothesis about the lexical sources of grams, it was important to extract from our reference material as much information as possible about the lexical sources of the grams we coded. We were able to identify lexical sources in two ways: through the author's comments about the relations of grams to lexical forms or other grams, and through our own observations made in reading the grammar or by checking glossaries and dictionaries for phonologically similar forms. A certain bias was probably introduced into this part of the data collection process since we had some idea of what lexical sources we expected to find, and this guided our search through lexicons and dictionaries. In addition to recording the form and meaning of the related elements, we entered a confidence rating to help us distinguish, if necessary, between relations explicitly noted by the author and those surmised by us on the basis of similarity of form.

2.7. Analysis

Our major goal was to characterize cross-linguistic gram-types in terms of their semantic content, their paths of development, and their modes of expression. The first step was to select commonly occurring meaning labels and to pull out of the database all the grams with a use characterized by that label.

Then we returned to the original source material to re-examine the description of the meaning of the gram to confirm that all the grams in the group were in fact similar in their meaning and could be appropriately characterized with that label. At the same time we noted what was actually said in the reference material about the meaning of the gram in order to refine our definition of the meaning label, if necessary.

We also examined the lexical sources found for the grams under consideration and attempted to categorize them and develop an understanding of how the lexical meaning changed into the particular grammatical meaning. We compared grams with different lexical sources, searching for correlations between the lexical source and the particular nuances of meaning attributed to individual grams.

Many of our grams have multiple uses, and many of our grams have the same or overlapping multiple uses. We studied these uses in order to postulate paths of development for grams of each type. We assumed that each use corresponds to a region of a diachronic path of development, and we used two types of evidence to postulate the order in which uses develop: First, direct evidence in the form of documentation that shows that one use was added after another; in this case, evidence from languages both inside and outside of our sample was used since we assume that the paths of development are universal. Second, we inferred an order of development on the basis of the relative generality of the meanings of the uses.

The diachronic paths we have postulated constitute hypotheses about the development of grams. We tested these hypotheses by comparing the uses of grams with their mode of expression. If a gram has uses that are considered to occur early in the development of a gram, then we expect the gram to have formal properties characteristic of early stages of grammaticization, namely, to be longer, more independent, and less fused with the verb. On the other hand, if a gram has uses indicative of a long process of semantic development, then we expect it to also have expression properties common to the late stages of grammaticization—greater reduction and fusion and loss of independence. This hypothesis is tested quantitatively in chapter 4 for grams relating to past and perfective.

The current work analyzes the most common gram-types in the semantic domains most exclusively associated with verbs—aspect, tense, and modality. The chapters are organized according to the proposed paths of development. The next chapter deals with grams with the meaning labels completive, resultative, anterior, perfective, and past, meanings that are shown to occur on the same diachronic paths. Chapter 4 presents the quantitative test of the hypothesis that form and meaning covary in grammaticization for the grams discussed in chapter 3. Chapter 5 considers grams with uses labeled as progressive, imperfective, habitual, frequentative, and iterative, as well as reduplicative grams. Chapter 6 considers agent-oriented and epistemic modalities, and chapter 7 deals with grams that have future as one of their uses.

Once gram-types and paths of development have been characterized, we should be able to refine certain general principles of grammatical meaning and semantic evolution by comparing our findings in the different domains. We hope to understand better the focal areas of semantic space that are commonly grammaticized across languages. These focal areas should represent some of the major, recurring communicative concepts used in structuring human discourse and human thought.

Anterior, Perfective, and Related Senses

This chapter examines the lexical sources and paths of development for **pasts** and **perfectives** and the meanings characterizing grams occurring along the paths leading to pasts and perfectives, namely, **completives, resultatives,** and **anteriors.** In the synchronic and diachronic data we examine, we find evidence for the source determination hypothesis in that grams from stative verb sources follow different paths of development from grams originating in dynamic verbs. In particular, auxiliaries from stative verbs go through a resultative stage while auxiliaries from dynamic verbs go through a stage of signaling completive or anterior before becoming past or perfective. We also examine the mechanism of lexical expansion during the development of these grams, looking particularly at the way these auxiliaries which are originally used only with active main verbs spread to uses with stative predicates and at what meanings they have when applied to stative predicates. This lexical spread creates the convergence in meaning that we hypothesize is typical of grams in later stages of development, although this convergence comes about through a variety of diachronic mechanisms.

Since pasts and perfectives develop from the same sources and in much the same way and have very similar semantic content, we must also ask how they differ from one another. The answer to this question seems to be that they differ from one another in the way they interact with imperfective and with semantic classes of verbs. Whether a particular gram is interpreted as past or perfective depends on whether the language in which it occurs has an imperfective and whether the gram in question contrasts with the imperfective, in which case it is a perfective, or co-occurs with it, in which case it is a past. In addition, the interaction with stative predicates distinguishes pasts from perfectives in some cases, as we shall see below.

Finally, we consider the form–meaning correspondences found among grams of these types. We hypothesize that completives and

anteriors with no other uses represent an early stage of semantic development, while anteriors with other uses and perfectives and pasts
represent the later stages, and that the semantically later uses are expressed by grams that have more reduced phonological and morphological form. Testing for the correlations predicted by this hypothesis
about the correspondence between form and meaning gives statistically very significant results. There is a strong tendency for the early
meanings to be expressed periphrastically, while the later meanings
overwhelmingly show inflectional expression. The strong association
between semantic development and the formal correlates of degree
of grammaticization—the degree of fusion, the length of the gram,
and its dependence on the stem—are presented in chapter 4. We also
find that while perfectives may have zero expression (as do seven perfectives in our corpus), pasts never do.

3.1. Preliminary grouping of meaning labels

The meaning labels we consider in this chapter—completive, anterior, resultative, perfective, and simple past—are similar conceptually
in that they all describe a situation that is completed prior to some
temporal reference point, but they differ in what other implications
they carry. Our reason for considering them together here is not so
much their conceptual similarity as the fact that we find both synchronic and diachronic relations among them.

Synchronically, we find the same grams expressing two or more
of these meanings in the cases shown in Table 3.1. Table 3.1 shows
(1) the language number, a number assigned on the basis of genetic
affiliation, which allows the reader to locate the language in the appendixes; (2) the language name; (3) the form number, which can be
used to locate more information about the form in appendix C. An x
in a column means that the gram in question has a use characterizable
by the meaning label named at the head of the column. Another
meaning label in a column means that that meaning label and the one
heading the column occur together to characterize a single use.

The evidence for diachronic relations among these meanings is of
two sorts. The strongest evidence is provided by documented cases
of grams having one of these meanings developing a use with another
of these meanings. Thus, for example, cases of anteriors and resultatives developing into pasts or perfectives can be found in French, Italian, German, Dutch, and Turkish. Evidence of a less direct sort
(especially useful for languages without adequate historical attestation) is available from the GRAMCATS survey. First, consider the data in
Table 3.1. For a gram to have two or more uses implies a diachronic
relation between the meaning labels in the adjacent uses, since it is

Table 3.1. Grams Having Two or More of the Meaning Labels Completive, Anterior, Resultative, Perfective, or Past

Language	Form No.	COMP	ANT	RESULT	PERF	PAST
32 Nakanai	02	x	x	x		
93 Buriat	38	x		x		
01 Inuit	05		x	x		
78 Kanuri	06		x	x		
42 Kui	25		x	x		
05 Agau	08		x	x		
48 Maithili	35		x	x		
10 Isl. Carib	18		x	x		
	41		x			x
03 Margi	34		x	x		x
33 Trukese	01			x	x	
25 Tahitian	03		FUT		x	
47 Latin	10		x	x	x	
46 Karok	16		x			x
52 Yagaria	21		x			x
49 Baluchi	13		x			REMOTE
68 Slave	54		x			x
86 Haka	05		x	x		x

Note. ANTerior, COMPletive, FUTure, PERFective, RESULTative.

reasonable to assume on the basis of our knowledge of documented cases that one use developed after, and probably out of, the other. The second indication of diachronic relations is provided by the lexical sources for grams. Thus we find 'finish' as a source for completives, anteriors, and perfective, and stative auxiliaries such as 'be' and 'have' plus participles as sources for resultative, anterior, past, and perfective. Thus we propose that these uses represent stages of development along some of the same paths, rather than each one representing an independent path. Given this assumption, the GRAMCATS data can be used to test the hypothesis that paths of development are similar cross-linguistically. Our proposal concerning the precise paths that involve these uses is presented in this chapter. Before proceeding to our analysis, however, we define the meaning labels in question and explain the coding criteria for each one.

3.2. Definitions

The initial definitions of the meanings expressed by grams were based on the current literature; for tense and aspect, this was primarily Comrie 1976, 1985b; and Dahl 1985. Of course, the choice of definitions orients the study in a particular way, but we changed the definitions if we found evidence in our data that did not fit the standard definitions. In some cases (as we will see in § 3.4), the descriptions in the reference material enriched our understanding of the grammatical categories, while in one other case, the data did not support the categories as defined in the literature (see § 5.4).[1]

Our working definition of **completive** is 'to do something thoroughly and to completion', as is expressed, for example, in 'to shoot someone dead' or 'to eat up'. Grams labeled as denoting a "completed action" by the reference grammar were not necessarily coded as completive. Unless the author's characterizations and translations included expressions such as 'thoroughly, completely, to completion' or the like, we regarded grams of this sort as **perfective.** For some languages, it was necessary to examine texts to discover the contexts in which the relevant gram was used in order to decide whether it should be coded as completive or with one of the other meaning labels.

Anteriors (or "perfects," as they are often called) differ from completives in being relational: an anterior signals that the situation occurs prior to reference time and is relevant to the situation at reference time. Anteriors are typically translated with the English Perfect and often accompanied by the relational adverbs 'already' and 'just'. Anteriors may occur with past or future tense marking.

Resultatives signal that a state exists as a result of a past action. The resultative is often similar to the passive in that it usually makes the patient the subject of the clause but differs in that a resultative may apply to an intransitive verb, as in *He is gone,* without a change of subject. Resultatives are compatible with the adverb 'still' and are used only with telic verbs, that is, verbs which describe events which have inherent endpoints.

Perfectives signal that the situation is viewed as bounded temporally. Perfective is the aspect used for narrating sequences of discrete events in which the situation is reported for its own sake, independent of its relevance to other situations (Hopper 1982). It is thus often used to refer to situations that occurred in the past. Anterior differs from perfective in that it would not be marked on several verbs in succession that are reporting a sequence of events but would only be used to show that some action is prior to the others in the narrative (Givón

1. Comrie's view of aspect, which we have adopted here, employs a spatial metaphor—perfective events are seen as bounded and imperfective ones are viewed from the inside. The other major view of aspect and time relates these notions to points or intervals on a time line (Bull 1971; Bennett and Partee 1978; Dowty 1979). The latter approaches take into account main verb semantics but otherwise deal exclusively with the temporal components of aspectual and tense meaning. Since our study traces the development of temporal meaning from non-temporal meaning, and since we view certain non-temporal components of meaning (such as current relevance) as important in the development of grams, we have not adopted these purely temporal definitions.

1982). Some terminological confusion arises due to the existence of the terms perfect and perfective. To alleviate this problem, we have decided to use the term "anterior" rather than "perfect" for what in English is called Perfect.

Past indicates a situation which occurred before the moment of speech. In a given use of a particular gram, the meaning label past may co-occur with one or more of a range of other meaning labels, such as imperfective, habitual, and progressive, among others. In this chapter we consider only grams which have past as the sole meaning label of a use, past perfectives, and those that signal remoteness distinctions in the past. A simple past resembles a perfective in that it is the tense of narration of sequences of past events.

The grammatical meanings just defined interact in ways that we discuss below with the lexical meanings of verb stems. Thus it is necessary for us to adopt a broad classification of verbs and to define the terms we use for these verb types in this and subsequent chapters. This classification is also useful in discussing differences among verbs that serve as lexical sources. This classification is based on Comrie 1976 and Quirk et al. 1985.

First, we use the term **situation** as a broad term for the action or state described by the lexical predicate. Then we divide predicates into types according to the kinds of situations they describe. A **stative** predicate describes an unchanging situation which will continue unless something happens to change it, such as *know, want, be tall, be ripe, be located.* A **dynamic** predicate typically describes a situation which involves some sort of change (Comrie 1976: 48–50), such as *write, walk, sneeze, ripen, drop.* Among dynamic situations, we can distinguish **telic** from **atelic.** A telic situation is one which has a built-in end point, such as *play a sonata,* while an atelic situation does not, as in *play the piano.* We will also have occasion to refer to **process** verbs, which are dynamic verbs describing a change of state, such as *grow, improve, ripen, turn red.*

3.3. Lexical sources

The lexical items which evolve into the grams discussed in this chapter are almost all verbs, which can be divided into two major types: stative verbs, usually copulas, but also 'have', 'remain', and 'wait'; and dynamic verbs, either movement verbs or verbs meaning 'finish' or 'be finished'. Non-verbal sources resemble movement verbs in being directional, as is the case with the adverbial sources 'away', 'up', or 'into'. There is also one case of a copula plus a proximal demonstrative (the demonstrative that points to things near the speaker) yielding an anterior (Tahitian).

The richest documentation of lexical sources can be found in the completives, resultatives, and anteriors, where about half the grams coded had indications concerning lexical sources. It must be emphasized again, however, that we do not have a uniform degree of confidence in our pairings of grams with sources. The pasts and perfectives, which are probably much older, had identifiable lexical sources in only one fifth of the cases. However, completives, resultatives, and anteriors develop into pasts and perfectives, and since we do have some evidence of the same lexical sources for these latter grams, we will assume that what we have to say about lexical sources is applicable generally to the grams of this group.

As source constructions, stative auxiliaries are typically combined with a form of the main verb that indicates past: either a past participle, as in the familiar European languages and also in Kui; or the perfective verb form, as in Tigre. The auxiliary is conjugated in the present for the present anterior and in many cases (e.g. Kui and Baluchi) can be put into the past or perfective to derive a past anterior. In some languages (e.g. Udmurt and Buriat), a non-finite form signaling past or passive is used with person/number endings for the anterior and/or resultative. Of course, these person/number endings may themselves derive from a copular or stative auxiliary, as they do, for instance, in Baluchi.

The most common dynamic verb source is 'to finish' or 'to be finished, ready, complete'. In such cases the relation between the lexical meaning and the grammatical meaning is very clear and direct. We find 'finish' as a source for completives in seven languages, and for anteriors in two. Similar suggestive evidence is available from other languages as well (e.g. the suffix -ile that occurs in several perfective verb constructions in Mwera is reconstructed as the proto-Bantu verb *gid-e 'finish + Perfect' [Voeltz 1980]).

Among directional and movement sources, there is a split between those that yield completive and those that yield anterior without a completive sense. As sources for completives, we have in our data three examples of 'into' or 'put into' and two examples of 'away' or 'throw away', but such lexical items do not occur as sources for any pure anteriors in the database.

Among the movement verbs that develop into anterior grams, the most common seem to be 'come' and 'come from'. Atchin shows a clear case of a past from 'come', which in the neighboring Vap and Wala dialects is an anterior, suggesting the developmental sequence 'come' > anterior > past (Capell and Layard 1980: 74ff.). In addition, 'come', 'come from', 'get up', and 'rise up' are found as sources of anteriors in three other languages.

'Go', on the other hand, is involved in the formation of a completive in Tucano, an anterior in Cocama, and in what is probably a perfective in Alyawarra.[2] The relations between each of these lexical meanings and the grammatical meanings derived from them are discussed below in the relevant sections.

Stative auxiliaries are attested as sources for resultatives and anteriors, but not for completives, which have only dynamic verb sources. One might argue that the stative auxiliary plus a past participle always goes through a stage of having resultative meaning before acquiring the anterior sense, but while it is true that most of our 'be' plus participle anteriors are also used for resultative, some of them do not have this use reported in the reference material.

3.4. Completives

Although our working definition of completive is 'to do something thoroughly and completely', it happens that in our reference material grams signaling an action performed completely and thoroughly are often described as having semantic nuances or other uses of three sorts.

1. The object of the action is totally affected, consumed, or destroyed by the action. To repeat, 'to eat up' is a good example.
2. The action involves a plural subject of intransitive verbs or object of transitive verbs, especially an exhaustive or universal plural, such as 'everyone died' or 'he took all the stones'.
3. The action is reported with some emphasis or surprise value.

The relation between completive and the first two senses is fairly obvious: if an action is done completely, it is likely to affect the object totally and may well involve multiple entities. We return to a further discussion of these senses below.

Emphatic value was especially mentioned in connection with the use of a completive in imperatives (e.g. in Gugu-Yalanji), but there is also a certain emphasis inherent in the notion of having brought an action to a thorough conclusion. Thus, the emphasis reported in the Tucano 'go' completive (Sorensen 1969: 272) seems parallel to the English 'went and did it' construction: *He went and told her the whole story*. Similarly, the Nakanai Perfective (Johnston 1980: 130), used as a completive, is reported to convey that "an event or process has been

2. The Alyawarra construction involves 'go' plus an unidentified linking element. The sense seems to be perfective, but it is not clear that this construction is frequent enough to be a perfective; that is, it probably does not occur on successive verbs in a narrative.

Table 3.2. Lexical Sources for Completives

Language	Form No.	Lexical Source	Expression Type
		Finish	
11 Cocama	23	'finish'	DERIV
14 Tucano	23	'finish'	DERIV
22 Koho	10	'finish'	AUX
28 Halia	45	CAUS + 'finish, be finished'	AUX
37 Buli	26	'finish, conclude, keep up, maintain'	AUX
	25	'whole, completed'	PARTCL
73 Tem	19	'finish'	AUX
74 Engenni	06	'finish'	AUX
84 Lao	39	'be complete'	AUX
86 Haka	09	'be finished, completed'	PARTCL
87 Lahu	29	'finish'	AUX
89 Cantonese	22	'finish, make perfect'	AUX
94 Tok Pisin	19	'finish'	AUX
		Movement, Direction	
14 Tucano	33	'go'	AUX
23 Palaung	15	'throw away'	AUX
33 Trukese	20	'away' (another use)	DERIV
	21	'up, east' (other uses)	DERIV
48 Maithili	44	'go'	AUX
	61	'go'	AUX
69 Krongo	47	'down, below'	PARTCL
		Move Into	
24 Car	06	allative, interior	DERIV
60 Yessan-Mayo	26	'to put into'	DERIV/INFL
89 Cantonese	24	'to bury'	AUX
		Other	
27 Atchin	18	'to lose, to be lost'	AUX
52 Yagaria	22	'to put'	AUX
46 Karok	24	'to be all gone'	DERIV
48 Maithili	55	'to fail'	AUX
85 Chepang	29	'to eat, devour, ingest' (the Satisfactual Completive)	DERIV/INFL
		Unknown Sources	
06 Touareg	17		DERIV
14 Tucano	22		DERIV
16 Gugu-Yalanji	16		DERIV
32 Nakanai	02		DERIV/INFL
42 Kui	21		PARTCL
60 Yessan-Mayo	07		DERIV/INFL
72 Mwera	09		DERIV
78 Kanuri	07		INFL
82 Maidu	25		DERIV
93 Buriat	38		DERIV

Note. AUXiliary, DERIVational, INFLectional, PARTCL = particle.

totally accomplished, in the face of lack of knowledge on the hearer's part of the perfected status of that event." The example Johnston gives is (1).

(1)   Eia   kora-le,   eia   taulai-ti!
      3.s   leave-that   3s   marry-PERF
      'Forget her, she's already married!'

In this connection, it is interesting to recall the "hot news" value of the English Present Perfect (which is an anterior, and thus related to completive), as in *Nixon has resigned!* (McCawley 1971). Hopper and Thompson (1980: 264) also mention that total affectedness of the patient is related to intensity. (See also Slobin and Aksu 1981 on the surprise uses of the Turkish Inferential.)

The lexical sources of completives differ from those of resultatives, which we discuss next, in that they are all dynamic verbs or directionals; that is, all suggest action or movement. Resultatives, on the other hand, all derive from stative verbs used with some non-finite form of the main verb. Such absolutely regular correlations support the source determination hypothesis in a particularly striking way.

Table 3.2 contains a list of forms with completive as their meaning, arranged according to their lexical sources, a gloss of their lexical sources, and, in the last column, an indication of their expression types.

Further, more specific support for the source determination hypothesis comes from an examination of the different sources for completives in relation to the extent to which they convey the senses described in §§ 3.1–3.3. Consider Table 3.3, where the number of times the nuance was mentioned is indicated for each type of lexical source, and where hyphens indicate that the sense was not mentioned in the reference material.

Table 3.3.   Semantic Nuances of Completive Grams

Source	Number of Grams from Each Source	Patient Affected	Plural	Emphasis
Finish	12	–	3	–
(Put) Into	3	3	1	–
Directions	7	–	–	–
Be lost	1	–	1	–
Be all gone	1	–	–	–
Dry in sun	1	1	–	–
Go	1	–	–	1
Put	1	–	–	–
Unknown	10	1	2	3

Completives from verbs meaning 'finish' are not reported to have the sense of totally affecting the patient, which is rather associated with the 'put into' completives. All three completives listed as '(put) into' signal that the object was totally affected. The Yessan-Mayo auxiliary *yuwa* 'to put in' is used with both intransitives and transitives: with intransitives it signals that 'the action was done by everybody'; with transitives it indicates a 'complete or thorough action of the verb to the object' (Foreman 1974: 99). The Cantonese auxiliary *maai*, originally from a verb 'to bury', signals that the remainder of the object of the action is affected. This contrasts with the Cantonese completive auxiliary *yun* 'finish', which signals only that the action is complete. The Car suffix *-n* is a directional marker in addition to a completive. It indicates 'direction toward the center of the island or into the jungle', as distinct from the direction 'toward the sea'. It also indicates that the object is completely done away with or destroyed by the action of the verb.

We suggest that the action of putting an object into a container, the jungle, or the ground (as in 'to bury') implies the disappearance of the object and hence, in one respect, the completion of the act. That is, the notion of a totally affected object comes directly from the source meaning and is not a sense developed later.[3] The source verbs 'put (into)', 'bury', and the like, inherently entail totally affecting the object or patient, and this flavor is retained as part of the semantic package in grammaticization. Completives from 'finish', on the other hand, could only have such nuances with particular, semantically accommodating main verbs and objects (e.g. perhaps 'to eat something') but not generally; since they are not part of the meaning of the source, daughter grams will not have such semantic flavors.

The sense of plural participants and, in particular, plural patients is found in completive grams from different types of lexical sources (cf. Table 3.3) and so is unlikely to be semantically an indication of the lexical antecedents. Perhaps plurality is associated with the completive sense because to carry an activity or process through to completion, in many cases, would involve affecting multiple patients.

We do not know much about 'go' as a source for completives, but this construction might resemble the English construction *go and*, which is usually used in the past to emphasize the deliberateness and finality of an action.

The mode of expression of completives falls into basically two

---

3. This conclusion in turn suggests that the one completive with this sense for which no source is known might have a similar source to the known ones. This is the Nakanai suffix *-ti*. A search of the directional suffixes which are used on verbs in this language turned up *-tivu*, which indicates 'the location of the shore or inland, from out on the sea' (Johnston 1980: 212).

types—periphrastic and derivational expression. Completives are relatively rich in lexical meaning and may be lexically restricted or simply not used frequently enough to have become inflectional. In Table 3.2 we have indicated the mode of expression by DERIV (derivational), AUX (auxiliary), PARTCL (particle) and INFL (inflectional). In some cases there was not enough information to decide which category the gram belonged to, and in these cases two possibilities are listed.

Because we find anteriors with 'finish' as a lexical source, we hypothesize that completives, especially those from 'finish', may develop into anteriors (see § 3.8). However, not all completives appear to take this course of development. The derivational completives in particular may not always continue their development by becoming inflectional; while it is apparently possible for derivational affixes to generalize in use and become inflectional, it does not appear to be common (see Comrie 1985a). Further, a difference between the 'finish' versus the 'put into' completives exists besides the one mentioned above: the 'finish' completives become more generalized anteriors, while our evidence suggests that the 'put into' completives do not; we have no instances of an anterior from a directional source hinting of 'into'.

3.5. Anteriors

Anteriors (or "perfects") have received considerable attention in the cross-linguistic literature on tense and aspect (Comrie 1976; Anderson 1982; Givón 1982; Li, Thompson, and Thompson 1982; Dahl 1985), as well as in the literature on English (McCawley 1971; McCoard 1976; Vermant 1983). The definition generally agreed upon for anterior is 'a past action with current relevance'. The English Perfect is a good example of an anterior: according to Dahl's analysis of the anterior in thirty-two languages of his corpus, the English Perfect has the second highest correspondence to his proposed universal prototype. Some examples of an anterior used to indicate a past action that is relevant to the current situation are in (2).

(2)   Carol has taken statistics. (So she can help us.)
      I've just eaten dinner. (So I don't want any more food.)

This very typical use of anteriors is the one most often mentioned in reference grammars. The indefinite aspect of a past tense so expressed is sometimes focused upon by authors (hence the label Indefinite Past); that is, the goal of the utterance is not to locate a situation at some definite point in the past, but only to offer it as relevant to the current moment. The evidence for this is the non-occurrence of the anterior with temporal adverbs that indicate a specific time in the past:

(3)   ?Carol has taken statistics last semester.
      ?I've gone to the bank at nine o'clock this morning.

Another similar use indicates a "new situation" or "hot news" (McCawley 1971; Anderson 1982):

(4)   Mt. St. Helens has erupted again!
      Nixon has resigned!

Though this particular use is not often directly mentioned in reference material, we suspect that the "emphasis" that is sometimes referred to in connection with anteriors and completives may in fact correspond to precisely this use.

Other senses often associated with the anterior are the **experiential,** in which certain qualities or knowledge are attributable to the agent due to past experiences, as in (5), and the **anterior continuing,** in which a past action continues into present time, as in (6).

(5)   Have you ever been to London?
(6)   I've been waiting for him for an hour.

Neither of these uses is frequently mentioned in reference material.

The most common non-anterior sense expressed by anterior grams is the resultative, in which a present state is described as the result of a past action. Such uses are discussed in § 3.6.

From the uses described here it is clear that the anterior would be frequent in conversational discourse, but according to Givón 1982, the anterior also plays a special role in narrative discourse. While the past, perfective, or a special narrative tense, such as the historical present, are typically used in clauses that are a part of the main narrative sequence, the anterior is used for events that are out of sequence, that is, events that occurred earlier but are relevant to the events located in the discourse "now." Consider the brief narrative (7) from Vermant 1983: 66.

(7)   Well . . . he turns on this woman . . . well he really lets her have
      it. And Mrs. Taylor, who's had a few herself by then, says—how
      did she put it now.

This narrative in the historical present in English uses a present perfect ([ha]s had a few [drinks]) to point to a prior event that is now relevant to the main narrative sequence. It is often the case that an anterior may combine with both present and past tense, and sometimes also future, to signal situations that precede and are relevant to these different temporal reference points. However, we also have in our material examples of anteriors that are restricted to the present as well as anteriors that are restricted to the past. These can be identified in Table 3.4 as grams that have PRES or PAST listed under Other Meanings. In the column labeled Other Meanings we list meanings that occur in the same use with anterior, except for the two that are marked with an asterisk. Definitions of meaning labels can be found in appendix B. The last column shows whether the gram is written bound to the main verb or not. This information will be of interest to us in § 3.10.

Table 3.4 shows only those anteriors that we hypothesize to be at an early stage of development, that is, anteriors with no other uses or with uses that we consider indicative of early rather than later stages of development, such as **quickly** and completive.

Table 3.4 also shows that anteriors derive from both stative sources (as do resultatives) and dynamic sources—in particular, movement verbs such as 'come' and 'come from'—as well as from verbs such as 'finish'. The changes leading to anteriors from these two different sources are discussed in §§ 3.7 and 3.8.

3.6. Resultatives

A resultative denotes a state that was brought about by some action in the past. This sense is similar to the sense of an anterior, which indicates that a past action has relevance in the present. In English the difference between resultative and anterior can be seen in constructions with *be* which are resultative versus those with *have* which are anterior.

(8) He is gone.　　　　He has gone.
　　　The door is closed.　　The door has closed.

A sentence such as *The door is closed* is often regarded as a "stative passive" in English since it describes a state rather than an action, and this is what in other languages is regarded as a resultative. This same construction with an expressed agent, or some other contextual indication of an agent, can be a regular passive, as in *The door is closed by the doorman*. The difference between resultative, passive, and anterior is that only resultative consistently signals that the state persists at reference time. Thus the sentences in (9) are acceptable, while those in (10) are not acceptable in the resultative sense. The second sentence in (10) is acceptable only with a passive reading.

(9) He has gone and come back already.
　　　The door has opened and closed several times.
(10) *He is gone and come back already.
　　　*The door is closed and opened several times.

Table 3.4.   Grams with Anterior as Their Only Use (Young Anteriors)

Language	Form No.	Other Meanings	Related String	Bound
01 Inuit	20		already	Y
37 Buli	17		all, already	N
Stative Aux				
02 Basque	04		be + perf part	N
08 Tigre	38		exist	N
	39		be	N
	40		wait	N
48 Maithili	21	PAST	remain	N
	24	PRES	be	N
	35	PAST	be	N
49 Baluchi	12		part + past + cop	Y
	14	COMP PAST	past + past + cop	Y
50 Mod. Greek	12		have	N
51 Danish	12		have	N
	13		be	N
75 Mano	07		be, do, make	N
93 Buriat	45	PAST	be + past	N
Movement				
03 Margi	40	PRES	to come from	N
	44	PRES IMM		N
	45		to get up	
			to come from	N
	46		to come	N
11 Cocama	14		go	N
23 Palaung	15		throw away	N
52 Yagaria	33	EX DUR	come	N
89 Cantonese	18	EXPER	to pass by	N
Finish				
59 Bongu	25		be ready, finished	
			completed	Y
71 Temne	19		finish	N
84 Lao	39	*COMP	complete	N
Other				
17 Alyawarra	03	PAST	clause conn	Y
25 Tahitian	07		medial demonstr.	N
			past copula	
26 Motu	11		past time, recent	N
Unknown				
03 Margi	48	*QUICKLY		N
08 Tigre	27			N
11 Cocama	15			N

Table 3.4. (*continued*)

Language	Form No.	Other Meanings	Related String	Bound
		Unknown		
13 Jivaro	25	PRES	zero	0
14 Tucano	03	PRES IMM		Y
	21	PRES		Y
24 Car	14	IMM		Y
35 Rukai	01			Y
38 O'odham	10			Y
40 Guaymi	08	ANT CONT		Y
	10			Y
46 Karok	40	PAST		H
	42			
50 Mod. Greek	17	FUT		N
69 Krongo	06			T
72 Mwera	44			N
73 Tem	17			N
	18	IMM		N
76 Bari	07	PAST		N
80 Tojolabal	08			Y
85 Chepang	39	IMM		Y
	40			Y
86 Haka	07			N
87 Lahu	48			N
88 Nung	11	PAST		N
90 Dakota	22	PAST		N
92 Uigur	19	PAST		Y

Note. ANTerior CONTinuing, COMPletive, EXcessive DURation, EXPERiential, FUTure, IMMediate, PRESent.

Nedyalkov and Jaxontov 1988 point out that the adverb 'still' is acceptable with resultative uses, but not with anterior. Consider sentences (11) and (12), where the resultative with *still* indicates that the state persists, but the anterior with *still* requires that *still* take on a non-temporal sense of 'nevertheless' as in *I still insist that he has gone.*

(11)   He has still gone.
       The door has still closed.
(12)   He is still gone.
       The door is still closed.

These facts are all consistent with the view that the resultative points to the state resulting from the action while the anterior points to the action itself.

A resultative sense is only compatible with a predicate that indicates a change of state or an action that produces a change of state. Thus resultative constructions may be lexically restricted, or a more gener-

Table 3.5. Other Uses of Resultatives

Language	Form No.	Result	Ant	Past	Compt	Pfv	State exist	Other
01 Inuit	05	PASS	x					INFER
03 Margi	34	x	x	x				
05 Agau	46	x						
10 Isl. Carib	18	x	x				x	
14 Tucano	17	x			x			EMP
	29	INFER						
32 Nakanai	02	x	x		x			
33 Trukese	01	x				x	PRES	INCHO
	39	x						CAUS, REC
42 Kui	06	x	x	x				
	25	x	x					
	26	PAST	PAST					
48 Maithili	34	x	x					
51 Danish	11	x					PAST	
68 Slave	10	x				x	x	
75 Mano	06	x						
78 Kanuri	06	x	x					
79 Palantla	10	x						
86 Haka	09	x	x	x				
93 Buriat	23	x						
	24	REM						
	38	x			x			

Note. CAUSative, EMPhatic, INCHOative, INFERential, PASSive, PRESent, RECiprocal, REMote.

ally used construction may have a resultative use only with change-of-state verbs. For example, Johnston's description of Nakanai is quite explicit about the change of sense when what he calls the Perfective is used with verbs of different lexical semantics. "On an action verb, perfective aspect (*-ti*) encodes the notion of an event having been entirely, or unexpectedly, accomplished, or completed in a way which involved the total consummation of its effect upon the patient" (Johnston 1980: 130). This sense is labeled completive above.

(13) ali-ti-a   'ate it all up'
     tuga-ti   'has already left'

"On a process verb, perfective aspect encodes the notion of a resultative, i.e. the idea of the utter completion of a change of state" (130).

(14) peho-ti   'dead'
     mate-ti   'extinguished'
     mapola-ti   'smashed, cracked'

"On a stative verb, perfective aspect indicates that the patient has undergone a process and is now totally affected" (130).

(15)   halaba-ti   'cleaned'
       mumugu-ti   'dirtied'
       kea-ti   'whitened'
       taulai-ti   'married'

In the GRAMCATS sample, twenty-one grams in sixteen languages were coded as marking resultative. Most of these have other uses, the most commonly occurring of which are anterior, completive, past, perfective, and state exists. Other uses which occur only once are also shown in Table 3.5. They are **emphatic, state commences, causative, reciprocal,** and **passive.**

The known lexical sources for resultatives tend to involve stative meaning. In three languages (Danish, Kui, and Tucano), the construction is made up of a conjugated form of the verb 'to be' plus a participial form of the main verb. In Mano, the gram derives from a main verb meaning 'to remain'. The only potential exception is in Kanuri, where the anterior, which also has a resultative use, is possibly related to the verb 'to come'. (See Table 3.6.) In the most common case, the resultative sense is the outcome of the combination of the stative auxiliary, which provides the sense of a present state, and the past and/or passive participle, which signals a dynamic situation which

Table 3.6.   Lexical Sources for Resultatives

Language	Form No.	Lexical Source
01 Inuit	03	
03 Margi	34	
05 Agau	46	
10 Isl. Carib	18	
14 Tucano	17	
	29 INFER	'be' + participle
32 Nakanai	02	
33 Trukese	01	
	39	
42 Kui	06	
	25	'be' + perfect participle
	26	'be' (past) + perfect participle
48 Maithili	34	'be' + past passive participle
51 Danish	11	'be' + past participle
68 Slave	10	
75 Mano	06	'remain'
78 Kanuri	06	'come'
79 Palantla	10	
86 Haka	09	'be, become'
93 Buriat	23	VN of passive
	24 REMOTE	VN of distant past
	38	

occurred in the past and is seen as affecting the object of the transitive verb or the subject of the intransitive. In the next section we will see how this meaning evolves into anterior meaning as a result of the discourse contexts in which it is used and its expansion to use with verbs of various types.

3.7. Resultative to anterior

Resultatives serve as sources for anteriors (which eventually evolve into simple pasts or perfectives) in a number of well-studied Romance and Germanic languages, including Spanish, French, Italian, English, Dutch, and German. Since earlier stages of these languages are available to us in written documents, we can be quite sure that the precursors of the modern Perfects were originally resultative in function. We will consider briefly here the history of these constructions in English and Romance.

According to Traugott 1972, Old English had two ways of forming resultative constructions: with intransitive verbs, an auxiliary *beo-* 'be' was used with an adjectival participle which agreed in number, case, and gender with the subject, and with transitive verbs, an auxiliary *habb-* 'have, take, get' was used with an adjectival participle agreeing in number, case, and gender with the object. Thus examples such as *He wæs gecumen* lit. 'He was come' are found. The *habb-* plus participle in earliest Old English was used only in possessive contexts, such as (16), in which *habban* retains its lexical verb meaning (Traugott 1972: 94f.).

(16)   Ic hæfde hine gebundenne.
       'I had him in a state of being bound.'

The modern Perfect develops out of these early resultatives as the participle loses its adjectival nature and becomes part of the verb rather than an adjective modifying a noun. This change is reflected in the loss of agreement on the participle and a change in word order by which the participle comes to always stand next to the auxiliary. The Perfect with *have* gradually replaces the instances of the *be* construction, which only survives with a few verbs such as *go* (see the examples in [8]).

The Perfect constructions in Spanish, Italian, French, and Portuguese have a similar history (Harris 1982; Vincent 1982). In Cicero, for example, sentences such as (17) are found (Vincent 1982: 82).

(17)   in ea   provincia pecunias magnas collocatas habent
       in that   province   capital   great   invested   have:3.P
       'They have great capital invested in that province.'

Here we find the participle agreeing with the object and the sense of possession of *habēre* still present as well as a stative sense. Latin also had a construction with 'be' plus the participle which yielded a sense of resultative with intransitive verbs. According to Harris, in some dialects, such as Calabrian and Sicilian, these constructions retain their resultative meaning, while in others, such as Spanish, they have developed into anteriors, and, in still others, such as French, they have become perfectives.

A resultative, as we have said, expresses the rather complex meaning that a present state exists as the result of a previous action. An anterior, in contrast, expresses the sense that a past action is relevant in a much more general way to the present moment. The semantic change that takes place between resultative and anterior can perhaps be seen as a generalization of meaning by which some of the specificity associated with the resultative stage is eroded. Such a generalization of meaning probably comes about in discourse contexts in which the resultative is expressed in order to set the stage for a subsequent action. If this discourse function is applied not just to actions that produce states but to actions that precede other actions, then the anterior sense evolves.

An important part of this evolution is the expansion of resultative grams to use with verbs of various semantic types. Usually, a resultative occurs with a change-of-state verb, and apparently early in their development they are most often found with change-of-state verbs. Thus Ernout and Thomas 1951 cite verbs such as 'discover', 'learn', 'persuade', and 'compel' as occurring with the *habēre* resultative in Ciceronian Latin. From this point, the construction spread to dynamic verbs of all types, which forces an interpretation not so much of a state resulting from an action but of an action with some lasting relevance. A construction that has spread to this point would be considered an anterior. The complete generalization of the construction would require that it come to be used with stative as well as dynamic predicates. However, the interpretation of an anterior with stative predicates presents certain problems, which we discuss in § 3.9.

3.8. Anteriors from dynamic verb sources

The development of anteriors out of resultatives has been studied in the languages of Europe in some detail, but very little information exists on the development of anteriors from dynamic verbs, such as the lexical verb 'finish'. What exactly are the ranges of uses of such anteriors and how do they compare with the anteriors from resultative sources? Dahl's questionnaire data suggest that anteriors from 'finish' may attain a range of use very similar to that of anteriors from resultatives: for example, the anterior in Kammu (a Mon-Khmer language) (*hóoc* < 'finish') is almost as close to the universal prototype as are the Swedish and English Perfects from auxiliaries meaning 'have'. Li, Thompson, and Thompson 1982 argue that the sentence-final particle *le* in Mandarin, which derives from the verb *liao* 'to finish', is used as a general marker of 'current relevance' in all tense contexts. It is thus similar but not identical to the English Perfect. Since such anteriors are less familiar, however, we will present here some examples of clear cases of anteriors from verbs meaning 'finish'. The first example is taken from a thorough description of Sango by Samarin 1967. Sango is a creole language of Central Africa based on the Ngbandi dialects and is not in the GRAMCATS sample. We have chosen it for illustration because Samarin presents the uses of the erstwhile verb *awe* 'be finished' in detail and supplies fifty-seven examples from tape-recorded speech and letters, which yield sufficient context to make good conjectures about the use of this gram.

The verb *awe* (*a* is a subject marker, *we* is the stem) is used both as a main verb and to indicate "an action antecedent to that of the verbs in the context" (Samarin 1967: 158), a use which fits our definition of anterior very well. Note in these examples that the anterior is past in one context and present in the other.

(18) tɛrɛ   amá   tongasó **awe,**   lo   kpé   tí   lo   bíaní.
      spider   SBJ:hear   thus   finish   3.s run   to   3.s truly
      'When spider had heard this, he ran away for sure.' (160)

(19) eh   bien, lo tɛ   ngunzá ní   kóé   **awe,**   mɔ goe
      well then 3.s eat   greens the.one   all   finish   2.s go
      mɔ   mú   na   lo   ngú . . .
      2.s   take with 3.s   water
      'Then, when he has eaten up the manioc greens, you go give
      him water . . .'

When used with change-of-state verbs, such as *gá pendere* 'to become beautiful' and *mbɔkɔ* 'to bruise', *awe* gives a resultative sense much as anteriors from stative auxiliaries do.

(20) jusqu'à,   mɛrɛngɛ́ wále   só,   lé   tí   lo
      for.a.while   child   female   this face of   3.s
      ambɔ́kɔ   **awe**   só,   lo   gá.
      SBJ:bruise finish   this 3.s come
      'Until the girl whose face was ulcerated, she came.' (161)

(21) lo   sí   gígí,   lo   tí   na   sése,   allé,
      3.s arrive outside   3.s fall with   earth   suddenly
      lo   gá   pendere   wále   **awe.**
      3.s come   beautiful woman finish

'She came out, she fell on the ground, and behold, she had become a beautiful woman.' (162)

Unlike anteriors from stative auxiliaries, however, *awe* also has a completive sense, both with change-of-state verbs and other actions verbs:

(22) fadesó   mbi   ça va   **awe.**
      now   1.s   recover finish
      'Now I am completely recovered.' (160)

(23) mais   mbi   lɛkɛ   ténέ   ní   **awe**   ngá,   si
      but   1.s   repair affair the.one   finish   also   so that
      mbi   tɛnɛ   na   mɔ   tí   má   sí.
      1.s   talk   with   2.s   of   hear so that
      'But I had fixed up the matter completely, and then I told you; so you would hear.' (161)

(24) kɔli   así   gígí   **awe,**   ála   zía   lɔrɔ   da,
      man   sʙɪ:arrive   outside finish   3.ᴘ   put   speed there
      akpé   na   wále   bíaní   **awe.**
      sʙɪ:run and   woman   truly   finish
      'When the man had come out, they put some speed into it, and ran away with the woman.' (162)

The predicates *ça va* (22) and *lɛkɛ* (23) are change-of-state verbs, meaning 'to recover' and 'to repair', respectively. In these cases *awe* adds the sense 'completely'. In (24), a simple action verb *así* 'to arrive' takes on an anterior sense in the first occurrence of *awe*, but in the last clause, with the verb *akpé*, *awe* adds the sense of 'away', that is, 'run to completion.'

The evidence suggests that *awe* is not used with stative predicates, for there is not one example in all the fifty-seven examples given by Samarin.

In Tok Pisin, an English-based creole that is in the GRAMCATS sample, the verb *pinis* 'finish' is used in very much the same way as *awe* is in Sango, but *pinis* may also be used with stative predicates. The sense conveyed by *pinis* is that the state applies completely or in a superlative manner (Mühlhäusler 1985: 380).

(25) ol namois ol i kristen pinis
      'The coastal dwellers are true Christians.'
(26) tupela i pren pinis
      'The two are real friends.'

An anterior from 'finish' that is perhaps more advanced in its semantic development than are the Sango or Tok Pisin anteriors is found in Palaung, a Mon-Khmer language from the GRAMCATS sample with no bound morphology and possibly no obligatory mor-

phology. The reference grammar available on this language (Milne
1921: 67–68) gives only the sparsest descriptions of the uses of the
grams, but the gram hwǭ-i̠, which is also a main verb 'be finished, be
ready', appears in a number of examples as well as in a few places in
a narrative, so that we may try to discern the range of its uses. Milne
labels this gram a Past Tense, indicating, for example, "I was going, I
went, I have gone, I had gone," but also states that it may be omitted
if another word in the context indicates past tense. In fact, in the
forty-page narrative at the end of the grammar, hwǭ-i shows up only
twenty-one times, counting both its main verb and auxiliary uses, despite the fact that it is clearly a past narrative. This suggests that its
main function is not to signal simple past tense, and thus we have
coded it with more specific functions.

The clearest examples of anterior uses of hwǭ-i are relational ones
in which an anterior in one clause signals a situation prior to and
relevant to the situation in the next clause, as in (27) and (28).

(27) bar   pan   kar-grāi   gē   hī   hwǭ-i   ta   ạn,
      as   what together-told 3.P finish finish to   3.s
      ạn   lọh   pwǫt.
      3.s   went away
      'They told him and he went accordingly.' (107)
(28) mī   hwǭ-i   hǫm   yǫ̆   pǫm   vēng   hā   ō.
      2.s finish eat   EMP rice return place   this
      'Come after you have eaten.' (107)

The antecedent clause may be lacking an explicit subject, in which
case hwǭ-i is described as an adverb.

(29) hwǭ-i   īt   ạn   chặng   vēng   ta   ngặr.
      finish sleep 3.s will   return to   fire
      'After sleeping, he will return to the fire.' (87)

In the narrative there is at least one case that might be called a "hot
news" use.

(30) nāng   hwǭ-i   pwǭ
      lady   finish birth
      'The lady has given birth.'

Somewhat less emphatic is (31).

(31) (Do not weep, O Queen.)
        ra-gwāi   ạn   ǭ   hwǭ-i   dēh   bī   rör   kyă kyă nă nă.
        dwelling   3.s 1.s finish give people make excellent
        'I have ordered the people to make an excellent dwelling for
        it.' (152)

There are no cases in the narrative where *hwǭ-i* could mean simple past, but there are some isolated examples where it is unclear whether a simple past or an anterior is meant (the translations are the author's).

(32)　kū-i　amīng　ǭ　ạn　hwǭ-i　bī-ɛr　do-ɛt
　　　　as　orders　1.s　3.s　finish　forgot　all
　　　　'He has quite forgotten my orders.' (103)

(33)　ǭ　hwǭ-i　grāī　ĕ
　　　　1.s　finish　tell　certainly
　　　　'Of course I told/did tell.' (84)

We did not find examples that suggest a completive sense.

The following example shows *hwǭ-i* with a change-of-state verb yielding a resultative sense.

(34)　ra-gwāī　hwǭ-i　rōr　lắlă
　　　　dwelling　finish　made　well
　　　　'The dwelling was well prepared.' (150)

Examples of *hwǭ-i* used with stative predicates are abundant, but there is no trace of emphasis or completion in the translations of these examples. Rather, the only implication beyond that of the simple existence of a present state is a sense of having achieved the state, but even this is not present in all examples.

(35)　hŭ　kīng　ạn　hwǭ-i　hrām
　　　　hair　head　3.s　finish　white
　　　　'His hair is already white.' (89)

(36)　ạn　hwǭ-i　hŭ
　　　　3.s　finish　is.full
　　　　'He has eaten enough.' (106)

(37)　kạn　hwǭ-i　jü̆　bạr　ō̆,　ka-dō-ɛ　bǖ
　　　　if　finish　is.long　as　this,　enough　still
　　　　'If it is as long as this, it is enough.' (107)

(38)　hwǭ-i　lă
　　　　finish　good
　　　　'It is good!' (176)

The lack of a completive sense in all these examples suggests a more advanced stage of semantic development for the Palaung anterior *hwǭ-i*.

Finally, consider the case of the Mwera suffix *-ile*, whose cognate in other Bantu languages is reconstructed by Voeltz 1980 as coming from the proto-Bantu verb **gid-e* 'finish' + Perfect. With dynamic verbs in Mwera, this suffix indicates that the action occurred in the immediate past, in particular, on the same day as the speech event.

With stative predicates, however, it indicates a present completed state, for instance, *nigonile* 'I am lying down, I am asleep' (Harries 1950: 94–95).

3.9. Interactions with stative predicates

As completives or resultatives develop into anteriors and further into perfectives, they must generalize to occur with verbs of all semantic types. We have just seen examples of the use of anteriors with stative predicates yielding a sense of 'present state exists'. However, this is not the only sense that anteriors can take with stative predicates. In this section we will see some evidence that the original (lexical) semantics of the gram determines the outcome of its combination with stative predicates, but that in later stages of development, there is a convergence among grams from different sources.

To begin with, in our sample are anteriors and completives which are apparently not used with stative predicates at all. Such is the case with the *have* Perfect in Modern Greek. While no explicit statement to that effect was found in the reference material for Margi, Kui, and Kanuri, in these languages as well no examples of statives with anterior grams were found. In languages that do allow an anterior or completive with stative predicates, we have found that two distinct situations are possible: one is associated with anteriors and completives from the main verb 'finish'; the other may be associated with anteriors from 'be' and 'have' auxiliaries, but there is very little evidence about the sources of the particular grams in question.

In the first situation, the completive or anterior gram has the sense of emphasizing the completeness with which the state applies to the entity. We just saw an example of this use in Tok Pisin, but it occurs in other languages as well. For instance, as Johnston describes the Nakanai completive (in [15]), it signals that the entity is totally affected by the state. In such cases, the tense and aspect of the clause remain unaffected so that the gram is compatible with a present state. It is sometimes difficult to distinguish such cases from instances of resultatives applied to change-of-state verbs. For instance, the Nakanai cases cited in (14) and (15) are distinguished only by the fact that the verbs in (14) are inherently dynamic or change-of-state verbs, whereas the verbs in (15) are inherently stative. Another example of a completive with this use is in Engenni. The Engenni completive is probably also from a verb 'finish'; although the author does not say so explicitly, she does consistently gloss *(pa)dhe* as 'finish' (Thomas 1978: 164).

(39) ọ   pẹ̌pìlè   dhẹ
      3.s   flat   finish
      'It is really flat.'

One hypothesis would be that this particular application of completives to stative predicates is characteristic of completives and anteriors derived from 'finish' and that it gives rise eventually to a simple marker of present state as the force of the completive sense is diminished with use over time. Thus we might speculate that the Palaung anterior, which has no more than a mild sense of achievement associated with it, has developed from the stronger completive sense.

(40) kạn   hwǫ-i   jŭ   bạr   ȫ,   ka-dō-ɛ   bṻ
      3.s   finish is.long   as   this, enough   still
      'If it is as long as this, it is enough.'
      hwǫ-i   lă
      finish good
      'It is good.'

In the second type of interaction with stative predicates, the anterior gram changes the aspect of the stative predicate to inchoative, that is, it makes the stative predicate signal a change of state. Clear examples of this type are found in Engenni, Trukese, and Island Carib. Note that the Engenni *ni* is described as signaling that 'the action has or will be completed before the next action begins' (Thomas 1978: 73), while *dhẹ* of example (39) indicates that the action is 'finished, completely, thoroughly' (170).

(41) Engenni
      ọ   mẹnimeni   nị
      it   sweet   ANT
      'It has become sweet.' (Thomas 1978: 164)
      ạdhè   bhi   nì   o
      day   be-black   ANT   in-fact
      'It has got dark, you know.' (Thomas 1978: 73)
(42) Trukese
      aa   semmwen   átewe
      3s-ANT   sick   fellow
      'That fellow has become sick.' (Goodenough and Sugita 1980: xlix)
(43) Island Carib
      sáditina   'I'm ill'
      sádihadína   'I've become ill'
      maráotu   'She is childless'
      maráoharu   'She has become childless' (Taylor 1956a: 23–24)

These same forms with dynamic verbs signal resultative or anterior.

(44) Engenni
      ọ   ta   ná   te   nì   ạkiè
      he   go   to   reach   ANT   town
      'He had reached the town.' (Thomas 1978: 109)

(45) Trukese
      aa   peyiyas
      3s-ANT   bury
      'She is buried.' (Dyen 1965: 24)

(46) Island Carib
      iódotibu   Thou didst go
      iódohadíbu   Thou art gone   (Taylor 1956a: 24)

The examples with statives show that these anteriors have the effect
of giving the stative predicate a dynamic change-of-state interpretation. Why is this so, and why do the 'finish' completives give such a
different interpretation?

We propose that this difference is due to a difference in the way
that completives and anteriors from different sources come to be used
with stative predicates. In the early stages it would not be normal for
constructions with 'finish' or anteriors from *be* or *have* auxiliaries to
be used with stative predicates. They are compatible only with dynamic predicates, and it is the meaning they develop with dynamic
predicates that is transferred in their use with stative predicates. That
is, the 'finish' constructions develop a meaning of completion and to-
tality which, when applied to a state, signals the completeness of the
state. The anteriors that were earlier resultatives have a different
sense—that of an action having taken place which is relevant to the
present. The requirement that it be an action which takes place is
apparently very strong, since when such grams are used with stative
predicates they take on a dynamic interpretation—that of the beginning of the state or becoming.

The anteriors with stative predicates of the second type are subject
to further development, since for an entity to have achieved a certain
state may imply that it is still in that state. Thus in Island Carib, certain
stative verbs in the Perfective, which is distinct from the anterior described above, denote a present state. For instance, *lamáali* 'he is hun-
gry' is a perfective form. Similarly, the stative *funatu* 'it is red' becomes
the perfective *funáali* 'it has turned red', with inchoative meaning,
which in turn when said of fruit gives the stative sense 'it is ripe' (Taylor 1956a: 24). Such inferential changes are not restricted to inherently stative predicates but also apply to the resultative reading of
change-of-state verbs. Thus, for example, *hiláali* 'he has died' can also
mean 'he is dead' (Taylor 1956a: 24).

Languages which apparently do not allow anterior to cooccur with
stative predicates develop a present state use of the anterior with
change-of-state verbs by this same process of inference. The compound anterior of Kui, which is made up of a conjugated verb *manba*
'to be' plus a participle, has a present interpretation with change-of-

state verbs. Thus 'be sitting down' is always expressed in the anterior, never in the present or progressive.

(47) īnu   koksa   manji
      3.s   sat   be
      'You have sat down, you are sitting down.' (Winfield 1928: 87)

Similar examples are found in Kanuri, where the Perfect suffix -na with certain verbs has a present stative interpretation (Lukas 1937: 43; see also Hutchison 1981: 121–22).

(48) nŏŋîn   'I learn, I shall know'
      ŏŋə́nà   'I know (I have learnt)'
      nâmŋìn   'I (shall) sit down'
      námŋənà   'I am seated (I have sat down)'
      ragə́skìn   'I am getting fond of, I shall like'
      ragə́skənà   'I like (I have got fond of)'

Such examples indicate that there are several routes by which a completive, anterior, or developing perfective can develop a use for present states:

    a. A completive with a stative predicate which indicates a complete present state weakens to indicate merely present state (e.g. Palaung hwọ̄-i, Mwera -ile);

    b. An anterior which indicates the beginning of state may come to assert the current existence of the state by inferential change (e.g. Island Carib -[h]a);

    c. A resultative, which indicates a past action producing a present state, may come to indicate only the present state (e.g. Kui manba and Kanuri -na);

And, finally, a case we have not yet discussed:

    d. A zero form, in languages in which the imperfective is overtly marked but does not occur on stative predicates, will indicate perfective for dynamic verbs, but present for stative ones (e.g. Ngambai and Nakanai zeroes).

In subsequent sections we turn to a discussion of the further development of anteriors, including their development into perfectives and pasts. Before leaving this section, however, we would like to point out that, given that anteriors develop into pasts and perfectives and that anteriors interact with stative predicates in such a way as to yield a present state meaning, we may be able to explain certain cases of residual morphology not otherwise explicable. In particular, the Preterite-Present verbs of the Germanic languages have present forms that are traceable to strong Preterites even though their meaning is clearly present. These were highly frequent verbs with primarily stative meaning: *agan* 'to possess', *witan* 'to know', *dugan* 'to avail', *unnan* 'to grant', *cunnan* 'to know, be able', *thurfan* 'to need', *durran* 'to dare', *sculan* 'to be obliged', *munan* 'to remember', *magan* 'to be able', *(ge)nugan* 'to suffice', *motan* 'to be permitted' (Moore and Knott 1955: 194). We suggest, then, that the Germanic Preterite was earlier an anterior, which, when applied to stative predicates, gave a sense of present state via one of the routes outlined in this section. While the Preterite eventually came to mark past tense even for states, these frequent verbs had already become lexicalized as presents, so that, in order for them to be used as pasts, new weak preterites were formed from them.

3.10. Old anteriors

In Table 3.4 we listed only anteriors that we consider to be at an early stage of their development because they have only the anterior use or (in only two cases) another use that is also considered an early use. We have also mentioned that anteriors tend to develop into pasts or perfectives. However, our material also contains grams which we hypothesize to represent an intermediate stage between pure anterior and past or perfective. These grams have anterior as a use but also have other uses suggestive of more grammaticized meanings. These grams and their uses are listed in Table 3.7. Table 3.8 shows the lexical sources of these grams and whether or not they are written bound.[4]

Note in Table 3.8 that these grams have their sources in approximately the same range of lexical items as the anteriors listed in Table 3.4, suggesting that the two sets of anteriors are on the same paths of development. To justify the hypothesis that these anteriors are at a later stage of development, we consider the meaning labels they express in addition to anterior. First, notice in Table 3.7 that eleven of these anterior grams also are used for resultative. Whether this combination of uses develops by an anterior from a dynamic verb source spreading to process verbs and taking on a resultative meaning, or by a resultative (from a stative verb source) spreading to dynamic (non-process) verbs and taking on an anterior reading, these grams are more grammaticized semantically than grams that are simply resultative or simply anterior. If we are correct in our hypotheses concerning the development of anterior meaning with stative main predicates, then those grams that have **state exists** as a use show even further development, since we take a present use with sta-

4. Some of the same forms are listed in these tables as in the RESULTATIVE tables, Tables 3.5 and 3.6.

Table 3.7. ANTERIOR grams with Other Uses (Old)

Language	Form No.	Past	State Exists	Result	Evidential	Other
01 Inuit	05	x		PASS	x	
03 Margi	34	x		x	PROB	
05 Agau	08			x		
	29		x			
10 Isl. Carib	18	x		x		
	41	x	x			
23 Palaung	05		x			
25 Tahitian	03	PERF	x			FUT ANT
32 Nakanai	02			x		COMP
39 Abkhaz	47	ALMOST				CF PROT
42 Kui	06	x		x		
	25			x		
46 Karok	16	x				PAST ANT
47 Latin	10	PERF		x		
48 Maithili	34			x		
49 Baluchi	13	REMOTE				
	15				PROB	REM ANT
52 Yagaria	21	x				IMM ANT
63 Baining	05	x				IMM FUT, IMP
68 Slave	54	SIM ACT				SUB CF
72 Mwera	31		x			
74 Engenni	09					FOCUS
						STATE COMMENCES
75 Mano	04					HYPO & CF PROT
78 Kanuri	06			x		
79 Palantla	03		x			
82 Maidu	41		x			IMM HOD
86 Haka	09	x		x		
87 Lahu	56					STATE CHANGES
91 Udmurt	05	AFF				FUT ANT
	07				x	

Note. AFFirmative, ANTerior, COMPletive, CF = counterfactual, FUTure, HODieranal, HYPOthetical, PASSive, PERFective, PROBability, PROTasis, SIMultaneous ACTion, SUBordinate.

tives to be a further derivation from 'a state completely affects on entity' or an inference from a resultative interpretation of a stative.[5] The majority of the anterior grams in this group have a use as a non-anterior past or perfective. The twelve grams that are also used for past are taken to be more grammaticized semantically, since we propose that anteriors become pasts and not vice versa. We return below to a test of this hypothesis.

5. Theoretically, then, we could make even finer distinctions in semantic age among these ANTERIORS, postulating that the ones with present state readings are older than the resultative–anterior combination. However, because of the small numbers involved it is not useful from a statistical point of view to try to make these distinctions.

Table 3.8.   Related Strings and Boundness for Old Anteriors

Language	Form No.	Related Strings	Bound
01 Inuit	03		Y
03 Margi	34		Y
05 Agau	08		Y
	29	have with oneself	N
10 Isl. Carib	18		Y
	41		N
23 Palaung	05	finish	N
25 Tahitian	03	be	N
32 Nakanai	02		Y
39 Abkhaz	47		Y
42 Kui	06		Y
	25	be + inf	N
46 Karok	16		Y
47 Latin	10		Y
48 Maithili	34	be + past passive part	N
49 Baluchi	13	past be + inf	Y
	15	past be + inf + past	Y
52 Yagaria	21		Y
63 Baining	05		N
68 Slave	54	perf of be	N
72 Mwera	31		Y
74 Engenni	09	?be	N
75 Mano	04		Y
78 Kanuri	06		Y
79 Palantla	03		Y
82 Maidu	41	be	Y
86 Haka	05	be or become	N
87 Lahu	56		N
91 Udmurt	05		Y
	07		Y

The remaining uses here are the ones listed under "Evidential," which are discussed in §3.15, and several uses that are easily related to anterior, such as **future anterior** and **past anterior, immediate anterior** and **remote anterior, completive** and **state commences.** It will also be noted that there are a few cases of anteriors used in counterfactual clauses; we discuss these later on.

Having proposed that this set of anteriors is semantically more developed or "older" than the set of anteriors with only one use, we would also expect that this older set of anteriors would have expression properties that are more grammaticized than anteriors in the "younger" group. In chapter 4 we test this hypothesis against the full range of formal properties of grammaticization, but for the moment, we would simply like to call attention to the fact that a clear difference is observable between the two groups in the tendency of the gram to

Table 3.9. Percentages of Young and Old Anteriors Written Bound

	Written Free		Written Bound	
Young anteriors	38	69%	17	31%
Old anteriors	11	37%	19	63%
Perfectives	7	23%	24	78%
Pasts	5	19%	21	81%

be written bound to the main verb. The relevant data to be compared are the last column of Table 3.4 and the last column of Table 3.8. The numerical and percentage counts of grams written bound and free are shown in Table 3.9, where the same counts for perfectives and pasts are also shown. (Cf. Tables 3.10 and 3.11.)

Note that the distinction we have made between anteriors with only one use and those with multiple uses is highly significant. The major shift from free to bound occurs between these two groups, with the percentage of bound grams increasing gradually after this major shift. The old anteriors, then, pattern more with perfectives and pasts than with the young anteriors in their form as well as in their meaning.

3.11. Anterior to perfective and simple past

The next development for anteriors along their diachronic path is the change from anterior to past or perfective. This change is well documented around the world, occurring or having occurred in Indo-European languages such as French, Italian, Rumanian, German, and Dutch; in African languages of the Kru and Bantu groups; and in Mandarin Chinese. Before discussing this particular change and its causes, it is necessary for us to discuss the notions of simple past and perfective in some detail, since these two gram-types have similar semantic content and discourse function and are mainly distinguishable by the way they interact with lexical classes of verbs and other grams present in the language.

Past is the most frequent temporal notion expressed grammatically in our material. In fact, in the GRAMCATS corpus, only meaning labels expressing agreement are more frequent than past. However, in the majority of cases, past occurs with other meaning labels in a given use and thus is not the only meaning expressed by the gram. For instance, we have cases of grams that are past progressive or past habitual. The English *used to* would be an example of the latter combination. It is true that the past in *used to* is marked by the regular Past Tense, but since there is no present habitual *he uses to*, the semantic notion past is inherent to this gram. Similarly, the French Imparfait and the Spanish Imperfect are inherently past, but past imperfective.

Table 3.10. Mode of Expression and Related Strings for Simple Past

Language	Form No.	Related String	Mode of Expression	Bound
05 Agau	10		SUF	Y
08 Tigre	20		STCH	Y
09 Cheyenne	64		PRE	Y
	67	away from speaker	PRE	Y
13 Jívaro	27		SUF	Y
15 Gugada	04		SUF	Y
16 Gugu-Yalanji	01		SUF	Y
18 Maung	05		SUF	Y
19 Worora	13		SUF	Y
27 Atchin	01	come	AUX-I	N
30 Tanga	08		PARTCL	N
35 Rukai	05		PRE	Y
48 Maithili	20		SUF	Y
49 Baluchi	11		SUF	Y
50 Mod. Greek	08		SUF	Y
51 Danish	02		SUF	Y
71 Temne	09		TNCH	Y
76 Bari	06	be	PRE	Y
78 Kanuri	03	be	SUF	Y
81 Zuni	01		SUF	Y
88 Nung	07	motion away	PARTCL	N
91 Udmurt	06	(negative)	SUF	Y
93 Buriat	02		SUF	Y
	22		SUF	Y
	46	to be	AUX-I	N
94 Tok Pisin	23	been	AUX	N

Note. AUX-I = auxiliary-inflected, PARTCL = particle, PRE = prefix, STCH = stem change, SUF = suffix, TNCH = tone change.

All these realizations of past express the meaning 'occurring before the moment of speech'. However, since we are not so much interested in the semantic component itself as in the grams that carry it, we are here restricting our interest to what we can call **simple past**: those grams which express only the notion that the situation occurred prior to the moment of speech. It is only these simple past grams that develop from anteriors and resemble perfectives. To isolate the group of simple past grams, we take all the grams from our corpus which have a use with past and no other meanings in the same use. These grams, then, have one use that is simple past. However, not all of these are classified as simple past because nine of these also have anterior as a use and are classified as **old anteriors**. Taking out the old anteriors, this leaves the twenty-six forms listed in Table 3.10 as simple pasts.

Since we have extracted the past grams that also express anterior or resultative (the old anteriors) and since we are not counting among the simple pasts those grams that have other aspectual functions in the same use, the simple past grams listed here tend not to have other uses. In fact, the only other uses mentioned for these grams are uses in conditional sentences in Tigre and Maung. Simple pasts, then, tend only to express simple past.

Perfective also designates a temporal notion, but not one that is reckoned deictically in relation to the moment of speech, but rather one that is determined by the viewpoint taken on the situation. That is, perfective presents the situation described by the clause as having temporal boundaries, as being a single, unified, discrete situation. Perfective is usually described in terms of its contrast partner, imperfective, which is said to present a situation without regard to temporal boundaries. Table 3.11 shows the perfective grams in our sample, with their related strings and mode of expression.

Dahl 1985 makes the important point that perfective grams, if not restricted to past time reference, typically describe events that are in the past. This generalization is true of our data as well: many of our perfective grams are restricted to the past, and for the rest the perfective use typically refers to past events. Of course, the reason for this is the fact that past situations are most naturally viewed as bounded. In fact, the notion of a perfective present event is anomalous, since by definition such a situation could not be viewed as bounded. Of course, future events can be viewed as bounded or unbounded, and a few of the grams listed above have 'immediate future' as another use, but it is more common for this distinction to be relevant for presenting narratives, and narratives are set in the past (or historical present), and not usually in the future.

In Dahl 1985 and Bybee and Dahl 1989 it is proposed that the typical system with a perfective aspect is a tripartite system with perfective restricted to the past, and the imperfective divided into present and past.

(49)

perfective	imperfective	
	present	past

That is, typically the tense distinction is only relevant in the imperfective.

Now we can see that the main difference between a language that has a simple past and one that has a perfective is the presence or absence of a past imperfective. The semantic content of simple past

84

Chapter Three

Table 3.11.   Mode of Expression and Related Strings for Perfective

Language	Form No.	Related String	Mode of Expression	Bound/Zero
02 Basque	07	be	AUX-I	N
04 Kanakuru	09		TNCH	Y
	10		AUX-I	N
06 Touareg	02		STCH	Y
10 Isl. Carib	21		SUF	Y
12 Chacobo	41	when	SUF	Y
17 Alyawarra	01	DATIVE	SUF	Y
	17	go and	SUF	Y
18 Maung	05		ZERO	0
19 Worora	33		ZERO	0
20 Alawa	29		SUF	Y
25 Tahitian	03	be	AUX-U	N
32 Nakanai	01		ZERO	0
33 Trukese	01		PARTCL	N
34 Pangasinan	06		PRE	Y
38 O'odham	39		AUX-I	N
39 Abkhaz	44		ZERO	0
	46		SUF	Y
40 Guaymí	01		SUF	Y
	02		SUF	Y
50 Mod. Greek	10		SUF	Y
	13		SUF	Y
52 Yagaria	31	PAST	SUF	Y
63 Baining	05		PART	N
68 Slave	10		PRE	Y
69 Krongo	07		PRE	Y
72 Mwera	13	finish	SUF	Y
	32	"	SUF	Y
	55	"	SUF/PRE	Y
73 Tem	15		ZERO	0
74 Engenni	14		TNCH	Y
77 Ngambay	01		ZERO	0
80 Tojolabal	03		ZERO	0
83 Shuswap	45		PRE	Y
85 Chepang	13		SUF	Y
89 Cantonese	13		PART	N
92 Uigur	18		SUF	Y
93 Buriat	25	PAST	SUF	Y

Note. AUX=auxiliary-uninflected.

and perfective is very similar—they can both be used to signal a completed past action and they are both used in the narration of past sequences of events. The simple past is semantically more general since it can also be used to signal past time for situations viewed imperfectively.

While the perfective interacts with imperfectivity by contrasting with it, the simple past may interact with notional imperfectivity in two ways, depending on the other grams existing in a language: (i) the simple past may be used in combination with an imperfective gram (e.g. *was sleeping*); or (ii) if there is no imperfective gram, the simple past may be used for all past situations, without regard for their notional aspect.

Another indication of the similarity between past and perfective is the considerable historical and comparative evidence showing that simple past and perfective develop from the same lexical sources and go through a stage of signaling anteriority. The developments in Indo-European languages are particularly well documented. Apparently independently, both Germanic and Romance developed a periphrastic resultative/anterior by combining an auxiliary meaning 'have' or 'be' with a past participle form of the main verb, as we explained in §3.7. In the modern Germanic languages, this construction can be seen in various stages of semantic development. In Modern English, as we said before, it is a good example of an anterior having the current relevance, experiential, and anterior continuing uses. In modern colloquial German, the comparable construction has extended its use and is taking over the functions of the older Past Tense. In the spoken language, this Compound Past construction can be used in simple narration, without a sense of anteriority.

In the Romance languages, a comparable situation exists. The 'have' or 'be' plus Past Participle construction originated as a resultative (see §3.7) and now in modern Castilian Spanish is used in very much the same set of contexts as the English Perfect (Harris 1982). However, the cognate construction in French, the Passé Composé, has generalized to perfective in the spoken language, completely replacing the older inflectional perfective, the Passé Simple.

In French (and Spanish), a past imperfective existed prior to the development of the anterior, so that when the anterior generalized to perfective, it did not also take over the functions of the imperfective and become a simple past, but rather took over only perfective functions and now contrasts with the imperfective. In the German case, however, no past imperfective exists, so that it appears that the anterior which is generalizing will become a simple past, like the older past that it replaces. Thus it appears that the existence of a past imperfective determines whether a generalizing anterior will become perfective or simple past. We will return to a test of this hypothesis below.

Outside Indo-European, there is also evidence for the development anterior > perfective or simple past. The Mandarin sentence-final particle *le*, which signals current relevance and other anterior-like functions (Li, Thompson, and Thompson 1982) is derived from a verb *liao* 'to finish'. After its sentence-final function was well established, it also developed a use in which it appears directly after the main verb (whether or not it is sentence-final) in which it functions to signal perfective action. Diachronically it is clear that the sentence-final function developed earlier than, and gave rise to, the verb-final function, even though they co-exist in the language today.

Heine and Reh (1984: 127–28) report, based on Westermann 1907: 139, that the verb 'finish' in the Dahome dialect of Ewe has developed from an anterior into a past tense marker. Presumably the pasts and perfectives from 'finish' in the GRAMCATS languages have gone through similar stages, although the evidence for the anterior stage may be missing.

Comparative dialect evidence from another part of the world shows the development of anterior > past from a lexical verb meaning 'come'. In Atchin, the auxiliary *ma* 'come' merges with pronominal forms to make a past tense auxiliary. In the neighboring dialects of Vao and Wala, however, this same auxiliary is still used as an anterior (Capell and Layard 1980: 74ff.).

Finally, Marchese 1986: 70 describes the Perfect or anterior auxiliary in both Eastern and Western Kru languages. The source of this auxiliary is not known. In one Eastern Kru language, Lozoua Dida, however, the cognate auxiliary is used for the perfective.

The evidence, then, for the passage of anterior to perfective or past is quite strong and distributed across various language families. It is also documented for anteriors from stative auxiliary sources as well as for anteriors from dynamic verb sources, which suggests that, as anteriors develop, the differences among them that are due to their sources gradually attenuate. This example illustrates the convergence of grams from different sources, as discussed in § 1.4.3, which accounts for the fact that the meanings associated with the most highly grammaticized categories are very similar across languages.

The change of an anterior to a past or perfective is typical of grammaticization changes. On the semantic level, the change is clearly a generalization of meaning, or the loss of a specific component of meaning: the anterior signals a past action that is relevant to the current moment, while the past and perfective signal only a past action. The specification of current relevance is lost. The meaning generalizes in the sense that the past or perfective gram expresses a more general meaning that is compatible with more contexts.

Such changes occur because of the way language is used. The anterior conveys the sense of past or perfective but includes a special flavor of relevance or proximity to the present or current situation. Thus if a speaker wishes to frame his or her contribution AS THOUGH it were highly relevant to current concerns, then the speaker might use the anterior more often than would be strictly necessary for the communication of the propositional content of the message. Such overuse weakens the force of the current relevance component, and eventually the hearer infers only past or perfective action from the anterior and no sense of current relevance.

Schwenter 1993 studies the ongoing change of the Spanish Present Perfect in the Alicante dialect, where it has come to be used as a hodiernal perfective, consistently signaling perfective situations that occurred on the same day. Schwenter argues that the frequent reporting of recent past events as currently relevant leads to the inference that the Present Perfect refers to the recent past, with the concurrent erosion of the current relevance meaning. Moreover, the fact that recent past is often on the same day as the moment of speech leads to the further inference that the Present Perfect signals past events on the same day, extending gradually to events more and more remote within the same day. Schwenter argues that once the Present Perfect is established as a hodiernal past rather than a past with current relevance, it will gradually extend beyond the limits of the day and will eventually become a general perfective, replacing the Preterite.

3.12. Perfective from bounders

Another very different source for the development of perfective is also attested, for instance in the Slavic languages. In these languages adverbs, comparable to English *up, down, over* and *through,* for example, with originally locative meaning, pair with verbs to create a sense of completion or, in Dahl's terms, "attainment of a limit." Thus *eat up* implies the attainment of a limit—the complete consumption of the object—which *eat* alone does not. *Write up, write down* have natural endpoints or limits that *write* alone does not. In Bybee and Dahl 1989, grams from such adverbial sources are referred to as **bounders** because of the semantic effect that they have.

The use of such adverbs to form lexical compounds may be highly irregular in a language, with verb–adverb pairs being restricted to certain combinations, or it may become very widespread in a language, with the adverbs becoming grammaticized and generalized to occur with many verbs. In such a case it may eventually happen that almost all verbs participate and have forms with and without bounders. In such cases, the verbs without bounders may be viewed as imperfective in aspect, while the verbs with bounders are perfective. A contrast develops that resembles the perfective/imperfective distinction. This has happened to varying degrees in the Slavic languages, in Georgian, in Margi (a Chadic language), and in Mokilese (an Oceanic language). However, in none of these languages is there only one bounder that has become productive; rather all these languages have a number of bounders in the class, and some verbs may combine with more than one and, consequently, have more than one perfective form. That is, in all these languages, the bounder formation remains derivational in nature, exhibiting much lexical idiosyncrasy.

The following are a few examples from Margi, which happens to be in the GRAMCATS sample. It can be seen here that even though the etymological source of the suffix is known, the meaning it adds to the verb is not always synchronically predictable.

(50) Derivatives in -bá 'out' (Hoffman 1963: 122–24)

ɗəm	'to pick, to gather'	ɗəmbá	'to pick out, to gather out of'
ndàl	'to throw'	ndàlbá	'to throw out'
ŋà	'to call'	ŋábá	'to call out'
'ùtlà	'to cough'	'útlábá	'to bring out by coughing'
dzànì	'to know'	dzànbá	'to know well'
pá	'to build, pile up, fold'	pábá	'to repair (partly broken down wall)'

Derivatives in -ía 'downward' (pp. 125–28)

ndàl	'to throw'	ndàlía	'to throw down'
dùgù	'to find, come upon'	dùgwía	'to come upon, to attack'
vəl	'to jump, fly'	vəlía	'to jump down'

Derivatives in -na 'away' (pp. 129–32)

ndàl	'to throw'	ndàlnà	'to throw away'
hù	'to take (one)'	hənà	'to take away, subtract (one)'
ŋgyù̥	'to burn (intr.)'	ŋgyìnà	'to burn (tr.), scorch, singe'

Among the examples of perfective derivatives that Hoffman gives are many with the same translation as the underived root, suggesting that in some cases little or no meaning in addition to perfectivity is added to the verb.

There are several differences between this type of perfective and the perfective that develops from an anterior (Dahl 1985; Bybee and Dahl 1989):

(1) The perfective derived from an anterior becomes inflectional in nature when it becomes affixal: that is, it is lexically general, applying to all verbs with very few idiosyncrasies of meaning. The perfective derived from bounders is derivational: not all verbs participate, not all verbs take the same bounders, and the bounders often add meaning other than perfectivity. The generalization of derivational morphology is probably accomplished by different mechanisms than the

grammaticization of inflection. Derivational affixes spread item by item through the lexicon, while the distribution of inflectional grams is conditioned by a much larger context—a clause or a section of discourse.

(2) Dahl's questionnaire revealed that the more common sense of 'perfective' is that associated with the inflectional perfective, which typically denotes "a single event, seen as an unanalyzed whole . . . located in the past" (Dahl 1985: 78). The derivational perfectives do not quite fit this prototype, since they emphasize that a limit has been attained, not just that the event is viewed as an unanalyzed whole. Of course, their grammatical meaning follows directly from their richer lexical meanings and gives us another instance of what we have called source determination.

The derivational perfectives resemble completives in their meaning. There are other points of similarity as well: many of our completive grams were themselves derivational, and some of the lexical sources for completives are directionals, such as 'away', 'up', or 'into'. Derivational perfectives, then, are probably just highly generalized and elaborated completives.

(3) The derivational perfective occurs with all tenses and is not necessarily restricted to the past as the inflectional perfective usually is. Unlike the inflectional perfective, which enters into the tripartite system in which perfective is always past and only imperfective has a tense distinction, in the derivational system perfective and imperfective cross-classify with tense to a much greater extent. For instance, in Russian, the non-past of a perfective verb expresses the future (although there is also a periphrastic future); of course, the non-past of the imperfective is present. In Margi, the present of the perfective verb also exists; it may be used for the future in a clearly future context, or it may be used to express root possibility, as in the following example (Hoffman 1963: 193):

(51)   nì   àhə́rí
       1   s PRES:take:PERF
       'I can take (it).'

However, even in such systems, the perfective is still more commonly used for reference to past occurrences.

(4) The derivational perfective has an overt marker, while the imperfective may be zero. In the inflectional system, the imperfective is always overtly marked, while the perfective may be zero. The distribution of zeroes is, of course, tied to the path by which the gram-type develops.

In fact, all these differences are attributable to the diachronic source of the grams in question. Grams developing from a derivational source have a different set of grammatical and semantic properties from grams that develop as inflection. These examples show that there is a strong correlation between the diachronic source of a gram and its synchronic use and distribution.

While the differences among perfective grams are of considerable interest, their similarities are probably even more worthy of attention. Dahl's analysis of his questionnaire material shows a close similarity between the derivational perfective of the Slavic languages and the inflectional perfectives of other languages. (E.g., the Slavic perfectives are only slighty further from the prototypical distribution of 'perfective' than the Spanish Preterite.) Considering the vast differences in paths of development of inflectional versus derivational perfectives, this convergence in meaning is quite noteworthy. It has been argued by Hopper 1979, 1982a that one of the major functions of aspect is a discourse function—the signaling of foregrounded versus backgrounded information in narrative discourse. We have already mentioned that one of the major functions of the simple past and inflectional perfective is the narration of simple sequences of events in the past. Hopper argues, citing Forsyth 1970, that the most characteristic function of perfective verbs in Russian is the expression of a sequence of actions. We are suggesting, then, that the similarities in the notions of perfectivity that languages express derive from the similarities in discourse function that perfectives are asked to perform.

3.13. Perfectives from zero

Another way that perfectives sometimes develop is as a consequence of the development of an imperfective. In such cases, the perfective has zero expression. Our sample contains seven examples of languages with an unmarked perfective: Maung, Worora, Nakanai, Abkhaz, Tem, Ngambai, and Tojolabal. In Nakanai, Ngambai, and Tem, the unmarked verb form is interpreted for dynamic verbs as perfective and for stative verbs as the context demands, with the default interpretation being present. This interpretation of zero-marked verb forms is also documented for pidgin and creole languages (Bickerton 1975, 1977), although Sankoff 1990 argues that these interpretations are not yet obligatory in some pidgin and creole languages. In Abkhaz and Tojolabal, the zero perfective is simply not applicable to stative predicates. For Maung the reference material did not contain a discussion of stative predicates, although it is reported that equational sentences lack a copula and are without tense.

Zero expression raises an interesting set of grammaticization questions, since zeroes "mark" categories that have not undergone the usual evolution from lexical to grammatical, but rather have arisen because some other contrasting gram has undergone this process. Dahl 1985 treats all zero-marked grams as default categories, that is, as not having a prototypical characterization, but only taking up the space left over by other overtly marked grams. Our data suggest that the semantic areas covered by zeroes are also systematic and quite comparable to those covered by overt grams (Bybee 1990b). For instance, it cannot be simply accidental that both overtly marked and zero-marked perfectives can signal the present with stative predicates. Rather, zeroes are attributed the same meanings as overt grams would have if they were available.

3.14. Differences between perfective and simple past

In §3.11 we pointed out that the perfective and simple past are very similar to one another, and we hypothesized that a developing anterior becomes one or the other depending on the presence or absence of a past imperfective in the language. In this section we offer a test of that hypothesis, and we point out other differences between simple past and perfective. We argue that some of these differences suggest that simple pasts are more grammaticized than perfectives and that there may even be a diachronic relation between these two gram-types in some cases.

If perfectives can only develop out of anteriors when a past imperfective already exists in the language, we would predict that a perfective will never contrast with an imperfective that has zero expression, for if the past imperfective is zero, that would mean that the perfective had developed even though there was no pre-existing past imperfective. This prediction is borne out in our data, where all twenty-five languages with a non-zero perfective also have a non-zero past imperfective.[6] The combinations of expression types in (52) are found in our sample for perfective and imperfective.

(52)	perfective	imperfective	n
	OVERT	OVERT	25
	ZERO	OVERT	07
	*OVERT	ZERO	00

In contrast with perfectives, simple pasts do not have zero expression in any of the languages of our sample. This suggests that a simple

6. A possible exception is the Athapaskan language Slave, where a zero is one realization of the imperfective. However, for many verbs a stem change also distinguishes perfective from imperfective, and due to the existence of numerous other aspectual markings, a true zero-marked imperfective occurs only very rarely (Keren Rice, personal communication).

past does not develop as a consequence of a present tense gram developing, but rather a past always develops via a grammaticization path from lexical material. At times a developing simple past may condition the establishment of a zero-marked present tense, giving the expression types shown in (53).[7]

(53)
	present	past	n
	OVERT	OVERT	18
	ZERO	OVERT	05
	*OVERT	ZERO	00

Thus despite the similarity in the notions expressed by simple past and perfective, their history of development may be quite different.

Other differences between simple past and perfective have to do with their interaction with lexical categories of verbs and with other grams, both of which point to differences in semantics. First, perfectives seem to interact with the lexical semantics of the verb more than pasts do, as we might expect, since perfective has more semantic relevance to the verb than past (Bybee 1985). That is, perfective offers a particular perspective on the action described by the verb and thus interacts with the verb's inherent semantics, while the past has scope over the whole proposition, which it locates in time with respect to the moment of speech, but without imposing any special perspective on the structure of the situation.

The actual manifestation of this difference can be seen in the way that perfectives apply to stative predicates. To begin with, in some languages, perfectives do not apply at all to stative predicates (as shown in Table 3.12 by NA under State Exists), while pasts commonly apply to all predicates, having the effect of signaling a past state with stative predicates. Further, when perfectives do apply to stative predicates, the effect is usually to signal a present state, not a past one, despite the fact that perfectives are usually past. We have already discussed the various ways that this situation arises diachronically. What is of interest here is that a similar situation does not obtain for pasts, even though they develop from the same set of sources as perfectives do. One hypothesis that would explain these facts is the hypothesis that pasts are more grammaticized than perfectives and, in some cases, are further developments from perfectives. The fact that pasts have a more general distribution among lexical classes of verbs than perfectives do is in perfect accord with this hypothesis. Diachronically this would mean that as perfectives develop into pasts, they gradually come to be used in a past sense with all classes of verbs, including stative verbs. If the presents of stative verbs have perfective marking,

7. Not all languages are counted here; in particular those with non-obligatory past markers may in some cases have neither overt nor zero presents.

Table 3.12. Other Uses of Perfectives

Language	Form No.	PFV	State Exists	Result	Other
02 Basque	07	PAST			
04 Kanakuru	09	x			
	10	x			
06 Touareg	02	PAST & FUT			HYPO PROT
10 Isl. Carib	21	PAST	x		
12 Chacobo	41	x			?COMP
17 Alyawarra	01	PAST			
	17	x			
18 Maung	05	PAST			
19 Worora	33	x			
20 Alawa	29	PAST			
25 Tahitian	03	x	x	x	FUT ANT
32 Nakanai	01	x	x		
33 Trukese	01	x		x	IMP
34 Pangasinan	06	x			
38 O'odham	39	x			
39 Abkhaz	44	PAST			IMM FUT, CONC, GNOM, OPT
	46	CONJ			
40 Guaymí	01	IMM			
	02	REMOTE			
50 Mod. Greek	10	x			
	13	PASS			
52 Yagaria	31	s 1ST			
63 Baining	05	IMM FUT, IMP			
68 Slave	10	x	x	x	
69 Krongo	07	IMM PAST			
72 Mwera	13	HOD	x		
	32	P-HOD	NA		
	55	P-HOD	PAST		
73 Tem	15	x	x		
74 Engenni	14	x			PURP, SUB, TEMP
77 Ngambay	01	x	x		
80 Tojolabal	03	x	NA		
83 Shuswap	45	x	x		
85 Chepang	13	x	NA		COMP
89 Cantonese	13	x			STATE CHANGES
92 Uigur	18	PAST			
93 Buriat	25	PAST			

Note. COMPletive, CONCessive, CONJunctive, FUTure, GNOMic, HODiernal, HYPOthetical, IMMediate, OPTative, pre-HODiernal, PROTasis, SUBordinate, TEMPoral.

this development might lead to double marking of stative verbs for past, as for instance in the Preterite-Present verbs of Germanic. Unfortunately, we know of no clear documented case of a perfective that has become a simple past. However, our database contains the case of Yagaria, which appears to have a perfective which is becoming a past.

In Yagaria there is a Present Tense, marked with zero, which is used for historical present in narration, and for medial verbs to indicate the same tense as the last verb. There is also a Progressive formed with a prefix *no-*, which is used for progressive and habitual, but only in the present. The Past form, the suffix *-d-* (which may be related to *hadó*, a word denoting completeness; Renck 1977: 115) is used for "all past actions, be they completive, perfective or habitual" (Renck 1975: 92). However, at the same time it appears to be used for what we would regard as resultative functions, as in (54).

(54)   beidie   'he has sat down = he sits, he is sitting'
       elidie   'he has taken = he is holding it'

The past tense suffix can also be used with the stative verb *hanó* 'to exist' with present tense reference, as in (55).

(55)   beite'na- ti   hogona   hano-d-   i-   e
       life   our   short   exist- PAST- 3s- IND
       'our life is short.'

With medial verbs with identical subjects, the Past indicates simple past, not necessarily perfective or anterior, while with non-identical subjects, it marks anterior, as in (56).

(56)   ba   do- d-   i-   ga- ta   hapei- d-   un- e
       sweet potato   eat- PAST- 3s- NI- we tell- PAST- 1P- IND
       'After he had eaten the sweet potato, we told him.'

This one suffix has a very wide range of use—wider perhaps than any of the other past or perfective grams we have examined. It can be used in some anterior and resultative senses with at least one stative verb to indicate present tense and for non-perfective past. If it is a perfective becoming a simple past, then we would expect to find it used to indicate past states. Indeed, in (57)–(58) are examples of past states with *-d* from Renck (1975: 151).

(57)   gei   da- hei-   d-   i-   e
       sickness   me- be.like PAST- 3s- IND
       'I was sick.'
(58)   l-   ago'yu ei-   d-   un- e
       we- be.angry- PAST- 1P- IND
       'We were angry.'

This Yagaria suffix, then, may be an example of a gram that is traveling through all the stages of anterior, resultative, perfective, and finally past. The Progressive prefix *no-* seems to be undergoing development as a present since it is used for both progressive and habitual, and there are examples of its use with stative predicates as well.

Table 3.12 also shows that perfectives have other, non-past, uses distinguishing them from simple pasts, which tend not to have other uses. In particular, perfectives may be used in future contexts, as in Tahitian, where with a temporal clause set in the future, the perfective signals future anterior, or as in Abkhaz and Baining, where the otherwise perfective gram can also signal immediate future. Simple pasts, on the other hand, are not used outside past contexts, with the possible exception of conditional sentences.

To summarize, then, we find the following differences between perfective and simple past in our data:

(i) Perfective contrasts with non-zero imperfective, while past either co-occurs with imperfective to make a past imperfective or is used alone to signal both perfective and imperfective past.

(ii) Perfective is sometimes zero-marked, but past is not.

(iii) Perfective is either not used with stative verbs or has the effect of signaling a present state with stative verbs. Past signals a past state.

(iv) Perfective is sometimes used for future or with future, but past is not.

3.15. Evidential uses of anteriors

Not all anteriors become perfectives or simple pasts, not right away at least. Another cross-linguistically documented path of development for anteriors involves their taking on certain evidential functions. Evidential grams indicate something about the source of the information in the speaker's assertion (see Chafe and Nichols 1986; Willett 1988). According to Willett's cross-linguistic study, the basic distinction among evidentials is between those that indicate that the speaker has the information via direct evidence of having witnessed the situation or via indirect evidence, which may be further divided into reported evidence (that is, the speaker has the information from another speaker) or inferred evidence (that is, the speaker has inferred the situation from its results or simply by reasoning).

The development of resultatives or anteriors into evidentials of indirect evidence is well known in Turkish, Bulgarian, Macedonian, and Georgian and is sometimes regarded as an areal phenomenon (Dahl 1985: 152). However, the same developments also occur in other parts of the world, as in Tibetan languages (Genetti 1986). In our sample, we have evidence for this development in three languages which lie outside the proposed "area": Udmurt (west-central Russia), Inuit (Greenland), and Tucano (Colombia).

In the cases where the sources of the constructions in question are known, they develop from auxiliaries meaning 'be' with participial forms of the main verb (e.g. in Armenian, Bulgarian, Macedonian, Georgian, and Tucano) or (in the case of Turkish) from the stative or passive participle without an auxiliary. Such sources suggest that a resultative stage gives rise to the evidential meaning. That is, the resultative indicates that a state exists due to a past action. This meaning is very close to the evidential meaning of an inference from results, which indicates that a past action is known or inferred on the basis of a current state. If in English we say *Mary is gone,* we state that she is not here and also that she has left. If this were an evidential marking inference from results, it would state that she has left and also that the speaker KNOWS because she is not here. That is, the relation between the two parts of the meaning of the resultative has changed.

In a way this change is similar to the change from resultative to anterior, in that the resultative focuses on the state resulting from the past action while the anterior describes the past action but from the point of view of its current relevance. The evidential also describes the past action, but with the added qualification that it is known through present results. In each case the change brings the gram closer to signaling a simple past action.

The diachronic relation of resultative and anterior to inferential is documented in some cases, namely Turkish (Slobin and Aksu 1982; Aksu-Koç and Slobin 1986) and Bulgarian and Macedonian (Friedman 1987), but it is also reconstructable from the languages of our sample on the basis of the sources and the range of use of the grams in question. The Tucano construction, consisting of the main verb root marked for gender (which we assume to be a participle) plus the verb 'be', signals that the speaker did not see the action but does see the result which verifies that it did happen (West 1980: 75). Thus one commonly uses this form upon receiving a letter (see [59]).

(59) Yu'u   pacó   ojáco   niámo.
     1.s.POSS mother   write:F   be:3.s.F
     'My mother wrote. (I didn't see her but here is the proof that she did it.)'

The Tucano construction is limited to an inference based on results, but in the other cases, the evidential use is considerably expanded and includes all kinds of indirect evidence.

The Inuit form *sima,* for instance, is used for anterior, or in Fortescue's words "relative past with continuing result" (Fortescue 1980: 272) and in such a use is incompatible with specific temporal words such as 'at 3 o'clock'. However, it is also used to indicate that the speaker did not witness the past situation himself. It can be used when the result is present, as in seeing a puddle of water outside the house (p. 294).

(60)   siallir-   sima-   vuq
       rain-   must.have-   3.s.IND
       'It must have rained.'

It can also be used for reported events that the speaker considers
reliable. Here it is compatible with specific time expressions (p. 294).

(61)   nalunaaqutaq   pingasut   tuqu-   sima-   vuq
       clock   three   die-   apparently-   3.s.IND
       'He died at three o'clock.'

It appears likely that from the inference-from-results use exemplified in Tucano, the evidential component can generalize to include
inference from reasoning (without direct results) and reported evidence, that is, the full range of indirect evidence. In fact, in Udmurt,
such a form is also used for the narration of folk tales, demonstrating
another path by which anteriors can come to be used in narrating
sequences of events.

Anteriors developing into pasts of indirect evidence do not take
over all the functions of simple past or perfective grams already existing in the language, but they do have the effect of restricting the
range of usage of the existing grams to reporting situations about
which the speaker has direct knowledge.

We have argued that the evidential use of anterior grams develops
from the resultative use, implying that only anteriors with resultative
uses—that is, anteriors from stative verb sources—develop into evidentials. This seems certainly to be the most usual route for this development, but there is also a case reported by Genetti 1986 of a
Newari anterior from a verb 'finish' which has evidential function.
Interestingly, however, Newari has another developing anterior with
evidential function, this one from a more stative verb, a verb translated as 'keep'. The latter verb yields a resultative construction and an
evidential indicating that the speaker witnessed the results of the past
action. The evidential sense of the anterior from 'finish' is different:
it indicates that the speaker sees no results but infers on other bases
that the past action occurred. Genetti argues that both the anterior
senses and the evidential senses are direct outgrowths of the original
lexical meaning of the two verbs, much as we would argue in support
of the source determination hypothesis.

Thus it appears that the most common source of evidential senses
for anteriors is the resultative sense that develops for anteriors coming from stative verb sources. However, at least one case of an evidential anterior from a dynamic verb source is also attested. Note also
that while evidential functions of anteriors are attested in widely distributed languages, such developments are less frequent compared to
the development of anteriors into pasts and perfectives.

3.16. Degrees of remoteness

In addition to past tense meaning combined with aspectual and evidential value and indications of current relevance or completion, past tense meaning can be divided into more specific indications of the degree of remoteness from the moment of speech. For instance, in Cocama, three degrees of remoteness are distinguished, as in the examples in (62) (Faust 1978: 42).

(62)   Ritama-ca   tuts-ui.   'I went to town today.'
       town-to   go-PAST
       Ritama-ca   tutsu-icuá.   'I went to town yesterday/a few days
       town-to   go-PAST   ago.'
       Ritama-ca   tutsu-tsuri.   'I went to town a long time ago.'
       town-to   go-PAST

In our data we find the same types of remoteness distinctions as those reported in Comrie 1985b and Dahl 1985. We use the following meaning labels to characterize remoteness distinctions:

   Those that have relatively non-specific cut-off points:
   Immediate past: the situation occurred in the recent or immediate past.
   Remote past: the situation occurred long ago, in the distant past.
   Ancient past: the situation occurred in ancient or mythic times.
   Those that refer to the daily cycle for cut-off points:
   Hodiernal past: the situation occurred on the same day as the speech event.
   Pre-hodiernal past: the situation occurred before the 'today' of the speech event.
   Hesternal past: the situation occurred yesterday, or on the day preceding the speech event.
   Pre-hesternal past: the situation occurred before yesterday.

The most common meaning component in our data is the remote past, but the exact span of time it may be used to refer to differs across languages according to what other past grams occur in the language. For instance, in Cheyenne none of the tense markers is obligatory, and there is a simple past in addition to the remote past. In Guaymí, on the other hand, tense is obligatory and divided into immediate and remote. In the Cocama examples given above and in Tucano, the remote past starts 'a few days ago' and continues into the distant past, while in Cheyenne and Uigur, translations such as 'a long time ago' suggest a period of time much more remote than a few days. Meanings such as hodiernal and hesternal are of course much more specific and uniform across languages.

   In our tables we divide languages into those that have distinctions

Table 3.13.   Degrees of Remoteness with Hodiernal and Hesternal

Language	Immediate	Remote	Hodiernal	Pre-Hodiernal	Hester-nal	Pre-Hesternal
11 Cocama		04	01	03		
12 Chacobo	37	38	35		36	
28 Halia			21	23		
58 Nimboran			08		08	07
60 Yessan-Mayo			12	13		
72 Mwera	31		13	32/55		
79 Palantla	07		06			

Table 3.14.   Degrees of Remoteness Not Referring to the Daily Cycle

Language	Immediate	Remote	Ancient
01 Inuit	13	14	
09 Cheyenne		65	
14 Tucano	02	01	
38 O'odham		38	
40 Guaymí	01	04	
49 Baluchi		13	
56 Ono	02	03	
59 Bongu		08/18	08/18
68 Slave	48		
82 Maidu		62/63	64
91 Udmurt		25	
92 Uigur	34	22	
93 Buriat		24	

based on the daily cycle (Table 3.13) and those that use the less specific division of immediate versus remote (Table 3.14). Languages with the latter type of distinction are much more common in our sample, but there are a few languages where the two types of distinctions occur together, as shown in Table 3.14. Note also that it is not uncommon for these languages to also have anterior grams (young or old) and perfectives. In other words, these languages tend to have fairly elaborate past marking.

In Table 3.13 it is clear that the most common cut-off point involving the daily cycle is today versus previous days, confirming the prediction of Dahl 1985: 125 (cf. Comrie 1985b: 93). A special past gram for 'yesterday' occurs only in Chacobo. In the Nimboran case the same past gram is used for 'today' and 'yesterday', and all other past contexts are considered pre-hesternal.

Sometimes it is difficult to be sure that reports of hodiernals and pre-hodiernals are accurate, since it is difficult to distinguish between a hodiernal past and a very immediate past. For instance, one description of Guaymí (Alphonse 1956) states that "the Immediate Past

Tense is used when an action is done within the limits of a day" (p. 27). Another description (Kopesec 1975) characterizes the immediate/remote distinction as relative, saying that once the situation time has been established, even if it is quite remote, the Immediate form may be used, as the actions of the narrative are considered to be close to the established scene (p. 22). It is possible that both descriptions are accurate, one dealing with narrative discourse and the other with non-narrative. However, we chose to follow the latter description, which in general we found to be more reliable.

Another case that is difficult to interpret is Chacobo, which has the following suffixes, translated as in (63) (Prost 1962: 117–18).

(63)   -ya-   'just now'
        -ʔita-   'yesterday'
        -yamï-   'short time ago'
        -ni-   'long time ago'

These suffixes co-occur with one member of an obligatory aspectual class, the member that "denotes that the action is complete or finished" (Prost 1962: 118), which suggests that they are not so much markers of tense as items that divide the past into segments. We have tentatively interpreted the first of these, -ya, as a hodiernal past, since the next degree of remoteness signals 'yesterday'. However, it might be the case that 'just now' actually means only 'just now' and 'earlier the same day' may be covered by another suffix, perhaps the one translated as 'a short time ago'.

One type of cut-off point not mentioned by Comrie or Dahl but reported for Maidu by Shipley (1964: 52–53) takes the speaker's lifetime as the relevant unit. Maidu has a periphrastic construction consisting of the verb stem followed by a morpheme kyʔym. The suffix wonó indicates a time long ago, but in the lifetime of the speaker or his/her parents, and the suffix paʔáje indicates a time "long ago in ancient or mythical times; long before my time" (Shipley 1964: 52).

We have already mentioned that the exact time period covered by immediate and remote may vary according to what other remoteness grams exist in the language. This fact implies that contrast is important in the evolution of the meaning of remoteness grams, and we will present evidence that this is so below. However, there are also cases, visible in Table 3.14, in which the principle of contrast appears to be irrelevant. For instance, in Bongu there are two forms that are synonymous, both signaling the remote and ancient past. In Mwera, shown in Table 3.13, there are two pre-hodiernal grams and no difference in their meaning is described in the reference grammar. On the other hand, in Slave there is an immediate past, but no remote past for it to contrast with. Rather, Slave has a perfective and what we have called above an old anterior. Thus the data show that it is not necessary to have only one marker of any stretch of the remoteness continuum, nor is it necessary to have a gram for one remote range just because there is a gram for its complement. On the other hand, remoteness grams do provide evidence for grammatical meaning being shaped in some cases by contrast, as we will see at the end of this section.

Unfortunately, our material contains very little information about the lexical sources of remoteness grams, and in general very little information is available concerning the way that remoteness grams develop. However, the material that is available is suggestive of certain tendencies, which we will outline here.

There seem to be three types of lexical sources for remoteness grams. First, remoteness grams may develop in the same way as simple pasts and perfectives develop, that is, from completives and anteriors. Second, remoteness grams may develop from temporal adverbs. Third, a small amount of evidence exists suggesting a relation to locative notions. We will consider the evidence for each of these sources.

In Mwera the hodiernal and pre-hodiernal pasts are restricted to the perfective, and no such distinction exists among the continuous and habitual pasts. The hodiernal past has the suffix -ile, which occurs generally in Bantu as a perfective suffix. It is reconstructed as coming from a verb stem *gid- meaning 'finish' plus an older perfective suffix -e (Voeltz 1980) (cf. Mambila gi(l) 'finish'; Heine and Reh 1984: 73). The evidence that this -ile suffix in Mwera was once an anterior or perfective is the fact that it signals a present when used with stative verbs (Harries 1950: 94–95).

The two pre-hodiernal grams in Mwera are formed with auxiliary prefixes, and one of them combines the auxiliary with the -ile suffix. By their formal properties we would surmise that the pre-hodiernal grams are more recent developments, suggesting that a formerly wider ranging anterior or perfective was restricted to hodiernal as the other constructions developed.

Remoteness distinctions may also arise from anteriors formed from stative auxiliaries plus a past participle. This type of development is reported in a number of Romance languages. For instance, in seventeenth century French, according to the Port-Royal grammar, the newly developed Passé Composé, which was formed with the auxiliaries avoir or être plus the past participle, developing from a resultative to an anterior, had become a hodiernal past, leaving the older Passé Simple as a pre-hodiernal past (Lancelot and Arnauld 1660: 104).

According to Comrie (1985b: 85), the Spanish Present Perfect (formed from the auxiliary *haber* plus the past participle), which we would characterize as an anterior, may be used as a simple past for situations taking place on the day of the speech event. The evidence for this is its compatibility with specific temporal adverbs, such as 'this morning'. Thus (64) is grammatical in Spanish (although not in English), while in (65) the reading must be anterior (involving current relevance) and is thus incompatible with the temporal adverb.

(64)   Lo he visto hoy a las seis de la mañana.
       *I have seen him today at six in the morning.
(65)   *Lo he visto ayer a las seis de la mañana.
       *I have seen him yesterday at six in the morning.

Dahl (1985: 125) reports the Romance languages Spanish, Catalan, and Occitan use the Present Perfect with 'this morning' in his questionnaire, but the Simple Past with 'yesterday'.

Apparently, it is common for the current day to serve as the frame for current relevance. Thus from a sense of a past situation with current relevance on the same day evolves the sense of a past situation on the same day. See Schwenter 1993 for a description of this usage in the Spanish of Alicante and for evidence concerning how the change from anterior to hodiernal past to perfective takes place.

Past anteriors which develop from the past forms of stative auxiliaries plus a past participle may develop uses for remote past. An example is found in Baluchi, where the past participle plus the past form of the copula produce a form used for past anterior but also for simple remote past time (Barker and Mengal 1969: 336). Since this gram parallels the present anterior, which is built on the past participle plus present forms of the copula, we assume that it originally had anterior meaning. The change of past anterior to remote past is a generalization of meaning and parallels the change of anterior to simple past. Since in a past narrative the past anterior is used for situations that are prior to those signaled in the simple past, past anterior situations are more remote than past ones, and at the same time, relevant in some way to the past situation. If the requirement that the more remote situation be relevant to the less remote one is lost, then the past anterior comes to be a simple remote past. Such a development probably also occurred in Udmurt, where a past form of the copula is used to form the remote past. (Cf. also the Baluchi Past Perfect Completive, which is used for "far past completion of an action or event . . . or likelihood of some remote past event"; Barker and Mengal 1969: 341.) Dahl 1985: 147 reports that Hindi, Bengali, and Amharic use the past anterior (pluperfect, in his terms) for the remote past.

Our material also provides some evidence that temporal adverbs may serve as sources for remoteness distinctions. The Cocama hesternal past suffix -icuá is apparently related to the word for 'yesterday', icuachi. Our information on Chacobo is rather limited, but the translations of the remoteness suffixes as shown in (63) above suggest a derivation from free adverbials of time.

Finally, there is some indication that remoteness notions may relate to locative notions. The remote past prefix in Cheyenne is identical to a prefix meaning 'toward the speaker' and similar to a prefix that refers back to something already established (Leman 1980a: 147, 191).

(66) énexho'ehne   'he's coming (toward speaker)'
     énehetóhoono   'that's what he said to him'
     énehesnéméne   'he sang that way'
     énehnéméne   'he sang long ago'

Another type of relation between remoteness and location is suggested by descriptions of the immediate and remote pasts in Tucano and Guaymí. We have already had occasion to mention the Guaymí case in which the immediate past is described as representing situations as close to the scene of the discourse, while the remote past represents situations as remote or distant from the scene (Kopesec 1975: 22). The Tucano immediate past (of direct experience) is described as representing a situation as either removed in time from the present or removed in space, so that for a third person subject, this form could signal a present action by someone not in sight at the moment (West 1980: 27).[8]

A final, unclassifiable lexical source for a remote past is found in Inuit, where the suffix riikatag meaning 'long ago' is made up of riir 'already' and the verb katag 'be bored with -ing'. Thus the form (67) would literally mean 'he is already bored with dying' (Fortescue 1984: 273).

(67) tuqu- riikatap- puq   'He died long ago.'
     die- long.ago- 3.s.IND

One final problem in the meaning of remoteness grams should be mentioned: there are cases of past grams that cover discontinuous sections of the temporal continuum. One such case is discussed in Comrie (1985b: 88). In Burera (Australia), one suffix may be used for present reference, 'I am eating now', or immediate past excluding the present day; another is used for situations occurring earlier on the same day and for those occurring more than a few days ago. Both

8. Another case of remoteness distinctions related to locative distinctions is found in Kiksht, discussed by Hymes 1975.

suffixes, then, have discontinuous meaning. In our sample, we also found a past gram with discontinuous meaning which is very similar to the first Burera suffix. In Palantla Chinantec, the two tense prefixes are na^2, which indicates an action completed earlier the same day (a simple hodiernal past), and ka^1, which is discontinuous, indicating an action just completed or an action completed on a previous day (Merrifield 1968: 25). Such meanings probably develop through the interaction of the meaning of the two grams. If a hodiernal past and an anterior (with current relevance) are both developing in the language, they would both have a claim to describe situations having just occurred on the same day. If the anterior wins for situations that just occurred but the hodiernal continues to function for situations earlier in the same day, then the result is a discontinuous meaning for the non-hodiernal gram.[9]

3.17. Form/meaning correlations

To summarize our discussion, we present a diagram (Fig. 3.1) showing the paths of development leading to simple past and perfective grams. The evidence from the frequency of occurrence in our sample points strongly to the main path of development as that of resultative or completive leading to anterior and then to perfective or simple past. The evidential path and the derivational one are minor in comparison, only occurring in a few languages of our sample. In the following we ignore these less frequently traveled paths and concentrate our attention on testing the unidirectionality hypothesis (§1.4.2) and the parallel reduction hypothesis (§1.4.6) using the main path of development.

These universal paths of development were hypothesized on the basis of documented changes occurring primarily in languages outside our sample, as well as from inferences based on the distribution of meaning components in the languages of our sample. If the unidirectionality hypothesis is correct, then all grams move along the path in the same direction. If the parallel reduction hypothesis is also correct, then the grams that are on early portions of the path will show lesser degrees of grammaticization than the ones that are on the later portions of the path. In order to test these hypotheses, we have assigned a semantic age to each of the grams we find occurring along this path according to its relative position on the path. In the next chapter, we use various statistical measures to search for an association between semantic age and three measures we have devised for rating the degree of formal grammaticization.

9. For other cases of discontinuous meanings caused by the interaction of two or more grams, see the discussion in chapter 7 on futures with habitual uses and Bybee 1988b.

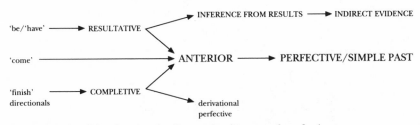

Fig. 3.1. Paths of development leading to simple past and perfective grams.

For the group of grams considered in this chapter, we refer to semantic age as **perfage.** Perfage 1 is assigned to completive grams that are not judged to be derivational in nature (see Table 3.2). We omit the derivational completives from consideration because they are not on the path leading to simple past or inflectional perfective. According to our path diagram, resultative grams should also be assigned a low perfage number, but in our data we have only four resultative grams that do not have other uses (see Table 3.5.). For the other resultatives, the range of uses they exhibit—anterior, past, perfective—suggests that they be grouped with grams at a later stage of development (perfage 3 or 4). Thus resultatives do not constitute a separate group for the purposes of our quantitative analysis.

Perfage 2 includes what we have called "young anteriors," anterior grams that have no other uses. These are listed in Table 3.4. Perfage 3 includes "old anteriors," or anterior grams with other uses indicating a more advanced semantic development, as shown in Table 3.7.

At perfage 4 are the perfective grams, as listed in Table 3.12, and at perfage 5 are the simple pasts of Table 3.10. As we said in section 3.14, we do not know of documented cases of perfective evolving into simple past, but there is some indication that simple pasts are older: they occur with a wider range of verbs, and their meaning has a broader scope.

(68) Perfage 1   completives
      Perfage 2   young anteriors
      Perfage 3   old anteriors
      Perfage 4   perfectives
      Perfage 5   simple pasts

In the next chapter we present our approach to the degree of grammaticization of form which allows us to test the correlation of semantic age with formal grammaticization.

CHAPTER FOUR

A Quantitative Approach
to Grammaticization

4.1. Introduction

In the last chapter we saw some correspondences between meaning and expression type when we compared affixal versus nonaffixal expression of anteriors, perfectives, and pasts (see Table 3.9). We found that the grams in the earliest stages of grammaticization, the young anteriors, were more likely to have periphrastic expression, while the other grams at more advanced stages of grammaticization had a greater tendency to be affixed. But affixation is not the only formal process that takes place in grammaticization; there are numerous formal processes of reduction and fusion that occur before and after affixation. The procedure we used in coding information about grams from the reference material included a number of formal variables which we can now use to test the hypothesis that grammaticization of form is concurrent with grammaticization of function.

Two types of formal changes occur in grammaticization—the reduction or loss of phonetic bulk and the fusion of the grammaticizing material to surrounding material. These two types of change are not specific to grammaticization but correspond to the two main types of phonetic change that affect all phonetic material over time, substantive reduction (the reduction of articulatory activity) and temporal reduction (the overlapping of articulatory gestures) (Pagliuca and Mowrey 1987). Furthermore, both types of formal change in grammaticization parallel the main types of semantic change in grammaticization. Phonetic reduction—the loss of specific phonetic properties—parallels reduction or generalization, which is also the loss of specific properties. The fusion of a developing gram to adjacent lexical material in affixation is parallel to the growing functional dependence of grams and their conceptual cohesion with lexical stems. Both of these processes create an iconic relation between meaning and form (as discussed in Haiman 1983 and Bybee 1985), but in our view the real insights into human language come not from examining the synchronic iconicity, but more from understanding the dynamic processes that create that iconicity.

In this chapter, we use the grams discussed in the last chapter to construct a quantitative test of the parallel reduction hypothesis. In the last chapter, we assigned perfages to the grams discussed, as follows:

Perfage 1	completives
Perfage 2	young anteriors
Perfage 3	old anteriors
Perfage 4	perfectives
Perfage 5	simple pasts

In this chapter, we propose three clustered measures of grammaticization of form and test for an association between each of these formal measures and the semantic measures of degree of grammaticization as manifested in the five perfages.

If the parallel reduction hypothesis is correct, then we will find an association between each of the three measures of grammaticization of form and the measures of grammaticization of meaning. This method of testing the parallel reduction hypothesis involves using the grammaticization path for perfective and past grams presented in § 3.17. Thus if the predicted associations are found in the data, the proposed path and corresponding perfages are also validated, providing an indirect test of the universal paths and unidirectionality hypotheses.

4.2. Phonetic reduction

Phonetic reduction can be manifested in any of the segmental or suprasegmental features of the phonetic string. Loss of stress and reduction to a neutral tone are early indicators of reduction, and these are often accompanied by the shortening and reduction of vowels. Consonants can also reduce by shortening, voicing, or loss of secondary features, and both vowels and consonants in grammaticizing material are subject to complete loss. The result of these processes is that grammaticized material will be shorter in terms of the number of segments present.[1] Since lexical material gradually develops into grammatical material, the degree of semantic grammaticization should be reflected in the degree of formal reduction or shortening. In the last

1. Another hypothesis is that grams will also tend to contain a restricted subset of the whole inventory of phonemes present in a language. English admittedly has a very small set of inflectional morphemes, but it is still interesting that a majority of them are composed of alveolar consonants and reduced vowels.

chapter we hypothesized five stages of development for grams on the path of development to past or perfective, and we called these perfages. In the following we use a method developed in an earlier work (Bybee, Pagliuca, and Perkins 1991) to give numerical values to the degree of the reduction of grams and correlate these measures with the five perfages.

For measuring reduction, or as we shall call it, **shortness,** we simply count the number of consonants and vowels present in the gram. For this count we use the longest allomorph in order to have a standard way of choosing among allomorphs of varying lengths. The longest allomorph is not chosen if it is clearly a marginal allomorph—infrequently used or suppletive.

Since shortness is intended as a purely temporal measure (with other aspects of reduction being treated as explained below), vowels are considered longer than consonants and given a numerical value of 2 while consonants are counted as 1. Long vowels are not double the vowel value, but rather counted as 3. Long consonants have been recorded as double consonants and thus would have a value of 2. For these purposes glides are counted as consonants.

The shortness parameter is formulated in terms of decreasing length because that is the directionality of change in grammaticization. The other parameters explained below, dependence and fusion, are also formulated to increase in value as grammaticization increases. Thus our measure of shortness is formulated so that the shorter the gram, the higher the number assigned to it. This is accomplished by starting with the number 10 and subtracting for each segment in the gram, as follows:

$$C = -1$$
$$V = -2$$
$$V: = -3$$

A second variable is also included in this scale. If the gram has, in addition to the longest allomorph, an allomorph that is a reduced version of it, then two points are added back in.

A certain arbitrariness is unavoidable in the calculation of shortness and the other formal variables, dependence and fusion. There is simply no fully principled way to assign particular numerical values to the presence versus the absence of certain morphological and morphophonemic conditions. What is not arbitrary, however, is the directionality of the assignments: every value that indicates a higher degree of grammaticization is assigned a higher number. Finer differentiations, such as between 1 and 2, are justified according to a general theory of grammaticization of form. We recognize, however, that a different assignment of values might yield different results.

We can illustrate the calculation of shortness by applying this procedure to the English Past Tense and Future *will*.

> *Past Tense:* The longest allomorph is [ɪd], which consists of one vowel (score -2) and one consonant (score -1). These subtracted from 10 yield 7. This gram also has a reduced allomorph, [d], so we add two points, yielding a total shortness score of 9.
>
> *Will:* The longest allomorph is [wɪl], which consists of a consonant (-1), a vowel (-2), and another consonant (-1). These subtracted from 10 yield 6. Since there is also a reduced allomorph, we add 2, yielding a total shortness score of 8.

Table 4.1 is a cross-tabulation of the shortness scores with the perfage scores for all the grams assigned a perfage value at the end of the last chapter. The perfages are listed across the top and the shortness scores on the left side. In this presentation it can be seen that the shortness score increases as the perfage increases. The significance values are calculated in three ways. Kendall's Tau-B and Tau-C provide a significance figure that rates the probability that the correspondence between the two variables occurred by chance. Since we have more cases than we have possible ranks, there are ties (two or more cases falling at the same rank). The Tau-B statistic takes into account

Table 4.1.   Cross-Tabulation of Shortness with Perfage

| | PERFAGE | | | | | |
SHORTNESS	1	2	3	4	5	TOTAL
1	1		1			2
2		2				2
3	1	8				9
4	7	6	2			15
5	2	7	3	1		13
6	5	9	1	5	1	21
7	5	15	7	10	7	44
8	1	1	5	2	6	15
9		4	7	11	6	28
10		2	2	5	2	11
11					3	3
12		1		1		2
Total	22	55	28	35	25	165

Statistic	Value	Significance
Kendall's Tau-B	.43	<.0001
Kendall's Tau-C	.44	<.0001
Gamma	.52	

ties for one variable and the Tau-C statistic takes into account ties for
both variables. Gamma tells us how well we can predict the pairing of
meaning and form if we know the perfage and shortness score for
each gram. Whereas random pairings would produce approximately
50% error, knowing the perfage and shortness for a gram reduces
the error by 52%. The values for these three statistics as given under
the cross-tabulation show that the correlation between shortness and
perfage is highly significant, supporting the prediction that semantic
reduction and phonetic reduction work in tandem.[2]

4.3. Loss of autonomy

Along with reduction in phonetic bulk comes a loss of autonomy and
growing dependence on surrounding phonetic material. We distinguish between the general loss of autonomy, which we call **dependence,** and the actual fusion of the gram with the verb, which we call
fusion. The reason for making this distinction is that some grams,
because of their syntagmatic position or their low relevance to the
verb, or both, become dependent on surrounding material but do not
ever affix to the verb. We do not want to consider such grams as less
grammaticized than those that do affix; thus we separate the measures of dependence and fusion.

Dependence, then, includes all those indices of loss of autonomy
that are not specific to a growing fusion with the verb. They are:

(1) The number of allomorphs of the gram, not counting those that
are purely phonetically conditioned. The number of allomorphs was
coded as 0, 1, 2, 3, or > 3. In calculating dependence, the following
numerical values were assigned:

Other allomorphs: $0 = 0$, 1 or $2 = 2$, $3 = 3$, $>3 = 4$

As the gram reduces in phonetic and semantic content, it is more
prone to coarticulation with other phonetic material in the environment and thus undergoes differential reduction according to surrounding material. This is reflected in the number of allomorphs that
the gram develops. The numerical values assigned for "other allomorphs" reflects our assumption that the difference between no allomorphs and one allomorph is greater than the difference between
one allomorph and two. Thus the minimum value for having allo-

2. Two grams have shortness scores of 12. This is somewhat anomalous but occurs
due to the situation in which the major form of expression is zero, so that the longest
allomorph was not chosen. However, the longest marginal allomorph had a reduced
version so that the calculation involved adding 2 points to the original 10, from which
nothing had been subtracted.

morphs at all is 2. In our coding procedure we recognized the dimin-
ishing value of counting allomorphs and did not distinguish numbers
greater than three.

(2) Conditioning for allomorphs. In coding we distinguished, as far
as possible, phonological, morphological, and lexical conditioning of
allomorphs of the gram. Lexical conditioning is, of course, directly
related to fusion with the verb and thus is included in that parameter.
Phonological conditioning may be by the verb or by some other element and thus is included under dependence, but it does not count
purely automatic alternations, such as between English /t/ and /d/ in
Past tense. These would not count as separate allomorphs. Morphological conditioning refers to allomorphy that is due to the presence
of another gram and, in effect, shows some fusion with that other
gram. The presence of phonological conditioning is given a value of
1 as opposed to the morphological conditioning which is given a value
of 2. The reasoning behind these assignments is that phonological
conditioning may be quite general and may develop early in the grammaticization process, while morphological conditioning requires a
special bonding between two grams that may indicate a higher degree
of grammaticization.

Phonological conditioning: No = 0, Yes = 1
Morphological conditioning: No = 0, Yes = 2

(3) Suprasegmental reduction. As we mentioned above, an early
indication of loss of autonomy and reduction is the loss of stress or
non-neutral tones. In our dependence variable, we include an indication of whether or not the gram can be stressed or have high tone.
In this case a negative answer is assigned; if the gram sometimes takes
stress (alternating), a value of 1 is assigned, and if the gram is always
unstressed, a value of 2 is assigned.

Stress: No = 2, Alternating = 1, Yes = 0

The dependence scale ranges from 0 to 9, and the higher number
indicates the greater degree of grammaticization.

The application of this parameter is illustrated again by comparing
the English Past Tense and Future *will*.

English Past Tense:
   1. We count the Past Tense as having more than 3 allo-
      morphs because it has [d] in addition to [ɨd], as well as
      several different vowel and consonant changes internal to
      the stem (score 4);
   2. The [ɨd] / [d] alternation is phonologically conditioned
      (score 1);

3. There are no allomorphs conditioned by other grammatical morphemes (score 0);
4. The gram is always unstressed (score 2).

Total dependence score: 7

Will:

1. If we count the reduced version of *will*, [əl], as an allomorph, and also its form which is contracted with *not* as an allomorph, then it has two allomorphs (score 2);
2. There are no phonologically conditioned allomorphs (score 0);
3. The allomorphy in *won't* is morphologically conditioned (score 2);
4. *Will* is normally not stressed (score 2).

Total dependence score: 6

As with shortness, the dependence scores for these two grams are very similar, even though *will* is not an affix. The difference between the two will become evident when we consider fusion.

Table 4.2 shows the highly significant cross-tabulation of dependence with perfage.

Fusion with the verb includes all the indices that give evidence for a degree of fusion of the gram with the main verb stem. They are:

(1) Written bound. Perhaps the best indicator of affixation is the way the gram is treated orthographically. If the gram is written bound to the verb, there are probably very good reasons for it. This ortho-

Table 4.2.   Cross-Tabulation of Dependence with Perfage

	PERFAGE					
DEPENDENCE	1	2	3	4	5	TOTAL
0	5	11		3		19
1	9	11	5	3	2	30
2	6	16	7	10	2	41
3		4	3	1		8
4	1	4	1	2	5	13
5	1	3	6	4	4	18
6		3	3	5	6	17
7		2	2	2	3	9
8		1		4	2	7
9			1	1	1	3
Total	22	55	28	35	25	165

Statistic	Value	Significance
Kendall's Tau-B	.39	<.0001
Kendall's Tau-C	.40	<.0001
Gamma	.47	

graphic decision would never be made if open class items came between the gram and the verb. On the other hand, written affixation is
demanded by fusional processes that occur between the stem and the
gram. Since these orthographic decisions are not arbitrary, we consider them good indicators of affixation. Of course, orthographies are
conventional and change slowly, so there may be cases where grams
that behave in every way as affixes are still written separately, but most
of the languages in our sample have fairly recently developed writing
systems, where long traditions are not a factor. For the fusion parameter, if a gram is written bound, it is assigned 2 points, and if it is
hyphenated or sometimes written bound, it is assigned 1 point.

Written bound: No = 0, Yes = 2, Hyphenated or sometimes = 1

(2) Open class intervening. A reliable indication that a gram is not
an affix is the possibility of open class items coming between the gram
and the verb. As grammaticization proceeds, positional variation becomes more restricted, and the gram tends to occur closer to the verb
more frequently until it is always in contact with the verb. If this does
not occur, affixation cannot take place. Thus even before affixation
takes place, the prohibition of intervening open class items indicates
a higher degree of fusion with the verb.

Open class intervening: No = 1, Yes = 0

(3) Phonological process conditioned by stem. Another indication
of fusion between the verb and a gram is the presence of allomorphy
in the gram conditioned by the phonological shape of the stem. This
type of allomorphy is possible even if the gram is not fully affixed to
the verb.

Phonological process conditioned by stem: No = 0, Yes = 1

(4) Lexical conditioning. Allomorphy that is lexically conditioned is
determined by the verb class. Thus the presence of different allomorphs for different conjugation classes, as in Romance languages, is
considered lexically conditioned allomorphy. Not only does the presence of lexical conditioning indicate co-dependence and thus fusion
between stem and affix; such situations usually take a long period of
time to develop, indicating an extreme degree of grammaticization.

Lexically conditioned allomorphy: No = 0, Yes = 2

(5) Conditions stem change. The converse situation, that of a gram
conditioning allomorphy in the verb stem, also indicates a high degree of mutual fusion. The assimilatory and reductive changes that
lead to stem allomorphy take place only when the stem and gram are
in close contact. It is our intuition that notable stress and tone changes

may take place more readily than segmental feature changes in vowels and consonants.

Stem change: No = 0, Tone or stress = 1, Vowel or consonant = 2

Once again applying these criteria to the familiar cases of English Past Tense and Future *will*, we find considerable differences between the two:

English Past Tense:
1. The Past Tense gram is written bound (score 2);
2. It allows no open class items to come between it and the verb stem (score 1);
3. It is affected by a phonological process conditioned by the stem, i.e. the devoicing found after voiceless consonants (*helped* [helpt] (score 1);
4. It has lexically conditioned allomorphy in the stem changes of irregular verbs (score 2); and
5. It conditions stem change in some verbs, such as *kept* (score 2).

Total fusion score: 8

Will:
1. *Will* is not written bound to the verb (score 0);
2. Open class items do intervene between *will* and the verb, in particular, manner adverbs (*I'll gladly help.*) (score 0);
3. There are no phonological processes conditioned by the verb stem (score 0);
4. There is no lexical conditioning—*will* does not vary according to which main verb it is used with (score 0);
5. *Will* does not condition any changes in the verb stem (score 0).

Total fusion score: 0

Table 4.3 presents the cross-tabulations for fusion and perfage, again with highly significant results.

All three of the formal variables for the degree of grammaticization of form yield highly significant correlations with perfage, which is a measure of the degree of grammaticization of meaning. These results are even stronger than those presented in Bybee, Pagliuca, and Perkins 1991 for the same formal variables correlated with the semantic age of future grams. This stronger correlation is predictable from the fact that all the grams tested in the earlier study had 'future' as one of their uses. Thus the range of meanings differentiated was much smaller than here in the perfage test, where the meanings range from completive to simple past. It is important to note, however, that future grams also yielded highly significant correlations between semantic age and degree of formal grammaticization, despite the smaller range of meaning involved.

Table 4.3.   Cross-Tabulation of Fusion with Perfage

| | PERFAGE | | | | | |
FUSION	1	2	3	4	5	TOTAL
0	8	10	2	1	1	22
1	6	18	6	3	3	36
2	2	2	2	4	2	12
3	5	23	12	16	9	65
4	1	1		3	4	9
5		1	1	1	3	6
6			4	1	2	7
7				3		3
8				1	1	2
9						
10			1	2		3
Total	22	55	28	35	25	165

Statistic	Value	Significance
Kendall's Tau-B	.37	<.0001
Kendall's Tau-C	.35	<.0001
Gamma	.47	

The data support the parallel reduction hypothesis: over a number of unrelated languages there is a strong association between meaning and the form of expression of particular grammatical morphemes that may be explained by postulating that the degree of dependence and the fusion of a gram with the verb increase and the length of the gram decreases as the meaning of the gram generalizes and becomes more abstract. Since the quantitative data yield significant results, we can also surmise that the proposed path of semantic change is correct in essence; moreover, the unidirectionality and universal paths hypotheses, which are crucial to the construction of the test of the hypothesis, are not falsified by the data.

4.4. Morphological typology

The well-known morphological typology classifies languages according to type of morphological expression used most often in the language. Languages with largely monomorphemic words are considered analytic or isolating languages; those with morphologically complex words in which morpheme boundaries are clearly discernible are called agglutinative; and those with multi-morphemic words and many word-internal fusional processes are fusional or inflectional.

Less often cited is Sapir's (1921) classification according to the types of meanings expressed in language. Sapir's hypothesis is that certain types of form express certain types of meaning, so that a typology of morphological form is also a typology of grammatical meaning. His semantic typology ranges from the concrete or lexical concepts to the most abstract and relational concepts, that is, the grammatical concepts. It is likely that the lack of follow-up on Sapir's semantic typology is due to the difficulty of classifying meaning into discrete categories. However, since his semantic scale involves many of the same parameters as a degree of semantic grammaticization scale—specificity versus generality, concrete meaning versus relational meaning—our classification of grams into perfages may provide the appropriate means of testing his hypothesis. Note, however, that when we distinguish five perfages, we are making distinctions toward the relational end of the scale, from COMPLETIVE, which is the most concrete, to PAST, which is the most abstract. Thus while we only test Sapir's hypothesis on grammatical morphemes, it is precisely on this end of the scale that the hypothesis is the most interesting and controversial. A further reason for testing Sapir's hypothesis is that if morphological typology is a significant factor affecting grammaticization, it may qualify the results presented in Tables 4.1–4.3.

Since we have information about the formal expression of all the verbal grams for the languages of our sample, we can calculate an overall mean for each language in terms of shortness, fusion, and dependence. These mean scores, especially those for dependence and fusion, amount to a quantitative measure of morphological typology, if we make the plausible assumption that verbal grams can be taken to be representative of the morphology of the language as a whole. That is, a language with high mean scores for dependence and fusion will be an inflectional language, while one with medium-range scores will be agglutinative and one with very low scores will be isolating. Shortness does not figure in traditional typologies; that is, to our knowledge no one has proposed a morphological typology based on the length of grammatical morphemes.

If morphological typology also involves a typology of grammatical meaning, then we would expect a correspondence between the type of meaning expressed grammatically and the overall formal type of the language. Let us call all the grams on the perfective or past path **perf** grams. Isolating languages would have perf grams with low perfages, namely completives and anteriors, while inflectional languages would have perf grams with high semantic ages, namely perfectives and pasts.

In Tables 4.4–4.6 we show the tests of this hypothesis which seek a correspondence between the mean scores for the formal variables and the mean perfage scores for each language. (The scores for the formal variables are calculated on all the grams coded, while the mean perfage is calculated only on forms assigned a perfage.) The number

Table 4.4.
Mean Perfage Scores for Each Language
by Mean Dependence Scores

Statistic	Value	Significance
Kendall's Tau-B	.31	<.0001
Kendall's Tau-C	.31	<.0001
Gamma	.33	

Table 4.5.
Mean Perfage Scores for Each Language
by Mean Fusion Scores

Statistic	Value	Significance
Kendall's Tau-B	.27	.0009
Kendall's Tau-C	.27	.0009
Gamma	.29	

Table 4.6.
Mean Perfage Scores for Each Language
by Mean Shortness Scores

Statistic	Value	Significance
Kendall's Tau-B	.07	.21
Kendall's Tau-C	.05	.21
Gamma	.07	

of cases for these tests is the number of languages in the sample having perf forms, sixty-eight.

The tables in this section are based on fairly continuous numbers rather than a few discrete categories, so cross-tables are no longer appropriate. Rank order statistics are still reported for consistency with the preceding results and because the resulting values do not meet the normality requirement for using interval statistics.

Tables 4.4 and 4.5 show a substantial association between the overall dependence and fusion scores for the language and the semantic ages of the perf forms, supporting the hypothesis that morphological type involves both formal and semantic parameters. Languages with a high degree of fusion and dependence also have perf grams that exhibit more grammaticization of meaning. Languages with little fusion or dependence tend to have perf grams with more specific meanings. Similar associations were found with future grams, as reported in Bybee, Pagliuca, and Perkins 1991; tests in other semantic domains would reveal the extent to which semantic typology pervades grammatical categories.

In contrast to Tables 4.4 and 4.5, Table 4.6 indicates that there is little or no relationship between the shortness score for all the verbal grams of a language and the degree of semantic development for the perf grams for that language. As we mentioned earlier, overall gram length has never been suggested as a significant typological parameter.

If the full range of grammaticization were taking place at a constant rate in all languages at all times, a kind of equilibrium would be reached in which all languages would have grams representing all stages of development. Thus there would be no typological differences among languages with respect to morphological form or meaning. The existence of types gives evidence for typological constraints on grammaticization: in some languages grammaticization does not proceed as far as it does in others. In particular, isolating languages do not carry grammaticization as far as fusional or agglutinating languages do. Not only do they not affix, they also do not have grams with meaning as abstract and generalized as synthetic languages do.

The stability of certain isolating languages, such as Chinese, over time further attests to typological constraints on grammaticization. The diachronic study of Lin 1991 shows anterior and resultative markers in Chinese developing and changing their meaning, but not generalizing to become pasts or perfectives, even over a time span of almost a millennium.

These results were anticipated in Bybee and Dahl 1989, where it was reported for two cross-linguistic samples that almost all languages that have inflection at all have a past or perfective gram. Again, this means that the presence of the most highly grammaticized morphemes depends on language typology. In the GRAMCATS sample we find that this generalization holds with only one exception.

Out of seventy-six languages, there are thirteen (17%) that lack a past or a perfective.[3] Eight of these languages are unquestionably analytic or isolating languages that have no inflectional grams. These eight are Haka, Lahu, Lao, Koho, Palaung, Motu, Tok Pisin, and Mano. It should also be noted that these languages are areally and genetically restricted: the first three are Sino-Tibetan; the second two are Austroasiatic; the others are Austronesian, Pacific creole, and Niger-Kordofanian respectively. Since all these languages have grammatical meaning expressed in non-bound particles or auxiliaries, we

3. We are also counting here languages that have degrees of remoteness in the past as containing a past gram. Pasts indicating degrees of remoteness were not, however, included in the quantitative study because it was not possible to assign them a perfage in a principled fashion, as little is known about their development. It was found, however, that their degree of formal grammaticization would place them between young and old anteriors, which is consistent with the specificity of their meanings.

expect that even though they lack pasts or perfectives, they would have the less grammaticized related meanings of completive and (young) anterior. Indeed all these isolating languages are reported to have either an anterior or a completive or both.

The other five languages cannot be considered analytic because they have a number of derivational affixes on verbs, primarily of the type that change the valence of the verb. Two of these languages, Car and !Kung, have no inflection whatever, and no reports of tense or aspect signaled periphrastically. However, one of the Car derivational affixes has a completive sense. !Kung appears to have neither an anterior nor a completive.

Dakota and Buli both have person/number inflection on verbs and a large number of valence-changing affixes in the derivational morphology, but tense and aspect are marked almost exclusively by auxiliaries and particles. For instance, Buli has a future auxiliary that is prefixed to the verb, but the other aspect grams are an anterior, two completives, and a gram meaning 'still', all of which are particles. Dakota has complex person/number marking and a set of derivational prefixes for valence-changing meanings, but all tense and aspect senses are coded in particles. The particle *k'un* in Dakota is a past anterior and is not used for simple past.

Finally, one language appears to present a counterexample to our generalization. Abipon (Macro-Panoan, Ge-Pano-Carib) has the future, habitual, progressive, and various directionals marked with suffixes, but there is no report of any past or perfective gram nor, for that matter, any completives or anteriors. Thus we can formulate the generalizations in (1).

(1)   With a few exceptions, if a language has inflectional tense or aspect, it will have a past or perfective gram.
      With a few exceptions, if a language has no inflectional tense or aspect, it will have an anterior or completive gram or both.

4.5. Controlling for language typology

Given that a substantial typological relationship between perfages and mean fusion and dependence is demonstrated in Tables 4.4 and 4.5 respectively, it is necessary to re-examine the results reported in Tables 4.1, 4.2, and 4.3 to determine if they are simply the result of the effects of typology or if there is an independent effect that remains even after the typological effect is controlled. In order to control for typology, we must adjust individual gram scores.

The individual formal grammaticization score for each perf form is adjusted to control for typology by subtracting the mean score on that parameter for all forms in the language and dividing the difference by the standard deviation of the scores for all forms in the language. This produces scores that are standardized in units of deviation from the mean. For cases where there is a single perf form in the language the standard deviation is 0, and since division would then produce an undefined result, a 1 is substituted for the standard deviation of 0. Similarly, if all the scores for a variable in a language are the same, a standard deviation of 0 would result and so a 1 is substituted in those cases also. These calculations and substitutions produce adjusted scores that are more directly comparable across languages since they take into account the possibility that there may be different means across languages as well as different spreads of the data as measured by the standard deviation.

Perfage scores are similarly adjusted, except that only the perf forms are taken into account when calculating the perfage means and perfage standard deviation values for each language. Tables 4.7, 4.8, and 4.9 are all based on adjusted scores for the formal and semantic variable values. These values are free of the typological influences of the sort determined above to exist (and can, in fact, be shown statistically to be so). These tables are based on the 165 perf forms found in the sample of languages.

Though the magnitude of the effects is definitely reduced when the

Table 4.7.
Perfage by Shortness Adjusted for Language Type

Statistic	Value	Significance
Kendall's Tau-B	.26	<.0001
Kendall's Tau-C	.26	<.0001
Gamma	.27	

Table 4.8.
Perfage by Dependence Adjusted for Language Type

Statistic	Value	Significance
Kendall's Tau-B	.22	<.0001
Kendall's Tau-C	.21	<.0001
Gamma	.27	

Table 4.9.
Perfage by Fusion Adjusted for Language Type

Statistic	Value	Significance
Kendall's Tau-B	.22	<.0001
Kendall's Tau-C	.21	<.0001
Gamma	.22	

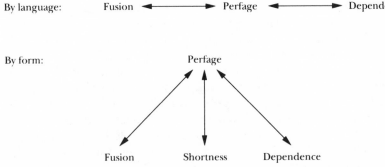

Fig. 4.1. Significant relationships with perfage.

scores are standardized, their values are still consistently substantial and they remain highly significant statistically. Taking the substantial typological effects into account does not reduce the association between form and meaning in perf forms to insignificance. Note that even shortness (Table 4.7) is reduced substantially by the adjustment for language type. The relationships between the variables is represented in Figure 4.1. Although not pictured here, it should be noted that the formal variables of fusion and dependence are also significantly associated with one another both across languages and across forms.

Figure 4.1 simply shows that the language means for fusion and dependence are highly associated with perfage, giving the typological dimension, while for individual grams, all three formal variables are associated with perfage, even when adjustments are made for language-specific tendencies for each of these four variables. Further tests of association between the adjusted scores and the mean scores confirm that grammaticization and the typological dimension are independent factors in our data.

Again, our interpretation of the relation between grammaticization and typology is that grammaticization is cross-linguistically similar in the course of development that it takes, both on the formal and semantic levels, but other language-specific factors determine how far grammaticization can proceed. Interestingly, whatever the constraint might be, it applies in parallel fashion in the formal and semantic domains.

4.6. Tests for causality and bias

We report in this section on other statistical tests we have applied to our data, in particular searching for causal effects and testing for sampling bias.

One of the central questions in the study of grammaticization concerns the issue of whether the semantic change leads and, consequently, causes the formal change, or whether the reverse relation holds. The data on fusion and perfage presented in Table 4.3 is suggestive of the former relation—that is, of semantic change leading fusion with the verb—since the distribution of grams in the cells is asymmetrical. There are forms occupying the upper right hand corner, where a high perfage is coupled with a low degree of fusion, and no forms in the lower left hand corner, where a low perfage would be coupled with a high degree of fusion. This table can be compared with Table 4.1, which shows the association of shortness with perfage to be much more symmetrical.

Further examination of the data reveals, however, that this asymmetry is not marked enough to suggest a causal relation for fusion, and that it is present only minimally for dependence and not at all for shortness. In fact, it appears that the asymmetry in the fusion table is due to the fact that some languages have highly grammaticized auxiliaries which express highly generalized meanings but which are not bound to the verb and thus would have very low fusion scores.

We conclude, then, that either formal and semantic grammaticization proceed in such close tandem that no distinction in order is detectable, or that our cross-linguistic data are too crude to pick up such a distinction. It is possible that a fine-grained language-specific study of grammaticization in progress would help to establish the causal dimensions in grammaticization.

Second, we examined our data in search of biases that might have been introduced due to our sampling method. Statistical analysis assumes that the individual cases are independent of one another; in cross-linguistic samples, that would mean that the languages are unrelated both genetically and areally. However, it is not known to what extent grammaticization is affected by genetic and areal factors; thus it is possible that a sample as large as ours may contain some nonindependent cases.

Dryer 1989 has argued that in word order studies areal effects that range over whole continents are discernible. Thus we need to make sure that the associations we have found between formal and semantic grammaticization are not due to each variable being independently associated with a particular continent or linguistic area.

Perkins 1989 presents a method by which sample sizes can be adjusted to eliminate bias caused by non-independent cases. This method yields different sample sizes according to the linguistic elements being studied. For instance, the phonological parameters of vowel and consonant inventories can be studied in larger samples than syntactic ones without the danger of areal bias, presumably because phonological change occurs more rapidly and with less influence from neighboring languages than syntactic change does.

Applying Perkins's 1989 method to the case of perf grams, we find that there is a significant association of mean shortness, fusion, and perfage with continent area. To eliminate this association, the sample size must be reduced to forty-nine. Using a sample that randomly reduced the number of languages from each continent based on the degree of variation of the mean scores within those continents, we retested the associations of mean shortness, fusion, and dependence with mean perfage and found that all associations that were previously significant remained significant. Similarly, the association of individual gram scores with continent was significant for fusion and shortness, so a sample of 107 of the 165 original cases was selected by continent based on the variation of the form scores within continents, and the associations were retested. Again, all associations remained significant, confirming that the form/meaning correspondence in grammaticization is not due to the similarities of languages and forms within continents.[4]

To check further for areal influence, associations in the adjusted samples were studied to determine whether they were in fact significant in each continental area and each hemisphere. The associations between the means for the languages (the typological variables) and the associations between the individual grams' properties remained similar (in the same directions and statistically indistinguishable except where there were too few cases to obtain statistical significance) across continents.

4.7. Conclusion

Because we used a stratified probability sample of the world's languages, we were able to test our hypotheses by quantitative methods. The primary hypothesis—that form and meaning covary in grammaticization—received overwhelming support from the quantitative analysis. In particular, the hypothesis we have named the parallel reduction hypothesis was supported by our data, as well as the hypothesis concerning the existence of universal paths of semantic development. The particular paths of development we proposed for perf grams also appear to be correct in essence.

The assignment of numerical values to both formal and semantic variables made it possible to apply statistical tests of the hypothesis that morphological typology is not just a matter of form, but also a matter of meaning. Languages that allow a high degree of formal reduction and fusion also allow a high degree of semantic reduction and generalization. Languages that have less fusion and less reduction on the formal side tend also to have less grammaticized meanings.

4. In neither subsample was there any association between perfage, fusion, or dependence and continental area.

While we have provided support for Sapir's conception of a typology of languages that includes both form and meaning, we have also shown that the sort of grammaticization under consideration in this study is an independent process operating cross-linguistically.

Sample sizes were adjusted so that it was possible to demonstrate that the cases used to test our hypotheses were independent. Both the primary variables and the typological variables were tested for continental and hemisphere effects, with the results strongly supporting the central hypotheses. We have, then, controlled for within-language, within-continent, and within-hemisphere variation. The results consistently provide overwhelming support for our hypotheses concerning the covariation of formal and semantic factors in grammaticization.

CHAPTER FIVE

Progressive, Imperfective, Present, and Related Senses

In chapters 3 and 4 we discussed the group of aspect and tense senses relating to situations viewed as completed, perfective, or past; in this chapter we take up the contrasting group of aspects and tenses, those relating to ongoing, repeated, or present situations. In particular, we discuss grams with commonly occurring **progressive, imperfective,** and **present** meaning. As in chapter 3, the meanings chosen to be treated together are diachronically related: we present evidence for a diachronic path beginning with progressive and eventually reaching imperfective or present. Another related sense discussed in this chapter is **habitual,** which is sometimes expressed by a more general imperfective or present gram and sometimes has its own expression. In addition, the less frequent but semantically related meanings of **iterative, continuative,** and **frequentative** are treated in this chapter. One mode of expression is singled out to be discussed here: reduplication, which is often associated with iterative meaning. We will argue that reduplication undergoes the same sort of semantic development in grammaticization as constructions made up of the more usual sort of lexical material.

5.1. Definitions

Our working definitions of the gram-types are based on the recent literature on aspect and tense, specifically Comrie 1976 and 1985b, and Dahl 1985 and other works cited in these.

Imperfective is treated in these works as the contrast partner of perfective, and thus views the situation not as a bounded whole, but rather from within, with explicit reference to its internal structure (see Comrie 1976: 24). In more concrete terms, an imperfective situation may be one viewed as in progress at a particular reference point, either in the past or present, or one viewed as characteristic of a period of time that includes the reference time, that is, a habitual situation. Imperfective forms are typically used in discourse for setting up background situations, in contrast with perfective forms, which are used for narrating sequences of events (Hopper 1979, 1982). Imperfectives may be applicable to either past, present, or future time, as in Russian, or, more commonly, restricted to the past, as for instance, the Imperfects of Spanish or French, which cover both ongoing and habitual situations, but only in the past. An imperfective restricted to the present is simply a present, since a present situation cannot be perfective.

Unlike Comrie (1985b: 36–41), we find it difficult to view the so-called present tense as a "tense," that is, as having to do primarily with deictic temporal reference. What present covers are various types of imperfective situations with the moment of speech as the reference point. That is, present includes ongoing activities, such as in Spanish (examples from Jorge Guitart).

(1) Qué haces? Estudias?   'What are you doing? Studying?'
     No, miro televisión.   'No, I'm watching television.'

Present also includes habitual situations.

(2) Qué haces por las noches?   'What do you do in the evenings?'
     Miro televisión.   'I watch television.'

The present is also typically used for gnomic situations, that is, those that apply to generic subjects and basically hold for all time, as in (3).

(3) Dogs pant to cool off.

Present and imperfective are the most general and abstract of the meaning labels treated in this chapter. The more specific ones are as follows.

Progressive views an action as ongoing at reference time. As Comrie 1976 defines progressive, and as we find it used in English, it applies typically to dynamic predicates and not to stative ones. Thus the progressive is typically used for actions that require a constant input of energy to be sustained, as in (4).

(4) Sara is reading.

However, states will continue without further energy input unless something occurs to put an end to them. Thus (5) is not used in English.

(5) *Sara is knowing the answer.

It is not uncommon to find progressives referred to as Duratives or Continuatives in reference grammars.

Continuous is defined for our survey, following Comrie 1976, as more general than progressive because it can be used in progressive situations but in addition with stative predicates. Thus continuous views the situation, whether it be dynamic or stative, as ongoing at reference time. As we shall see in §5.4, no cross-linguistic gram-type 'continuous' emerged from our study despite the logical position of this sense in Comrie's system.

Habitual situations are customarily repeated on different occasions. Comrie's (1976: 27–28) definition of habitual is well put:

> [Habituals] describe a situation which is characteristic of an extended period of time, so extended in fact that the situation referred to is viewed not as an incidental property of the moment but, precisely, as a characteristic feature of a whole period.

Habitual grams may also be restricted to either present or past, or applicable to both. Alternate terms for habitual found in reference grammars are Customary and Usitative and sometimes Iterative, although this term is more properly used as follows.

Iterative describes an event that is repeated on a particular occasion. The notion of iteration is particularly relevant to telic predicates—those that have a well-defined end point. Thus iteratives will have lexical restrictions. In reference grammars iteratives are sometimes called Repetitives.

Frequentative includes habitual meaning—that a situation is characteristic of a period of time—but additionally specifies that it be frequent during that period of time.

Continuative includes progressive meaning—that a dynamic situation is ongoing—and additionally specifies that the agent of the action is deliberately keeping the action going. Continuative is the meaning of 'keep on doing' or 'continue doing'.

5.2. Progressive sources

For several reasons we view progressive meaning as the specific meaning that feeds into the chain of developments leading eventually to the highly generalized imperfective or present meanings. First, progressive meaning is more specific, and it is included in the more general meanings of imperfective or present. Thus our general theory of grammaticization would predict that progressive is a sense that occurs early in the process of grammaticization and might develop into the more general meanings. Second, historical and comparative evidence exists in Turkic, Dravidian, and Celtic languages, as well as in dialects of Yoruba, which shows constructions with progressive meaning developing into presents or imperfectives. (This evidence is reviewed

Table 5.1. Lexical Sources and Mode of Expression of Progressives

	Language	Form No.	Related Strings	Expression
			Location	
02	Basque	02	verbal noun in locative + be	AUX
10	Isl. Carib	17	here	SUF
11	Cocama	08	be located + complement of Place	AUX
13	Jivaro	68	be, sit	SUF + AUX
17	Alyawarra	19	sit, stay, be	AUX
		20	lie, be	AUX
25	Tahitian	01	be here	PRE + PART
26	Motu	32	this	PARTCL
38	O'odham	12	sit, stay for a while	SUF
39	Abkhaz	53	in < mouth	AUX
49	Baluchi	09	loc + be	AUX
72	Mwera	47	loc + VN + aux	AUX
77	Ngambay	02	be seated + aorist	AUX
		03	be seated + verbal N	AUX
		04	be standing + aorist	AUX
		05	be standing + verbal N	AUX
83	Shuswap	08	be there, stay	AUX
86	Haka	36	place, participle	PARTCL
87	Lahu	24	be in a place, live	
89	Cantonese	28	stay, reside	AUX
90	Dakota	23	stand	SUF
		24	sit	AUX
94	Tok Pisin	16	stop, stay	AUX
			be + Nonfinite form	
40	Guaymí	23	be	AUX
42	Kui	23	be, live, exist + pres part	AUX
82	Maidu	70	be + participle	AUX
88	Nung	10	be + and (?)	AUX
90	Dakota	25	be + infinitive	AUX
93	Buriat	40	be + gerund	AUX
			Movement	
26	Motu	20	come toward speaker	AUX
40	Guaymí	15	go (away from speaker)	AUX
		16	come (toward speaker)	AUX
75	Mano	02	to, toward, side	PARTCL
		08	direction	
80	Tojolabal	01	to go	AUX
94	Tok Pisin	18	walk + loc	AUX
			Reduplication	
16	Gugu-Yalanji	08		
26	Motu	32	2p reduplicates first syllable of stem	
32	Nakanai	04	reduplication + completive -*ti*	
34	Pangansinan	02		

Table 5.1. (*continued*)

Language	Form No.	Related Strings	Expression
		Other	
02 Basque	46	to be engaged in, to continue	AUX
14 Tucano	24	gerund + do	AUX/SUF
73 Tem	16	to continue	AUX
89 Cantonese	14	be hard, be tight	AUX
94 Tok Pisin	17	'now'	PART
		Unknown	
01 Inuit	21		SUF
04 Kanakuru	11		AUX
12 Chacobo	19	translated 'now'	SUF
	20	translated 'now'	SUF
56 Ono	17		SUF
58 Nimboran	32		SUF
59 Bongu	17		SUF
68 Slave	12		PRE
69 Krongo	05		TNCH
	09		AUX
81 Zuni	20		SUF

below.) Third, our own data contain some cases that appear to be intermediate between the more specific progressive and the more general imperfective or present senses. Finally, our data also show that the same range of lexical sources gives rise to progressive, imperfective, and present. Thus we begin our discussion of the path of development that produces imperfective and present by discussing the lexical sources for progressive grams.

Table 5.1 shows that progressives resemble what we referred to in chapter 3 as young anteriors in their abundance (they occur in 38 languages in our database), in that some languages have more than one and in the transparency of their lexical sources. The majority of progressive forms in our database derive from expressions involving locative elements (cf. Blansitt 1975; Comrie 1976; Traugott 1978; Heine and Reh 1984). Our data, then, corroborate as a world-wide trend the strong tendency in Africa for progressives to derive from locative expressions: Heine, Claudi, and Hünnemeyer 1991a report that they found over a hundred African languages with locative sources for progressive grams. The locative notion may be expressed either in the verbal auxiliary employed or in the use of postpositions or prepositions indicating location—'at', 'in', or 'on.' The verbal auxiliary may derive from a specific postural verb, such as 'sit', 'stand', or 'lie', or it may express the notion of being in a location without reference to a specific posture but meaning only 'be at', 'stay', or, more specifically, 'live' or 'reside'. The Abkhaz construction uses the post-position 'in', which derives from the noun 'mouth', as an auxiliary by adding inflections to it and couples it with a nominal form of the main verb. The form of the main verb is usually nominal (cited as a verbal noun or a gerund), although serial constructions are attested: Ngambay, for example, has two constructions expressing the progressive meaning, one using the verbs 'be seated' and 'be standing' with verbal nouns, and one using the same auxiliaries with Aorist (unmarked) verb forms. The meaning of the locative construction which gives rise to the progressive is probably 'be in the place of verbing' or 'be at verbing'. The meaning of the serial construction would be 'sit verbing' or 'stand verbing'.

An interesting question that arises with regard to these sources concerns the range of possible variation in the degree of specificity of the postural or locative notion included in the construction. We know that the elements that enter into grammatical periphrases are always among the most frequently used items in the language; that is, they are already highly generalized in semantic content before entering into grammatical constructions. Lexical items that qualify for grammatical constructions are more often 'go' and 'come' than the more specific and less frequent 'swim' or 'exit'; more often 'have' or 'get' than 'buy' or 'steal'. However, in some languages, the postural or locative notions of the progressive seem quite specific, such as Ngambay 'sit' contrasting with 'stand', but both yielding a progressive sense. In other languages, the auxiliaries are the more generalized 'be located' or 'be there,' and the locative elements are generalized to 'place' or simply 'locative'. The Spanish auxiliary that produces a progressive construction with the present participle is *estar,* which comes from the Latin *stare* meaning 'to stand'. However, by the time the Spanish Progressive developed, probably very little of the specific postural meaning of *estar* remained. On the other hand, the uses of *estar* in contrast with the other Spanish copula, *ser,* retain some locative and postural nuances, as it is *estar* that is always used for location and temporary states.

The question is, If some sense of location is necessary in these progressive constructions, how specific can they be and still be grammatical, and how generalized can they be and still impart enough of the locative sense to yield the progressive meaning? Of course, such a question cannot be answered until we have a means of quantifying specificity and generality of meaning, but the question is important if we want to determine whether there must be some sense of location in any progressive derived with a stative verb auxiliary.

Against the twenty-one cases of progressives derived using a locative element, we have only six cases of progressives from *be*-auxiliaries plus a non-finite verb form (see Table 5.1). Even for these six cases, it is possible that a locative notion is involved in the periphrasis but not reported explicitly in the grammar. For instance, while the auxiliary in the Nung construction, *al*, is glossed simply as 'to be', another 'to be' verb also exists in Nung, and examination of examples of their use shows *al* used in sentences asking for or giving locations, while the other *be*-verb is used in equational sentences (Barnard 1934: 39–40). The Guaymí 'be' verb, *tä*, may be a borrowing from Spanish *está*, which is of locative origin, as we mentioned above. Like *está*, it is used to describe temporary or transient states and situations. Even where such distributions are not found, it is still possible that the auxiliary involved in the construction has locational meaning, since copulas often derive from locational or postural verbs. An intermediate case is the Kui progressive auxiliary *man-*, which means 'live, exist', suggesting again a locative origin.

The participial or gerundive forms of the main verb present an analogous situation: since such non-finite verb forms are sometimes derived diachronically from locative elements, the form of the main verb itself may carry some locative meaning. For instance, the Haka present participle particle is also a noun meaning 'place'. From outside our sample, the Godié noun *dʌ*, meaning 'place', is added to the verb to produce the verbal noun that is used in the progressive construction (Marchese 1986). In some of our cases where no locative element is reported as a part of the progressive construction, it may be that it resides in the element used to form the non-finite main verb. Thus the Kui Present Participle suffix has two allomorphs, *-i* and *-ki;* the first is homophonous with the ending on nouns and the other with the dative, both of which could themselves have derived from locative elements. It is also possible that the Maidu Participle suffix *-dom* and the Buriat gerund suffix *-za* are both originally locative elements, though no additional information is available for either in the reference material. The other element involved in the Nung construction, *der*, glossed as 'and' (but only for joining 'actions', not nouns), also occurs in other combinations producing subordinating conjunctions. It could certainly have earlier had a more concrete locative meaning.

Thus one strong hypothesis for sources of progressives would be that a progressive involving a stative auxiliary always derives from a construction which originally included an element with locative meaning. Or, stated another way, aside from movement sources, reduplications, and constructions with verbs meaning 'to keep on', all progressives derive from locative constructions. Heine 1990 explicitly disagrees with this position, claiming that progressives can also be derived from equational sentences of the form, 'X is a Y' as in 'He is (an) eating (one).' The only example he offers of progressives deriving from this construction is the case of Italian, which like Spanish uses a descendent of Latin *stare* 'to stand' with a present participle. Since *stare* is originally a locative verb, this construction could as well be interpreted as having a locative source.

This hypothesis bears on our attempts to understand developments in languages with which we are more familiar, such as English. The present-day English progressive appears to be made up of a copula with no particular locative meaning and a gerund, again with no evidence of a locative meaning. However, one hypothesis, put forth by Jespersen 1949: 168 about the origins of this construction in Middle English, postulates the presence of a locative preposition before the gerund, as in (6) and (7).

(6)   He is on hunting.
(7)   He was a-coming home.

This preposition has now been deleted in most dialects. Another hypothesis (see Scheffer 1975 and Traugott 1972) points to a construction found—but not too frequently—in Old English, which combined the copular verbs *beon* and *wesan* with a present participle. The Present Participle forms in *-ende* were gradually replaced by the *-ing*, so it is conceivable that our modern Progressive is a continuation of this old, non-locative construction. One could argue that since historians of the language have not solved the problem, a general theory of grammaticization may be invoked. If so, of course, the preponderance of locative sources for progressives in other languages would suggest a locative source for the English Progressive as well.[1] We will see later that the semantics of the English Progressive point in the same direction.

The conclusion concerning stative sources for progressives, then, strongly points to location as a necessary semantic element, and no clear cases of progressives formed with a copula without a locative element have been found in our data.

Other sources for progressives appear less frequently in our data. Movement sources with verbs meaning 'come' and 'go' are found in widely separated languages. These constructions presumably resemble periphrases possible in English (8) or Spanish (9).

(8)   He goes around bragging about his promotion.
(9)   Andaba   escribiendo   para   los   periódicos.
      go:IMPF:3.S   write:GER   for   the   newspapers.
      'He was writing for the newspapers.'

---

1. Note that the nascent progressives in other Germanic languages have locative elements: Dutch *Ik ben aan het studeren*, literally, 'I am at the studying'.

The similarity between the movement sources and the locative sources is that they both contain a locative element: they both say something (albeit quite vague) about the location of the subject and the activity, either that the subject is located somewhere doing something or the subject is moving (around) doing something.

The other lexical source for progressives is auxiliary verbs which have a fairly literal meaning of 'continue' or 'keep on doing something'. Such sources need little comment, except to say that they themselves may at times be descendants of movement verbs. For instance, the Spanish verb *seguir*, which is used with a gerund to mean 'keep on doing', as a main verb means 'to follow' in both the literal movement sense and the figurative sense.

In the next section we discuss the nature of early progressive meaning and how it evolves from the various periphrastic constructions we have discussed in this section.

5.3. Progressive meaning

García 1987 points out that new periphrases develop to express meanings that are more specific than the meanings already expressed grammatically in the language at the time. All languages have means of expressing present ongoing activities, but in languages without an explicit progressive gram, the same device is usually used for habitual actions, ongoing states, and all other present occurrences.

If we look at the meaning elements that go into the formation of the progressive periphrasis, it would appear that the original function of the progressive is to give the location of an agent as in the midst of an activity. In fact, this function seems to persist, even in well-developed progressives such as the English one. Dwight Bolinger (personal communication) points out that the English Progressive makes a very appropriate answer to a location inquiry.

(10)   A: *Where's Lou?*
       B: *He's taking a bath (having a nap, etc.).*

On the other hand, Bolinger continues, an answer naming the actual location, such as *in the bathroom* or *in bed,* gives less information.

As expressions of location, progressive constructions would most appropriately be used with main verbs that describe activities that have some characteristic and overt location, rather than with predicates describing internal and non-observable states. Thus the oft-cited restriction of progressives to use with dynamic verbs follows directly from the source from which they develop.

The richly detailed description of the English Progressive by Hatcher (1952) makes it appear that the meaning of this gram derives from a locative source, although she by no means intends to make this point. Hatcher contrasts the Simple Present with the Progressive in the description of 'a single occurrence'. She points out that the Progressive is typically used with predicates that describe an overt activity (11) or a state that is 'developing by degrees' (12) (Hatcher 1952: 268).

(11)   She is washing dishes, tending the furnace.
       I'm slipping. I'm losing my hold.
       Your teeth are chattering. Your nose is running.
       She's chewing gum, picking her teeth, yawning.
(12)   I'm developing a cold, getting hot.
       One of my headaches is coming on.
       This is driving me nuts, getting us nowhere.
       I'm beginning to understand.

On the other hand, the Simple Present is typically used for states or activities that are not overt (13) or in performative statements (14) (Hatcher 1952: 266–67).

(13)   It stings. It tickles. My new shoes hurt me.
       Does this light bother you?
       I smell something funny. I see it. I hear it.
       I remember her. I understand. I love your hat!
(14)   I insist that she will come. I tell you I won't.
       I warn you that I won't. I beg you.
       I give my consent. I refuse. I bet five dollars.

While these appear to be the usual pairings of gram with predicate, in cases where the Progressive and Simple Present are used with the same predicates, Hatcher notices that the difference seems to reside in the fact that the Progressive implies a greater involvement of the subject in the activity: either the subject is an active agent or the subject is affected by the action. In (15) the development by degrees involves the subject; in (16) the Progressive changes the interpretation of the predicate to a dynamic one that involves an agent; in (17) the interpretation of the predicate is not dynamic, but the involvement of the subject is increased by the use of the Progressive where the Simple Present is more normal (examples from Hatcher 1952: 269–72).

(15)   I see it.
       I'm seeing it more clearly now.
(16)   I taste something bitter.
       I'm only tasting it (I'm not going to eat it).
(17)   Imagine: at last I'm seeing the Mona Lisa.
       I'm hoping and praying that he'll come.
       He thinks he's being entertaining, but he's only boring her to death.

Even though the English Progressive has advanced considerably from its origins and is used in a wider range of contexts than progressives in other languages (Comrie 1976: 33; Dahl 1985: 90), it still conveys much more than simple aspectual meaning. What it conveys seems to be directly derivable from a locative source, from a meaning 'the subject is in the midst of doing something'. As we mentioned above, if the original function of the progressive periphrasis is to give a location, then the activities expressed by the main verb must be overt and have a characteristic location. The implication of the subject being located in the midst of this activity is that the subject is actively involved, probably originally as the agent in the activity, but perhaps later extended to predicates in which the subject is an experiencer. The application of the progressive to states that are developing by degrees (an application that is mentioned or exemplified for other languages in our corpus) is probably a later development, since these states do not typically involve a particular location for the subject.

The semantic relation between the English Progressive and the locative periphrasis that leads to progressive suggests to us that the English gram should be reconstructed as deriving from a locative construction (rather than from the copula plus a present participle). The fact that a number of the progressive grams in our sample which are from locative sources are reported to be roughly equivalent to the English Progressive (Shuswap, Tucano, etc.), and the fact that non-locative progressives are very rare (if they exist at all), also point to a locative source for the English Progressive.

The only real argument in favor of regarding the diachronic origin of the English Progressive as simply *be* plus the Present Participle is the fact that such a construction did exist in Old English. However, it was not very frequent and it had a meaning very different from progressive meaning. It used a form of 'be' and the participle with adjectival force. It expressed a habitual or characterizing state, not active involvement in an activity. According to Curme 1913, our expressions such as *peace-loving* and *god-fearing* are modern survivors from this usage. A typical Old English example is from Ælfric's *Lives*, I, ll. 52–55, where the author has stated that the creator has made creatures of various forms and gaits.

(18) Sume **syndan creopende** on eorðan mid eallum lichoman, swa swa wurmas doð. Sume gað on twam fotum, sume on feower fotum, sume fleoð mid fyðerum.
'Some creep on the earth with their whole body, as worms do. Some go on two feet, some on four feet, some fly with wings.'

Curme (1913: 163) notes it would destroy Ælfric's meaning to translate the first verbal form as 'are creeping', since he intends a generic characterization, not the active progressive meaning of the modern construction. If the general theory of grammaticization is correct, it is highly unlikely that the meaning of the modern Progressive could have evolved out of the sense illustrated in (18). We therefore side with those who propose that this older construction disappeared, and the modern Progressive is a more recent development from a locative construction.

The semantic nuances for the English Progressive that we have described here, following Hatcher 1952, are not verifiable for most of the languages in our sample, due to the nature of the reference material. However, the grams we have labeled as progressives in our database are all exemplified in our material with prototypical dynamic verbs, suggesting active involvement of an agent. Moreover, Dahl's questionnaire survey shows the English Progressive to be close to the universal prototype, despite the fact that it is more frequently used in the questionnaire than most other progressives.

The semantic changes that take place in the development of the progressive are gradual erosions of the original, fuller meaning of the construction. We propose that the original meaning of the progressive construction is 'the subject is located in the midst of doing something'. The function of this locution is to give the location of the subject. As we suggested earlier, it is used at first for activities that imply a specific location for the subject and the activity. Thus the construction contains either explicitly or implicitly the following elements of meaning:

        a. An agent
        b. is located spatially
        c. in the midst of
        d. an activity
        e. at reference time.

As these particular components of meaning weaken, the construction becomes appropriate in more and more contexts.

Among other things, the requirement that the subject be an agent is gradually expanded, probably at the same time as the notion of activity expands to include developing states. As these co-occurrence tendencies weaken, the sense remaining in the construction as a whole is the sense of an ongoing action or state of affairs.

In some languages the progressive construction is restricted to activities that are actually ongoing at the moment of speech. Thus in Spanish (Jorge Guitart, personal communication) the progressive implies that the subject is involved in an activity and cannot or should not be interrupted.

(19)   No puede venir al teléfono; se está bañando.
       'He can't come to the telephone; he's taking a bath.'

Similarly, the Dutch progressive is appropriate only for activities that are actually ongoing. In these languages, "in the midst of" is interpreted very narrowly. In English the interpretation is much broader: the activity can be ongoing in an extended sense, that is, characteristic of a time period, and need not be actually in progress at the moment.

(20) I'm writing a book about poltergeists.

In Spanish this broader sense can be obtained with the help of temporal adverbs:

(21) Elena está jugando volibol   este año.
      'Elena is   playing volleyball this year.'

Progressive constructions are often cited as examples of temporal categories that are based on locative ones (Anderson 1973; Traugott 1978). The intriguing question about such categories concerns the apparent shift from locative to temporal meaning, and whether it involves an inferential leap or a metaphorical shift. Our examination of the meaning of progressives suggests that no great step is involved in a progressive becoming aspectual. Rather, the temporal meaning is present from the beginning, since to be located spatially in an activity is to be located temporally in that activity. The change that occurs is the gradual loss of the locative meaning. What is of interest here is the fact that it is the locative rather than the temporal meaning that undergoes erosion. This particular direction of change is closely tied to the fact that grammaticization requires the broadening of contexts of use: if a construction means 'to be in the midst of doing,' the only change that would give it more contexts of use would in fact be the erosion and loss of the strict locative meaning, which would then allow the expression of temporal meaning in a wider range of contexts.

5.4. Comrie's analysis of imperfective, continuous, and progressive

Comrie (1976: 24–40) provides an analysis of the relations among the various subcategories of imperfective and definitions of these subcategories. His classification of aspectual oppositions is exemplified in Figure 5.1 (his Table 1, from p. 25).

Since we have dealt with the perfective in chapter 3, we are concerned here only with the subdivisions of imperfective and their definitions. As Comrie defines the imperfective, it makes "explicit reference to the internal temporal structure of a situation, viewing a situation from within" (1976: 23). Habitual is defined in a way we have already cited, by saying that habitual situations are characteristic of an extended period of time (1976: 28–29). These are the only positive definitions offered; continuous and progressive are defined by the

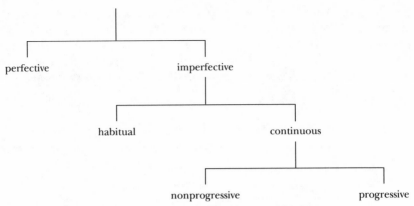

Fig. 5.1. Classification of aspectual oppositions (Comrie 1976: 25).

absence of properties. Continuous is defined as "imperfectivity that is not occasioned by habituality" (1976: 33), and progressive is continuousness combined with non-stative meaning (1976: 35). (Nonprogressive is not defined.)

While we sympathize with the goal of coming up with succinct yet adequate definitions of the functions of grammatical morphemes, our own theory leads us to reject a negative definition of the progressive. In our view, grams have inherent semantic context which is a continuation of the original semantics conveyed by the lexical item or periphrasis from which the gram has evolved (Bybee and Pagliuca 1987; Bybee 1988a). This view is well supported by Hatcher's analysis of the English Progressive, as well as other analyses, such as Bolinger 1947 or Goldsmith and Woisetschlaeger 1982, which propose that the Progressive makes a content-ful contribution to the utterance. In fact, the English Progressive appears to be very rich in meaning, supplying the sentence both with aspectual and non-aspectual nuances.

While definitions citing the absence of properties may yield economical descriptions of grams, we feel they are inappropriate, since the diachronic development of grams shows that they have real semantic content. Definitions citing the absence of features might appear appropriate for grams expressed by zero, but Bybee 1990b has argued that even zeroes have real semantic content, which they absorbed from the context. Even the English Simple Present, which has had much of its domain of use taken over by the newly developed futures and progressive, is not rendered a NON-category, since it still expresses the content—habitual, generic, and stative—that it expressed before. Later in this chapter we will see more examples of the effect of a developing gram on other grams, as well as examples of the development of zero expression.

The hierarchical organization of Figure 5.1 shows perfective and imperfective to be the broadest ranging categories, with habitual and continuous dividing up the imperfective range. Of course, Comrie (1976: 26) argues that imperfective is not made up of two separate meanings, but rather is a single general, more abstract meaning that covers both. We have adopted this view of imperfective and have coded as imperfective only those grams with uses in both habitual and continuous contexts.

We have also attempted to follow Comrie's analysis of continuous as divisible into progressive (for dynamic verbs) and nonprogressive (for statives). Cast in a diachronic light, Figure 5.1 suggests that a progressive would become a continuous by generalizing to apply to stative predicates as well as dynamic ones:

progressive > continuous > imperfective

In our data, however, while progressives stand out very clearly, no equally clear category of 'continuous' emerges. One problem is the lack of explicit mention of co-occurrence restrictions, so that we do not know for sure whether progressives are restricted to dynamic verbs. Moreover, the language of reference grammars is unclear: a gram described as used for 'ongoing actions or states' may not mean that it can be used with stative predicates; rather it may mean it signals an ongoing 'state of affairs', which could be described with a dynamic predicate.

We should not be surprised that no coherent continuous gram-type arises from our data since, despite Comrie's classification of aspects, he cites no examples of a continuous marker (nor a non-progressive marker, for that matter). Further, Dahl's (1985) study turned up a cross-linguistic gram-type of progressive but no 'continuous'.

Our conclusion, then, regarding Comrie's classification and definition of aspectual oppositions is that a gram-type for each node of Figure 5.1 does not exist. We have strong evidence for progressive, habitual, past imperfective, imperfective, and present as cross-linguistic gram-types in our material, but a clear distinction between a progressive which is restricted to dynamic verbs and a continuous which is not does not emerge from our data.

5.5. Lexical restrictions

Given our analysis of the development of progressive meaning, the fact that progressives are preferred with dynamic verbs—either activity or process verbs—is a consequence of the fact that progressive meaning is originally most compatible with activity predicates and only gradually extends to other predicate types. In fact, we argue in this section that the various co-occurrence restrictions we found for progressive (and in some cases, continuous) follow from the source meaning of the construction.

As mentioned above, we expected to find progressives described in our reference material as co-occurring only with dynamic predicates, but in fact, such descriptions are not commonly made explicit. Despite this, we suspect that such restrictions are in place in many cases, since several of the progressives were described as equivalent to the English Progressive and since all of them were illustrated with canonical dynamic predicates. In some cases in which the progressive gram is described as indicating an 'ongoing state or action', the illustration of the 'ongoing state' is one of development by degrees, as in 'it's getting dark' (Tucano: Sorensen 1969: 267–69). It appears that the lexical analysis needed to find the restrictions on the progressive gram was simply not attempted by many of the authors of the reference material.

On the other hand, in a few cases interesting details on the lexical co-occurrence of progressive gram-types are given. In these cases the restrictions give information about the original source of the progressive construction. For instance, progressives that definitely are not restricted to dynamic situations occur in Motu, where the form is derived directly from a demonstrative meaning 'here (or there) now', and in Chacobo with a progressive translated as 'now'. The Motu construction neither nominalizes the verb nor uses a copula, suggesting that it is a different type of periphrasis than the 'subject is located in an activity' type of progressive. Less information is available on the Chacobo progressive, but a similar analysis, in which the temporal element (which may perhaps derive from a locative one) is added directly to the verb phrase, appears reasonable.

In some cases more specific lexical restrictions are the result of a progressive developing from a locative source. In Island Carib the progressive suffix -ia is used only with verbs of action or process, except for the fact that it is used with bases indicating position or quantity. The latter uses are indicative of a lexical source as a locational, such as ia(ha) 'here', and when it indicates location (and quantity), it apparently does not indicate aspect (Taylor 1956a: 24; 1956b: 138).

5.6. Progressives evolving into presents and imperfectives

Situations which are simultaneous with the moment of speech, and thus present, may be of several different aspectual types. Present situations may be viewed as progressive activities that are ongoing at the moment of speech. Habitually occurring situations may be viewed as simultaneous with the moment of speech if the moment of speech is included in the period of time which is characterized by the occurrence of the habitual situation. States may be described as in effect during the moment of speech. Generic or gnomic situations are often regarded as timeless because they hold for all time, but they still can be regarded as in effect at the moment of speech. Thus it is possible to find grams of 'present tense' which express all these meanings: progressive, habitual, state exists, and gnomic. It is also possible to find grams that express various subsets of these four meanings. In the course of this chapter, we will try to explain how various types and combinations of present meanings arise diachronically.

In some sense it is accurate to say that a 'present tense' expresses the meaning of present imperfective. Since imperfective, as we have defined it, expresses both ongoing progressive action and habitual occurrence (at some reference time) and may also be used for states and gnomic situations, an imperfective that is restricted to the present would be indistinguishable from a present tense. Or, as we put it in chapter 3, a present gram expresses a subpart of imperfective meaning.

Since both present and imperfective meaning include the possibility of describing a situation as progressive, it is plausible to suppose that the more specific progressive grams may undergo development into either a present (in cases where the progressive was restricted to the present) or an imperfective (in cases where no temporal restrictions were in effect). A major step in such a development is the extension of the progressive to express habitual meaning. Cases of such developments have been proposed in the literature on the basis of historical and comparative evidence. Comrie 1976: 101 mentions the case of dialect variation in Yoruba, where some speakers use the periphrastic locative construction only for progressive, while others use it for habitual situations as well. He also discusses the case of Scots Gaelic, in which a locative periphrasis has generalized to express habitual and thus may be regarded as an imperfective. Another case is the Turkish suffix -yor, from the verb 'to walk, go', which formerly in the spoken language and currently in the written language expresses progressive meaning only but in current spoken language is also used for habitual (Underhill 1976: 145ff.; see also Dahl's 1985 questionnaire results for Turkish -yor, which classify it as an imperfective marker). Dahl 1985: 93 mentions the case of the older Punjabi and Hindi-Urdu progressives that have extended to general imperfective usage. Finally, Heine 1990 mentions the case of the Chamus dialect of Maa (Eastern Nilotic), in which the progressive has assumed the function of a present tense marker with dynamic verbs.

In our data we find cases of presents and imperfectives with lexical sources similar to those found for progressives, although our data yielded relatively few lexical sources for these more highly grammat-

Table 5.2.   Imperfectives

Language	Form No.	Related String	Expression
03 Margi	27	in the place of	PARTCL
06 Tuareg	03		PRE
32 Nakanai	03		REDUP
35 Rukai	04		REDUP
50 Mod. Greek	07		STCH
68 Slave	09		ZERO
72 Mwera	15		SUF
74 Engenni	15		TNCH
78 Kanuri	01	'in' or 'at'	SUF
83 Shuswap	27		PRE

Table 5.3.   Past Imperfectives

Language	Form No.	Related String	Expression
02 Basque	06	be	AUX
04 Kanakuru	13		AUX
05 Agau	30	be, pass the day	SUF
08 Tigre	42	exist, be located	AUX
17 Alyawarra	02		SUF
18 Maung	06		PAST P/N PRE + SUF
20 Alawa	33		SUF
25 Tahitian	02	distance particle	PARTCL
39 Abkhaz	46		SUF
42 Kui	24	past of be + PresPart	AUX
47 Latin	08	be	SUF

icized markers (cf. the paucity of related strings for perfectives and pasts reported in chap. 3). For instance, as shown in Table 5.2, the sources for imperfectives in our data include two cases of reduplication, one zero, and two related strings with locative meaning. We deal with zeroes and reduplication later in this chapter. The fact that the only other sources are both locative is compatible with the hypothesis that progressive meaning develops into imperfective meaning.

Past imperfectives (Table 5.3) also provide evidence that progressive meaning may generalize into imperfective meaning. The Kui past imperfective is formed, parallel to the present progressive, with the verb *man-* which earlier meant 'live, exist', conjugated in the present tense, plus a Present Participle of unknown origin. While the present version of this construction is restricted to progressive meaning, the past version has both habitual and progressive uses (Winfield 1928: 87). Of course, this suggests that the past imperfective began as a past progressive but has subsequently generalized its meaning. The loca-

Table 5.4. Presents

Language	Form No.	Related String	Expression
02 Basque	01	be	AUX
05 Agau	07		SUF
08 Tigre	17	exist + imperfect verb	AUX
	21		STCH
12 Chacobo	42		SUF
13 Jívaro	24		SUF
15 Gugada	03		SUF
16 Gugu-Yalanji	02		SUF
17 Alyawarra	04		SUF
	05	participle/locative	SUF
18 Maung	04		PRE
20 Alawa	34		SUF
25 Tahitian	01	copula	PARTCL
27 Atchin	02		AUX
35 Rukai	08		ZERO
39 Abkhaz	01		SUF
40 Guaymí	05		SUF
47 Latin	07		ZERO
48 Maithili	15		AUX
49 Baluchi	01		ZERO
50 Mod. Greek	07		ZERO
51 Danish	01		SUF
52 Yagaria	19		STCH, ZERO
	20	exist	PRE
56 Ono	01		SUF
58 Nimboran	05		SUF
59 Bongu	36		SUF
60 Yessan-Mayo	11		SUF
71 Temne	08		TNCH
73 Tem	13		PRE
76 Bari	08		ZERO
81 Zuni	02		SUF
85 Chepang	11		SUF
86 Haka	38		ZERO
88 Nung	06		PARTCL
91 Udmurt	01		SUF
92 Uigur	35		SUF
93 Buriat	01		SUF

tive nature of the Tahitian imperfective is also suggestive of progressive origins.

Among the present grams shown in Table 5.4 are a few locative sources: the Tigre verb *halla* is used in existential sentences and also in locational sentences (Raz 1983: 48f.); the Yagaria prefix is probably from a verb *hano* which is also used in existential and locational sentences (Renck 1975: 53, 57, 90, 201); the Alyawarra suffix *-iyla* is reported to be of participial origin (Yallop 1977: 52) and, not surpris-

ingly, resembles the locative suffix -*ila* which indicates 'near', 'beside',
'by', or 'along' and has the same form as the ergative and instrumental
(Yallop 1977: 76f.). The sources of the Basque and Baluchi presents
are discussed in §5.7.

These few locative sources suggest progressive origins for at least
some presents, but the existence of several cases of zero expression
for presents indicate that they also develop as the result of a developing past tense, as explained in §3.13.

5.6.1. Implications of languages with two present grams

It can be seen in Table 5.4 that some languages have two grams that
we have classified as presents. In all these cases, it is clear that one is
an older, more grammaticized (or zero) gram and the other is a
younger developing gram, and in three out of four cases, it appears
that this younger gram has developed from a progressive. Such a
situation should come as no surprise to us after examining the data
on the English Progressive and Present, since the Progressive appears
to have been generalizing and taking over some of the functions of
the Present for several centuries (see also the discussion of 'layering'
in §1.4.7). In three cases in our data the newer gram has gone beyond
its earlier more restricted meaning (presumably of progressive) and
now functions in most present contexts without, however, having
completely replaced the older present. We turn now to an examination of the facts reported in these three languages—Yagaria, Alyawarra, and Tigre—as well as a discussion of Margi, which apparently
has a progressive developing into an imperfective.

In Yagaria the Present Tense has zero expression and in main
clauses "relates actions in the present, or, as 'historic present', actions
which took place in the past" (Renck 1975: 86). As a medial verb
form, "it relates successive actions without denoting whether the action described is completed or still in progress as the anticipated action starts" (p. 106). In such cases, it takes its tense from the final
verb form.

If the examples presented throughout Renck 1975 are any indication, the Progressive, formed with the prefix *no-* (probably from *hano*
'to exist') is much more commonly used than the Present Tense. According to Renck (p. 90), the *no-* prefix can describe situations as either progressive or habitual. Thus (22) can have two interpretations.

(22) ba   no-   d-   on-   e
      potatoes sweet. PROG- eat- 1.P- IND
      'we are eating sweet potatoes now' or 'we usually eat sweet
      potatoes'

Furthermore, the *no-* prefix is used in present tense expressions that
are semantically stative. For instance, 'I am angry' is expressed with

no- in both an impersonal (23) and a personal construction (24) (Renck 1975: 147).

(23)	da-	hei'	no'-	v-	ei-	e	'I am angry.'
	l.s-	anger	PROG-	wrap-	3.s-	IND	
(24)	da-	hei'	no'-	v-	ou-	e	'I am angry.'
	l.s-	anger	PROG-	wrap-	1.s-	IND	

In these examples, however, the finite verb appears to be a dynamic one, 'wrap', so it could be argued that these are cases of the progressive occurring with dynamic verbs. The same construction occurs also with the highly generalized verb *hu-* (allomorphs *hi-*, *si-*, and *su-*), which means 'to do, to be, to make, to speak', as in (25) and (26) (Renck 1975: 147).

(25)	d-	oubibi	no-	s-	i-	e	'I am tired.'
	l.s-	tired	PROG-	DO-	3.s-	IND	
(26)	d-	oubibi'	no-	s-	u-	e	'I am tired.'
	l.s-	tired	PROG-	do-	l.s-	IND	

Furthermore, while the prefix *no-* seems to be normal in such constructions in the present tense, the past equivalent is expressed with the simple past suffix. In other words, the construction with *no-* in the present tense seems to be aspectually identical to an expression with no overt progressive marker in the past (examples from Renck 1975: 146, 152).

(27)	alaga	no-	da-	h-	a-	e	'I am bored.'
	boredom	PROG-	l.s-	shoot-	3.s-	IND	
(28)	alaga	da-	hao-	d-	i-	e	'I was bored.'
	boredom	l.s-	shoot-	PAST-	3.s-	IND	

Such examples suggest that the *no-* prefix is much more than a progressive marker; it appears to be approaching the generality of a present marker, but without having completely replaced the zero present.

The Alyawarra case appears in some ways to be similar to the Yagaria case. In Alyawarra two suffixes, *-ima* (Present) and *-iyla* (Present Continuous), are described as used for many of the same present tense functions. We hypothesize that *-ima* is the older of these two since it also occurs in the other Arandic languages described by Yallop (1977: 58), while *-iyla* does not have cognates in the other languages. Further, *-ima* is used spontaneously by the speakers when verbs are given in their citation form, suggesting that it is taken to represent a default meaning. Yallop suggests that *-iyla* might be related to the` locative and participial forms in *-ila*.

Yallop (1977: 52) states that the uses of *-ima* parallel those of *-iyla*, but that the latter is preferred for the description of present happenings. Such a description would suggest that *-iyla* is a progressive (as in

English), but further examples show that it is much more generalized than a typical progressive since it can be used with stative predicates, as in the following examples (Yallop 1977: 51–52, 81).

(29) atha   nginha   itilariyla
      1.s.ERG   2.s.ACC   know:PRES.CONT
      'I know you (i.e., we've met before).'

(30) akira   intiyla
      meat:NOM   smell:PRES.CONT
      'The meat smells.'

(31) arntitjiriyla   ayinga   intingipirna
      sick:INTR:PRES.CONT   1.s.NOM   rotten:after
      'I'm sick after (eating) rotten (meat).'

There are also examples of -*iyla* in habitual contexts, in a main clause in (32) (p. 51) and in a relative clause in (33)(p. 137).

(32) nga   angkiyla   alyawarra,   ra
      2.s.NOM   speak:PRES.CONT   Alyawarra,   3.s
      angkiyla   arirnta
      speak:PRES.CONT   Aranda.
      'You speak Alyawarra, he speaks Aranda.'

(33) angkina   ayinga   artuka,   urala
      talk:PAST.CONT   1.s.NOM   man:DAT   fire:NOM.REL
      ayrtirniyla
      chop:PRES.CONT
      'I was talking to the man who chops the firewood.'

These examples suggest that -*iyla* is not simply a progressive but is closer to a general present, since it is used in these additional contexts. It appears from the examples cited in Yallop 1977 that -*iyla* may be more frequently occurring than -*ima*; however, despite the general distribution of -*iyla*, it has not completely replaced -*ima*. Thus the language appears to have two very general present tense grams.

A third case of overlapping present forms is found in Tigre. Here what is traditionally labeled the Perfect/Imperfect distinction is described as actually representing a past/non-past distinction. This distinction is signaled by stem changes familiar from other Semitic languages. In addition, there are a number of periphrastic constructions, among which are two with progressive, habitual, and stative uses, one in the present and the other in the past. For instance, one is formed with the Imperfect of the verb plus the auxiliary *halla*, which is the present existential verb, also used to give location. The other is formed with the past existential and locational verb *'ala* and is used for past contexts (Raz 1983: 48–49).

The Imperfect is described as expressing "a state of existing or an action whose period of time includes the present moment" (Raz 1983: 70). This use is illustrated with a stative predicate and with habitual situations. Second, it is described as indicating futurity, and the third use is as an historic present used in narratives about past time. The periphrastic constructions are used for in-progress actions and states and also for habitual situations. There is no indication that the periphrastic constructions may be used for future or historic present. Nor is it clear what the difference is between the periphrastic and the Imperfect forms in the case of present occurrences or habitual and stative situations. Note, however, that the past version of the construction has no past imperfective to compete with; in fact we have designated it as a past imperfective (see Table 5.3).

Again we have a case of considerable overlap in the expression of the present. The Imperfect is clearly the older, more grammaticized form, since it is expressed by stem changes that go back to a common Semitic source. The periphrastic constructions are clearly more recent formations and could possibly come from progressive constructions that have generalized their use, being formed as they are with verbs that are also used in locative sentences.

Finally, we consider Margi, which has a periphrastic construction formed with locative elements that appears to be generalizing from a progressive to an imperfective. According to Hoffman (1963: 177), the preverbal particle *ə́və̀r* "probably originated from a combination of *wú* 'in' + *ìvì* 'place' in an *r*-genitive construction, meaning 'in the place of . . .' (cf. the preposition *ə́və̀r* 'instead of')." This particle (which Hoffman labels 'progressive') indicates an action in progress at present or in the past. In addition, it indicates an habitual action in the past. Its path of generalization (from progressive only to progressive plus habitual) is similar to that of the presents we have just examined. The only difference is that this form is compatible with past contexts (and it apparently does not need past tense marking to be so compatible) and thus appears to be developing into an imperfective.

One of the forms that this Progressive is apparently replacing is the Present, which is expressed with a prefix *a-*, and which has a very general range of use. It is used with stative predicates in the present, for generic and habitual situations, as well as for certain future and subjunctive functions.

Despite the fact that we have found several cases of what we believe to be progressives evolving into presents or imperfectives, it is difficult to make generalizations concerning the way that progressives develop due to the lack of synchronic detail and explicit diachronic information. The data available do suggest, however, a few tentative generalizations.

First, as the progressive takes over functions of the present, the present seems to retain its use as historic present and its use in generic statements the longest. In Tigre and Yagaria the older present forms are still used for past narratives, while none of the newer presents in any of the four languages has this use. Generic sentences are less often mentioned, but it appears that the Tigre Imperfect and the Margi Present are the preferred expression of generic statements, and the newer progressive forms are not used in this way.

We have used the generalization to habitual contexts and generalization to use with stative predicates as the criteria for classifying a gram as present or imperfective, but it is not clear from the data at hand which of these generalizations precedes the other. In Yagaria, Alyawarra, and Tigre, the forms in question are used in both contexts. However, we do have two cases of a generalization to habitual in a past context but not in a present one. These cases are Margi, mentioned just above, and the Past Progressive of Kui, which is used for habitual while the Present Progressive is not. Neither of these forms is used with statives, as far as we can tell. Thus, at least in the past, the use in habitual contexts precedes the use with statives.

5.6.2. Implications for theories of grammatical meaning

The examples discussed in the previous section, along with the example of the English Progressive and Simple Present, demonstrate that grammatically expressed meaning categories do not necessarily have to form maximal contrasts. In all these examples we have seen that two constructions have considerable overlap in their usage. Our analysis of these situations is that a more recently developed construction is gradually taking over some of the functions of an older, pre-existing construction. Of course, we do not believe that the two constructions are actually identical in their meaning, despite the fact that they may both be appropriate and express the same meaning in certain contexts. Rather, we believe that in the cases discussed here, as in the English case, there are probably subtle differences that are very difficult to discover and describe (especially for a non-native speaker). In particular, our hypothesis that grammaticizing elements retain parts of their lexical meaning well into the grammaticization process predicts that the newer constructions are richer in the meaning that they contribute to the utterance than are the older constructions.

The considerable overlap we find in constructions developing in the same semantic domain means that at any particular synchronic stage the contrasts found will not necessarily represent opposite poles on an abstract semantic dimension that represents some basic dichotomy in the speakers' world view. Rather, it seems to us that there are certain major contrasts of universal validity—such as the basic distinction between the perfective domain (which we have discussed in chap. 3) and the imperfective (which is the subject of the present chapter)—but that within these domains there are successive waves of grammaticization which may follow upon one another at such a rate as to produce only very small and subtle semantic distinctions.

This view implies that to find the exact meaning of a gram at any particular stage of development requires careful, detailed, language-particular grammatical study, for differences among languages in the retention of lexical meaning and the interaction of existing grams may produce considerable cross-language variation in meaning. It does not vitiate, however, the goal of a large cross-linguistic study such as that reported on here. Rather, if we draw an analogy with phonological and phonetic study, we might say that our cross-linguistic study is turning up universal entities on the level of the notion of a "voiceless dental stop." Such a notion provides a useful frame of reference: we may go from language to language identifying such an element, the IPA provides a symbol for it, theories of phonetic evolution may predict paths of change for it, and so on. However, to say that a language has a voiceless dental stop does not by any means exhaust the descriptive possibilities or capture the native speaker's command of such an element. From language to language we may find important differences in the timing of voice onset, in the position of the tongue at the teeth, in the duration of closure, and in the contextual variants of the voiceless dental stop. We argue, then, that the study of grammatical meaning, like that of phonological elements, requires both the broad cross-linguistic perspective and the detailed language-specific perspective.

5.7. New form without new meaning

In some languages of our sample (as well as in some other well-known languages), a newer formation appears to have equivalent semantics to an older, more synthetic construction. For instance, in Basque, as we saw above, the present and past imperfective of most verbs are formed with the present and past, respectively, of the auxiliary meaning 'be, have'. However, for a half dozen high-frequency verbs, these same meanings are expressed by a synthetic formation that is not a derivative of the periphrastic one but apparently represents an older system in which all verbs had synthetic or inflectional forms. The layering hypothesis and the parallel reduction hypothesis predict wrongly that the difference in form corresponds to a difference in meaning.

In Kanuri there are two major verb classes, one formed with inflectional suffixes and prefixes and the other with these same affixes attached to a formative that derives from the verb 'say, think' and attaches to the lexical root. Again, it is clear that the inflectional formation represents an older expression type, and yet there appears to be no difference in meaning. The newer formation with the verb 'say, think' is the productive formation that applies to loanwords and derived verbs (Lukas 1937; Hutchison 1981).

Another comparable example, from outside the sample, is the case of the English past tense suffix -ed, which is a later development than the past tense formed with ablaut vowels. Apparently this suffix was formed before the Old English period from the past tense of the verb 'do', which in Old English was dyde. In Old English, both the ablaut formation and suffixation existed with the same meaning. Of course, the suffixation has become productive and applies to new verbs in English.

Since these cases represent counterexamples to the hypotheses proposed here, we need to consider how they differ from the more usual cases that we have presented in our discussion so far. The difference may be that these newer periphrases begin as devices for creating new verbs, both for handling borrowings and for creating new verbs from nouns, adjectives, or adverbs. In all the cases examined, the inflectional forms being replaced were highly fused, complex, and irregular, which makes the extension to new forms difficult and the creation of a periphrasis helpful.

The Kanuri case is especially interesting because of the choice of the auxiliary, the verb ngin meaning 'say, think'. Hutchison 1981: 102–11 argues that the formation originated with this verb used with ideophones or onomatopoetic words, comparable to the English phrase go boom. Ngin is still the verb used in such expressions in Kanuri. Thus bàdák is the word for the beating of the heart, and the phrase bàdák shìn means '(the heart) is going badak'. But bàdák is also the root of a verb formed with the affix derived from ngin, bádákcìn 'is beating (distinctly).' With onomatopoetic words it is natural to use a verb meaning 'say'. The formation increased in productivity and generalized so that it could apply to adverbs, nouns, adjectives, compounds, and loanwords from Arabic, Hausa, and English. What was originally a derivational process has become a major inflectional class, but because it did not have independent inflectional meaning, it is equivalent to the older inflectional system in the expression of tense, aspect, and mood.

Thus we might say that if a new construction provides a means of forming a new verbal notion rather than of modifying the tense, aspect, or modality of the predicate, it can replace the older inflection without introducing any new grammatical meaning.

5.8. Habitual meaning

According to the scheme we adopted above, based largely on Comrie 1976, one half of the imperfective spectrum is occupied by progressive meaning, the other half consists of habitual meaning. An examination of our cross-linguistic data and what historical information is available on the development of habitual grams suggests that habitual is not a homogeneous piece of imperfective, but rather is highly affected by tense (Bybee 1990b). In our data we observe a clear asymmetry between the expression of habitual meaning in the present and its expression in the past. In particular, while our corpus contains plenty of examples of overt grams which express habitual in all tenses (19 cases) and also examples of specifically past habitual grams (10 cases), the two cases of specifically present habituals in our data are both cases of zero expression.

A gram with zero expression arises as the result of the development of an overt gram in the same semantic domain. The absence of an overt marker in a particular semantic domain (such as the tense/aspect domain) allows the hearer to infer from context the intended interpretation or to infer a default interpretation if the context is also vague. When the overt marker becomes obligatory, the default sense associated with the absence of a marker becomes conventionalized as the meaning of zero.

Our data suggest that while paths exist for the development of general habituals and past habituals, no grammaticization path leads to a strictly present habitual. The only way to arrive at a present habitual is by developing a progressive that cuts out part of an originally more general present and leaves the present habitual as a default reading. Such a course of development has restricted the English Present to habitual and generic readings, for example.

The reasons for the asymmetry in the development and consequent expression of habitual in the past and present are pragmatic. We have already argued that there is a strong overlap between perfective and simple past meaning, since both are used to narrate simple sequences of events. We have also argued that present tense is really the same as present imperfective. It follows then that habitual may be one of the basic or default aspectual readings of present tense, but not of past. Thus explicit expression of habitual meaning will be more frequent in the past than in the present, leading to the development of explicit grammatical marking of habitual in the past.

When we described present tense meanings in §5.6, we noted that present covers several different aspectual types: progressive, habitual, present state, and generic statements. However, these distinctions—particularly the distinction between habitual, stative, and generic—

are not nearly so clear as one might expect. For example, the generic statement (34) differs from the so-called habitual one (35) only by having a generic rather than specific subject.

(34)   Dogs pant to cool off.
(35)   My dog pants to cool off.

Both (34) and (35) make characterizing statements about the subject, statements whose validity extends over more than the actual moment of speech. Similarly, the difference between habitual and stative is minimal. Present states characterize a situation for a period of time that includes, but is not necessarily restricted to, the present moment. The difference between habitual and present stative resides entirely in the lexical meaning of the predicate: the present habitual reading of dynamic predicates covers many different instances of the same situation, while the present stative covers one continuous situation.

Our analysis of progressive meaning as describing an agent actively involved in an overt activity shows that that part of present meaning is distinct from habitual/generic/stative meaning, and indeed, the cross-linguistic data support this point, since we have many cases of explicit markers of progressive in the present. Analyses of the English Progressive/Simple Present distinction help to illustrate what is meant by the statement that habitual/generic/stative are the default meanings of present.

Calver 1946 analyzes the uses of the English Simple Present as referring to "the constitution of things (logical, physical, psychological, essential, etc.)," which is echoed by Goldsmith and Woisetschlaeger (1982: 80), who propose that the Simple Present describes "how the world is made such that things may happen in it." Bolinger 1947 and Hatcher 1952 both point out that such characterizations simply reflect the fact that the Simple Present carries no explicit meaning at all; it refers to the default situation from which all other tenses represent deviations. Gerhardt and Savasir (1986) find confirmation for this understanding of the Simple Present in the interactional usage of this tense by three-year-olds, who use it to describe and even constitute normative behavior and situations. The absence of any explicit tense or aspect meaning in the Simple Present, then, leaves it open to absorb the meaning inherent to normal social and physical phenomena, and this meaning, if described and broken down explicitly, consists of habitual occurrence and behavior as well as ongoing states.

None of this can be said to hold true for the simple past in English or in any language. First, the simple past does express an explicit temporal relation, that the narrated events occurred before the moment of speech. This fact is reflected in the associated fact that simple past is not marked by zero in any languages of our sample or any language that we know of. Second, while simple past encompasses various aspects—including perfective, habitual, and progressive—the default correlation is between perfective and simple past. That is, while present tense principally tells of the way things are, the past tense principally narrates what happened. In order to explicitly talk about habitual or ongoing situations in the past, one needs to add extra elements into one's utterance, hence the grammaticization of past habitual and progressive.

5.8.1. Habitual grams

Given what we have just said about the interaction of habitual with tense, it is not surprising that our coding procedure turned up only two present habitual grams which were not also progressives or more general presents. One of these grams occurs in Kui, a Dravidian language, which has developed some compound tenses which overlay an older, inflectional, present/past marking. The Present Progressive has in effect cut into the Present domain, leaving the old Present to encode present habitual and future, now called Future. That this Future is an older present is supported by comparative evidence: in other Dravidian languages the cognate forms still signal a general present tense (Subrahmanyam 1971: 313–16).

The other occurs in Tucano, where the lack of an inflection indicates "habitual, customary action or state" (Sorensen 1969: 157). Tucano has a periphrastic progressive, so again we can assume that the zero marking formerly signaled general present and now has been restricted to habitual/stative/generic.

Despite the scarcity of explicit mention of such cases in the reference material, we know that there are a number of other very similar cases. In fact, the English case is one. In our sample any of the languages in which a progressive gram was reported which also have a present tense are potential cases. If the progressive gram is the regular expression of progressive, then the present is left for marking habitual and allied senses. We suspect that such a situation obtains in Abkhaz, Baluchi, Bari, Basque, and perhaps some other cases.

As we mentioned above, our corpus also contains habitual grams that are compatible with both past and present, and in some cases, future. In cases in which these grams occur in languages with obligatory tense, the habitual gram co-occurs with the tense markers, as in Cocama, Atchin, Yessan-Mayo, and Worora. In languages without obligatory tense, the habitual occurs in all temporal contexts, as in

Table 5.5.   Habituals without Tense Restrictions

Language	Form No.	Related String	Expression
01 Inuit	10		SUF
	29	all the time	SUF
	50		SUF
	91		SUF
04 Kanakuru	36	to sit	AUX
19 Worora	31		SUF
27 Atchin	17		PARTCL
28 Halia	41		PRE
33 Trukese	41		PARTIAL REDUP
40 Guaymí	21	be, go	AUX
43 Abipon	12	to live	SUF
46 Karok	29		SUF
52 Yagaria	46	to see	REDUP SUF
56 Ono	16	to be used to	SUF
60 Yessan-Mayo	10		SUF
68 Slave	02		PRE
	38		PRE
69 Krongo	18		PRE
80 Tojolabal	02		PRE
90 Dakota	26		PARTCL
94 Tok Pisin	10	to know	AUX

Inuit, Abipon, and Karok. Table 5.5 displays the general habitual grams found in our sample. Some of these general habituals are derivational in nature, such as those in Halia, Abipon, and Karok.

In languages where habitual expression is restricted to the past, it obligatorily co-occurs with explicit tense marking. We suspect that these past habitual grams began as more general habitual locutions that were compatible with either past or present (cf. English *used to*, discussed just below). However, since explicit reference to habitualness is necessary in the past, but not in the present, the habitual construction was used more frequently in the past than in the present. Hence it grammaticized in the past and was lost in the present.

5.8.2. Lexical sources

Tables 5.5 and 5.6 show the lexical sources for habituals that we found in our sample. The two lexical verbs that serve as sources for habitual auxiliaries, and eventually for affixes, mean 'to live' and 'to know'. Tok Pisin uses *savi* 'to know' (presumably from Portuguese *save* 'he knows') for both the expression of ability (know how to) and for habitual. Yagaria uses a reduced and reduplicated form of the verb 'to see' in its habitual construction. It is possible that this verb 'to see' is conceptually related to 'to know' in Yagaria as in other languages.

Table 5.6.   Past Habituals

Language	Form No.	Related String	Expression
08 Tigre	16	to live	AUX
12 Chacobo	34		SUF
20 Alawa	02		SUF
71 Temne	17		AUX
73 Tem	20	usually	AUX
82 Maidu	43		SUF
91 Udmurt	27	was + future	SUF
92 Uigur	26		SUF
93 Buriat	43		AUX
	44		AUX

Additional cases of 'know' developing into a habitual are found outside our sample. In Haitian Creole, the French verb *connaitre* 'to know, be acquainted with' gives rise to the verb *kône* 'to know', and its shortened form *kôn*, which means 'used to' (Phillips 1983). In Mon Khmer the verb *ceh* 'to know' can be made into an auxiliary meaning 'always' (Huffman 1967: 109, 184).

While little is known about how these lexical verbs develop into habituals, it might be that the meaning of these two verbs converges very early in a general sense of 'to experience'. The English locutions in (36) and (37) may perhaps be close to the source meaning of these constructions.

(36)   I lived working on a boat.
(37)   I knew working on a boat.

Other lexical sources for habituals have lexical meaning that is very close to the grammatical meaning of habitual. For instance, English *used to* is derived with the verb *use*, which entered English through Old French. From the earliest documentation of this verb according to the *Oxford English Dictionary* (Murray et al. 1884–1933), it had as one of its meanings 'to follow a usage or custom'. Starting around 1400 the verb became very frequent in a construction with a following infinitive, with the meaning 'be accustomed to doing'. This construction was used with human subjects and appeared in both present and past tense. In the 1600s it was extended to occur with inanimate subjects as well. The phonological reduction undergone by *used to*, from [yuzdtuw] to [yustə], distinguishes it from the lexical verb *use* when followed by *to*.

The use of this construction in the present tense eventually disappeared, leaving it as a strictly past habitual gram. We propose that the present tense use was less frequent than the past tense use, for reasons we presented earlier, namely, that explicit mention of habitualness is less necessary in the present, where the default meaning includes habitualness, than in the past, where it does not. The higher frequency in the past led to its grammaticization, while the lower frequency in the present led to the disappearance of the construction.

The semantic change undergone by *used to* is not great, since its original meaning is so close to its grammatical meaning. However, some generalization of meaning must have occurred, since it has extended its domain in two directions from its original use. As we just mentioned, it generalized from use with only human subjects to use with subjects of all types, and in addition it has come to be employed with stative verbs, giving the sense of a past state.

(38)   I used to be able to play the Minute Waltz in a minute.
(39)   My father used to have a car like that.

The natural resemblance of habitual occurrences and states that accounts for this extension has already been discussed.

Notice that the Past Habitual, *used to,* is not obligatory in English, in the sense that it is not necessary to use this gram to render a past habitual reading. The Simple Past is also acceptable in a habitual context, such as (40).

(40)   When she lived with him, she sang to him every day.

Either *used to* or the other Past Habitual *would* (discussed below) could be put with *sing* in (40) with no discernible change in meaning. Similarly, the Past with stative verbs is essentially equivalent to statives with *used to*.

(41)   My father had a car like that.

If either of the English Past Habituals were to continue its development and become the obligatory expression of habitual in a past context, this would contribute to the development of the Past tense into a perfective, especially since the Past Progressive does seem to be the obligatory expression of progressiveness in the past.

Turning to other sources, cases in which the habitual appears to be related to future are particularly intriguing. We have already seen one way that such a situation may arise. In Kui the old Present was used for habitual, progressive, and future. With the development of a periphrastic progressive, this older form came to signal just habitual and future.

Even more interesting are cases in which the overt expression of future appears to resemble that of past habitual meaning. One such case is the English form *would,* which in Old English was the Past tense of *will.* The Old English verb *willan* meant 'wish, want, be willing, be disposed to', and its Past form expressed the same range of meaning in the past. The combination of a modal sense with tense is a particularly volatile combination, and *would* has undergone considerable semantic change to the point that in Modern English its modal use is as a marker of the conditional apodosis (and for some speakers, the protasis as well). In its modal sense it no longer expresses tense (see Bybee 1990a). On the other hand, in its habitual use it still clearly expresses past time. What is the relationship between these two uses?

The evidence suggests that the modal and aspectual sense of *would* have been unrelated since very early in the development of this form. The uses of both *will* and *would* in an habitual sense date from the earliest documented stages of Old English. For instance, in Beowulf, in addition to expressing volition, *will* is occasionally used to describe characteristic or habitual behavior in the present as in (42), and *would* is used for the same thing in the past, as in (43).

(42)   Ic minne can glædne Hroðulf thæt he þa geogode wile arum
       healdan. (l. 1181)
       'I know my gracious Hrothulf, that he will treat the young
       men well.'

(43)   Þonne he swulces hwæt secgan wolde. (l. 880)
       'Then he would tell of such things.'

Again it appears that the grammatical meaning of habitual is not too far from the earlier lexical meaning of *willan*. This verb expressed volition, and what one wants to do, one is inclined or disposed to do. While in certain contexts this does not have to imply that one habitually does something (e.g. 'He was inclined to tell her off, but he didn't'), in many contexts it is safe to infer that the inclination is followed, especially in the past.

Modern English *will* can still be used for what can be called 'characteristic behavior', as in (44).

(44)   Water will boil at 100 degrees Celsius.

The use of *would*, however, does not parallel this use, but rather expresses the sense of having gone through the action on many different occasions in the past, as in example (45), from Coates 1983: 209.

(45)   The thing was, he **would** concoct anecdotes and he'd tell them
       to me over and over again, you know, obviously not realizing
       that he'd told them to me before.

This case and the example of *used to* are both cases in which there are parallel present and past forms, but only the past form develops into a grammatical habitual.

In our database is another case of past habitual formed with the same material as future grams plus a past marker. This occurs in

Udmurt, where the combination of *val* 'was' with the future tense gives a past habitual. A different type of case occurs in Inuit, where the future marker *ssa* signals past habitual when it is used in a past narrative context. In the face of grams that can be used for both future and habitual, some linguists have wanted to subsume both under the label "irrealis." However, the diachronic evidence we have examined here makes it clear that the two uses are not the result of a single category but are rather the result of divergent paths of development. Other arguments against the category "irrealis" are presented in §6.12.

5.8.3. Habitual on other paths of development

By examining other uses of habitual we can hypothesize some other means by which habitual meaning comes to have overt expression. In particular there are a number of cases in which habitual meaning is but one use of a gram that has other senses as well. In §5.6 we discussed the evolution of progressives into presents and imperfectives. In this development the progressive extends to cover habitual functions, and the result is a gram of very general meaning. Interestingly enough, in two of these cases we find evidence for an asymmetry between present and past.

In Kui a periphrastic progressive has developed, comprising the Present Participle plus the inflected forms of the verb *manba* 'to live, exist'. The construction with the Present of the auxiliary gives a present progressive meaning, leaving the older simple Present to express habitual and future, as we mentioned above. The Past forms of the auxiliary in this construction, however, are used for both progressive and habitual meaning in the past (Winfield 1928: 86).

In Margi the Progressive particle *ə́və̀r* "indicates that the action is/was in progress or being done at a certain time, whether the present or in the past. It also indicates habitual action in the past" (Hoffman 1963: 176). In Margi, no explicit marking of past is necessary in the clause containing *ə́və̀r* but if it is in a past context it may signal habitual. Present states, generic statements (and presumably present habituals) are expressed by what appears to be a much older marker, a prefix *a-*.

The development of a habitual reading for a progressive in the past before the present is again due to the difference between default readings of present versus past. The default reading of present continues to include habitual, but since the default reading of past does not include habitual, the progressive comes to be used in that capacity.

Six of the grams in our database which mark habitual also may be used to indicate iterative action. These are all among those that are used without tense restrictions, for none of the past habituals are used for iterative. These iterative/habituals are found in Inuit (form no. 10), Atchin, Halia, Rukai, Yessan-Mayo, and Krongo. Both habitual and iterative indicate that an action is repeated, but in the case of iterative, the action is repeated on the same occasion, while habitual means that the different occurrences are on separate occasions.

Our theory would lead us to expect that one of these specific meanings is the earlier meaning of the gram, and the other is added as the meaning of the gram generalizes. We do not have direct evidence concerning the directionality of this development, that is, whether iterative generalizes to include habitual or habitual generalizes to include iterative. However, it is possible to infer that iterative is probably the earlier more specific meaning of these grams, using formal and semantic evidence.

Two of the grams expressing both habitual and iterative are formed by partial reduplication (Trukese and Rukai). In §5.11 we argue that iterative is the earliest aspectual meaning of reduplication. Our argument is based on the fact that iterative is the most iconic aspectual sense for reduplication, and on the fact that in our data iterative is the most common meaning expressed by total reduplication, which we assume precedes partial reduplication diachronically. Thus for reduplicated forms, we reconstruct a path from iterative generalizing to include habitual.

Such a generalization is conceptually well motivated. Iterative means that an action is repeated on a single occasion. In order to include habitual, the only change necessary is the loss of restriction that the repetition be on a single occasion. The other direction of generalization is much more difficult to motivate. The early sources of habitual grams that we have examined do not actually denote repetition of an action. They denote that the subject is accustomed to or disposed to perform a certain action. The grammatical meaning of habitual emphasizes that certain situations characterize a subject during a certain period of time which incidentally covers multiple occasions. In the case of dynamic verbs (but not stative), repetition can be inferred from habitual, but it is not repetition on a single occasion. Therefore, we would suggest that as habitual generalizes it is not likely to encompass iterative meaning.

5.8.4. Conclusions concerning habituals

Specific, overt grams coding habitual meaning are much less common in our data than other aspectual grams of similar specificity of meaning, namely, progressive or anterior grams. Habitual meaning is more commonly included in the meaning of a more general gram, such as imperfective or present, than expressed separately. Where separate expression occurs, the lexical sources are typically very close to the grammatical meaning of habitual. They include lexical items such as 'live', 'know', and 'be accustomed to'.

A striking asymmetry exists in the expression of present habitual versus the expression of past habitual. While our database contains ten examples of overtly expressed past habituals and eighteen examples of habituals that are not restricted by tense, the only two cases of present habitual that we have coded both have zero expression. Contributing to this asymmetry is the fact that developing habitual grams that may occur in both the present and past tend to be lost in the present rather than developing into present habitual grams, as occurred for example with the English cases of *used to* and *would*. A further asymmetry occurs in cases where a developing progressive takes on habitual meaning in the past before it does so in the present.

We argued earlier that while several grammaticization paths exist for past habitual and general habitual, none exists for present habitual. What would be the present counterpart of past habitual—that a certain state or activity characterizes a time period that includes the present moment—is the default meaning of present, and therefore no special locutions are created to describe it.

5.9. Iteratives

The iterative is a commonly occurring aspectual gram of rather specific meaning. It signals that an action is repeated on a single occasion and differs from the habitual and frequentative, which both signal that the repetition occurred on different occasions. The matter of distinguishing a single occasion from multiple occasions is, of course, not always straightforward. In the Mwera examples in (46), in which a polysyllabic stem is reduplicated while a monosyllabic stem is triplicated, the first three examples are clearly interpretable as on a single occasion, while the last two are less clear out of context (Harries 1950: 77).

(46)	lya	'eat'	lyalyalya	'eat and eat and eat'
	gwa	'fall'	gwagwagwa	'fall and fall and fall'
	taŵa	'tie'	taŵa-taŵa	'tie over and over again'
	pinga	'want'	piŋga-piŋga	'search for'
	jenda	'travel'	jenda-jenda	'wander about'

However, as with other aspectual notions, whether or not a situation is viewed as comprising one or more occasions is a matter that can be manipulated by the speaker. Thus 'search for', which inherently covers multiple activities, can be used in contexts in which one occasion is described (as in [47]), or in cases in which multiple occasions are described (as in [48]).

(47)   He searched for his keys all morning.
(48)   He searched for his brother in every city he visited.

The notion of repetition applies best to a situation that comprises a single cycle—that is, a situation with an inherent beginning, middle, and end, such as winking, hitting, kissing, and so on. However, an iterative gram may also apply to a predicate that describes a situation with multiple cycles, such as walking or swinging, and in such a case it closely resembles what we have called continuative meaning, that is, the sense of 'keep on doing'. Thus the Atchin example (49) has a continuative sense, while (50) has an iterative sense, due apparently to the nature of the main verb (Capell and Layard 1980: 83).

(49)   Ko   m'ok   wiel.
       but   CONT   walk
       'He kept on walking.'
(50)   Ko   i-si   le ni   m'ok   wits?
       but   who   here   CONT   throw
       'But who is it here keeps on throwing?'

Thus in some cases we have coded an iterative gram with an additional sense of continuative, while in other cases we must admit that it is difficult to distinguish the two senses.

The plurality or repetition in iterative meaning does not apply just to the action itself, but often has consequences for the participants in the action. As seen in Table 5.7, a gram used for iterative action may also convey the idea that multiple participants were involved in the action or that the action was distributed over several separate agents, goals, or locations. For plurality of action to include plural participants is common in Native American languages (Mithun 1988), but as can be seen in Table 5.7, it also occurs elsewhere in the world (see also Bybee 1985: 102–5).

The expression of iterative grams is for the most part by reduplication or affixation. Since reduplication of the verb offers such an appropriate icon for repeated action, it is not surprising that our sample contains eight cases of stem reduplication for expressing iterative and one case of a reduplicated suffix. These grams are mostly expressed by total reduplication, although the Karok and Rukai reduplications are partial. Our hypotheses concerning the diachronic development of reduplicative grams will be discussed in the next section.

Given the fact that iterative meaning is rather specific, in contrast, say, to imperfective or present meaning, it might appear surprising

Table 5.7. Iteratives

Language	Form No.	Other Uses	Expression
01 Inuit	10	Habitual Plural participant Gnomic	SUF
	37		SUF
10 Isl. Carib	26	Plural participant	SUF
12 Chacobo	09		SUF
17 Alyawarra	16	While moving	SUF
20 Alawa	36		REDUP
27 Atchin	17	Habitual Continuative	PARTCL
28 Halia	41		PRE
30 Tanga	01	Emphatic	REDUP
33 Trukese	42		REDUP
34 Pangasinan	20	Distributed	PRE
35 Rukai	04	Progressive Habitual	REDUP
42 Kui	20	Distributed	SUF
46 Karok	17	Again	PRE
	19		REDUP
	20	Distributed Plural participant Continuous	SUF
49 Baluchi	19	Continuative	SUF + AUX
52 Yagaria	34		SUF
	35	Excessive duration	REDUP SUF
58 Nimboran	28	Distributed by turns	SUF
59 Bongu	05	Frequentative Ceaselessly	SUF
60 Yessan-Mayo	10		SUF
68 Slave	16	Iterative	PRE
69 Krongo	18	Habitual	PRE
71 Temne	29	Frequentative	SUF
72 Mwera	12		REDUP
74 Engenni	12		SUF
82 Maidu	03	Distributed	SUF
91 Udmurt	22		SUF
92 Uigur	36		REDUP
94 Tok Pisin	13	Continuative	REDUP

that the non-reduplicated grams for iterative are almost all affixes. In fact, Atchin presents the only real case of a nonbound expression for iterative in our sample, since in Baluchi all finite verb forms take the auxiliary *bu-* 'be', and thus the iterative meaning must reside in the suffix. The reason this more specific meaning is expressed by an affix rather than by a periphrasis with an auxiliary (as is the progressive meaning) is that a good many of these grams are derivational rather than inflectional in nature. In many cases, the authors of the grammars explicitly describe these iterative affixes as derivational. In other cases, we can infer their derivational status based on the fact that they occur in an inner layer of affixation and have lexical idiosyncrasies, that is, lexical restrictions, or lexicalized meaning in some cases (see the examples in [46]).

Derivational grams undergo a different sequence of developments in grammaticization than inflectional grams do. Heine and Reh 1984 and Heine and Claudi 1986 argue that verbal derivational affixes arise from the compounding of a verb plus an adposition or two verbs, one of which develops into a grammatical morpheme. Compounding is also known to be the source of derivational morphemes in English. For instance, adjectival and adverbial -ly of *friendly* and *slowly* come from earlier compounds comparable to modern *friend-like* or *slow-like*.

Heine and Reh 1984: 141–46 point out some important differences between the evolution of inflectional and derivational grams. Affixation of inflectional grams occurs after the gram has generalized its meaning and come to be used with a large number of verbs or nouns, if not all. Then the gram and its lexical host are taken to be a single unit, that is, they are lexicalized together. The lexicalization which results in the formation of an affix occurs for all main verbs at about the same time, with perhaps more frequent verbs leading the way.

The development of derivational affixes differs, however, in that lexicalization occurs before extensive generalization and, moreover, may occur at different times for different lexical verbs. Since the two elements—the verb that will become the main verb and the verb that will become the affix—are in a compound construction, they are taken to be a lexical unit early in their development, even before the developing affix undergoes much semantic and phonological erosion. Then, if a number of such compounds develop, the meaning of the developing affix may generalize, its form may reduce, and it may come to apply to a large number of individual verbs. The important point is that the generalization process which is necessary for grammaticization tends to follow, rather than precede, the lexicalization process. The result is, of course, that grams that develop in this way will have to be affixes rather than free grams.

The diachronic development of iterative meaning is difficult to piece together given the data available to us. None of the iterative grams we surveyed had known lexical sources. A few had other meanings that suggest possible chains of development, however. The

Alyawarra iterative also means to do something while moving, suggesting a source from a motion verb. Here we should compare the Yessan-Mayo continuative *yi*, which is identical to the verb 'go', and recall that some of our progressive grams also have movement verb sources.

Those iteratives which are also used to signal plural or distributed participants might have come from quantifiers. The Island Carib iterative can also be used to pluralize nouns, and the Baluchi iterative suffix -*an* is the same as the plural definite suffix used on nouns. In some cases of reduplication, the effect on verbs is iteration, while the effect on nouns is pluralization. The implication of this is that plural or distributed meaning is probably original to the constructions and not a later development during grammaticization.

5.10. Continuatives and frequentatives

We have already seen the close semantic connection between iteratives, continuatives, and frequentatives, and this relation is examined in more detail in the next section, where we discuss reduplication. In the current section we present the data on continuatives and frequentatives and offer a few comments about them.

Continuatives are not frequent in our data (see Table 5.8), but this meaning label was coded wherever we found a gram whose meaning was translated as 'continue' or 'keep on' doing. The other uses for these grams are all clearly in the imperfective domain: Atchin, Baluchi, and Tok Pisin forms have iterative as another use, the Bongu and Shuswap forms have frequentative as their other use (see

Table 5.8. Continuatives

Language	Form No.	Related String	Expression
01 Inuit	30		SUF
	31		SUF
	32		SUF
04 Kanakuru	36	sit	AUX
10 Isl. Carib	28	all	SUF
27 Atchin	17		PARTCL
48 Maithili	32	remain	AUX
49 Baluchi	19	plural	AUX + SUF
59 Bongu	33		REDUP
60 Yessan-Mayo	24		REDUP
	31	go	SUF
82 Maidu	28		SUF
86 Haka	14	play + progressive	AUX
87 Lahu	24	be in a place, live	AUX
89 Cantonese	17	go down	AUX
94 Tok Pisin	13		REDUP

Table 5.9.   Frequentatives

Language	Form No.	Other Uses	Expression
18 Maung	09	Habitual	REDUP
19 Worora	32		SUF
39 Abkhaz	55	Plural	SUF
42 Kui	30		AUX
56 Ono	14		SUF
59 Bongu	05	Iterative	SUF
	33	Continuative	REDUP
		Again	
68 Slave	38	Habitual	PRE
		Gnomic	
69 Krongo	18		PRE
	45		TNCH
	46		REDUP
76 Bari	30		REDUP
83 Shuswap	29	Continuative	SUF
85 Chepang	43		SUF

Table 5.9), Kanakuru has habitual, and the Cantonese and Lahu forms can signal the continuation of a state as well as an action. The Lahu gram also has a progressive sense.

The lexical sources for continuatives, which are shown in Table 5.9, are similar to those found for iteratives, namely, 'all' and plural, or to those found for progressives, 'sit', 'remain', 'live', and 'go'.

Frequentative was coded as a use when the author's description or translation gave the sense of 'frequently' or 'often'. At times it was difficult to tell if iterative or frequentative was the best coding. We have almost no lexical sources for frequentatives, although we do know that the Abkhaz form is also the non-human plural marker, and the Kui auxiliary is a general one with other uses. The other uses of frequentatives resemble the other uses of iteratives and continuatives, attesting again to the close relation between these senses.

While it appears clear that both continuative and frequentative meaning can develop directly from lexical meaning of the sort expressed by auxiliaries such as 'keep on' or adverbs such as 'often', we also postulate a diachronic relation between iterative and each of these senses. We consider the following a plausible sequence of development of the sense of iterative grams. The difference between iterative and continuative is largely a matter of the type of verbs with which they occur, since iteration applies better to punctual or telic predicates and continuativity to both telic and atelic. It is therefore conceivable that an iterative might generalize to a continuative. Frequentative implies that the situation occurred on different occasions and thus also may be an extension from a specifically iterative meaning. Habitual and progressive are more general still, and we would suggest that habitual develops out of frequentative meaning, while progressive comes from continuative meaning. We find some support for these hypothesized paths among our reduplicative grams, which we discuss next.

5.11. Reduplication

Reduplicative morphemes[2] are a problem in many morphological theories because they do not have a constant phonological shape or even a small number of allomorphs, but rather a different allomorph for every stem with which they occur. In our theory, the principle that they challenge is the principle that all grams develop from a fuller lexical source, since it is not possible to trace a reduplicative gram back to a single word or even a specific phrase. However, there is an obvious way to apply our theory as developed to this point to reduplicative grams, and that is to consider the fullest, most explicit form of reduplication, total reduplication, to be the originating point for all reduplications, with the various types of partial reduplication as reductions and thus later developments from this fullest form.

Some support for this hypothesis may be found in the observation by Spagnolo 1933: 141 on the source of the partial reduplication in Bari:

> The reduplication of the verb stem, as used in the Present and Future Tenses (e.g. *Nan dodoto* ['I am sleeping'], *rerembu* ['stabbing'], *kɔkɔndya* ['doing'] . . . *Nan dé dodoto* ['I shall be sleeping']), is a contracted form of a primitive, now almost absolete [sic], Frequentative construction, which would sound like this: *Nan doto doto, rembu rembu, kɔndya kɔndya . . . Nan dé doto doto.* . . . [translations added]

Looking at Gugu-Yalanji, we get some idea of how the reduction of total reduplication to partial reduplication might occur. In this language, there is total reduplication with the two occurrences of the stem connected by a linking morpheme -*l*- or -*n*-. The inflection follows the final stem (Patz 1982: 175).

(51)   dinda-l-dinda-l   'keep roasting'
       karrba-l-karrba-l   'keep holding on'
       dunga-n-dunga-y   'keep going'
       yirrka-n-yirrka-y   'keep shouting'

---

2. We are grateful to Noriko Watanabe for help in analyzing the material used in this section.

Patz (1982: 176–77) also reports that six intransitive verbs have reduplication according to other patterns.

(52)
jana-y	'stand'	badi-y	'cry'
janjana-y		bandadi-y	
warri-y	'run'	bunda-y	'sit'
wanarri-y		bundanda-y	
kada-y	'come'	wuna-y	'lie down'
kankada-y		wunana-y	

It is easy to see that these are reductions of the fuller form with the linking *n;* for instance, *jana-n-jana-y* loses the second vowel and coalesces the nasals to become *janjana-y; warri-n-warri-y* loses the *w* following the *n* and the *rri* syllable preceding it to produce *wanarri-y.* And so on for the other examples.

We consider it entirely plausible that partial reduplications result from the phonological erosion and assimilation of totally reduplicated forms. Of course, once a partial reduplication pattern becomes well established in the language, it can become productive and extend to new forms, such as loanwords. However, we would contend that the original source of such reduplications is in total repetition of the verb.

If this is indeed the formal evolution undergone by reduplicative grams, then our theory would predict that total reduplication expresses the earlier, fuller meaning of reduplication, while the partial reduplications express more general meanings and meanings that occur later on the evolutionary path. Given this framework, we can attempt to chart an evolutionary path for reduplicative grams by examining the meanings that are expressed by total versus partial reduplication. We expect to find that total reduplications express the most specific meanings, while partial reduplications express more general meanings or have a greater variety of uses or functions.

We also begin with the assumption that total reduplications are maximally iconic at their origins, that is, that repetition of the verb signals repetition of the action described by the verb. In terms of our meaning labels, the earliest meaning of reduplication could be iterative (repeated action on one occasion), frequentative (often repeated action, not necessarily on the same occasion), or continuative (to keep on doing something, on one occasion, but applicable to atelic situations), since all these senses very explicitly express repetition. As can be seen in Table 5.10, these are the senses most commonly expressed by total reduplication in the languages of our sample.

Iterative is the meaning we found most commonly associated with reduplication, and most commonly associated with total reduplication. Thus the evidence for iterative as the original meaning of

Table 5.10. Meanings Expressed by Total (T) and Partial (P) Reduplication

Language	Form No.	Iterative	Continuative	Frequentative	Distributive/ Plural	Progressive	Habitual	Intransitive
16 Gugu-Yalanji	08	T/P	T/P			T/P	T/P	
18 Maung	09			P			P	
20 Alawa	36	T						
30 Tanga	01	T						
33 Trukese	42	T						
	41							
	37						P	P
32 Nakanai	03				P	P	P	P
34 Pangasinan	03				T[a]			
	02					P		
35 Rukai	04	P				P	P	
46 Karok	19	P						
59 Bongu	33		P[b]	P				
60 Yessan-Mayo	24	T	T					
69 Krongo	46			P				
72 Mwera	12	T						
76 Bari	30			T				
	01				P	P		P
92 Uigur	36	T						
94 Tok Pisin	13	T	T					

[a] Uncontrolled distributed.
[b] To do something ceaselessly; another use expresses 'again'.

reduplication is strong. We offer the following comments on the other senses we coded as expressed by total reduplication.

In Tok Pisin and Yessan-Mayo, total reduplication expresses both iterative and continuative. Consider the Tok Pisin example (53) from Hall 1943a: 32, which expresses repetition on one occasion, while (54) from Mühlhäusler 1985: 383 expresses continuative.

(53) ju faitim pig, faitim faitim.
      'You strike the pig, and keep on striking it.'
(54) ol i tingting tingting.
      'They kept thinking.'

As we mentioned in the preceding section, much of the difference between iterative and continuative has to do with the nature of the main verb: a predicate describing a situation which typically involves a single cycle, such as shooting, if continued, will involve the repetition of the cycle. A less well defined activity, such as thinking, if continued, is not so much repeated, as increased in duration. If iteration is the original meaning of reduplication and it occurs originally with verbs having only one cycle, then as it expands to application with verbs of other types, its meaning would generalize to include continuative meaning. Thus we propose that one step in the semantic development of reduplication is (55).

(55) ITERATIVE > CONTINUATIVE

Reduplication in Gugu-Yalanji supports that portion of the path, since it is used for both iterative and continuative depending on the verb type. It has extended as well to progressive and habitual, as we will see below.

The other cases of total reduplication are Pangasinan and Bari, and in these two cases the available information seems inadequate. In Bari, total reduplication is not common, but it does occur with passive verbs with the meaning 'always being done', that is, frequentative. The expression that Spagnolo says is nearly obsolete in the quote above is not translated, but it is labeled as Frequentative. It should be noted, however, that the term Frequentative is often used for what we are calling iterative, that is, repetition on a single occasion.

Pangasinan is the only case we have of a total reduplication expressing distributed action, and in this case it is specifically distribution that is uncontrolled, as seen in (56) (Benton 1971: 127).

(56) manbása   '(will) read'
      manbásabása   'reading anything and everything'
      manpasiár   'go around'
      manpasiárpasiár   'go around all over the place, with no special
                        destination in mind'

This type of aspect includes the notion of iteration. However, we have no information on how or why total reduplication in this language has this particular specific meaning. It should be noted, however, that Pangasinan also has a partial reduplication that has a very generalized function.

As we mentioned above, it seems very plausible that iterative is the original meaning of reduplicative constructions and that continuative might be an extension of iterative meaning. We further hypothesize that progressive meaning may derive from continuative meaning. That is, from a sense of 'keep on doing,' which involves a continued input of energy and implies that the situation is continued longer than normal, the meaning generalizes to signal simply that a situation is in progress. This would explain the Gugu-Yalanji reduplication, which spans iterative, continuative and progressive.

(57) ITERATIVE > CONTINUATIVE > PROGRESSIVE

There is perhaps another path of development from iterative in which the direction of generalization is toward including repetitions on different occasions under the purview of reduplication. This path would lead to frequentative meaning—that something is done often—and eventually to habitual meaning—that the situation is characteristic of an extended period of time. In our data there are four languages that express habitual meaning with partial reduplication, and one of these (Maung) has both frequentative and habitual, suggesting the link between the meanings. Thus we propose a second path for reduplication.

(58) ITERATIVE > FREQUENTATIVE > HABITUAL

Notice that the semantic developments hypothesized in these two paths are fully supported by the formal distinction between total and partial reduplication: the number of total reduplications decreases toward the rightward direction of the paths, and the number of partial reduplications increases, as shown in Table 5.11.

Table 5.11.
Ratio of Total to Partial Reduplications
Expressing Different Meanings

	T/P
Iterative	6/2
Continuative	2/1
Frequentative	1/2
Progressive	1/4
Habitual	0/4

Our data, limited though they are, suggest further that the two paths may converge in later developments, so that both progressive and habitual may be expressed by the same reduplicative form. Once this has happened, the meaning expressed by the form is imperfective meaning, as in the case of Nakanai (Johnston 1980: 131).

(59) Eia   o-io   sa-sapa.
      3.s   at-there   REDUP-sweep
      'She is there sweeping.'
(60) Eia   sa-sapa   te   la   kavikoki.
      3.s   REDUP-sweep   PREP NCL   morning
      'She sweeps in the mornings.'

What we do not know is whether it is just as likely for a habitual to generalize to an imperfective as it is for a progressive to generalize to an imperfective. We have evidence for the latter occurrence in non-reduplicated forms but no evidence for the former.

In Table 5.10, three languages are shown as having an intransitivizing use for partial reduplication. The uses of reduplication as described for Bari (an Eastern Sudanic language) and Nakanai (an Oceanic language) are nearly identical. In both cases, reduplication has a very general aspectual sense of continuous or imperfective and is also used to agree with plural participants. In addition, the reduplicated transitive verb does not require an overt object noun phrase but only implies the existence of an object. Consider (61)–(62), from Nakanai (Johnston 1980: 155–56).

(61) La sobe hugu la obu.
      NM girl carry NM wood
      'The young woman carried the wood (on her head).'
(62) La sobe hugugu.
      NM girl carry-REDUP
      'The young woman is carrying (something on her head).'

Hopper and Thompson 1980 have argued for a discourse relation between imperfectivity and intransitivity. Imperfective forms are typically used in backgrounded clauses where the focus is on the situation as continuing (while something else occurs) and not on the outcome of the situation with respect to a particular object. For this reason, backgrounded clauses are often intransitive as well as imperfective. Our data suggest that the intransitivizing function of reduplication is a very late development, preceded by the complete generalization of the aspectual functions of reduplication. In the three languages that have this function for reduplication, the reduplicative form is quite reduced. Consequently, we are led to the conclusion that the intransitive function derives from the imperfective meaning of reduplication.

The intransitivizing function of reduplication in Trukese may be even more developed than in Nakanai and Bari. In Trukese there are three distinct reduplication processes, which we describe in more detail below: one is a total reduplication, one reduplicates the initial syllable, and a third one, the one used for intransitivizing, is so formally reduced that it consists only of doubling the initial consonant of the root. Goodenough and Sugita (1980: xxiii) make the following comment about the form of this reduplication process: "Comparison with other Pacific languages shows that such doubling of initial consonants reflects an old doubling of the first syllable with subsequent loss of the unstressed first vowel."

About the function of this reduplication, they say the following (ibid.): "It seems to impart a stative or adjectival meaning to verb bases, especially to object focused verbs, converting them into inactive verbs (often best translated as passives)." Some examples are given in (63).

(63) ffót   'be planted'   cf.   fótu-ki   'plant it'
      ppos   'be stabbed'   cf.   posu-u-w   'stab him'
      ttong   'love'   cf.   tonge-e-y   'love him'
      fféér   'be in a state of having cf.   fééri   'do it'
               been done'

Of course, we do not know if this use of reduplication could derive from a function such as those found in Bari and Nakanai, but it is worth noting that they share the property of being intransitive and would be equally appropriate in backgrounded clauses.[3]

On the basis of the scanty information we have available, then, we would propose the tentative paths in (64) for the development of reduplication.

(64)
ITERATIVE > CONTINUATIVE > PROGRESSIVE
                                                         ↘
                                        IMPERFECTIVE > INTRANSITIVE
                                                     ↗
ITERATIVE > FREQUENTATIVE > HABITUAL

3. If the sequence of developments leading to a passive or stative sense for reduplication could be worked out, we might then have an explanation for the seemingly anomalous use of reduplication in Greek and other Indo-European languages for the expression of anterior or perfective. The explanation would be that the anterior is formed from a passive participle, which is a very highly developed reduplicated form, and an inflected auxiliary.

The modern situation in Trukese suggests that reduplication can grammaticize more than once in the history of a language, and that forms produced by successive waves of grammaticization can co-exist, although the form and meaning of each one identifies its age. In this sense, grammaticization of reduplication is identical to the more usual sort of grammaticization of lexical items or phrases (see §1.4.7 and §5.6.1).

We have already mentioned the doubling of initial consonants which Goodenough and Sugita regard as a reduction of an earlier reduplication of initial syllables. We would propose that the reduplication of initial syllables ultimately derives from a total reduplication. In addition to this highly reduced form of reduplication, Trukese also has a reduplication pattern by which the first syllable is doubled as well as the first consonant.

(65) rúrrúr   'slipping back and forth'
      fáffátán   'be accustomed to walk', cf. *fátán* 'walk'
      pwúppwúnú   'treat as a spouse'

Goodenough and Sugita argue that this pattern originated in a total reduplication which was reduced in case the first and second consonants of the verb base were identical or articulated in similar positions. In these cases, the unstressed (second) vowel was deleted and "the first of the resulting adjacent consonants assimilated to the second, if they were not already identical, to produce a double consonant" (1980: xxiv). Thus *nananan* became *nannan* 'to chatter', *rararar* became *rarrar* 'be trampled down'.

According to Goodenough and Sugita, this partial reduplication has spread to other forms and has taken on the meaning of repetition on different occasions—that is, habitual, as in *fáffátán* 'be accustomed to walk'. At the same time, there is a fuller reduplicated form which has the meaning of repetition on one occasion *fátánátán* 'go on walking'. Goodenough and Sugita suggest that these two reduplications are originally the same and the meaning has split. Our theory, on the other hand, would suggest that the fuller reduplication is a newer development. In any case, the three formal types of reduplication in Trukese have meanings corresponding to three different stages of semantic development: the fullest form signals iterative or continuative, the reduplication of the first syllable signals habitual, and the doubling of the first consonant is intransitivizing.

This study of reduplication is sketchy and tentative since it is based only on the cases of reduplication that turned up in our stratified probability sample. However, it does show a clear association of meaning with form which reflects the diachronic development of reduplicative grams. A fuller study that selected languages known to have reduplication and that distinguishes types of partial reduplication according to degree of reduction and assimilation as well as more nuances of meaning should reveal an even greater association of meaning with form.

5.12. Conclusion

In this chapter we have examined a variety of meanings in the domain of imperfective. The most widespread and frequently occurring of these is progressive, which is usually periphrastic in expression and usually has transparent lexical sources. The most frequent meanings expressed inflectionally are present and imperfective (either past or general), and we have presented evidence that progressives provide a source for these two inflectional gram-types. Some cases in which a progressive developing into a present occurs in the same language with a present illustrate the layering principle and show that contrasts among grams need not constitute maximal contrasts.

We have also examined some gram-types that are more often periphrastic or derivational in expression, such as iterative, continuative, and frequentative, emphasizing that each of these senses is appropriate only with verbs of certain lexical semantics. Reduplication is a major way of expressing these notions, and reduplication was studied in the languages of our sample. Our analysis supports the hypothesis that reduplicated forms undergo grammaticization in much the same way as other lexical forms do.

The study of the grammaticization of tense and aspect has yielded some results that bear on our general understanding of how these temporal notions are expressed grammatically. First, while we relied heavily on Comrie's 1976 analysis of aspect in our study of perfective and the subdivisions of imperfective, our data did not wholly support his hypothesis, especially with regard to the types of imperfectives. In particular, we found no evidence for a 'continuous' gram-type, nor for a 'non-progressive'. Second, our theory, which claims that grams have inherent semantic content, requires definitions of categories in positive rather than negative terms. Thus we disagree that progressive should be defined in terms of continuousness, which in turn is defined as imperfectivity without habituality. We present instead a rather rich, content-ful definition of progressive.

On the other hand, most properties of Comrie's theory are found to be suitable for the analysis of the diachronic development of tense and aspect. Comrie's basically spatial metaphor for understanding imperfective—that the situation is viewed from the inside—is confirmed by the overwhelming occurrence of locative sources (meaning 'to be in or at an activity') for progressives, which then develop into imperfectives. A second, less common expression of aspect likens verbal aspect to nominal number; for example, we found many cases of iteratives expressed by reduplication (which is often also used for noun number) and two cases of markers that can also be used to pluralize nouns. Iteratives also sometimes have uses that indicate a plural absolutive argument, or distribution over several entities. However, it should also be remembered that completives (which give rise to anteriors and perfectives) also may have uses indicating multiple participants. Thus although there is some indication that iterative can be viewed as parallel to noun plural, the overwhelming evidence from grammaticization supports the spatial metaphor for the understanding of aspect.

Finally, in our study of tense and aspect across languages, we have found substantial interactions between the two notional domains. Like Dahl 1985, we found that inflectional perfective is usually restricted to the past and, in fact, resembles the past tense in both meaning and function. We have also argued that present 'tense' is in fact the present imperfective, since most situations that are contemporaneous with the moment of speech are imperfective. Progressives may be restricted to the present or co-occur with all temporal reference points. On the other hand, habituals may be general or restricted to the past. The only present habituals in our database have zero expression.

An important feature of the grammaticization of tense and aspect is the changing interactions with the lexical semantics of the verb. Our reference grammar survey has turned up a number of tantalizing details of this interaction but more frustrating gaps in the descriptions. More detailed language-specific studies need to be made of the lexical co-occurrence patterns of these developing tense and aspect grams.

Mood and Modality

6.1. Introduction

Mood and **modality** are not so easily defined as tense and aspect. A definition often proposed is that modality is the grammaticization of speakers' (subjective) attitudes and opinions. (See for instance, Palmer 1986: 16, based on Lyons's 1977 discussion of modality.) Recent cross-linguistic works on mood and modality, such as Palmer 1986, however, show that modality notions range far beyond what is included in this definition. In fact, it may be impossible to come up with a succinct characterization of the notional domain of modality and the part of it that is expressed grammatically. In Bybee 1985: 191–96 it was argued that the category of mood is best viewed as a set of diachronically related functions, and it was suggested there that a real understanding of modality would emerge from a study of these diachronic relations.

It is such a study that we are now pursuing. As in the other chapters of this book, we will discuss the grammatical meanings in the modality domain in terms of their progression on certain diachronic paths. It is not the goal of this chapter to define an overarching category of mood or modality, any more than it was the goal of previous chapters to define tense or aspect, but rather it is our goal to establish the major paths of development for mood and modality notions, and to try to determine how and why particular grammatical meanings arise in this domain.

Chosen for inclusion in this chapter are grams with uses that are traditionally associated with modality—for instance, those indicating obligation, probability, and possibility—and those traditionally associated with mood—imperative, optative, conditional, and subordinate verb forms. Previous research led us to expect that the same gram might express two or more of these senses, and that expectation was borne out in our data, as we will see below. Because our study is diachronic in nature, we also include in this chapter some semantic notions that are diachronically related to the traditional notions of modality, such as ability and desire.

Previous research (Bybee 1985; Bybee and Pagliuca 1985; Bybee, Pagliuca, and Perkins 1991) also suggests that it is useful to distinguish various types of modality, both because certain diachronic generalizations can be made using these distinctions, and because these types of modality correlate with types of formal expression. We will begin, then, with defining and exemplifying four types of modality—**agent-oriented**, **speaker-oriented**, **epistemic**, and **subordinating**. We will also give our working definitions of the meanings expressed in each of these types.

6.2. Types of modality

6.2.1. Agent-oriented modality

Agent-oriented modality reports the existence of internal and external conditions on an agent with respect to the completion of the action expressed in the main predicate. As a report, the agent-oriented modality is part of the propositional content of the clause and thus would not be considered a modality in most frameworks. However, it is important for us to include agent-oriented modality in our study, since these modal senses are the diachronic sources of most senses that DO qualify as modality in other studies.

Agent-oriented modality can be expressed by lexical or grammatical morphemes. Some of the most semantically specific notions in this set are the following: **Obligation** reports the existence of external, social conditions compelling an agent to complete the predicate action, as in (1), which expresses strong obligation, and (2), which expresses weak obligation.

(1) All students **must** obtain the consent of the Dean of the faculty concerned before entering for examination.

(Coates 1983: 35)

(2) I just insisted very firmly on calling her Miss Tillman, but one **should** really call her President.

(Coates 1983: 59)

Necessity reports the existence of physical conditions compelling an agent to complete the predicate action, as in (3).

(3) I **need** to hear a good loud alarm in the mornings to wake up.

Ability reports the existence of internal enabling conditions in the agent with respect to the predicate action, as in (4).

(4) I *can* only type very slowly as I am a beginner. (Coates 1983: 92)

Desire reports the existence of internal volitional conditions in the agent with respect to the predicate action, as in (5).

(5)   Juan Ortiz called to them loudly in the Indian tongue, bidding them come forth if they **would** (= *wanted to*) save their lives.

(Coates 1983: 212)

Diachronic relations exist between some of these senses. For instance, necessity can develop into a sense of desire, as for instance in the English word *want*, which came from an Old Norse verb meaning 'to lack or miss', from which it developed the sense of 'need'; only beginning in the eighteenth century has it been used to express desire.

These most specific semantic senses can generalize over time to express broader meanings which are nevertheless agent-oriented in the sense that they report on conditions governing the agent. For instance, in the formation of the future (see chap. 7, and Bybee and Pagliuca 1987), both desire and obligation can come to be used in sentences expressing the intentions of the agent, especially in the first person. Thus in Middle English, both *will* (from a desire source) and *shall* (from an obligation source) are used to express first person intentions (examples from *Sir Gawain and the Green Knight*).

(6)   I **wyl** nauþer grete ne grone . . . (line 2157)
      'I will not shout or groan.'
(7)   And I **schal** ware alle my wyt to wynne me þeder. (line 402)
      'And I shall use all my wit to find my way there.'

Modern examples are in (8), which can be used to express an **intention**, although literally they report an obligation.

(8)   I have to go now. I gotta go now.

Desire also gives rise to expressions of **willingness**, as in (9).

(9)   I'll help you.

Ability generalizes to **root possibility**, which reports on general enabling conditions and is not restricted to the internal condition of ability, but also reports on general external conditions, such as social or physical conditions. (See §6.4 for further discussion of root possibility.)

(10) I actually **couldn't** finish reading it because the chap whose shoulder I was reading the book over got out at Leicester Square.

(Coates 1983: 114)

The agent-oriented modalities can also be used in directives—utterances that are intended not to report, but to elicit action. Such uses are considered to be within the domain of modality, and because the speaker is involved in creating the obligation or granting the permission, these uses are described as subjective (Palmer 1974, Lyons 1977, Coates 1983: 32).

(11)   "You **must** play this ten times over," Miss Jarrova would say, pointing with relentless fingers to a jumble of crotchets and quavers.

(Coates 1983: 34)

(12)   You **can** start the revels now.   (Coates 1983: 88)

6.2.2. Speaker-oriented modality

The last two sentences are examples of directives, which according to Lyons 1977: 746 are "utterances which impose, or propose, some course of action or pattern of behaviour and indicate that it should be carried out." Directives include commands, demands, requests, entreaties (all of which are **mands**) and warnings, exhortations, and recommendations. Our term 'speaker-oriented' is meant to include all such directives as well as utterances in which the speaker grants the addressee permission (as in [12]). Speaker-oriented modalities do not report the existence of conditions on the agent, but rather allow the speaker to impose such conditions on the addressee.

The grammatical terms used in our study for speaker-oriented modality are

imperative: the form used to issue a direct command to a second person;
prohibitive: a negative command;
optative: the wish or hope of the speaker expressed in a main clause;
hortative: the speaker is encouraging or inciting someone to action;
admonitive: the speaker is issuing a warning; and
permissive: the speaker is granting permission.

6.2.3. Epistemic modality

Epistemic modality applies to assertions and indicates the extent to which the speaker is committed to the truth of the proposition. The unmarked case in this domain is total commitment to the truth of the proposition, and markers of epistemic modality indicate something less than a total commitment by the speaker to the truth of the proposition. The commonly expressed epistemic modalities are possibility, probability, and inferred certainty. **Possibility** indicates that the proposition may possibly be true, as in (13), and should be kept distinct from root possibility, as illustrated in (10).

(13)   I **may** have put them down on the table; they're not in the
       door.

(Coates 1983: 133)

Probability indicates a greater likelihood that the proposition is true
than possibility does.

(14)   The storm **should** clear by tomorrow.

A stronger sense of probability is found in the notion of **inferred
certainty**, which strongly implies that the speaker has good reason for
supposing that the proposition is true.

(15)   There **must** be some way to get from New York to San Fran-
       cisco for less than $600.

We will also have occasion to mention in this chapter the expression
of propositions as contrary to fact, which we will refer to as **counterfactual**. An example of counterfactual obligation, for instance, is
in (16).

(16)   I should have mailed this yesterday, but I forgot.

We will not discuss evidentials directly in this chapter, although certain evidential senses are mentioned as they relate to epistemic modality. In particular, an indirect evidential, which indicates that the
speaker has only indirect knowledge concerning the proposition being asserted, implies that the speaker is not totally committed to the
truth of that proposition and thus implies an epistemic value. (For
more on evidentials in this framework, see Willett 1988.)

6.2.4. Subordinating moods

The same forms that are used to express the speaker-oriented and
epistemic modalities are often also used to mark the verbs in certain
types of subordinate clauses. In this chapter we discuss complement
clauses (17), concessives (18), and purpose clauses (19).

(17)   I suggested that he should call you immediately.
(18)   Although he may be a wise man, he has made some mistakes
       in the past.
(19)   We are working now so that we can take the summer off.

The reader should note, however, that our treatment of subordinate clauses is restricted to those containing special finite verb forms.
Complementizers and non-finite verb forms were not within the
scope of our study, although they surely constitute interesting objects
of study. Our focus is simply on understanding how special verb
forms become associated with certain types of subordinate clauses.
For a fuller treatment of complementation, see Noonan 1985, Ran-

som 1988; for a discussion of infinitives in the current framework, see Haspelmath 1989.

6.2.5. Form/meaning correspondences

The cross-linguistic survey reported on in Bybee 1985 revealed that agent-oriented modality is very rarely expressed by inflectional affixes, while the three other modality types very frequently are. This correlation suggested a diachronic scenario whereby as agent-oriented modalities grammaticize, they develop into the other types and gradually take on inflectional expression. It also suggests a way of distinguishing mood from modality: modality is the conceptual domain, and mood is its inflectional expression.

Our study of modality is hampered by gaps in our data and by the fact that many of the phenomena we wish to study are represented by only a few cases in our database. It is also limited by the fact that much less work has been done on the grammatical expression of modality than on the grammatical categories of tense and aspect. Nevertheless, we will present here the ideas that emerge from the analysis of our data, in an attempt to provide, at the very least, a framework for future research. We first discuss agent-oriented modalities and show how they evolve into epistemic and speaker-oriented modalities. We then go on to show how these latter modality types come to be used in subordinate clauses.

6.3. Obligation

In our data, obligation is the most frequently expressed agent-oriented modality. Approximately three fourths of the grams expressing obligation are auxiliaries or particles, and one fourth are affixes. Obligation can also be expressed by main verbs that show little grammaticization, as for example, the Spanish verb *deber*, or by auxiliaries that show considerable grammaticization, such as the English auxiliary *should*. In our comparison of reference material it was not always possible to apply a consistent cut-off point between lexical and grammatical forms, so in some cases we may have included forms that are more lexical than grammatical, and in others we may have failed to code a partially grammaticized form because it was neglected in the reference material. It is precisely on these outer margins of grammar that we expect the boundaries to be the least clear.

6.3.1. Lexical sources

As shown in Table 6.1, many of the constructions that are grammaticizing as expressions of obligation in our data contain lexical items that refer explicitly to concepts related to obligation. Thus Danish

Table 6.1. Related Strings and Mode of Expression
for Grams Expressing Obligation

Language	Form No.	Types of Obligation	Related Strings	Expression
01 Inuit	06			SUF
02 Basque	19		need	AUX
05 Agua	16	Weak		AUX
09 Cheyenne	39	Weak		PRE
14 Tucano	31		want + impersonal subject	AUX
16 Gugu-Yalanji	20			SUF
	21		dative	SUF
19 Worora	18			PRE, SUF
22 Koho	07	Strong		AUX
23 Palaung	10	Weak	good	AUX
	13	Weak		AUX
28 Halia	03			AUX
	22	Strong		PARTCL
33 Trukese	04	Weak	(negative)	PARTCL
	14			PARTCL
34 Pangasinan	22			PRE
37 Buli	15		'be, sit, stand'	PRE
39 Abkhaz	56	Strong	'be'	SUF
40 Guaymi	07			SUF
42 Kui	31	Strong	inf + become + imp subj	AUX
48 Maithili	43	Weak	see	AUX
	50	Weak	understand	AUX
49 Baluchi	03	Weak		PRE
	08	Strong	fall, befall	AUX
	10	Strong	be + subj in accusative	AUX
	21	CF	(past subjunctive)	PRE, SUF
50 Mod. Greek	14	CF		PARTCL
	16	CF		PARTCL
51 Danish	04	Strong	owe	AUX
	09	Strong	mete, measure	AUX
	16	Weak		AUX
60 Yessan-Mayo	21		(negative) don't know	PARTCL
68 Slave	45		(negative)	PARTCL
	47	CF		PARTCL
	50	Strong		AUX
	53	Weak CF	optative of 'be' with perfective verb	AUX
71 Temne	34		have + noun class prefix	AUX
72 Mwera	42	Strong	be fitting	AUX
76 Bari	04	Future	do	AUX
81 Zuni	04	CF	past + x + future	SUF
84 Lao	33	Strong		AUX
	34	Weak		AUX

Table 6.1.   (*continued*)

Language	Form No.	Types of Obligation	Related Strings	Expression
85 Chepang	26		be, have + irreal	AUX
	44	Indefinite	be, have + x	AUX
86 Haka	40	Strong		PARTCL
87 Lahu	04		get, obtain, catch	AUX
	20	Weak	be fitting, be proper	AUX
88 Nung	13	Strong	ʔloc part, collective plural	PARTCL
89 Cantonese	05	Weak	owe	PARTCL
93 Buriat	21		future in nominal construct	SUF
	47	CF	perfect + future	SUF
94 Tok Pisin	09	Strong		AUX

Note. CF = counterfactual.

skulle, cognate with English *shall,* derives from a verb meaning 'owe'; the Cantonese phrase *ying goi* includes the verb *goi,* meaning 'owe', with another obligation word, *ying.* The Basque construction uses the uninflected verb *bear* meaning 'need'. The Mwera and Lahu auxiliaries of obligation are glossed as meaning 'be fitting, be proper'. The Palaung particle for obligation means 'good', perhaps giving the implication 'it is good, fitting to'.

Another large set of obligation constructions is formed using the highly generalized auxiliaries meaning 'be', 'become', or 'have'. Abkhaz uses the copular verb plus the Conditional suffix in an obligation construction, and Baluchi uses the verb *buəg* 'be, become'. Buli uses a prefix *bo-*, which is the same as the verb 'to be', with emphatic person/number inflection on *bo-* and an inflected main verb stem. Slave uses the Optative forms of the verb 'to be' with an inflected main verb in the Optative as well. The Slave Optative is the verb form used in main and subordinate clauses for various types of non-asserted propositions. (With Perfective forms of the main verb, the same construction gives a sense of past counterfactual obligation.) The Kui construction uses the verb *ane* '3s becomes' with the infinitive form of the main verb. The Chepang verb *kheʔ* 'be, have' occurs with the Irrealis Nominal in some obligation constructions. The Temne obligation construction uses the verb *-ba* 'have' plus a noun class prefix on the main verb, creating a nominalized or infinitive verb form. The Bari construction of future obligation uses the auxiliary verb meaning 'do' with an unmarked main verb.

Such constructions may be parallel morphologically and semantically to the various obligation periphrases found in English using the generalized verbs *be* and *have*. (Cf. also Spanish *haber de* and *tener que*). The English *be to* construction as in (20) indicates that the agent has been set or scheduled to do something by some outside forces, and is thus obliged. However, the agent's commitment to the obligation is left open.

(20)   She **is to** see the dean tomorrow at 4.

A more common periphrasis for obligation in English is structurally parallel to *be to,* but uses the verb *have,* as in (21).

(21)   What a student **has to** pay for housing these days is
       outrageous.

Have to expresses more general obligation, not just situations which are scheduled, and the agent's commitment to the obligation is often apparent, as in (22).

(22)   I have to go now.

Have got to is the other common periphrasis for obligation in English. Despite the fact that it appears to be a Present Perfect in origin, it expresses a present state. This is due to the same sort of implication that was discussed in §3.9; what one has got, or has obtained, one now possesses. Lahu also has an obligation construction using a verb *ga* meaning 'get, obtain, catch'. Coates 1983: 57 points out that *have got to* is more common in spoken language than *have to*. While her data are all from British English, the same appears to be true for American English, where uses such as (23) would be normal.

(23)   I've got to study tonight. (or reduced: I gotta study tonight.)

How does the obligation sense arise in constructions such as these, with a very generalized auxiliary of being or possession? In Bybee and Pagliuca 1985 we argued that the obligation sense in the *have to* construction (and this would hold for the *be to* and *have got to* constructions as well) derives in part from the sense imparted by the infinitival verb forms. Expanding our discussion there to include 'be' auxiliaries, we can say that these constructions indicate that an agent possesses ('has') or is associated with ('is') an activity. In temporal terms there are at least three ways that one may have or be associated with an activity—either one has completed an activity, one is currently engaged in an activity, or one is projected to engage in an activity. In some languages this temporal dimension is expressed in the main verb form—the past participle gives the completed sense, the gerund or present participle gives the progressive sense, and the infinite gives the projected sense. The 'have' or 'be' verb associates the agent with a projected activity (in the infinitive).

Even given the presence of this kind of future projection, we still need to consider why the resulting sense is one of obligation rather than some other modality or even future tense. Our discussion in chapter 7 explains why the resulting sense is not future at first (it could develop into future later). The basic sense of future is prediction, which has the whole proposition in its scope. The constructions we are examining here have a finite verb linking an agent with a projected predicate, giving agent-oriented meaning. Further, we would not expect the modality of ability to come out of these constructions, since ability is not so future-projecting as obligation—if you are able to do something, you probably already have done it at some point. (We will see below that some ability constructions are related to perfective.) On the other hand, desire is future-projecting, but more internal. Desire seems to be too specific a meaning to be expressed by auxiliaries meaning 'be' and 'have'.

This explanation relies heavily on the assumption that some part of the construction signaling obligation has the sense of non-past and non-present, the sense of an activity being projected. In English we attribute this sense to the infinitive, but can we find a source for this temporal projection in the other constructions? This is a difficult question to answer without knowing more about the languages under investigation. Clearly in the case of Slave, where both verbs are in the Optative, the future or unrealized projection is present; similarly, the Kui construction uses an infinitive, the Chepang an Irrealis Nominalization, and the Abkhaz a form used in conditional protases. The sense of the Temne nominalization is 'name of action', but, as commonly occurs (according to Woodworth 1991), this type of nominalization can also have a future-projecting infinitive sense in certain syntactic contexts. In the Bari construction the future sense is clearly present (although its source is unknown), since the meaning is future obligation.

Because obligation is externally imposed, some of the source constructions for obligation are passive-like in structure; that is, the one who is obliged is treated like the object or patient in the clause. This is true for instance in Baluchi, where the strong obligation reading of the construction that uses 'be' and a possessive suffix on the infinitive also has the semantic subject in the accusative case, and the semantic object, if it is a noun, in the nominative case (Barker and Mengal 1969: 240).

(24) ayra   ji(h)əgi   ynt
      3.s.acc   run:INF:POSS   be:3.s
      'He has to run away.'

(25) məna   ai   ləngar   joʀ   kənəgi   ynt
      1.s.acc   3.s.POSS   plow:NOM   build   do:INF:POSS   be:3.s
      'I have to fix his plow.'

In another Baluchi construction signaling obligation, the infinitive is used with the auxiliary *kəp*, meaning 'fall, befall', with the semantic subject in the accusative case again (Barker and Mengal 1969: 198).

(26)   məna   rəvəg   kəpit
       1.s.ACC   go:INF   fall:3.s
       'I have to go.'

Similarly, Kui uses the auxiliary meaning 'become, happen' in the 3s neuter form, *ane*, with the infinitive to express a passive obligation meaning. Also in Tucano, where the auxiliary verb *ia* 'want' takes an impersonal subject, the sense is one of an impersonal obligation.

(27)   baʔa-ro   ia-ʔa
       eat-PART   want-PRES:IMPRS
       'One should eat.' (West 1980: 78)

Another obligation construction from a passive source is the English *be supposed to* construction. From sentences such as *They suppose him to be qualified*, a passive *He is supposed to be qualified* can be derived. In this passive sentence, some external bodies impose a supposition upon a subject. When this passive construction comes to be used with dynamic main verbs, *He is supposed to go tomorrow*, then it takes on an obligation sense. The idea that the conditions are imposed from the outside upon the subject is maintained although it does not really retain its passive syntax, since, for example, the agent cannot be expressed in such a sentence.

Two apparently idiosyncratic lexical sources for obligation markers may be similar to *be supposed to*. They are the Maithili auxiliaries *caks* 'to see' and *bujh*, 'to understand', both of which are used in their Optative forms to express weak obligation. The construction with *caks* in Early Maithili had the auxiliary in its Present Passive Optative form. The forms of this auxiliary may also be used with the Past Passive Participle of the main verb (Jha 1958: 534).

6.3.2. Types of obligation

An examination of familiar and well-documented languages suggests that the major distinctions within obligation have to do with gradations of strength of the obligation; that is, an obligation may be either strong or weak. If a weak obligation is not fulfilled, the consequences are not too serious; but the consequences of not fulfilling a strong obligation are much more severe. As we mentioned in §6.2.1, English distinguishes strong obligation, expressed with *must* and *have to*, and weak obligation, expressed with *should*.

Another sense closely related to obligation and often conflated with it is the sense of destiny or what is to be. While we did not find this sense mentioned often in reference grammars, it appears to be important diachronically. Benveniste's (1968) description of the sense of the Latin periphrastic construction of infinitive + *habēre*, which became the Romance synthetic future, is that it referred to situations which were destined or prearranged to happen (cf. chap. 7).

A similar sense is clearly evidenced for *should* in Old and Middle English. In Old English, both *shall* and *should* (the Present and Preterite forms of *sculan*) were used to report both moral and physical obligations and inevitabilities. In Middle English, *shall* was used more frequently in the first person to make promises and state intentions, but *should* continued to be used primarily in the third person to report past destiny and inevitabilities, as in examples (28)–(29) from *Sir Gawain and the Green Knight*.

(28)   þere watz much derue doel driuen in þe sale þat so worthé as
      Wawan schulde wende on þat ernde
      (ll. 558–9)
      'There was much severe lament arising in the hall that so worthy a man as Gawain was to go on that errand . . .'
(29)   (he was dreaming about) How þat destiné schulde þat day dele
      hym his wyrde.
      (l. 1752)
      'How destiny was to deal him his fate that day.'

Such usage contrasts with Modern English uses of *should* for weak obligation, because now *should* is used in present time without the sense of destiny and with more of the sense of personal obligation.

6.4. Ability and possibility

The second most frequent agent-oriented modality occurring in our sample of languages is **ability**. As with obligation, there is no clear boundary between lexical and grammatical expression of ability, so some of the forms we have included in the study may be bordering on lexical forms. Table 6.2 shows the grams in our database that express the related agent-oriented notions of ability, root possibility, and permission. Indeed, Table 6.3, which we discuss below, attests to the relatedness of these notions since it shows that a single gram is very likely to express two or more of these notions. It should also be pointed out that, given the nature of our reference material, it was not always possible to distinguish confidently between ability and root possibility.

6.4.1. Lexical sources

Table 6.2 shows the lexical sources for grams expressing ability, root possibility, and permission in our database. We do not include here

Table 6.2. Lexical Sources for Ability, Root Possibility, and Permission

Language	Form No.	Related String	Expression
01 Inuit	66		SUF
	69		SUF
02 Basque	12		AUX
	17		PARTCL
03 Margi	49		AUX
	50		AUX
18 Maung	07		PRE
19 Worora	19	finish	AUX
20 Alawa	35		SUF
22 Koho	06		AUX
	08		AUX
26 Motu	17	know	AUX
28 Halia	03		AUX
	22		PARTCL
34 Pangasinan	07		PRE
39 Abkhaz	61		AUX
40 Guaymí	19	arrive, be there	AUX
42 Kui	30		AUX
48 Maithili	51		AUX
	52		AUX
49 Baluchi	06	know how to	AUX
	10	be + plural possessive	AUX
	16	do, make	AUX
51 Danish	08	know	AUX
	09		AUX
59 Bongu	11		SUF
71 Temne	16		AUX
72 Mwera	46	know how to	AUX
76 Bari	24		AUX
83 Shuswap	12		SUF
84 Lao	12	anterior	AUX
	35		AUX
	41	be	AUX
86 Haka	21		PARTCL
	36		PARTCL
87 Lahu	16	be, become	AUX
	17		AUX
	18	get, obtain	AUX
	19	reach, arrive at	AUX
	25	send	AUX
88 Nung	11		PARTCL
	22	know	AUX
89 Cantonese	01		AUX
	02		AUX
	03		AUX
	04		AUX
	25	fall down	AUX
92 Uigur	31	take	SUF
94 Tok Pisin	02	know	AUX
	10	know	AUX
	22	enough	PART

Table 6.3. Grams Expressing Ability, Root Possibility, and Permission

Language	Form No.	Ability	Root Possibility	Permission	Epistemic Possibility	Other
01 Inuit	66	x				
	69	x				
02 Basque	12	x	x	x	x	
	17	x	x			
03 Margi	49	x	x			
	50	x	x			
18 Maung	07		x			(NEG) FUT, PRES
19 Worora	19	x				
20 Alawa	35	x				PAST
22 Koho	06	x				
	08			x		
26 Motu	17	x				
28 Halia	03	x	x	x		OBL
	22		x			OBL
34 Pangasinan	07	x	x			
39 Abkhaz	61	x	x			
40 Guaymí	19	x				
42 Kui	30			x	x	HAB, FREQ
48 Maithili	51		x			
	52	x				
49 Baluchi	06	x				
	10	x				OBL, INTEN
	16	x	x	x		
51 Danish	08	x	x	x		IMP
	09			x		OBL, IMP
59 Bongu	11		x		?x	
71 Temne	16	x				
72 Mwera	46	x				
76 Bari	24	x				
84 Lao	12	x	x	x		
	41	x				
	35		x		x	
86 Haka	21	x				
	36	x	x	x		
87 Lahu	16		x	x		
	17	x				
	18	x				
	19	x				
	25			x		CAUS
88 Nung	11	x				ANT
	22	x				
89 Cantonese	01		x			
	02		x	x		FUT, WILLING
	03	x	x		x	
	04	x				FUT
	25	x				
92 Uigur	31	x				
94 Tok Pisin	02	x	x	x		
	10	x				HAB
	22	x				

Note. INTENtion.

related strings that are reported to mean 'to be able' or 'to be permitted', since we are searching for the more specific lexical sources for precisely these meanings.

The most commonly documented lexical source for ability is a verb meaning 'to know' or 'to know how to'. The Motu verb *diba* means 'to know' as well as 'can, be able' and is used to speak of physical as well as mental ability. The Baluchi auxiliary *zǝn* means 'to know how' and is used with the infinitive to signal mental ability. The Danish auxiliary *kunne* (cognate with English *can*) formerly meant 'know' and thus signaled mental ability. The Mwera auxiliary *manya* is glossed as 'know how to'. The Nung auxiliary *sha* also means 'to know' and signals mental ability. Tok Pisin *kæn* is from the English auxiliary *can*, which like Danish *kunne*, is derived from a verb meaning 'know'. Tok Pisin also uses *savi*, a pidgin word from the Portuguese verb 'know', for ability.

The use of 'know' with a verb phrase complement yields the sense of 'know how to'. In some cases, 'know how to' would cover primarily mental ability, as in *I know how to speak French,* but in many cases a physical ability necessarily accompanies a mental one, as in *I know how to shoot a crossbow.* Thus a verb originally restricted to mental ability is extended to apply as well to physical ability, and thus becomes a general signal of ability.

There are also documented cases of auxiliaries predicating physical ability being extended to cover mental ability as well and thus becoming general markers of ability. One such case is English *may*, which formerly predicated physical ability or might, and later expressed general ability. Another example is Latin **potere* or *possum* 'to be able', which is related to the adjective *potens* meaning 'strong or powerful', and which gives French *pouvoir* and Spanish *poder*, both meaning 'can' as auxiliaries, but 'power' as nouns. Presumably these verbs generalize in the same way as the mental ability verbs: since physical and mental ability often overlap, they would be used in many cases where both types of ability are intended and thus come to predicate both (Bybee 1988a).

Another group of auxiliary verbs that comes to signal ability is dynamic, telic verbs of various sorts. Two languages, Guaymí and Lahu, use the movement verb 'arrive at' to signal ability. Matisoff 1973: 233 describes the Lahu verb *gà* 'reach, arrive at' as meaning 'managed to do' when used after a main verb, implying that there were difficulties that had to be overcome. The Guaymí auxiliary *reb* means 'to arrive at' or, when used in the perfective with a verbal complement, 'to arrive at a state' or 'to begin'. However, in the present imperfective with a verbal complement, *reb* means 'to be able'. Since 'arrive at' implies the successful completion of an act, it is not a long step to the expression of the ability of the subject to complete that act. The exact mechanism by which this meaning arises would have to be discovered in a more detailed analysis, however.

Lahu also uses a verb *gä* meaning 'get, obtain' in a construction whose meaning is to manage to complete an act. The Uigur Potential suffix is derived from an auxiliary verb *al-* meaning 'to take'. Again we have the notion of successful attainment in the semantics of these verbs. Matisoff 1973: 233, 551 points out that this same Lahu verb is used in another construction to signal obligation and observes that English 'get' also has such a dual use, as an obligation marker in *gotta*, and meaning 'manage to' or 'be permitted to' as in *I get to sit on Santa's lap*.

Perhaps related to these auxiliaries that express successful attainment of a goal are four cases in our database in which an ability gram is related in some way to the expression of anterior or perfective. The Worora ability construction uses the particle *kolε* meaning 'finished' with the Irrealis suffix and prefix on the main verb. The Alawa construction uses the Present Punctiliar Subjunctive, which, when used in the negative, signals simple past. The Lao form *dai:*[5] (colon indicates short vowel) means 'can' but also 'did, already'. The Nung ability construction uses the same particle as found in the anterior, *ngut*. At this point, we do not know exactly how these constructions arise or why they contain elements signaling anteriority. We can only point to the fact that successful completion implies and in fact demonstrates ability.

We argue below that the permission sense can develop out of the root possibility sense, as it has in English for *may* and *can*. However, it is also possible to arrive at the grammatical sense of permission more directly, by the grammaticization of a verb meaning 'be permitted to' or, as in Lahu, through the extension of the semantics of causation. For instance, the Lahu auxiliary verbs *cɨ* 'to send (someone)' and *pi* 'to give' express causative meaning as well as permission. The phrase *vɔ̀ʔ cɨ* means both 'make someone wear' and 'let someone wear' (Matisoff 1973: 237). Similarly, *vɔ̀ʔ pî* means both 'dress someone' and 'let someone wear'.

6.4.2. Ability, root possibility, and permission

The development of grams signaling ability demonstrates nicely the way meaning change in grammaticization may be characterized as the loss of specific semantic features. We have already pointed out that ability grams may come either from verbs such as 'know', which express mental ability, or verbs such as 'have the power or might', which express physical ability. If we examine the semantic development of

an auxiliary such as English *can,* we can see how semantic generalization takes place. In Bybee 1988a it was argued that the meaning of
can goes through the stages shown in (30).

(30) *Can* predicates that
        (i)   mental enabling conditions exist in the agent
        (ii)   enabling conditions exist in the agent
        (iii)   enabling conditions exist
      for the completion of the main predicate situation.

The earliest examples of *can* used with a verb complement show it
used to express mental ability (example from Murray et al. 1884–
1933 [*OED*]).

(31) Your aun bok yee can nought spell. Cursor M 14692 (c. 1300)

Around 1300, according to the *OED*, examples of *can* with predicates
requiring physical ability are found, such as (32) with the Past form.

(32) So yung that sho ne couthe Gon on fote. Havelock III
      (c. 1300)

When both mental and physical ability are possible, the meaning of
can is as in (30.ii).

The transition from mental ability to general ability is easy enough
to understand. Since most activities that require mental ability also
require some physical ability, *can* would very often be used where
both types of ability are required. The idea that *can* was predicating
only mental ability would soon be lost. From use with main verbs
meaning 'paint', 'read', 'spell', 'speak French', 'tell a tale', the use of
can would spread to be used with all types of activities.

The third step in the progression in (30) is the generalization from
ability to root possibility. As shown in (30), this step can also be seen
as the loss of a specific component of the meaning, the component
that requires that the enabling conditions reside in an agent. This
generalization resembles the one just described: since the enabling
conditions for an agent to perform an act do not lie entirely in the
agent, but also depend on the external world, *can* would also be used
in cases in which the enabling conditions are both in the agent and
outside the agent, as in *I can ride that horse* or *I can play that sonata.* In
these cases the properties of the horse and the sonata are of some
significance in determining the agent's ability, since horses can be
more or less difficult to ride, sonatas can be more or less difficult to
play. Thus *can* generalizes to predicate all sorts of enabling conditions—those internal to the agent as well as external conditions, as
examples (33)–(34) from the *OED* show.

(33) Thou canest not with one view peruse the wide compasse of it.
      (1561)
(34) Thou cannest not haue of Phocion a frende & a flaterer bothe
      to gether. (1548)

May started with a meaning of physical ability or power and went
through a similar development. In Old English we find examples of
may ⟨mæg⟩ used for general ability, as in (35), and even for root possibility, as in (36).

(35) á mæg God wyrcan wundor æfter wundre
      'God can work wonder after wonder.'   (Beowulf l. 930)
(36) thær mæg nihta gehwæm nith-wundor seón
      'A wonder can be seen there every night.'   (l. 1365)

Both *may* and *can* have come to be used to report permission—that
an agent is permitted to do something. In both cases, the permission
use developed after the root possibility use was firmly established. In
Bybee and Pagliuca 1985 it was argued that the permission use developed out of the root possibility sense. The general enabling conditions expressed by root possibility include both physical conditions
and social conditions, and permission is simply the presence of social
enabling conditions.

Thus a general root possibility sense would automatically include
the sense of social permission. The use of the form to ask and grant
permission is, then, just a special instance of root possibility. This
hypothesis is supported by the fact that in our data (as shown in
Table 6.3) nine of the thirteen grams expressing permission also
are used to express root possibility. Moreover, our hypothesis predicts that a gram expressing ability would not move directly to the
expression of permission without also being able to express root possibility. In synchronic terms that would mean that we would not expect to find a single gram whose uses included ability and permission,
but not root possibility. As shown in Table 6.3, we uncovered no such
situation.

Another way to arrive at the grammatical expression of permission
would be for a verb meaning 'be permitted' to grammaticize directly
to a permission sense. In this case, the gram would not be expected to
have root possibility as another use. This occurred with the Greek
particle *as* from the Ancient Greek Imperative *áphes* 'let!', and it may
be the case with the Koho auxiliary *di*.

As Table 6.3 shows, our data reveal a strong cross-linguistic pattern of overlap among the uses labeled ability, root possibility, permission, and epistemic possibility. We have just presented diachronic

Fig. 6.1. A path to permission.

data from English to support a path as in Figure 6.1. A gram expressing root possibility can undergo further development, by which it comes to be used to express epistemic possibility. Since grams meaning obligation can also undergo a shift to epistemic meaning, we treat all agent-oriented–to–epistemic changes together in the next section.

6.5. Paths of development for agent-oriented modalities

In the following sections we sketch out the paths of development that agent-oriented modalities can take. As before, our method is to examine multiple uses of a single gram and postulate that these uses are in a diachronic relation, one developing out of another. The proposals concerning the directionality of the relations are based on the directionality of documented changes and on the general principles derived from what is known about the course of semantic change in grammaticization. On the basis of diachronic evidence, we assume that the agent-oriented sense is earlier than the epistemic, speaker-oriented, or subordinating senses.

Our examination of the data and consideration of plausible sequences of changes has suggested to us that in the case of agent-oriented grams, we have multiple diverging paths of development, rather than a single sequence into which all uses of these grams may fit. We propose that the development of epistemic and speaker-oriented senses are independent developments. Further, the use of these modality grams in subordinate clauses grows out of their use in epistemic and speaker-oriented senses, and the type of subordinate clause for which they are appropriate depends on the epistemic and speaker-oriented senses that they have already developed. The consequence of this is that the use of modality in subordinate clauses may develop independently according to the type of subordinate clause. If this hypothesis can be supported, it has consequences for our understanding of the synchronic status of categories such as 'subjunctive mood' or 'irrealis'.

In the next section, then, we take up the development of obligation and root possibility into epistemic modality, and in §§6.7–6.9 we discuss their development into speaker-oriented and subordinating uses.

6.6. Agent-oriented and epistemic meaning

The fact that some of the English modal auxiliaries have both agent-oriented or root meanings and epistemic ones is well known (Horn 1972; Lyons 1977; Palmer 1979). The fact that other languages have a similar overlapping of agent-oriented and epistemic senses was reported in Steele 1975. The diachronic implications of this polysemy have been discussed in Shepherd 1981; Sweetser 1984, 1990; Bybee and Pagliuca 1985; and Traugott 1989. It is clear that the epistemic senses develop later than, and out of, the agent-oriented senses. In fact, for the English modals, where the case is best documented, the epistemic uses do not become common until quite late.

Horn 1972, Steele 1975, and Coates 1983 all point out that the force of the epistemic sense expressed by a modal is directly related to the force of the agent-oriented sense from which it derives. Horn further points out that the strength of the modal meaning in both domains is scalar:

agent-oriented		epistemic	
strong obligation	gives	inferred certainty	(*must*)
weak obligation	gives	probability	(*should*)
ability	gives	possibility	(*may*)

Though there is not a large number of grams in our database that express both agent-oriented and epistemic senses, the ones that do conform to this pattern. A case of a marker of strong obligation expressing inferred certainty is found in Abkhaz, cases of a marker of weak obligation expressing probability are found in Baluchi and Modern Greek, and cases of a marker of ability or root possibility also expressing epistemic possibility are found in Danish, Lao, and Cantonese.

(37) Strong obligation (Abkhaz)
    s- cà- r-   o- w+p'
    l.s- go- COND- be- STAT
    'I must go.'   (Hewitt 1979a: 192)
(38) Inferred certainty (Abkhaz)
    a-   y°nə   də- q'a- za+r- ò-   w+p'
    ART- house 3.s- b3- COND- be- STAT
    'He must be at home.'   (Hewitt 1979a: 195)
(39) Weak obligation (Baluchi)
    če, a   e   drwst satā   bỳbart?
           3.s this all   jewelry SUBJ:take.away:3.s
    'Should he take away all this jewelry?'

(h)ā,   a   ešā   bỳbart.
yes,   3.s   3.p   subj:take.away:3.s
'Yes, he ought to take them away.'

(Barker and Mengal 1969: 179)

(40) Probability (Baluchi)
      ma   bəkly   adda   kəssa   bỳzanən.
      l.p   perhaps there   someone subj:know:1.p
      'Perhaps we know someone there.'

(Barker and Mengal 1969: 185)

(41) Root possibility (Lao)
      khɔɔj   aat   paj   haa   cau   myynii
      l.s   can   go   see   2.s   today
      'I can come to see you today.'

(Morev, Moskalyov, and Plam 1979: 79)

(42) Epistemic possibility (Lao)
      láaw   âat   cáʔ   bɔɔ   sábaaj   lăaj
      3.s   may   be   ill   very
      'He may be very ill.'   (Yates and Sayasithsena 1970: 390)

This regularity lends further support to the hypothesis that grammaticization paths are universal and predictable on general semantic principles.

6.6.1. Metaphor versus inference as the mechanism of change

Especially with regard to changes in modal meanings, a controversy has arisen in the literature over whether the mechanism of semantic change in grammaticization is metaphorical extension or change by the conventionalization of implicature. Sweetser 1984, 1990 argues that the image schematic structure of the sense of the modal is maintained during the shift of meaning from the sociophysical world to the world of reason and belief. Thus she argues that *may* represents "an absent potential barrier in the sociophysical world," and in the world of reasoning, *may* means that "there is no barrier to the speaker's process of reasoning from the available premises to the conclusion expressed in the sentence qualified by *may*" (1990: 74).

Traugott 1989 and Traugott and König 1991 along with Bybee 1988a argue that the shift from agent-oriented to epistemic meanings involves the conventionalization of implicature, by which the inferences that can be made from the meaning of a particular modal become part of the meaning of that modal. First consider the way inferential change operates in a different domain, the development of causal meaning in the originally temporal connective *since*. In earlier English, as described by Traugott and König 1991: 194–95, *since* was used only in cases such as (43), expressing only 'time after'.

(43)   I have done quite a bit of writing since we last met.

However, since a cause usually precedes an effect, and since speakers often link clauses to show cause, a causal inference can be made in many cases where *since* is used. Thus sentences such as (44), where both a temporal and causal interpretation are possible, arose.

(44)   Since Susan left him, John has been very miserable.

Once the causal sense is firmly established as part of the meaning, then the connective can be used in cases where only causal meaning is expressed.

(45)   Since you are not coming with me, I will have to go alone.

In order to establish a mechanism for change for any particular form, it is necessary to examine the way that form is used at the point at which the new use is developing. As Faltz 1989 argues, in order for an inference to be taken as part of the meaning of a form, situations in which the inference is present must occur frequently enough for the language-users to assume that the inference is a necessary part of the meaning of the form. The historical progression will be similar to that illustrated by examples (43)–(45), where at the first stage the early meaning implies the new meaning, then cases arise in which both meanings are expressed, and finally, cases arise where the new meaning is used alone.

On the other hand, if metaphorical extension is the mechanism of change, there need not be such a progression. The shift to a new domain can be abrupt, as it often is in lexical change. Further, there will be very few instances of use in which the older and newer meanings overlap, as in (44). The only way to determine the mechanism of change in any particular case is to find evidence for the way the new meanings arose. Some exemplifying cases are discussed in the next two sections.

6.6.2. Root to epistemic possibility

Bybee 1988a examined the occurrence of *may* in a Middle English text in search of early uses of epistemic *may* and found many occurrences of a sentence type that has a root possibility meaning but implies an epistemic meaning as well. First, consider that in Modern English some sentences with a root possibility meaning imply epistemic possibility. Consider (46).

(46)   It **can** take me up to four hours to get there.

In a context in which someone is estimating an arrival time, (46) implies (47).

(47) It **may** take me up to four hours to get there.

In the Middle English text *Sir Gawain and the Green Knight*, there are many examples of *may* used to express root possibility in a context in which epistemic possibility is also implied. (48) is an example.

(48) ȝe ar a sleper ynslyȝe, þat mon *may* slyde hider;
      'You are so unwary a sleeper that someone can sneak in here;'
                                                          (l. 1209)

Here *may* is translated with modern *can* to convey the root possibility reading. Note that, as shown in (49), the root possibility reading implies the epistemic reading of the sentence, so that it could be argued that (48) is ambiguous.

(49) 'someone can sneak in here' implies 'someone may sneak in here'

There are also uses of *may* in *Gawain* that have only the root possibility reading. In (50), the first use of *may* may be either root or epistemic (and thus may be translated into current English as either *can* or *may*), but the second occurrence, with the negative, is only root, and can only take *can* in present-day English.

(50) For mon may hyden his harmes, bot vnhap ne may hit.
      'For a man may/can hide his misfortunes, but he cannot undo them.'
                                                          (l. 2511)

Again, the first clause shows the implication (51).

(51) 'a man can hide his misfortunes' implies 'a man may hide his misfortunes'

About one third of the examples of *may* in *Gawain* can be interpreted as either root or epistemic possibility; the rest are unambiguously root, like the negative clause above and other affirmative clauses.

   This means that in a substantial number of cases, the hearer is entitled to infer a sense of epistemic possibility along with the literally expressed root possibility sense. We do not know how frequent the cases where such inferences are appropriate must be before the inference becomes part of the meaning, but the frequency of such cases in this one text suggests that the inferential mechanism is highly likely to be involved in this case of a shift to epistemic meaning.

   A shift from agent-oriented to epistemic meaning involves a change in scope. The agent-oriented modal is part of the propositional content of the clause and serves to relate the agent to the main predicate. The epistemic modal, on the other hand, is external to the propositional content of the clause and has the whole proposition in its scope. It seems apparent that most semantic changes in grammaticization are gradual changes, but it is at first difficult to see how such a scope change could be gradual. However, if we look at the particular examples in which root possibility implies epistemic, the manner in which such changes could be gradual becomes apparent.

Consider the two examples presented above. Both involve the non-specific pronoun *mon*. In these cases, the modal *may* has the verb phrase in its scope, but since the subject noun phrase contributes almost no semantic information to the proposition, *may* actually has the whole of the semantic content of the proposition in its scope. Of the nine clear cases in the *Gawain* text in which a root possibility meaning implies an epistemic one, four use the pronoun *mon* 'one' as subject; five (including some that use *mon*) occur in relative clauses with non-specific heads; and the others are either in passive clauses or use non-agentive verbs. Consider the passive sentence in (52).

(52)   (give me your word) þat þou schal seche me þiself, where-so
       þou hopes I **may** be funde vpon folde . . .
       'that you will seek me yourself, wherever you think I can/may
       be found on the earth . . .'   (ll. 395–96)

Note that the subject is semantically the patient, and thus part of the verb phrase, which is within the scope of the root possibility modal, but since there is no agent explicit in the clause, verb phrase scope is equivalent to propositional scope. Thus we would suggest that even scope changes can occur gradually, given certain types of clauses, in this case clauses without explicit, specific agents.

Note that a modal signaling ability would not be able to occur in such clauses, implying that the change from ability to root possibility is a necessary precondition to the development of epistemic possibility. Thus we continue the path started earlier as in Figure 6.2.

Fig. 6.2. A path to epistemic possibility.

6.6.3. Obligation to probability

To understand the way markers of obligation take on epistemic meaning, we can study both *should* and *must* in English. We will see here that their epistemic senses arise in different contexts, suggesting different mechanisms of change. First we consider *should*.

Should can be used to express future, present, and past probability, the latter with *have* + Past Participle. Examples (53)–(55) show the three tenses with epistemic *should*. Each of these examples can have an obligation reading as well as a probability reading.

(53)   The letter should arrive sometime next week. (future)
(54)   The letter should be in the mail. (present)
(55)   The letter should have come last week. (past)

In order to have only an epistemic reading, the context must disallow the obligation reading, as in the following case where a dummy subject precludes an agent-oriented reading.

(56)   It should take me about four hours to get there.

What we see in these examples is that the obligation sense of *should* implies the probability sense, suggesting that an inferential mechanism might have been or still is at work here. The present obligation sense of *should*, from which the epistemic sense arises, has developed fairly recently. We have already said that it is not mentioned in the *OED*. It would follow, then, that the epistemic sense has arisen even more recently, and that Modern English examples such as those in (53)–(56) show how the change has taken place: since the obligation sense implies the probability sense, *should* gradually is coming to be used for probability as well as obligation.[1]

The situation with *must* is quite different, however. The contexts in which *must* has an obligation reading and the contexts in which it has an epistemic reading are mutually exclusive. In the future, *must* has only an obligation reading.

(57)   The letter must arrive sometime next week.

In present and past sentences, however, *must* has only an inferred certainty reading.

(58)   The letter must be in the mail.
(59)   The letter must have been in the mail.

In fact, in the past tense and in the present tense with a stative verb, *must* can ONLY have an epistemic reading. Thus even with a dynamic verb in the past, *must* is epistemic.

(60)   He must have called three times while you were gone.

And in the non-past with a dynamic verb, *must* is epistemic with progressive situations.

---

1. However, as Traugott 1989 has pointed out, *should* had some past epistemic (or evidential) uses even in Old English.

(61)   He must be trying to call me right now.

In a restricted set of cases, the reading of *must* can be ambiguous between an epistemic and an obligation reading. One such case is (62).

(62)   He must play tennis a lot (or he won't win the tournament).
                                (and that is why he is so good).

In this case the epistemic reading has present habitual aspect, while the obligation reading is future-projecting. The two readings have different implications. The epistemic reading implies that he (probably) does play tennis every day, while the obligation reading implies that he probably does not. Neither reading implies the other.

Similarly, consider (63), which can also have two readings.

(63)   He must understand what we want (or we'll never get it).
                                    (we've told him so many
                                    times).

In (63) the epistemic reading calls for a stative interpretation of the main verb, but the obligation reading requires a dynamic interpretation, such as 'he must be made to understand'. Again the obligation reading does not imply the epistemic; in fact, they imply two distinct states of affairs, one in which the subject probably does understand and one in which he does not.

In other words, the contexts in which *must* has an obligation sense (future contexts only) and the contexts in which it has an inferred certainty sense (present with a stative verb or Progressive and Past) are largely mutually exclusive. This, along with the fact that the obligation sense does not imply the inferred certainty sense, argues strongly that the conventionalization of implicature cannot be the source for the epistemic sense (cf. Traugott 1989).

Since the epistemic use of *must* arises in contexts with aspectual interpretations distinct from the obligation uses, it appears that metaphor may be at work in this change. Metaphorical change involves a shift to a different domain—in this case from the domain of social obligations and physical necessities applied to an agent, to the epistemic domain that speaks of the necessary conditions under which a proposition can be true. This sort of change more closely resembles change in lexical meaning, and in fact, *must* more closely resembles a lexical item than, say, *should* does. That is, the meaning of *must* is not as eroded as that of *should; must* expresses strong obligation and in that sense has more semantic content than *should*. In addition, *must* has not generalized to the wide set of uses that *should* has (see below, the discussions of subjunctives and conditionals). We suspect, then, that the mechanism of change involving metaphorical extension occurs more readily with words or phrases that are less grammaticized, and still more lexical in their semantic content.

Another way that a probability sense can develop in a modal that earlier had an agent-oriented sense is through the sense of prediction, which we argued was the defining sense of a future gram. A future that has reached the stage of prediction can be used to make predictions about the present, which can be interpreted as an expression of probability. For instance, if the phone rings, one can say *That'll be Mary*, predicting that it will be revealed in the future that the caller is (right now) Mary. It appears that futures from various sources can have this use. For this reason, Bybee and Pagliuca 1987 argued that this use derives from the prediction sense.

In our database, we have found a present probability use of future reported in Basque and Haka. A well-attested case of a future gram that has become primarily a marker of probability of this sort is the Spanish synthetic Future. The suffixes for this Future derive historically from the Latin auxiliary *habēre* used with the infinitive form of the verb. The original sense of this construction was one of destiny or obligation. It has long been used for future prediction in Spanish, but now, especially with the development of the future from 'go' (*ir a*), the modal uses of the synthetic future are more common than the simple prediction uses in most dialects (Moreno de Alba 1977). Thus examples like (64)–(65) are characteristic of this set of suffices.

(64) Ya   tú   comprenderás   cómo   nos   reímos.
      Now   2.s   understand:FUT   how   REFL   laugh:PERF.1.P
      'Now you probably understand how we laughed.'
(65) Tendrá   veinte   años.
      Have:FUT.3.s   twenty   years
      'She's probably about twenty years old.'

It is significant that the probability sense of this erstwhile future applies only to present tense, suggesting that this probability sense did not develop in the same way as either *should* or *must* in English. This means that there is more than one path an obligation gram may follow to arrive at a sense of epistemic probability.

6.6.4. Obligation and epistemic meanings in the GRAMCATS sample

In the languages of the GRAMCATS sample, there are five forms that are reported to have both obligation and epistemic uses. Since they present an interesting range of variation, we discuss each one briefly.

The Abkhaz construction that expresses obligation and inferred certainty was exemplified above in (37) and (38). The suffix *r*, which is glossed as 'if' in conditional sentences, expresses both strong obligation and inferred certainty with stative predicates.

Two other similar examples are from Basque and Haka (Bawm). In Basque the obligation construction using the uninflected verb *bear* 'need' can be used with a stative predicate to give the sense of 'must be'. The Haka obligation particle *ding* with the assertive particle *asi* 'it is so' signals inferred certainty (Reichle 1981: 59, 67).

(66) a   hawng   ding
      3.s   come   OBL
      'He must come.'

(67) mi   rep   a   si   ding   asi
      man   honest 3.s   be   OBL   it.is.so
      'He must be an honest man.'

The Guaymí suffix -*re* gives a sense of strong obligation when used with the immediate future perfective -*di*, but when used with the immediate past perfective -*ba*, the resulting sense is that the speaker is reporting a non-witnessed situation (Kopesec 1975: 24).[2]

(68) Tigwe   blitadre   ben
      1.s:ERG   speak:FUT.PERF:OBL   with
      'I must talk with him.'

(69) Niaragwe   blitabare   ben
      3.s:ERG   speak:PAST.PERF:OBL   with
      '(They say that) he spoke with him.'

The description indicates that the sense of (69) is evidential, referring to the source of the information, rather than strictly epistemic. However, with a general non-witnessed evidential, the implication is definitely an epistemic one—that the speaker does not vouch unconditionally for the accuracy of the information.

The Baluchi prefix *bỹ*- is characterized as a general subjunctive, being used in complement clauses and certain other subordinate clauses. In main clauses it signals weak obligation, or if accompanied by the adverb 'perhaps', it signals probability (Barker and Mengal 1969: 179, 185).

(70) če, mən e   mə(h)aria   pər   ai   býəbərin?
            1.s this   riding.camel   for   3.s   SUBJ:take:1.s
      'Shall I take this riding camel for him?'
      [h]ā,   təw   [h]ər Dəwla   ešyra   bỳbərəy.
      yes   2s   in   every.way   3.s   SUBJ:take:2.s
      'Yes, you must certainly take it.'

2. P. D. Young (personal communication) indicates that in his data, the agent in this construction is in the Dative: *mä blit-a-dre ti-e* 'I must talk with him.'

(71) təw   bəlky   ayra   bỳzanəy
      2.s   perhaps   3.s.OBJ   SUBJ:know:2.s
      'Perhaps you may know him.'

In three languages, Abkhaz, Guaymí, and Baluchi, the obligation forms that also express epistemic senses show signs of having undergone a great deal of grammaticization. Formally they are extremely eroded, consisting of not more than a single syllable, and they are affixed. Each of these forms has multiple uses besides the two we have been considering here; they can all be used in subordinate or conditional clauses. These facts suggest that the development of epistemic meaning for these forms came very late in the grammaticizing process. On the other hand, the Basque and Haka forms are less eroded phonologically and not bound. Not coincidentally, they also have their epistemic sense only with stative predicates, suggesting that their development into epistemics is by metaphorical extension, as with English *must*.

6.6.5. Root possibility and epistemic meanings in the GRAMCATS sample

Our sample also includes four languages that show evidence of epistemic possibility developing from root possibility. We suspect there may be more cases, but because of the difficulty in distinguishing these two senses, and because of the polysemy of English *may*, it is often difficult to be sure from secondary sources which meanings are intended.

The Lao form *aat* appears to occur in both root and epistemic senses, as we noted above in examples (41) and (42). In closely related Thai, the cognate form, also *aat*, has only epistemic uses, according to Steele 1975.

The Basque construction, which consists of the subjunctive form of the auxiliaries *edin* or *ezan* and the infix *-ke* at the end of the auxiliary, is used for all kinds of ability, as well as for root and epistemic possibility as shown here (Saltarelli et al. 1988: 235, 236).

(72) hamarr- eta- ko   pelikula- ra   joa- n
      ten-   LOC- REL   film-   S.ALL   go- PERF
      g-   a-   ite-   z- ke
      1.P.ABS- PRES- AUX(SUBJ)- AP- POT
      'We can go to the ten o'clock film.'
(73) hemen ego- n   d-   a-   ite-   ke
      here   be- PERF   3.ABS- PRES- AUX(SUBJ)- POT
      'She can be here.'

The Cantonese auxiliary combination *hó nàng* seems to have only epistemic possibility and future as its meanings (according to Kwok 1971: 77), but each part of the combination derives historically from a verb meaning 'to be able'.

(74) yǎu   di   hó nàng   ngaam   gé
      there be some   may   right   SP
      'Some may be right.'

The Kui auxiliary *duhpa* expresses permission, as in (75), as well as epistemic possibility, as in (76) (Winfield 1928: 125).[3]

(75) ānu īra gipki duhi gina?
      'May I be doing this?'
(76) earu dapa katta vessa duhteru
      'They may have told lies.'

A slightly different scenario must be reconstructed for the Modern Greek particle *as*, derived historically from the Imperative form in Ancient Greek *áphes* 'let!' from *aphiēmi* 'I let.' Since this form derives from an imperative form, there is probably no stage at which this particle or its predecessor had root possibility meaning. However, from this closely related sense, a group of uses developed which resemble the normal development of root possibility: permissive, optative, and concessive.

6.7. Possibility and probability

Quite a number of languages in our sample have grammatical markers of the epistemic notions of possibility and probability. We hypothesize that many of these developed through the grammaticization of auxiliaries with agent-oriented meaning in the ways illustrated in preceding sections. Since epistemic meaning appears relatively late on the grammaticization path from agent-oriented meaning, we would expect epistemic markers to be highly grammaticized and their lexical sources to be unknown except in cases where an extensive historical record is available (as in English). A high degree of grammaticization is evident for many of the epistemic markers in our data, but not for all. Taking affixation as a rough guide to grammaticization of form, we find a fairly even split for the grams in Tables 6.4 and 6.5: twenty-one are expressed by affixes and twenty-five by particles and auxiliaries. Despite the number of auxiliaries (seventeen), information about lexical sources was scarce in our reference material. That which was available, however, suggests that not all epistemic meaning originates with agent-oriented meaning. Rather, some

3. The etymological source for this auxiliary is not given in the grammar or in Emeneau and Burrow 1961. However, the form has a very interesting range of usage, including, besides the permission and epistemic possibility senses, uses for habitual and frequentative action when used with the present verbal participle. This range of meaning suggests that the auxiliary may have derived from a verb meaning 'know', since 'know' can develop into ability and related meanings as well as into habitual and related meanings.

of the auxiliary source meanings may give epistemic meaning rather directly.

The source constructions that can be identified are the auxiliary verbs meaning 'to happen' and 'to be possible' for possibility in Abkhaz, 'to seem' for possibility in Maidu, 'to befall' for passive possibility in Maithili, 'to stand' plus the past anterior giving past possibility in Uigur, and a construction in Tigre involving 'to become' and an adposition meaning 'if' giving probability. The Slave possibility particle may derive from the phrase meaning 'I don't know.'

Tables 6.4 and 6.5 list the grams meaning possibility and probability found in our database. The tables also show, to the extent determin-

Table 6.4.   Other Uses of Grams Expressing Epistemic Possibility

Language	Form No.	Possibility (tense)	Future	Protasis	Other
02 Basque	12	pres			
	13	past			
10 Isl. Carib	42	fut	x	real/hypo	state changed
11 Cocama	13	all tenses			apodosis
12 Chacobo	48	fut			
17 Alyawarra	11	fut			apodosis
19 Worora	20	?			
20 Alawa	31	fut			(neg) present
32 Nakanai	13	fut	x	real	apodosis, purpose comp to want
33 Trukese	03	fut	x		comp to want
38 O'odham	37	pres, fut			reality
39 Abkhaz	65	pres, fut			
	66	fut			
42 Kui	30	all tenses			permission
47 Latin	11	fut		real	comp to want, order purpose, concessive optative, hortative exclamation
48 Maithili	29	pres			
	36	past			
	49	all tenses			
59 Bongu	23	all tenses			
68 Slave	43	fut			attempt
82 Maidu	45	pres, fut			real/hypo
84 Lao	35	pres			root possibility
	36	pres			
85 Chepang	12	pres, fut	x		admonitive prohibitive
88 Nung	09	pres			
89 Cantonese	03	pres	x		
92 Uigur	23	past			
93 Buriat	41	pres, past			

Table 6.5.   Other Uses of Grams Expressing Probability

Language	Form No.	Probability (tense)	Future	Other
01 Inuit	74	present		
02 Basque	05	present	x	
	08	past		subsequent apodosis hypo
08 Tigre	15	all tenses		protasis hypo
12 Chacobo	23	future		
13 Jivaro	30			
14 Tucano	16	all tenses		
	34	future		
39 Abkhaz	50	future		
40 Guaymí	04	remote future		
47 Latin	09	future	x	request
49 Baluchi	03	present		subjunctive
	15	remote past		remote past anterior
82 Maidu	46	all tenses		apodosis hypo
84 Lao	37			
86 Haka	10	present	x	future obligation apodosis
	40	present		obligation apodosis
87 Lahu	51	future		desire
92 Uigur	21	past		

able from the reference material, the tenses which the epistemic meaning may apply to (in the third column) and the other uses of these grams (in the remaining columns). The tenses which the modality applies to were determined largely by the illustrative examples and do not necessarily exclude uses in other tenses. The tense may not be explicitly expressed; that is, *I may go* would be counted as referring to future time.

When no other tense indicator is present, the possibility and probability markers make future time reference. Present temporal reference is possible only with stative predicates or with a progressive sense for dynamic predicates. Past time reference always occurs with an explicit marker of past. Thus the normal or default interpretation for epistemic possibility and probability with dynamic predicates is that the situation is expected to take place in the future.

In a few cases, the expression of simple future is another use of the epistemic marker. For probability, the future use is coupled with present probability, as in Basque and Haka, where the sense of the future gram with a stative predicate is 'is probably'. Consider the uses of Haka *lâi*, and compare it to the Spanish synthetic future discussed in §6.3 (Reichle 1981: 67).

(77) ka   nan   umpî   lâi
     1.s   2.s   marry FUT
     'I shall marry you.'
(78) buh   an   ei   liau   asi   lâi
     rice 3.P eat PROG   be   FUT
     'They are probably eating rice.'

Grams that can express either future possibility or future occur in five languages, Island Carib, Nakanai, Trukese, Chepang, and Cantonese. In these five languages the same form is glossed sometimes with 'may' or 'might' and sometimes with 'will' or 'shall'. Without knowing what other elements in the clause or the context select the possibility or the future reading, it is best to assume that these grams express meanings along a range from prediction to possibility. It is interesting to note that all five grams with these uses also have other uses indicative of a long history of development, i.e. uses in complements, in protases, and as speaker-oriented moods.

Five of the grams expressing possibility can also be used in protases, primarily of reality conditions, but in some cases also in hypothetical conditions. In four of the five cases, these grams are used along with a marker meaning 'if'. Of course it is reasonable that a gram indicating possibility would be used in an *if*-clause, since an *if*-clause sets up a possible world. Note, however, that a modal must have most of its meaning eroded before it can obligatorily occur in a protasis, since the environment of a protasis tends to bring out the full meaning of a modal. Thus in English, when we put *will* in an *if*-clause it does not signal a prediction, but rather tends to indicate 'willingness', as in (79). Similarly, *may* indicates permission rather than epistemic possibility, as in (80).

(79) If you will help me, we can finish faster.
(80) ?If he may help me, I would finish sooner.

Would in an *if*-clause formerly and still indicates volition or willingness, as in (81), but now in American English it is increasingly heard in the protasis replacing the simple past, as in (82).

(81) If you would help me, we would finish sooner.
(82) If he would buy it, he wouldn't have any money left.

It appears that in order for a modal element to occur in a protasis without contributing lexical meaning to the clause, it must already have a very reduced semantic content. We would hypothesize, then, that these possibility markers which can be used in protases are highly grammaticized. This hypothesis is supported by the form of these grams: the Latin Present Subjunctive is a single vowel with three lexically determined allomorphs, and the O'odham suffix *p* is a single consonant; the Island Carib and Nakanai forms are both very small particles, each of a CV shape, *me* in Island Carib and *ge* in Nakanai.

The case is somewhat different if the modal element occurs without an element meaning 'if'. In that case, all the conditional meaning is contributed by the modal element itself. Such appears to be the case in Maidu, where an auxiliary verb 'to seem' is conjugated in the Subjunctive Mode to indicate that the condition of the protasis is being given. (This auxiliary and one other are the only verbs that appear in the Subjunctive Mode; Shipley 1964: 48–49).

Only two of the probability grams appear in protases, suggesting that their stronger meaning tends to exclude them from this position. Of the two that do appear in protases, one, the Baluchi Subjunctive, only has the meaning of probability in a main clause when accompanied by a word meaning 'perhaps', indicating that it is sufficiently devoid of meaning to fit appropriately into a protasis. The other probability form, a periphrastic construction in Tigre, actually includes the gram meaning 'if' in its construction and thus resembles the Maidu form just discussed in that it is the very marker of conditionality.

A tentative conclusion concerning modals in protases emerges from these considerations. While the semantics of possibility (and to a lesser extent, probability) are compatible with the epistemic status of conditions stated in a protasis, modals expressing epistemicity must be very generalized and devoid of meaning in order to occur in a protasis with an overt element meaning 'if' without being interpreted as contributing additional meaning. On the other hand, more recently formed auxiliary constructions, such as the Tigre and Maidu ones, which explicitly signal that a situation is hypothetical, may do so without help of another 'if' element and in fact could become the 'if' element themselves.

In apodoses, modal elements occur with greater freedom, since it appears that most (if not all) agent-oriented and epistemic meanings are consonant with the main clause of a conditional sentence. Consider some English possibilities.

(83)   Reality conditions:
       If I see Mary, I want to tell her.
                       I have to tell her.
                       I'm going to tell her.
                       I'll tell her.
                       I may tell her.
                       I might tell her.

(84)   Hypothetical conditions:
       If I saw Mary, I would tell her.
                     I could tell her.
                     I might tell her.

In these sentences, the different semantics contributed by the distinct
modal elements are all appropriate and express possible contrasts.
Thus in our database, we find forms that express both probability and
possibility (as well as future) occurring in apodoses, while protases
mostly contain forms signaling the weaker notion of possibility.

Examples of probability forms in apodoses are found in Basque,
Maidu, and Haka. Consider the Haka (Bawm) form *ding*, whose other
uses are for obligation and probability. *Ding* and *lâi*, which was exemplified earlier, are used in phrases that are required in apodoses
(Reichle 1981: 69).

(85)   nî   a   sâ   selê,   fâng   ka   dêng   kho   ding mi
       sun   3.s   hot   if   paddy   1.s   husk   can   COND
       'If the sun were (shining) hot, I could husk paddy.'

The other major uses of epistemic markers occur in subordinate
clauses, especially complement clauses and concessive clauses. These
are discussed in §§6.9 and 6.10.

6.8. Agent-oriented modalities to speaker-oriented moods

Imperative is one of the most common meaning labels in our database, occurring 136 times. More than half the languages in our database have more than one grammatical means of signaling imperative.
Within a language, imperatives may be distinguished by features such
as polite, emphatic, immediate, or delayed.

It is a common observation that imperatives may have zero expression, especially in the singular (Greenberg 1966: 47). Such cases exist
in our database, but not in large proportions: 11 imperatives out of
136 have zero expression. Interestingly enough, these zero imperatives have no other uses; that is, they are not also used for other
default functions, such as perfective or present habitual. This fact
suggests that zero imperatives arise directly as imperatives and not via
some other functions (Bybee 1990b).

Non-zero expression of imperative must arise as overt material
grammaticizes. Some possible evidence of their sources can be found
in the other uses that they have. The other meanings that appear most
commonly in imperatives in our database are future and obligation.
Indeed, in our database, future is the most commonly occurring other
use for imperatives. We have thirteen languages in which a gram used
for future may also be used as an imperative. We suggested in Bybee

and Pagliuca 1987 and Bybee, Pagliuca, and Perkins 1991 that the future sense gives rise to the imperative function through an indirect speech act. In a situation in which the speaker has authority over the addressee, a prediction about the addressee can be interpreted as a command.

(86)   You're gonna take off your shoes before you come in here.

The evidence that imperative develops in this way out of the prediction use of futures is the fact that futures from all possible lexical sources can be used as imperatives. For instance, in our database we have the following lexical sources for futures used as imperatives: 'go' in Atchin; 'come' and 'want' in Danish; 'do, make, be' in Yagaria; and an adverb in Motu (see chap. 7).

Our database also contains four cases of grams used for the agent-oriented sense of obligation which can also be used for imperative. Again we would claim that use of an obligation marker in second person can easily be reinterpreted as an imperative. For instance, sentence (87) can be interpreted as the speaker issuing a directive.

(87)   You must call your mother.

It is common for the forms used in imperative sentences to also occur in subordinate clauses, particularly the protases of conditional sentences, complement clauses to main verbs of ordering or wanting, and purpose clauses. These latter two uses are considered in §§6.9 and 6.10.

Our database also contains a number of other speaker-oriented grams, such as optatives, hortatives, prohibitives, and admonitives. Because of the small number of cases, it is much more difficult to hypothesize paths of development for these grams.

A rather unexpected set of examples of a shift to a speaker-oriented modality is found in the development of an admonitive mood out of a marker of possibility. In most of these cases, the sense of possibility (either root or epistemic) carries with it the notion that the possible situation is unpleasant, dangerous, or deleterious in some way. Grams signaling possibility with this additional deleterious flavor are found in Gugada, Alyawarra, Ono, and Slave. In Alyawarra and Slave, and also in Chepang, where the possibility marker does not carry the deleterious implication, the gram in question can also be used to issue warnings or (in other words) as an admonitive. Consider the Slave particle sáná (var. sóné) in the deleterious possibility use (88) and the admonitive use (89) (Rice 1989: 412).

(88)   wǫt'ée   sáná
       2.s:OPT:burn   PROH
       'You might get burned.'

(89) goǫts'í   sóné
      2.s:OPT:lie   PROH
      'Don't ever lie.'

This same particle is further used for negative obligation.

(90) tu   gá   náguyee   sóné
      water   near   3.s:OPT:play   PROH
      'He must not play near the water.'

In Chepang, the Indefinite Future, which can be used for future and possibility, can also be used to issue a warning in the second person, as in (91). Caughley 1982: 102 explains that this warning use is original in sentences in which the addressee is not intentionally involved, as in (91), but was extended to cases where the addressee could have some control, such as (92). In these cases, it could be interpreted as a prohibition and has consequently come to be used in that way with sentences where the addressee is clearly intentionally involved, such as (93).

(91) naŋ   has-teʔ-caʔ
      you   vomit-CIF-IFUT
      'You may be sick!'
(92) baŋ- sey   ton-teʔ-caʔ
      stone-ABL   fall-CIF-IFUT
      'You may fall from that rock!'
      'Don't fall from that rock!'
(93) jugaŋ- ma- teʔ   giyuŋh-caʔ- jə
      every-CNJ-CIF   go.out-IFUT-2D
      'Don't you two ever go out!'

Such a sequence of events would explain the set of uses that the Slave particle has as well. (But see Lichtenberk 1992 for another view of 'apprehensional' forms.)

Finally, we mention the role of aspectual forms in expressing the imperative. We might expect that one of the basic aspectual forms of the verb could be used for the imperative function, and indeed this is the case in a small number of languages. In our database, both perfective and imperfective forms perform the imperative function: in Baining and Trukese the perfective form can be used for imperative, while in Danish and Tahitian, an imperfective form (the present in Danish) can be used for imperative.

6.9. The development of subordinating moods

Subjunctive is the term given to special verb forms or markers that obligatorily occur in certain types of subordinate clauses. The analysis of subjunctives has often been controversial because it is unclear whether subjunctive forms actually carry meaning, or whether they are semantically empty elements that show up by virtue of syntactic requirements. On the one hand, in the familiar languages that have subjunctive verb forms, a large majority of their uses are dictated by the surrounding context, leaving no room for semantic contrast. Thus in Spanish, main verbs such as *querer* 'to want', *mandar* 'to order', and *sentir* 'to regret' always have a subordinate verb in the subjunctive when its subject is not the same as the main clause subject. In contrast, affirmative main predicates such as *creer* 'to believe', *es verdad* 'it is true', *estar seguro de* 'to be sure of' always have indicative subordinate clauses. This predictable distribution accounts for the vast majority of subjunctive occurrences. On the other hand, there are a few cases where the subjunctive/indicative contrast produces a difference in meaning.

(94) Dice   que   vienen   ahora.
     say:3.s   that   come:IND:3.P   now
     'He says they are coming now.'
(95) Dice   que   vengan   ahora.
     say:3.s   that   come:SUBJ:3.P now
     'He says for them to come now.'

Such contrastive examples, and the fact that the distribution of moods in noun complement clauses is not arbitrary but determinable by the semantic content of the main predicate, suggest that the mood contrast is meaning-bearing. But if it is, then our task is to determine what meanings the indicative and subjunctive carry. The literature on this topic demonstrates that the meaning of this type of mood distinction is so highly generalized and deeply embedded in context that it seems impossible to give it a characterization that is valid across different clause types without making the characterization itself so weak as to be vacuous.

While the approach offered by grammaticization theory does not solve this synchronic problem, it can at least cast the problem in a light which allows us to better understand why subjunctives exist at all and why they have the distribution that they do. If we view the uses of subjunctives as links on a grammaticization chain, we can accept the possibility that a gram might be meaningful in one context but not in another, and we can stop searching for the one meaning that inheres in all the uses and start examining the processes that lead speaker/hearers from one use to another.

Subjunctives from different sources all have in common the fact that the subordinating uses show up very late on the grammaticization paths. In fact, after the generalization of subordinating uses, the only further development for such grams is their gradual loss from the language. Our attention in this section is directed toward explaining how forms originally signaling agent-oriented modality eventually come to serve as subjunctive, and in §6.11 we discuss cases in which former tense forms become restricted to subordinate uses and thereby become subjunctives.

In the following we present historical and cross-linguistic data that suggest that agent-oriented and perhaps epistemic modalities are originally used in complement clauses with the same meaning as they have in main clauses. Of course, they would most frequently be used in complement clauses where they are semantically appropriate, but in just such cases, their meaning can be viewed as a weaker reflection of the lexical meaning of the main predicate. As such uses become more common, the semantic contribution of the subordinate modal becomes less important, until it is analyzed not so much as making a semantic contribution as being an obligatory concomitant of subordination of a certain type. From this point, the subordinate form is free to spread to other subordinate clause types, where it would not have originally been semantically appropriate. In such clauses it makes little or no semantic contribution.

6.9.1. *Subjunctives in complement clauses: The case of* should

One common syntactic context in which subjunctive verb forms are found is complement clauses, sometimes also referred to as noun clauses because the clause behaves syntactically as though it were the object of the main verb (or at times, the subject). The hypothesis we want to pursue here is that the appearance of a modal element in a complement is originally motivated by a certain harmony between the meaning of the modal and the meaning of the main verb. As evidence for this hypothesis, in this section we discuss the evolution of *should* into a subjunctive in British English, and in the next section we present data from our sample languages which show a high correspondence between main clause uses of grams and their distribution in complement clauses.

Lyons 1977: 807 uses the term "modally harmonic" for situations in which a modal verb and an adverb express the same degree of modality. Coates 1983 expands the use of the term to include all cases of a modal and another word or phrase that express the same degree of modality. The interesting point about such harmonic combinations is that the two elements seem to be in concord, rather than doubling the modal effect or setting up a situation in which one modal element is within the scope of the other. For instance, *He may possibly come* expresses the same degree of certainty as *He may come*. Expressing possibility twice neither increases nor decreases the possibility. A non-harmonic combination, however, forces an interpretation in which one modal is within the scope of the other, as in *He may certainly come*, which is best interpreted as *may* meaning permission within the scope of the epistemic *certainly*.

In her 1983 study of the English modal auxiliaries, Coates discusses the use of *should* in complement clauses and finds a variety of environments in which *should* is used, ranging from cases where *should* has its usual main clause force of weak obligation, to cases in which it can be regarded as subjunctive because it does not appear to express any meaning at all. Consider first some examples from Coates 1983: 68 in which *should* can have its full sense of weak obligation.

(96)   It is essential that on this point the churches should learn
       from each other.
(97)   I suggested that they should put (a)round each carriage door
       a piece of beading.

In these examples the main predicate expresses necessity or imposes an obligation, and it thus creates a harmonic context for the use of *should*. Coates points out that these examples may be interpreted with *should* in its weak obligation sense, or in its semantically empty quasi-subjunctive function, without changing the meaning or implications of the sentences. In Coates's data such examples are common.

However, Coates also identifies cases in which *should* in a subordinate clause does not have the explicit meaning of weak obligation, and thus is described as semantically empty, as in (98)–(99).

(98)   Is it legitimate that they should seek to further that aim by
       democratic and constitutional means?
(99)   It was inevitable that Peter Ustinov should join the exclusive
       four-star club by writing, producing, directing and starring in
       one film.

Even though *should* is not contributing positively to these sentences, the main predicates with which it occurs here have some semantic affinity to *should*. *Legitimate* refers to what is legally allowed, while *inevitable* harkens back to an earlier use of *should* to talk about what was destined to be.

A purer example of a semantically empty *should* was recorded from British television in February of 1984.

(100)   The police are expecting that the Libyans should make the
        first move.

Here an interpretation of *should* to mean weak obligation gives the wrong interpretation.

Table 6.6.   Predicates with *that*-Clauses with Subjunctive *should*
in Coates 1983: 69

Adjectives	Verbs	Nouns
Listed by Coates as harmonic with weak obligation:		
essential	*suggest*	*suggestion*
fitting		
important		
necessary		
right		
Considered by us as also possibly harmonic with weak obligation:		
appropriate	*agree*	*determination*
better	*ask*	
expedient	*decide*	
inevitable		
legitimate		
natural		
Not harmonic with weak obligation:		
distasteful	*think*	*basis*
funny		*condition*
ironical		*danger*
keen		*idea*
sad		*notion*
shameful		*wish*
understandable		
undesirable		

Table 6.6 lists the main predicates that occur with subjunctive *should* in Coates's corpus. In the first group of predicates are the ones that Coates lists as compatible with the weak obligation reading of *should*. In the second group are, in our opinion, predicates that may also be harmonic with the fuller meaning of *should,* although we have not seen all the examples in which these predicates occurred in Coates's corpus. Among the adjectives, it seems that *appropriate, better, expedient, legitimate,* and *natural* are compatible with weak obligation in the same way that *fitting* and *right* are. The remaining adjectives are evaluative: *funny, ironical, sad,* and presuppose the truth of their complement clauses.

Most of the verbs on the list describe speech acts that communicate how things ought to be and are thus harmonic with *should.* The one that does not, *think* (like *expect* in example [100]), has as its complement the speaker's opinion. The nouns are more difficult to evaluate out of context, and some of them, especially *condition,* may also be compatible with weak obligation. The observation that emerges from this table is that about one half of the predicates used with subordinate *should* have meanings harmonic with a sense of weak obligation or destiny.

From the current situation in British English, we can reconstruct three stages in the diachronic development of *should* as a subjunctive.

In Stage 1, *should* is used in contexts in which it can express weak obligation (or destiny) because it is harmonic with the main predicate, as in (96) and (97). Since it is harmonious, however, it need not be interpreted as adding any meaning to the proposition, and thus can be extended to other environments where it is not meaningful. This extension takes place gradually, via Stage 2.

In Stage 2, *should* is used with harmonic predicates, but it does not itself contribute to the meaning of the sentence, as in (98) and (99). These examples contain the adjectives *legitimate* and *inevitable* respectively, and yet are categorized as "quasi-subjunctive" by Coates. While the meaning of *should* is compatible with their meaning, *should* does not add any meaning to these sentences, as can be seen by substituting an infinitive construction in (98) or using *would* instead of *should* in (99).

The reanalysis of *should* as a concomitant of subordination rather than a modal expressing weak obligation leads to Stage 3, in which *should* comes to be used with predicates that are not only not harmonic with weak obligation, but in fact express a meaning contrary to the earlier meaning. These are the evaluative or factive predicates such as *funny* or *distasteful*. At this stage also, the mental attitude predicates, such as *think* and *expect,* come to use *should* in their complements, as in (100).[4]

Let us now look back at the history of *should* to see if there is any diachronic support for the hypothesis that the subjunctive use of *should* developed from harmonic contexts. First note that in Middle English, *should* was quite common in subordinate clauses. In one Middle English text, *Sir Gawain and the Green Knight,* there are thirty-four occurrences of *schulde,* and two thirds (twenty-two) of them are in subordinate clauses. Table 6.7 shows the complement clause uses of *should* according to the Oxford English Dictionary. Here we see that *should* occurred in past tense noun clauses complementing predi-

---

4. The harmonic use of modals in subordinate clauses is occasionally encountered in current American English. Example (i) was a quote in the Albuquerque *Journal.* When speakers were asked informally what was wrong with it and how to correct it, one suggested that *would* belonged in the main clause, as in (ii). That is, *would* is harmonic with *preferred.*

    (i)   *We preferred if a private organization would buy it.*

    (ii) *We would prefer that a private organization buy it.*

Example (iii), which was heard on network news, has a harmonic *may* in the subordinate clause that is in concord with *could* of the main clause.

    (iii) *It could be years before the FDA may approve it.*

Another example of the phenomenon of harmony is the use of the Latin Subjunctive in a clause dependent on a subjunctive or infinitive.

Table 6.7. Actual Stages of Development of *should*, According to the *OED*

	Past	Present
Harmonic:		
Complements to will, desire, command, request	1000 A.D.	1200 A.D.
Non-harmonic:		
Complements to evaluation, surprise, approval	1350 A.D.	1350 A.D.
likelihood, expectation, hope, fear	1350 A.D.	1600 A.D.

cates of will, desire, command, advice and request from 1000 AD. About two hundred years later *should* began to appear in the complements to these same types of clauses, but without the restriction that the context be in the past tense. These main predicates, which impose or seek to impose an obligation on the subordinate subject, are harmonic with the weak obligation sense of *should*.

A full century later, in the mid 1300s, *should* began to appear in the non-harmonic context of evaluative predicates, those expressing surprise or its absence, approval or disapproval, without regard for the tense of the main predicate. About the same time, *should* began to occur in the complement to predicates in the past tense expressing likelihood, expectation, hope, or fear. By 1600 this use, however, was further conventionalized, since by that date examples in non-past tense began to appear. Thus, around 1350 there seems to have been a rapid expansion of *should* into non-harmonic contexts, which affected complements to predicates of two major types: those expressing evaluation, and those expressing belief or opinion. While all these uses continue into current British English, their first appearance in the language represents a diachronic progression of precisely the type we predicted—from harmonic to non-harmonic contexts. Since both harmonic and non-harmonic uses remain in the language, the analyst of the synchronic situation faces the difficulty of determining whether *should* is meaningful in complement clauses or not. From a diachronic point of view, we can see that *should*, like other grams we have studied, retains its older meaning in certain contexts while it expresses a more generalized meaning in other contexts.

6.9.2. Subjunctive in complement clauses: Cross-linguistic study

Palmer 1986: 132 in his chapter on complement clauses notes that subordinate moods often reflect the mood of an independent clause, especially that of a semantically similar independent clause. If subjunctives have their source in the frequent use of harmonic combinations of main verb and subordinate verb, then the situation Palmer describes is precisely what we would expect: many cases where the subordinate clause uses of a subjunctive reflect its main clause uses. However, it should be noted that we are not proposing a synchronic constraint on grammars, but rather a diachronic mechanism for the creation of subjunctives that will be reflected to some extent in the synchronic distribution of subjunctives. In fact, our proposal is that from the originally harmonic uses of subjunctives, there is a generalization to non-harmonic contexts, when the subjunctive is reanalyzed as a concomitant of subordination. Given a series of diachronic changes, situations could arise in which all traces of a harmonic origin for subjunctives would be lost. For example, the main clause uses could be replaced by some newer construction, or the harmonic subordinate uses could be replaced, leaving only the non-harmonic uses. Despite these possibilities for obliterating the harmonic correspondence between main and subordinate clause uses, we expected to find some evidence for our hypothesis concerning the origin of subjunctives in our database. In fact, the evidence we found overwhelmingly supports our hypothesis.

In our database, there are twenty-five languages reported to have special finite verb forms or markers (usually particles) that occur in complement clauses. The reason there are not more such forms is that many languages use non-finite forms in complement clauses, and we did not code non-finite forms. In six of the twenty-three languages, the marker in question reportedly has no main clause uses, contributing nothing to the test of our hypothesis. In three of these cases (Abkhaz, Agau, and Krongo), the marker in question functions like a quotative; that is, it is used primarily in complements to verbs of saying or reporting. Such markers may have developed in a different way from the subjunctives being discussed here.

If we take the languages in which there are finite grammatical elements that have both main and subordinate clause uses, the hypothesis predicts that the main clause meanings will be harmonic with the subordinate clause contexts, as shown in Table 6.8.

For the purposes of the table, "order/command" stands for verbs of telling or requesting someone to do something, as well as for expres-

Table 6.8. Hypothesized Relationship between Main Clause Uses and Subordinate Clause Uses

Main Clause Use	Subordinate Clause Use: Complement to Verbs of
1. obligation	order/command
2. imperative	order/command
3. optative	want/desire
4. possibility/probability	think/believe

Table 6.9. Main and Complement Clause Uses of Subjunctives

Complements to predicates of:		
'order'	'want'	'think'
Imperative:		
Motu	Motu	
Mwera	Dakota	
Dakota		
Yagaria		
Mod. Greek		
Optative:		
Basque	Basque	
Mod. Greek	Tigre	
	Slave	
Obligation:		
Halia	Nakanai	
	Haka	
Future:		
Motu	Motu	
Touareg	Nakanai	
Dakota	Atchin	
Yagaria	Trukese	
Yessan-Mayo	Yessan-Mayo	
Epistemic:		
	Nakanai	Mod. Greek
		Trukese
		Baluchi

sions of what one should and should not do; "want/desire" stands for verbs of desire or volition; and "think/believe" for mental states in the range of belief or opinion.

In three cases, Gugu-Yalanji, Inuit, and Latin, the mood in question is very general, so that the range of complement clauses it occurs in includes both harmonic and non-harmonic contexts. These cases are discussed below. In the fifteen other languages, a strong case can be made for regarding the main clause uses as harmonic with the complement clause uses. Consider Table 6.9, which shows the main and complement clause uses for subjunctives for these fifteen languages.

Table 6.9 indicates that the co-occurrence of main and complement clause uses is not quite as neat as that hypothesized in Table 6.8. In particular, imperative and optative do not always pair up with ordering and wanting respectively. Rather, it seems that complements to ordering and wanting cannot be so easily distinguished, since they both occur with modal elements used in imperatives, optatives, and statements of weak obligation. Their similar behavior is most likely due to the similarity in their semantic implications: ordering or telling someone to do something is the overt attempt by the main clause subject to get the subordinate clause subject to act, while wanting or desiring is the covert state upon which ordering is based.

Thus a weaker version of the harmony hypothesis is supported by the cross-linguistic data, that is, the main predicates indicating ordering or wanting are harmonic with the main clause functions of imperative, optative, and weak obligation. This more general hypothesis is supported by eleven languages in our database.[5]

The other main clause function that correlates with complements to 'want' and 'order' is future, which we also view as harmonic from either of two perspectives. First, it could be that these future grams derive from modals of obligation or desire, since these are among the most common sources for futures. In that case, the harmony between main and complement clause uses would be due to an earlier meaning of the future grams. An alternative view is that the semantics of future time reference is compatible with complements to both 'want' and 'order' since the situations described in these complements will take place subsequent to reference time, if they take place at all.[6]

Counting these languages that have future complements to ordering and wanting, and Gugu-Yalanji, Latin, and Inuit, which will be discussed shortly, all nineteen of the languages in our database with a special modal element or verb form in complement clauses to verbs of ordering and wanting use that same modal element or verb form in main clauses that express imperative, optative, weak obligation, or future. Only two languages, Kanakuru and Tahitian, with special elements in complements to ordering and wanting reportedly have no main clause uses for these forms. Such support for the harmony hypothesis, albeit in weakened form, is much stronger than originally anticipated, given that there are so many ways in which the harmonic pairings can be obscured by further diachronic developments.

The other complement-taking predicate type that occurs in our data with a special verb form that also occurs in main clauses is the type in which the complement expresses the beliefs or opinions of the subject of the main clause. In each of these cases the main clause use

5. Given the secondary nature of our data, the test of this hypothesis is somewhat crude. It is certainly possible that a closer examination of the distribution of subordinating moods in these languages would support the stronger version of the harmony hypothesis.

6. One of the Yessan-Mayo forms that is followed by the future is *kap*, glossed as 'shouldn't' in the expression of a warning; we are analyzing this as negative ordering. The Greek complement-taking verbs of thinking take the particle referred to in the table when they are negated.

is an epistemic one: in Baluchi the Subjunctive can express probability in main clauses (aided by the adverb meaning 'perhaps'), in Trukese the *pwe* particle expresses future or possibility, and in Modern Greek the modal particle *na* expresses inferred certainty in main clauses. These examples are especially valuable because they demonstrate that the harmony principle is operative in the epistemic domain as well as the domain of obligation and desire.

In three languages in our sample, we found subjunctives used more generally in complement clauses, such that they appear in both harmonic and non-harmonic contexts. The Latin Subjunctive has main clause uses in optative and hortative sentences, as well as for the expression of weak obligation and epistemic possibility. Its complement clause uses under verbs of wanting, ordering, and obligation are thus harmonic with its main clause speaker-oriented uses, and its complement clause uses under verbs of doubt and fear are harmonic with its main clause epistemic uses. But the Latin Subjunctive is used in other complements as well: it occurs with verbs meaning 'hinder', 'prevent', and it also appears in indirect questions. If hindering and preventing are regarded as negative counterparts to ordering, then the use of Subjunctive under these verbs could be taken as harmonic with the use of the optative in negative clauses. However, its use in indirect questions is not explainable in any comparable way. We suggest that this use and others that develop later in Romance languages, such as the use of Subjunctive in presupposed evaluative clauses in Spanish, is the result of the reanalysis of the Subjunctive as a general concomitant of non-assertive complement clauses (see Table 6.10).

The Inuit Participial Mood is finite despite its name, since verbs in this mood take person/number inflection. This mood has a wide range of uses in complement clauses, though it is not obligatory in every case. The main clause use is speaker-oriented and, similar to the Latin case, expresses the wish or strong suggestion of the speaker. In complement clauses, it is used in indirect commands (a harmonic use), but also in the complement to mental state and activity verbs, as well as verbs of sensory perception and experience, and verbs of saying, reporting and asking. In addition, the Participial mood is possible in the complements to evaluative predicates.

The Gugu-Yalanji form -*nkV* is called a Purposive by Hershberger 1964b and by Patz 1982, as one of its most common uses is in purpose clauses. Its main clause use signals need or obligation, according to Patz 1982: 273, and it is used in the complements to verbs of ordering and wanting. It is also used with the main predicate 'be afraid to', which might be regarded as a negative version of 'want to', but its use in the complements to 'know how to' and 'be good at' does not reflect need or obligation.

Table 6.10.   Harmonic and Non-harmonic Uses of the Latin Subjunctive,
Inuit Participial Mood, and Gugu-Yalanji Purposive

Main Clause Use	Complement Clauses
Latin	
Harmonic:	
Optative	want
Hortative	order
Weak obligation	obligation
Possibility	doubt
	fear
Non-harmonic:	hinder, prevent
	indirect question
Inuit	
Harmonic:	
Optative/suggestion	order, command
Non-harmonic:	mental states and activities
	sensory perception and experience
	saying and reporting
Gugu-Yalanji	
Harmonic:	
Obligation	want, order
Non-harmonic:	be afraid to
	know how to, be good at

While the distribution of the Gugu-Yalanji Purposive is not at all
unusual, further information about Purposives in Australian languages shows that their development is not from modal auxiliaries
and does not parallel the development of *should* or other subjunctives
from modal forms. As in other Australian languages (Dixon 1980:
458), the Gugu-Yalanji Purposive suffix -*nkV* is cognate with the Dative marker in the same language and most probably is derived from
it. Thus from the nominal use of the Dative, as illustrated in (101),
the verbal use of (102) can develop (Patz 1982: 274).

(101)   yubal   wuju   mana   milkul-ku
         2.D.NOM   grass:ABS   get:IMP   soup-DAT
         'You two get some grass for the soup!'
(102)   yubal   wuju   mana,   milkul   nuka- nka
         2.D.NOM   grass:ABS   get:IMP   soup:ABS   eat-   PURP
         'You two get some grass for eating the soup!'[7]

7. According to Patz 1982: 274, "This type of grass was made into a little brush to
soak up and eat soup or honey with."

This phenomenon is not restricted to Australian languages. Haspelmath 1989 discusses a number of cases where infinitives that were derived via purpose markers come from nominal inflections such as dative and benefactive. Heine 1990 discusses similar cases in Ik and Kanuri.

In the case of purposive from a dative marker, the main clause use would derive from the subordinate clause use, and not vice versa. After the dative marker comes to be used on verbs, it can then enter into constructions parallel to the English 'is to' or 'has to' construction. (Note that the meaning of the Gugu-Yalanji constructions is similar to this one in English.) Since Gugu-Yalanji has no copula, such a construction would be formed by juxtaposing the subject and verb with purposive marking, in effect, making the purposively marked verb the main verb.

Another similar development has occurred in the evolution of Modern Greek. The modal particle *na*, with the uses shown in Table 6.9 and many more besides, derives from *hína*, a conjunction whose earlier meaning was 'in order to'. The main clause uses of this particle would also be derived from the subordinate clause uses. Thus, along with the harmony principle, which accounts for the development of subordinate clause uses for modals, we must also recognize that main clause uses can develop from subordinate clause uses.

Finally, we will say a few words about one developing complement clause use of the Spanish synthetic future, since it appears to follow the principle of making its first complement clause appearance in a harmonic context. As we have mentioned before, the Spanish synthetic Future developed from a Latin construction which used the auxiliary *habēre* 'to have' with an infinitive main verb. The construction originally signaled obligation or destiny and gradually developed into a future. More recently, the synthetic Future has developed epistemic uses; in particular it signals present probability, as illustrated in §6.6.3, with examples (64)–(65), repeated as (103)–(104).

(103) Ya   tú   comprenderás   cómo   nos   reímos.
       Now   2.s   understand:FUT   how   REFL   laugh:PERF.1.P
       'Now you probably understand how we laughed.'
(104) Tendrá   veinte   años.
       have:FUT.3.s twenty   years
       'She's probably about twenty years old.'

Since the *ir a* (go-future) construction in Spanish has been increasing in frequency, this epistemic use of the synthetic Future is becoming its primary use. It is also becoming more frequently used in the complement clause to the main predicate *no sé* 'I don't know' with an embedded question referring to present time, as in (105)–(106).

(105) No sé   si será   que ellos eran   tímidos.
       NEG know:PRES.1.S if be:FUT.3.S that 3.P   be:IMPF shy
       'I don't know if it might be that they were shy.'
(106) No sé   quien será. (Looking at a photo album)
       NEG know:PRES.1.S who be:FUT.3.S
       'I don't know who that is.'

This use is a harmonic one, since the uncertainty expressed in the present probability sense is compatible with the main predicate 'I don't know'. As the newer go-future is taking over the main clause uses of future, we might expect this older future, if it remains in the language at all, to become a subjunctive. Indeed, Urdiales 1966 reports that for the peninsular dialect of León, the synthetic Future is restricted to subordinate clauses. (See §6.10.1 for a discussion of this form in concessive clauses.)

6.10. Subjunctives in adverbial clauses

Among forms used for functions we have now established as common for subjunctives—imperative, optative, epistemic, and uses in complement clauses—three adverbial clause uses are also often cited: uses in purpose, concessive, and conditional clauses. In this section we briefly discuss the way in which the use of subjunctives in such adverbial clauses relates to the other uses of subjunctives. Conditionals were mentioned briefly in §6.7, and will not be further pursued here.

6.10.1. Concessive clauses

Special verb markers that occur in concessive clauses were reported in ten languages of our database. A concessive or adversative relation involves two clauses: the main clause is, as usual, asserted, while the concessive clause describes a situation which would ordinarily lead to a negative implication about the main clause. The function of the concessive clause is to say that in spite of the negative implication, the main clause assertion stands. English typically marks concessive clauses with the conjunction *although*, as in example (107) from König 1988: 146.

(107) Although John had no money, he went into this expensive restaurant.

König notes that not all languages have specific concessive conjunctions or verb forms. Instead, many languages have only the adversative conjunction 'but', which can be interpreted as expressing the concessive relation. The fact that the concessive relation is not always explicitly expressed, and when it is, it may be expressed by a conjunction, explains why only ten of the sample languages were reported as having verb forms marked for concessive, since in many languages conjunctions are not attached to, nor positioned with, the verb.

Most of the concessive markers we coded occur without an accompanying conjunction and without other uses, suggesting that they are functioning specifically as concessive conjunctions. However, since there may be a diachronic continuum from separate conjunction to affix, it is difficult to make a clear distinction between conjunction and verb form. It appears, nonetheless, that most of the forms for which we have lexical sources are more conjunction-like, while the forms that we consider below that also occur in other subordinate clauses are more mood-like.

Not many lexical sources were mentioned in the reference material, but the ones that were mentioned exemplify four of the five types proposed by König 1988: 152–56. Thus free-choice quantification plays a role in the Cheyenne concessive prefix, where the form *ho?* 'whenever' is one of the elements in the form *ho?ese* (Leman 1980a: 111). In Agau, one of the concessive suffixes co-occurs with the marker used in Imperfect Protases (Hetzron 1969: 26). As König (1988: 154) points out, the use of conditional markers in concessive constructions provides evidence that concessive conditionals (expressing 'even if') are a source for concessive constructions (expressing 'even though'). Another Agau construction uses the focus marker from the cleft construction with a form described as the ablative suffix to mark the verb of the concessive clause (Hetzron 1969: 20). The Abkhaz suffix *g'ə* can also be used as a conjunction meaning 'even, also', which fits either König's category of concessive markers from conditionals or that of markers signaling 'remarkable co-occurrence'. One concessive marker found in our database that does not fit any of König's source categories is the Cocama suffix *-huiri*, which is also a nominal postposition meaning 'under, below' (Faust 1971: 139).

Of primary interest to us here are the cases in which the concessive clause contains a special verb form functioning not so much as a conjunction but rather as a mood form which is used in other subjunctive contexts. The interest of these cases derives from the fact that concessive clauses contain factual statements (see [107] above), while subjunctive contexts are usually regarded as containing non-factual or irrealis statements. Thus concessives stand as evidence that the indicative/subjunctive distinction is not about reality and irreality, as some would claim (see §6.12), but rather about assertion and lack of assertion.

In our database a subjunctive occurs in concessive clauses in Classical Latin with the Present Subjunctive, and in Modern Greek with the modal particles *na* and *as*. These three grams have, among others, epistemic and optative uses in addition to their concessive use. The Abkhaz suffix *nda(z)* has optative uses in addition to its concessive use, and the Jivaro suffix *-ta* may present a parallel case.

Outside our sample we find a possible link between concessive and epistemic functions. The Spanish synthetic future, which is commonly used for present probability, as illustrated above at the end of §6.9, can also be used in present concessive clauses. Gili y Gaya (1964: 165–66) argues that the concessive use derives directly from the probability use in interactional contexts in which the speaker wants to concede to the opinion of the addressee. He gives (108) as an example.

(108) —Fulano es un sabio.
       —Lo será; sin embargo, se ha equivocado algunas veces.
       'Fulano is a wise man.' 'He may be (FUT); nevertheless, he has been mistaken at times.'

The probability use indicates that the speaker has reservations about the truth of the proposition, but the concessive use expresses reservations about unconditionally accepting the ordinary consequences of the proposition. In other words, the epistemicity applies to the connection between the two propositions, rather than to the proposition which contains the epistemic marker. Such a change appears to be a further instance of the broadening of scope that is so characteristic of grammaticization.

Another possible example of the development from epistemic to concessive is English *may*, whose concessive sense, as in the translation of (108) above, seems closely related to its epistemic sense.

Are there other paths of development for subjunctives in concessive clauses? In our data all concessives that have other uses have optative as a use. We also note that English *may* has (or had) an optative use as well, but the Spanish synthetic future does not. The frequent co-occurrence of optative and concessive suggests that we should consider whether an optative use might give rise to a concessive use or vice versa. However, in the absence of any documented case of a change from optative to concessive, or vice versa, we are leaving this possibility uninvestigated. It should be observed that it is also plausible to suppose that optatives and concessives frequently derive from the same sources, in particular modals with meanings such as 'ability' or 'permission' as, for example, English *may*, which could account for one form having these two uses.

Another possible source for subjunctives in concessive clauses is the protasis of a conditional sentence. König argues that concessive conditional sentences, expressing the meaning 'even if', can by inference evolve into concessive sentences. The concessive conditional relates a series of protases to the apodosis (König 1988: 147).

(109)   *Whether or not he finds a job, he is getting married.*
        Even if I try very hard, I won't manage.

Due to the hearer's tendency to infer as much as possible from the
speaker's utterance, such conditional protases tend to evolve into factual concessives, where, for example, 'even if' is taken to mean 'even
though' (König 1988: 159–60).

In our database, only the Latin Present Subjunctive occurs in both
concessive clauses and the protasis of reality conditions (presumably
counterfactual conditions would not give rise to concessive conditionals). In addition, as we have already mentioned, the Agau concessive
form uses a protasis marker. Thus there is some evidence in our database for this path of development for concessives, but the whole issue
of the spread of subjunctives to concessive clauses is an area where
more research is required.

6.10.2. Purpose clauses

Another commonly described subordinate clause type is the purpose
clause, traditionally known as the "final clause". We coded all the
grams associated with verbs that marked purpose clauses, as long as
we were reasonably sure that they were not non-finite forms. In languages without person/number inflection it is difficult to distinguish
a finite and a non-finite form, so our coded forms may include some
non-finite forms. Here, as in the case of concessives, we have some
grams that are more conjunction-like on the one hand, and grams
that would be considered mood forms on the other. Thus in Yagaria,
the purpose clause has the suffix *ge'* as the last suffix on the verb, and
this suffix has no reported uses other than to mark purpose clauses.
It thus resembles a conjunction. The purpose clause also contains
the Intentional Future form, which is positioned close to the stem
and is also used to express imperative, hortative, and intention (Renck
1975: 131).

(110)   dote'na eli-na   folo'ei-s- i - e - ge'   hoya no'- el - i - e
        food   take.3s appear.FUT.3.S.IND.PURP work PROG.make.3s.IND
        'He is working in order to find food.'

In eleven languages we found purpose grams that had no other
uses reported; most of these are probably conjunctions specific to the
purpose construction. Their lesser degree of grammaticization is evident in their size—seven of the eleven are polysyllabic, while only two
of the fifteen forms with multiple uses are polysyllabic. Unfortunately,
our material contained no information about the lexical sources of
these grams.

Table 6.11. Purpose Markers with Other Uses

Language	Form No.	Agent-oriented	Future	Purpose	Complement	Speaker-oriented
01 Inuit	16		x	x		
02 Basque	14			x	want order	optative
04 Kanakuru	33			x	want	
06 Tuareg	15	intention	x	x	want order	
08 Tigre	22	intention		x	want	imperative
15 Gugada	08	desire/intention		x		
16 Gugu-Yalanji	21	obligation		x	want order	
27 Atchin	03		x	x	want	imperative
32 Nakanai	13	obligation	x	x	want	
39 Abkhaz	59	intention	x	x		
40 Guaymí	07	obligation		x		
47 Latin	11			x	want order	optative hortative
50 Mod. Greek	14	intention		x	order	imperative optative
52 Yagaria	23	intention	x	x	order	imperative
60 Yessan-Mayo	14		x	x	want	
68 Slave	08			x	want	optative
90 Dakota	03	willingness obligation	x	x	want	imperative

Note. Two languages, Inuit and Agau, have purpose markers that can also function as causal connectives.

In the seventeen other languages with special verb forms used in purpose clauses, other uses of these same forms were reported, and, as shown in Table 6.11, these other uses are remarkably similar across languages. Furthermore, they are all uses that we have discussed in connection with the development of agent-oriented modality into mood. Table 6.11 is arranged to reflect our hypothesis about the diachronic progression from one use to another. As before, we hypothesize that agent-oriented uses reflect the earliest meanings of modal grams, and that subordinate and speaker-oriented uses develop from these. As we argue in chapter 7, the use of future grams to signal prediction occurs before such grams find their way into subordinate clauses or speaker-oriented contexts. Thus we propose that agent-oriented and future uses are precursors to the purpose, complement clause, and speaker-oriented uses, and that the latter three uses develop in parallel.

Intention is the most commonly mentioned agent-oriented use that gives rise to purposive forms. As we point out in chapter 7 and also in Bybee and Pagliuca 1987, intention is a generalized agent-oriented sense that can develop out of desire, obligation, or movement toward a goal. While intention can develop into prediction, which is the criterial use for futures, and from there come to be used for purpose clauses, it is apparently not necessary for future to serve as an intermediate step between intention and purpose. Rather, in Tigre the intention marker appears to move into purpose clauses without first being used for future. In Tigre the gram in question (the Jussive) is highly grammaticized, suggesting that it does not appear in purpose clauses with its full meaning of intention, but rather that a purpose clause presents a harmonic context for this element.

The most striking pattern in Table 6.11 is the strong tendency for the verbal gram used in purpose clauses to also be used to mark the complement clause of main verbs expressing wanting and ordering.[8] At least two avenues of explanation for this correspondence present themselves. First, the complements to 'want' and 'order' could be viewed as a slight extension of the purpose relation, since these complements, like the purpose clause, mention a goal to be reached. In fact, Haspelmath 1989 presents evidence that both finite and nonfinite purposive markers can generalize to infinitives and general subordination markers respectively. Second, both the agent-oriented meaning of intention and the future meaning are harmonic with complements to 'want' and 'order' and with purpose clauses. Both types of clauses are set in the future with regard to the temporal reference point of the main clause, and both mention, as we said just above, a goal or intention. Under the first proposal, the development of the complement marker would depend on the prior development of the purpose marker, while under the second proposal the two developments are independent. More detailed data than that which we have at our disposal would be necessary to further clarify the mechanisms underlying this correspondence.

6.11. Indicative sources for subjunctives

Subjunctives may also arise from indicative tense forms which have no modal value, such as present, past imperfective, or past anterior (pluperfect). Examples also exist of futures becoming present subjunctives. How do such cases arise? How do grams which previously had no modal meaning take on a mood function? We will argue in this section that when new tense and aspect grams arise, they do so primarily in main asserted clauses and only gradually take over the functions of the previously existing tense and aspect grams. Since

8. We expect that this correlation would be even stronger if infinitives had been included.

non-assertive subordinate clauses are not used for the expression of focus or topic (Hooper and Thompson 1973), they tend to be conservative grammatically, retaining older syntax and morphology (Givón 1979a: 85). Thus a consequence of the gradual spread of new grams to more environments is that some subordinate clause environments will not be affected immediately, and here the older grams will continue to be used—trapped, so to speak, in these conservative environments. Since in these contexts the surrounding semantic material has modal content, the old indicative forms themselves come to be associated with modality.

A good example of the development of a present subjunctive from a present indicative and a conditional from a past imperfect indicative is found in Armenian.[9] Classical Armenian had a synthetic present tense, a past imperfective, and a perfective, as well as subjunctive forms (Thomson 1975). In the centuries between the Classical and the Modern periods, a periphrastic progressive arose which consists of a non-finite main verb (with suffix -um) and forms of the verb 'to be'. This periphrasis exists in both the present and past tenses, and in the present it has apparently extended its usage in the way discussed in chapter 5, beginning as a progressive and gradually taking on habitual functions as well. The forms of the older present indicative still exist, but they are not used with indicative function. Rather, these 'simple verb forms' show up in the following contexts: (a) in future formations, where they occur with a prefix kʰə or a particle pʰitʰi; (b) in purpose clauses; (c) in protases of reality conditions; (d) with future time reference following the conjunction 'until'; (e) in the complement to 'to be necessary'; and (f) in main clauses in a function described as 'present optative' (Fairbanks and Stevick 1958).

This set of environments seems a characteristic enough distribution for a subjunctive form, yet how this distribution would arise from indicative forms is not clear until we consider the circumstances surrounding the development of a new progressive. First, the future grams use the old simple present probably because the new progressive was developing at about the same time as these futures developed, and combining future with progressive would give future progressive meaning. Second, the subordinate clause uses—purpose, protasis, complement to 'be necessary', and adverbial temporal clause—all present situations viewed, not as in progress even at some future time, but more as bounded entities, as the English examples (111)–(113) illustrate.

9. We are grateful to Martin Haspelmath for bringing to our attention the Armenian and Arabic examples discussed in this section.

(111)   He is saving his money so that he can buy a car.
        *He is saving his money so that he can be buying a car.
(112)   If I find it, I'll give it to you.
        *If I am finding it, I'll give it to you.
(113)   Please wait here until he comes back.
        *Please wait here until he is coming back.

Since a progressive sense is usually inappropriate in clauses fulfilling
these functions, the Modern Armenian Progressive cannot move into
these contexts until it has generalized in meaning to signal only present tense. Of course, it has apparently now reached this stage, but
only recently, so it will take some additional time before it makes its
way into these subordinate contexts. (Another candidate for these
subordinate contexts would be future, but again, it appears that these
futures are too recently formed to be used in these contexts.)

Another interesting development for the Armenian simple present
forms is that they no longer can be used in main clauses for simple
assertions of present tense. Rather, in main clauses a simple present
expresses weak obligation, 'I am to' or 'I should' (Fairbanks and Stevick 1958: 118, 150), as in (114) and (115), or hortative, as in (116).

(114)   pᶜaymanóv   vor   ušadrutyámb   varèk   mekenèn
        condition   that   carefully   drive.2s   car
        'On condition that you drive the car carefully.'
(115)   inč   lezvòv   gərèm   hascèn
        what   language   write.1s   address
        'In what language should I write the address?'
(116)   gənank   mez   mòtᶜ
        go.PRES.1.P   POSS.1.P   house
        'Let's go to my place.'

Such a main clause use can only develop as a result of the association
of the simple present forms with subordinate clause functions of obligation and purpose. As we saw in our discussion of complement
clauses and purpose clauses, it is possible for a form, such as the
Gugu-Yalanji Purposive, to originate in subordinate clauses (as a nominalized form marked with a suffix related to the dative marker),
but to be used in main clauses with a sense of obligation. In these
instances, it is almost as if a main clause verb of obligation goes un-
expressed.

A parallel development seems to have occurred with the Classical Armenian Imperfect, although no main clause uses of this form
are reported in Modern Armenian. A new periphrastic form, the Past
Progressive, consists of the main verb with the suffix -um and the
past forms of the verb 'to be'. This newer formation has taken over

both the past progressive and past habitual functions which were formerly signaled by the Imperfect and contrasts, like the old Imperfect did, with the Preterite. In Classical Armenian the Imperfect was used in both clauses of hypothetical and counterfactual conditionals (Thomson 1975: 106), and the Imperfect remains in the protases of such conditionals in Modern Armenian (Fairbanks and Stevick 1958: 211). The reason for this is the same as that given above for the old Simple Present remaining in protases: progressive and habitual meaning are not usually intended in protases. Note that if a newer grammaticization from a progressive meaning were put into a protasis, the context would tend to highlight its fullest meaning, thus emphasizing the progressive sense.

Not surprisingly, the old Imperfect is used with the future prefix *k'ə* to form what is termed the Past Future by Fairbanks and Stevick (1958: 132). This form, which is like English *would* in both form and function, is used in the apodoses of hypothetical and counterfactual conditionals and in phrases such as 'I would like . . .'.

In Armenian, then, the development of a progressive into an imperfective in both the present and the past has left the older Present and Imperfect forms stranded in primarily subordinate contexts, yielding new subjunctive and conditional forms. A similar development is under way in some varieties of Arabic.

The Classical Arabic Imperfect was a general present tense that was also used for future time reference, as Classical Arabic lacked an explicit future marker. Some colloquial dialects of Arabic have developed progressive grams and future grams that are gradually restricting the contexts in which the old Imperfect can be used. For instance, in Iraqi Arabic (Erwin 1963: 335ff.), the progressive with the prefix *da* is used for ongoing situations, including some stative ones, such as may be described by mental process verbs, and also some recurrent habitual situations. The Imperfect is used for general habitual situations and also in purpose clauses and temporal clauses introduced by 'before'.

In Cairene Arabic the simple Imperfect is much more restricted in main clauses. It is no longer used for any indicative present tense functions. The prefix *bi-* is used on the Imperfect verb form for present progressive, habitual, and generic statements. Now in main clauses the simple Imperfect (like the Armenian simple Present) is used for exhortations ('Let's go') or for statements of weak obligation ('he is to let them know'). In subordinate clauses, the use of the Imperfect is widespread: it is used in the complements to predicates meaning 'be able to', 'know how to', 'like to', 'let', 'continue to', and 'begin to'; it is used in purpose clauses following verbs of motion; it is used after many temporal conjunctions (Mitchell 1956: 83–85). Thus the new construction with the prefix *bi-* has all the characteristics of a present indicative, while the older simple Imperfect has all the characteristics of a present subjunctive.

The case of Cairene Arabic appears then to be parallel to the Armenian case: as a new present progressive generalizes to become a present, the old present that is being replaced loses its main clause functions and is gradually restricted to subordinate clauses of certain types—in particular those in which a progressive or habitual aspect is not appropriate. In both cases, new non-assertive main clause functions develop, presumably out of the subordinate clause uses.

Another change of indicative to subjunctive, studied in progress by Klein-Andreu 1990, supports the hypothesis that competition between newer and older grams can lead to the development of subjunctive forms. Klein-Andreu discusses the change of the Latin Pluperfect Indicative into the Spanish Imperfect Subjunctive in *-ra*. She argues that two semantic changes take place in this process: a temporal change, from past-before-past to simple past; and a modality change, from assertive to non-assertive. Klein-Andreu attributes these changes to the development of the periphrastic Perfects in Spanish. The newer past anterior competed with and took over the main clause functions of past anterior, leaving the old Pluperfect in embedded non-asserted clauses, such as the protasis of conditional sentences.

Klein-Andreu's study shows that in a text written in the transition period in the 1300s, the new periphrastic past anterior tends to be used most often in contexts with high 'focus', while the old Pluperfect tends to be relegated to clauses with lower focus.[10] Klein-Andreu identifies clauses of high focus as those which describe transitive events, have animate subjects and objects, and are first mentioned in sequences of events. Low focus is associated with negation, description of states, and occurrence in relative clauses. The text count shows that even though the old Pluperfect is at this period still more frequent than the new periphrasis (occurring about three times more often), it has a higher than average occurrence in low focus environments, while the periphrastic construction has a higher than average occurrence in high focus environments. This tendency apparently persisted and grew stronger as the periphrastic past anterior continued to develop. The result was that the old Pluperfect was eventually restricted to subordinate clauses and thus became a past subjunctive.

Competing future forms might also be the source of some subjunctives. As we mentioned before, the Spanish synthetic future is

10. See also Hyman and Watters 1984 on the tendency in African languages for new tense/aspect grammaticizations to be associated with focus constructions.

gradually being replaced in Modern Spanish by a periphrastic future formed with the verb and preposition *ir a* 'to go to'. As Moreno de Alba 1977 reports for Mexican Spanish, the 'modal' functions are much more common with the synthetic future than with the periphrastic one. That is, intention and prediction are most commonly expressed by the periphrastic future, while the synthetic one is more common in generic statements, concessives, and suppositions. We have already illustrated the concessive use and the use in suppositions, and we have pointed out that the supposition or probability use leads to a use in subordinate clauses, especially complements to phrases such as *no sé*. In at least one Iberian dialect, that of León, the synthetic future is reportedly used only in subordinate clauses (Urdiales 1966). It is easy to see, then, that a future gram could take on subjunctive uses, especially as a new future develops in main clauses.

Here it is important to note that the reason the old future resides in subordinate clauses is that the new future can only develop in main clauses. The crucial stage in the development of future meaning is the expression of prediction, and prediction occurs necessarily in an asserted clause. Recall also that one of the reasons new periphrases grammaticize is that they express in a stronger fashion the meaning that has eroded and weakened in the older gram. Such stronger senses are the ones most favored in main asserted clauses.

We have seen, then, the changes in (117) of indicative to subjunctive due to the development of new indicative forms.

(117) present indicative → present subjunctive
       past imperfective   → conditional
       past anterior   → past subjunctive
       future   → present subjunctive

In each case the conditions governing the spread of the newer grams is somewhat different but the general principle is the same: the new grammaticization has fuller semantic content and is more appropriate for asserted, focused clauses and is used more for the central functions of the particular gram-type, namely, prediction for future, progressive and habitual for present. Thus out-of-focus and more marginal uses (generic statements for present, probability for future, protases for past anterior) can retain the older gram long after the new gram has taken over the central, focused functions.

If we compare subjunctives that have developed from modal elements to those that develop from indicatives, we again see a remarkable convergence. Many of the same uses are covered by subjunctives from these different sources: complement clauses (especially non-assertive ones), purpose clauses, optative, imperative and hortative, conditional protases, and so on. This convergence suggests a universal gram-type for subjunctive as we have proposed for the various tense and aspect grams. Yet here the cross-linguistic similarity among grams is less focused; it is more difficult to identify the semantic content of the gram-type. There seems to be a greater divergence among the uses; the uses of subjunctives have clearer diachronic interconnections than synchronic ones. There are two reasons for this: first, subjunctive uses occur near the end of grammaticization paths; whether they are from indicatives or from modal elements, their restriction to subordinate clauses comes very late in their development. A related point is that they are more semantically reduced, they contribute less to the semantics of the clause, and they are used more because they are strongly associated with the syntactic configuration than because of the semantic contribution they make. Second, subjunctives do not uniformly cover the same set of uses across languages because other devices exist to fulfill some of the same functions: complement clauses, purpose clauses, and concessives may use infinitives or participles. Thus other constructions may interfere with the coherent distribution of subjunctives. In sum, their highly eroded meaning and their non-contiguous distribution in a language makes subjunctives differ more cross-linguistically and makes them the subject of much debate and controversy.

6.12. Irrealis

Precisely because of the difficulty in analyzing the meaning and functions of subjunctive and related modalities, alternate ways of categorizing mood distinctions arise. A recent development (not found in our material until 1970) is the postulation of a distinction between 'realis' and 'irrealis'.[11] This distinction is defined as distinguishing between actual and non-actual events (Chung and Timberlake 1985: 241), or as indicating 'unreal time' (Bickerton 1975). This terminology is often used in the description of creole languages (Bickerton 1975; Givón 1982), Australian languages (Capell and Hinch 1970; Dixon 1980), and the languages of New Guinea (Foley 1986; Roberts 1990). We do not know who originally proposed this terminology nor what the motivation was for using realis/irrealis rather than the more traditional mood terms applied to European languages. However, examination of the earliest use in our corpus, in a description of Maung by Capell and Hinch 1970, helps us to see what kind of language situation the distinction is meant to describe.

In Capell and Hinch's analysis of the Maung verb system, the forms that are labeled irrealis have uses that we would consider modal—the

11. The term 'irrealis' has also been found as early as 1938 in description of Blackfoot by C. C. Uhlenbeck (1938: 169–71).

expression of possibility, hypothetical, and imperative, but these same forms are used in the present and past indicative sense with the negative particle. In other words, the normal way of negating indicative statements uses the same forms that in the affirmative are clearly non-indicative in their force. If one sits and thinks about what negative, possibility, hypothetical, and imperative have in common, one could well come up with the idea that they all describe situations that are unreal or non-actual in some sense. One might then proceed, as Capell and Hinch have done, to divide the verbal inflections of Maung into two major categories—realis and irrealis. This decision would be supported by some formal similarity between the suffixes for present and past irrealis (that is, the verb forms used in the negative present and negative past).

Capell and Hinch 1970: 67 use the realis/irrealis distinction as the highest level distinction in their inflectional categorization.

(118)
REALIS
{
PRESENT: Indicative, Present, Future
IMPERATIVE: Negative only
PAST: Past simple or complete, and Imperfect
}

IRREALIS
{
PRESENT: Potential, Indicative Negative Present and Future
PAST: Indicative Negative, Hypothetical (protasis), Imperative Positive
}

A problem with using realis/irrealis at this level to divide the whole system is that the negative and affirmative are split in a way that does not accord with the usual definitions of realis. The negative imperative is considered realis and the affirmative imperative is considered irrealis, while if the definition were applied as usual, they would both be considered irrealis. Note also that the future affirmative is classified as realis here, while in some other systems it figures as irrealis. These facts suggest that realis/irrealis is not really explaining why the same forms are used for modality-related functions and for negation. Another hypothesis is available: since negative contexts are among those that tend to be conservative (Givón 1979a), the 'irrealis' forms could be used in both modal and negative contexts for the same diachronic reason, namely that they are older forms whose range of use has been restricted by the development of new forms.

The misalignment between irrealis as defined and the actual distribution of forms in languages occurs quite often. Consider Foley's statement (1986: 158) in his book on Papuan languages: "Status expresses the actuality of the event, whether it has been realized or not. The basic distinction here is a binary one, realis versus irrealis, but few languages express it in just this way." That is, realis/irrealis is rarely realized in a language as a binary morphological distinction. It appears to be more common to have multiple markers in both domains. Thus in Givón's 1982 discussion of tense, aspect, and modality in five languages—Hawaiian Creole, Early Biblical Hebrew, Bemba, Chuave, and Krio—he finds that none of these languages has a single marker for irrealis. And, we might add, in the GRAMCATS survey of seventy-six languages we did not find any in which a single gram could adequately be described as marking off all the irrealis territory.

Even where there is a binary distinction, as might be the case in Maung, not all members of the realis or irrealis categories fit the proposed definitions. Some authors wish to get around this problem by interpreting irrealis differently in each language. Thus Chung and Timberlake (1985: 241) say, "It is also clear, however, that languages differ significantly as to which events are evaluated as actual (and expressed morphologically by the realis mood) vs. non-actual (and expressed by the irrealis mood)." For instance, Roberts 1990: 399 confronts the problem of Bargam (a Papuan language), which treats the past habitual as irrealis. Roberts suggests that the interpretation of the notion 'real world' differs across languages. We suggest that if this binary distinction differs so much across languages that a past aspect, which is usually considered one of the prototypical case of realis (Foley 1986: 158f.), can be irrealis in some languages, this binary distinction is not cross-linguistically valid.

Compare realis/irrealis to perfective/imperfective, which is a distinction drawn on approximately the same level. Dahl 1985 and our own survey reported in chapter 3 have shown that perfective is a coherent category with a cross-linguistically valid definition, which usually has a single marker in languages where it occurs. Imperfective may be subdivided into progressive and habitual, but each of these is also a coherent category. One never finds statements to the effect that perfective/imperfective represents the bounded/non-bounded distinction, but languages differ as to what they consider bounded. One does find differences in the application of perfective and imperfective in languages, such as the difference between Slavic perfectives and inflectional perfectives. Such differences correspond, as we have shown in Bybee and Dahl 1989 and in chapter 3 above, to differences in sources for grammaticization. But languages do not whimsically decide, for instance, that habitual is going to be perfective.

Why would a past habitual have 'irrealis' marking? Chung and Timberlake 1985: 221 also try to explain such a case, citing English *would* in past habitual sentences. Their explanation is that since habitual sub-events are indefinite both in number and in time, they can be viewed as extending over possible worlds. But if we look at the history of English, we find that *would* in past habituals and 'irrealis' *would* are entirely independent developments. The past tense of *willan* 'to want' in Old English was already used for past habitual in texts such as *Beowulf* (see chap. 5), centuries before the future uses of *will* or the conditional uses of *would* developed. Taking these two unrelated uses of *would* and trying to construct some common semantics does not improve our understanding of linguistic categories.

What does improve our understanding of grammatical categories is a knowledge of the mechanisms that bring them into existence and that shape their subsequent evolution. In this sense, mood categories are extremely difficult and extremely interesting, as they represent long chains of diachronic developments, and they interact with semantic, syntactic, and discourse parameters. Imposing binary distinctions and looking for the one semantic element that all uses have in common will not always yield useful results.

A final point we would like to make is about the semantic content of the realis/irrealis distinction. When grams are described in terms of realis/irrealis, the claim is made that these grams are categorizing events as actual or non-actual, as occurring or not in the real world, as though the speaker's choice of a mood depends on the truth value of the proposition. Considerable evidence suggests that it is not the domain of truth or fact that is the relevant domain for mood, but rather the domain of assertion and non-assertion that is relevant (Hooper 1975; Klein 1975). That is, mood does not index the truth value of a proposition in any abstract sense, but rather tells us the extent to which the speaker is willing to ASSERT the truth of a proposition. Inherent in the function of epistemic modality is the expression of the degree of commitment that the speaker is willing to admit concerning truth of the proposition. Speaker-oriented moods are also not about truth, but rather about the function of the utterance in the context: an imperative has a different function from an assertion and is thus often marked differently. Even subjunctives are not pointing to actual versus non-actual events. Concessives express true propositions and yet are often in the subjunctive because their propositions are not being asserted. Main predicates that take presupposed complements, that is, evaluative predicates, take subjunctive complements in Spanish, as in (119) and in British English can take *should,* as in (120).

(119)   Lo   siento   que   esté   enferma.
        PRO   regret.1s that   be.SUBJ.3s   ill.FEM
        'I'm sorry that she is ill.'

(120)   It's a shame that she should be so late.

Both of these complements express propositions that are true in the real world at the moment and yet have subjunctive markers. Finally, we can cite the fact from Klein-Andreu 1990 discussed above, that a Pluperfect Indicative which commonly occurred in non-asserted or backgrounded clauses was reinterpreted as a subjunctive. We conclude, then, that mood is not about truth values, but about the speaker's choice between assertion and contrasting functions.

6.13. Conclusion

One way to summarize this chapter is to present the cumulative paths of development that we have presented evidence for along the way (figs. 6.3–6.5). The paths for modalities are separated here according

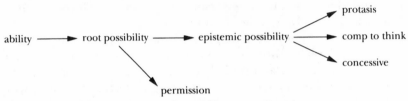

Fig. 6.3. The path of development from ability.

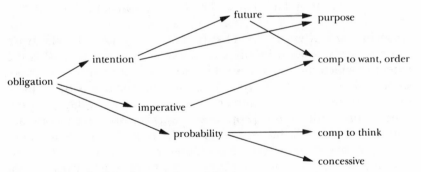

Fig. 6.4. The path of development from obligation.

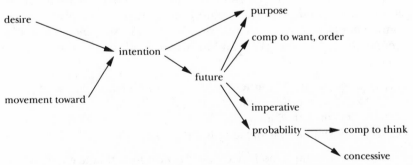

Fig. 6.5. The path of development from desire and movement toward.

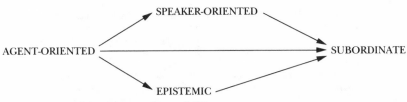

Fig. 6.6. Paths of development for modalities.

to agent-oriented source in order to simplify the diagram, but it can be seen that there is considerable convergence in the late stages of development, especially in the subordinating uses.

Figure 6.6 summarizes these paths in terms of the types of modality represented at different stages. One interesting point here is that all three types of modality can feed into subordinate clauses, if the subordinate clause type is harmonic with their meaning in other uses. As we pointed out before, this means that a single gram can develop multiple subordinate clause uses by separate paths. Thus all the uses of a subjunctive may not be contiguous on a single path, and may not be closely related semantically.

At the beginning of this chapter we mentioned the findings reported in Bybee 1985 that agent-oriented modalities tend to have non-bound, periphrastic expression while the other modality types tend to have bound expression. We are now prepared to test this correlation on our current database. Table 6.12 shows the percentage of grams written bound and non-bound for the various modal senses examined in this chapter.

The table shows that ability grams are the least likely to be bound, while imperatives are the most likely to be bound. Probability and subjunctive grams have about the same likelihood of being bound—approximately a fifty-fifty chance. The grammaticization path shown in Figure 6.6 would predict that subjunctives would be more grammaticized and thus more bound than imperatives, but the percentages in Table 6.12 show that imperatives are more likely to be bound.

Table 6.13 shows the percentages for the modalities grouped together so that agent-oriented modalities may be contrasted with the other three types.

This table shows a strong correlation between expression type and the type of modality, as predicted. This correlation supports the hypothesis that agent-oriented modalities generally are at early stages of grammaticization, while the other modalities are generally at later stages.

Finally, we can compare the extent to which the most grammaticized modal grams are affixal with the extent to which past and perfective grams are affixal. In §3.10, Table 3.9, we saw that in our

Table 6.12.   Non-bound and Bound Grams by Modalities

Modality	Non-bound	Bound
Agent-oriented:		
Ability, root possibility, permission	84% (42)	16% (8)
Obligation	74% (37)	26% (13)
Epistemic:		
Possibility	59% (16)	41% (11)
Probability	47% (9)	53% (10)
Speaker-oriented:		
Imperative	32% (44)	68% (93)
Subordinate:		
Subjunctive	45% (10)	55% (12)

Table 6.13.   Percentages of Agent-oriented and Other
Modalities Written Bound or Non-bound

Modality Type	Non-bound	Bound
Agent-oriented	79%	21%
Other modalities	36%	64%

database, 78% of perfective grams were written bound, and 81% of past grams. Thus there seems to be a much greater tendency for these tense/aspect grams to be affixal than the epistemic and subordinating modal grams we have considered here. As Bybee 1985 pointed out, the tendency of a gram to affix to a stem is partly governed by the semantic relevance of that gram to the stem. Since the modalities with propositional scope are not directly relevant to the verb stem, but rather modify the whole proposition, they have a lesser tendency to become affixed to the verb. (See also Bybee, Pagliuca, and Perkins 1990.)

CHAPTER SEVEN

Future

The focus of this chapter is on grams which mark future, a topic which we have addressed in earlier publications (Bybee and Pagliuca 1987; Bybee, Pagliuca, and Perkins 1991). Here we refine our earlier analyses and extend their scope to include all the relevant forms in the now-complete database.

In the database are 156 forms which have at least one use as a future; future uses are mentioned for grams in seventy languages, making future the most widely distributed meaning in the languages of the sample.

As the numbers suggest, it is not uncommon for a language to have more than one gram which has future as a use. In fact, forty-nine of the seventy languages have two or more futures, and of these, sixteen have three, three have four, four have five, and three have six such forms. As we have argued here and elsewhere (Bybee and Pagliuca 1985, 1987; Bybee, Pagliuca, and Perkins 1991), such apparent duplication may be viewed as a consequence of the independent development of grams from distinct sources and from similar sources at different periods, which produces layers of relatively old markers underlying layers of more recently evolved ones. As we shall see, the continued viability of multiple forms in a given language is insured by differences in the range of uses to which each may be put.

Range-of-use differences are attributable to one or more of the following: specialization of future uses; the presence of retained earlier non-future uses; and the presence of late-developing non-future uses. Differences in future uses exist when one gram is specialized (e.g. as an immediate future) and the other is not, or when one is specialized in one way, a second in another way, a third in yet another, and so on. Retained uses are non-future uses which are remnants of earlier stages along the developmental pathways leading to future. Since such uses are source-specific, with each displayed only by futures from a particular source, two grams may have similar uses as futures but differ in non-future uses by virtue of having distinct retained uses. Similarly, because late-developing uses, such as subordinate clause uses, are characteristic of the most mature future grams and are not displayed by younger future grams, two grams may have similar future uses but differ in late-developing non-future uses. Theoretically, so long as any two future grams within a language differ in any of these ways—so long as any distinct uses are viable—the forms are in effect removed from being in direct competition.

We have argued in earlier publications that, cross-linguistically, futures evolve from a fairly restricted range of lexical sources—from constructions involving movement verbs, from markers of obligation, desire, and ability, and from temporal adverbs. In addition to futures from these sources, which we here refer to as **primary futures**, future may arise as one use of a form whose principal function is the marking of present tense or perfective or imperfective aspect; we refer to such forms as **aspectual futures**.

7.1. Definitions

7.1.1. Future

Our working definitions of the meaning labels relevant to pathways to future are in part derived from and in part designed to be consistent with the recent literature on futures in particular languages and language families and cross-linguistically, and on more wide-ranging studies of tense and modality. These include Abraham 1989; Bybee and Pagliuca 1985, 1987; Bybee, Pagliuca, and Perkins 1991; Comrie 1985b; Fleischman 1982a; Heine, Claudi, and Hünnemeyer 1991a; Palmer 1986; and Ultan 1978.

We regard the focal use of future as equivalent to a prediction on the part of the speaker that the situation in the proposition, which refers to an event taking place after the moment of speech, will hold (Bybee and Pagliuca 1987). Each of the following English sentences refers to a future event, and though the nuances may vary, in each one the speaker is making a prediction about an event which is yet to occur.

(1)   We shall no doubt live to see stranger things.
(2)   I think the bulk of this year's students will go into industry.
(3)   At this rate of development, Paris is going to look like London and London like New York.

7.1.2. Immediate future

A future gram restricted to referring to events which are imminent or about to occur is an immediate future. The database contains thirty-nine grams which have immediate future as a use, making immediate futures the most commonly occurring type of future gram after simple futures. Thirty of these are primary futures; the other nine are aspectual futures. While in many cases the designation of 'immediate future' may indeed mark a temporal distinction, we suspect that in some cases other modal or aspectual nuances that are difficult to describe may be involved. A distinction between immediate and simple future—manifested by the presence of a separate primary future gram for each—is made in sixteen languages of the sample: Inuit, Basque, Margi, Motu, Halia, Trukese, Yagaria, Bongu, Yessan-Mayo, Slave, Krongo, Mwera, Chepang, Haka, Cantonese, and Tok Pisin. In another six languages—Tigre, Alyawarra, Abkhaz, Baining, Tem, and Engenni—future uses of aspectual forms (aspectual futures) contrast with the uses of primary futures along similar lines.

For example, Margi has two futures: one used for events which are imminent or about to take place in the near future, the other for non-imminent events. Each is formed with the present forms of two auxiliary verbs: *ləgərì* (from a main verb meaning 'approach, come near to') for immediate future, and *rà* (from a main verb meaning 'go') for simple future (Hoffman 1963: 212–17, 222). Margi also has an aspectual future—in this case a present which can have a future reading in certain contexts (Hoffman 1963: 190–196).

In Abkhaz and Baining, simple primary futures are supplemented by immediate future readings of perfectives. The simple future of Baining is a prefix *i-*, illustrated in (4) in the form used for first and second person, but immediate future may be expressed by the perfective particle *sa* (cf. the double gloss in [5]); *sa* also has imperative as a third use (Rascher 1904: 62ff.).

(4) ik   ğoa   tes
     FUT:1/2   1.s   eat
     'I will eat.'

(5) sa   ğoa   tes
     PERF/IMM FUT 1.s   eat
     'I have eaten'/'I will eat immediately.'

Chepang, too, distinguishes immediate future and simple future, but here the situation is considerably more complicated (Caughley 1982: 92, 105, 109). Simple future may be expressed by suffixing *-ca²* to the main verb, as in (6), immediate future by *-khe²*, as in (7) and (8). *-ca²* has two alternate readings—epistemic possibility, as the double gloss in (6) indicates, and admonitive. But while *-ca²* by itself indicates future, it is not *-khe²* alone that marks immediate future, but rather *-khe²* in conjunction with one or the other of two tense/aspect suffixes: *-²a,* which Caughley labels the Past (cf. [7]), in which, as

Caughley notes, it is properly functioning as a perfective), or -*na*ʔ, the Non-past or general imperfective (8). Caughley characterizes the difference in meaning in the following way: for (7), "the action as a completed unit is about to occur"; for (8), [the action] "is about to begin."

(6) ŋa-ʔi   goʔ-ceʔ-na-ŋ
     1.s-AG   call-FUT-2-1.EXCL
     'I will/may call you.'

(7) jaʔ-ʔi   mak-kheʔ-ʔa-thəy
     tiger-AG   devour-IMM-PAST-GOAL
     'A tiger is about to devour him.'

(8) kim-taŋ   dah -kheʔ-naʔ
     house-ALL   arrive-IMM-NONPAST
     'He is about to arrive at the house.'

On the basis of this distinction, it would appear that the most accurate description of the construction in (7), *V -kheʔ -ʔa*, is immediate perfective future, and of the second, *V -kheʔ -na*ʔ, immediate inceptive future.[1] To complicate matters further, -*ʔa* and -*na*ʔ may combine to form a second way of expressing simple future (cf. [9]), and -*ʔa* followed by the future suffix -*ca*ʔ produces an emphatic future, as in (10).

(9) ŋa-pay   nuk -ʔa-na-ŋʔ
     1.s-DIF   hide-PAST-NONPAST-1.EXCL
     'I will hide.'

(10) dyah   to -ʔa-ca-ŋʔ
     now   tell-PAST-FUT-1.EXCL
     'I will indeed now tell him!'

In addition, Chepang has another form, -*dhan*, which, cooccuring with -*ca*ʔ, produces what may be regarded as yet another immediate future; compare (11), in which it is attached to both the verb and the subject. Caughley, who refers to *dhan* as a "Near Future marker," suggests that it may be a grammaticized version of the temporal adverb *deni* ('just now', 'about now'); it also occurs with the Chepang Nonpast with the meaning 'yet' or 'still' (1982: 105, 108).

(11) na-ʔi-dhaŋ   yo -dhaŋ-ca-ŋʔ
     1.s-AG-IMM.FUT   look-IMM.FUT-FUT-1.EXCL
     'I am about to look'/'I will look now.'

In one language of the sample, Mwera, the near future is divided into two distinct chunks, today or tomorrow, indicated by the preposed auxiliary *ci* as in (12) and (13), and immediately after tomor-

---

1. Without Caughley's characterization of the difference between (7) and (8), the glosses would have led us to code both as simple immediate futures.

row, indicated by the auxiliary *cika* as in (14) (Harries 1950: 98f.). Harries calls these the Immediate Future Indefinite and the Middle Future Indefinite, respectively, and contrasts them with a Remote Future Indefinite, consisting of the auxiliary verb *jiya* ('come') in its Immediate Future Indefinite form followed by the stem of the main verb, used for "actions at remote time, but not confined to remote time" (p. 99); cf. (15) and (16).

(12)   cinummalanjile naino
       'I will tell him now.'
(13)   cinyende malaŵi
       'I will go tomorrow.'
(14)   cinyie-ika cikambinje kwalola wānace
       'When I come I shall want to see the children.'
(15)   manyanyi cigajiewa
       'The grass will die.'
(16)   pāna ula cijijenya
       'Perhaps the rain will fall.'

Our labels for the uses of *ci* are hodiernal future and crastinal future; for *cika*, immediate post-crastinal future; and for the construction with *jiya*, future. It is worth noting that in our sample, against this single language with futures divided according to the daily cycle are seven languages with pasts divided according to the daily cycle, and Mwera is one of them (see Table 3.14). Thus not only is it more common to have past time reference divided by the daily cycle, it appears that the presence of daily cycle distinctions in the future implies the presence of such distinctions in the past. Note, however, that is not simply degree of remoteness that is at issue (contrary to Comrie 1985b). In fact, immediate futures far outnumber immediate pasts—our database contains nine immediate pasts compared to thirty-nine immediate futures (see Table 3.15).

On the other hand, remote pasts far outnumber remote futures. Only one gram in the database is used to refer specifically to future events which are remote from the moment of speech, as against sixteen which code events which occurred in the remote past (see Table 3.15). Moreover, the remote future in question, which occurs in Tem, is not a primary future, but instead one use of a general imperfective, and it is not entirely clear that it codes events which are exclusively remote. The frequency of immediate futures in our database may be a result of the use of this label in reference grammars for other modal or aspectual nuances of futures.

7.1.3. *Epistemic qualification of future*

In six languages of the sample, we find pairs of future grams which, in addition to expressing prediction, bear an indication of how

convinced the speaker is that the event will come about. We label these
uses as **future certainty** and **future possibility**. Future certainty indicates that the speaker is emphasizing that the future event is sure to
come about, and thus has absolute confidence in the prediction. Future possibility indicates that the speaker is indicating that s/he is un-
sure as to whether the future event will come about, and hence in
effect that s/he is not confident in making an unqualified prediction.
As we saw in the previous chapter, possibility markers are often restricted to future interpretations (see Table 6.4).

Future certainty grams occur in Inuit, Agau, Tucano, and Pangasinan; future possibility grams occur in Agau, Krongo, and Engenni.
In Agau, future certainty is the sole use of the suffix -aɢa, which
Hetzron (1969: 12–13) calls the Imperfect Definite form. Future
possibility, however, is the alternate reading of a general imperfective suffix, which Hetzron labels the Imperfect Indefinite (pp. 12f.);
cf. (17), with an allomorph of -aɢa, and (18), with the same form but
with the adverb *nessi* 'now' adding immediacy to the certainty.

(17) táq- áɣá
      know-2.s:IMPF.DEF
      'You will [certainly] know [it].'
(18) án ŋə́šší des-áɣá
      I now study-l.s:IMPF.DEF
      'I am going to study now.'

In (19)–(21), the Imperfect Indefinite suffix -e has a continuous
reading with 'now', a future possibility reading with 'tomorrow', and
a habitual reading when no temporal modifier is present.

(19) án   ŋəšší des-é
      I   now   study-l.s:IMPF.INDF
      'I am studying now.'
(20) dəngéta   ča   des-é
      perhaps   tomorrow study-l.s:IMPF.INDF
      'Perhaps, tomorrow I shall study.'
(21) *des-té*
      study-2/3.s.FEM:IMPF.INDF
      'You study/she studies.'

7.1.4. *Definite and indefinite future*

Definite and indefinite also qualify predictions of future events, but
rather than the speaker's confidence in making the prediction, what
is at issue is whether the speaker is offering an assurance that an event
will take place at some definite time or is not offering such an assur-

ance. Grams with these functions are rare; at best, only one language (Nung), has a definite future, and two others (Inuit and Buriat) have indefinite futures.

Clear examples of language-internal distinctions between a simple future and an indefinite future are found in Inuit and Buriat. In Buriat, the plain future is built from the suffix -*xa*, which marks the verbal noun of the future, combined with predicative suffixes for person and number, producing a finite form; compare (22) (Poppe 1960: 55ff.). The second gram, which Poppe refers to as the simple finite future, is the suffix -*uuža*, which has the indefinite future reading, as in (23).

(22) jaba-xa-b
      go-FUT-l.s
      'I shall go.'
(23) jab-uuža-b
      go-FUT-l.s
      'I shall go (sometime, at an indefinite time).'

Among the six grams which have future uses in Inuit are two indefinite futures. These are the suffixes -*jumaar*, which is a simple indefinite future, and -*llarumaar*, which is built up from -*jumaar* and an intensity marker and codes indefinite future certainty (Fortescue 1984: 275, 296, and passim). Compare (24), with -*jumaar*, and (25), with -*llarumaar*, to the simple futures marked by -*ssa* in (26) and -*niar* in (27).

(24) takuqqikkumaarpugut
      see-INDF.FUT-l.p:IND
      'We'll see each other again (sometime/someday).'
(25) tikillarumaarpuq
      come-INDF.FUT.CERT-3.s:IND
      'He will come (someday), just you wait and see.'
(26) tuqussaatit
      die-FUT-2.s:IND
      'You will die.'
(27) siallirniarpuq
      rain-FUT-3.s:IND
      'It's going to rain.'

7.1.5. Expected future

Also relatively rare are **expected futures**, grams which refer either to events which are expected to occur in the near future, or to those which have been pre-arranged, which are sometimes referred to as "scheduled futures." In English, expected future is expressed by the use of either the present, the present progressive, or the 'be to' construction with an appropriate temporal expression, as in (28)–(30).

(28) We fly to Irkutsk on Wednesday.
(29) We're flying to Irkutsk on Wednesday.
(30) Maria is to sing in *Aida* tomorrow night.

Only four grams in the database, three of which are aspectual futures, have expected future as a use. The sole case of a primary expected future is the suffix *sussaa* in Inuit, which has expected future as its only use (Fortescue 1984: 292); compare (31).[2]

(31) aqagu   avalattussaavunga
      tomorrow   go.to.Denmark.is.to.l.s:INDIC
      'Tomorrow I am to go to Denmark.'

The three aspectuals are imperfectives. Two (the forms in Latin and Modern Greek) have Present as their principal use, and in this respect are akin to the English of (28); compare the Latin examples (32) and (33) and the Modern Greek examples (34) and (35).

(32) Cras   est   mihi   judicium.
      tomorrow   be.3.s   l.s:DAT court
      'Tomorrow I have a case in court.'
(33) Quam   mox   irruimus?
      how   soon   attack-l.p:IMPF
      'How soon do we attack?'
(34) ti   deftera   fevgo   ja   tin   elada
      ART   Monday   leave-l.s:IMPF for   ART-ACC Greece
      'On Monday I leave for Greece.'
(35) avrio   vlepo   to   jatro
      tomorrow   see-l.s.IMPF   ART-ACC   doctor
      'I see the doctor tomorrow.'

The third form is the Baluchi Continuative construction, built up from the infinitive plus the 'singular definite' suffix -*a* and an inflected form of the verb *buəg* 'be, become' (Barker and Mengal 1969: 233ff.). The principal use of this construction is progressive, and its future use is most accurately characterized as expected future progressive; compare (36) and (37), which recall (29).

(36) mən   svarəga   koha   ləgg-əg-a   bin
      I   lunch   mountain   climb-INF-DEF   be:l.s
      'I shall be climbing the mountain at lunch(time).'

___

2. It is tempting to assume that -*sussaa* is built up from -*ssa* and another element, but we cannot be sure.

(37) če,   təw   ymšəpi   van-əg-a   bəy?
     you   tonight   study-   be:2.s
                       INF-DEF
     'Will you be studying tonight?'

In all three cases, the sense of expectedness or scheduledness would appear to be attributable to the presence of temporal expressions which locate the event in the future. However, as Comrie (1985b: 118) points out in his discussion of the use of the English Present with future reference, since sentences such as *It rains tomorrow* do not normally have such interpretations, an appropriate temporal expression by itself is not sufficient to guarantee an expected future reading. In fact, Comrie suggests that Presents have future readings of this sort only when they refer to scheduled events. That is, he regards the temporal expressions as merely consistent with, and not the locus of, the future sense in such cases, which is why events which are not normally schedulable, such as a rainfall, cannot have such readings. But since it is also true that the Present cannot be used to report a planned event in the absence of a temporal modifier placing it in the future (*I fly to Chicago* cannot be used to report the fact that one holds a ticket on a scheduled flight to Chicago yet to occur) it would appear that neither future nor expectedness can be said to reside in either the verb used to report a planned event or in the temporal modifier. Rather, only the combination of a planned event and an appropriate modifier together can produce an expected future reading of a Present.

Whether all the instances of this use of imperfectives are in Indo-European languages because they tend to enjoy more comprehensive descriptions than non–Indo-European languages is unclear. It may be that all imperfectives with future uses allow what is in effect an expected future reading when the predicate refers to a plannable event and an appropriate temporal expression is present. Note that the temporal expression is present even in the example of Inuit's specialized expected future gram, although from Fortescue's description we assume that *-sussaa* could occur without it. It is not clear, however, whether in the absence of the temporal expression it might not be an expected future with an obligation flavor—something like the reading of English *be to* in sentences such as *I am to sing the part of Gandhi.*

7.2. Lexical sources of primary futures

We have relatively reliable information about the lexical sources of 46 of the 119 primary futures, that is, those grams which code for future which are not principally aspectual forms, as indicated in Table 7.1.

Table 7.1. Sources and Expression Types for Primary Future Grams

Language	Form No.	Sources	Expression
A. Movement Verbs			
1. 'come'			
03 Margi	42	approach	AUX-I
14 Tucano	28	come	SUF SUF SUF AUX-I
	32	come	SUF SUF
40 Guaymí	18	come to	AUX-I
51 Danish	18	come	AUX-I PART PART
69 Krongo	12	come	AUX-I
72 Mwera	36	come	PRE
73 Tem	14	come	AUX-I
75 Mano	03	come	AUX-U PART
80 Tojolabal	04	return	AUX-I
89 Cantonese	20	be near to, reach	PART
2. 'go'			
03 Margi	37	go	AUX-I
11 Cocama	06	go	AUX-I
18 Maung	03	going to	PRE
27 Atchin	03	go	AUX-I
43 Abipon	07	go	SUF
69 Krongo	08	go to	AUX-I
75 Mano	05	go	AUX-U
76 Bari	05	go	PART
81 Zuni	03	go	SUF
88 Nung	08	go	AUX-I
B. Desire			
01 Inuit	18	want to, desire	SUF
51 Danish	05	want to	AUX-I
94 Tok Pisin	07	like, be willing, ready	AUX-I
C. Ability			
89 Cantonese	03	be able to	PART
	04	be able to	PART
D. Other Verbal Sources			
1. 'be, become'			
02 Basque	05	genitive suffix + Aux 'have' or 'be'	SUF SUF AUX-I
08 Tigre	41	be 3sg.	PART STCH AUX-U
37 Buli	15	be, be located	PRE
47 Latin	09	be, become	SUF
52 Yagaria	23	be, do, make, speak	SUF
60 Yessan-Mayo	14	be	SUF
68 Slave	50	object is located	AUX-I
82 Maidu	42	be	SUF SUF
85 Chepang	41	be, have	SUF SUF

Table 7.1. (*continued*)

Language	Form No.	Sources	Expression
		2. Other Verbs	
01 Inuit	17	try to	SUF
02 Basque	19	need	SUF AUX-U AUX-I
51 Danish	04	owe	AUX-I
51 Danish	06	get, have	AUX-I
60 Yessan-Mayo	32	do, make	AUX-I
76 Bari	04	do	PART
	23	look for	PART
		E. Temporal Adverbs	
33 Trukese	03	then, thereafter	PART
76 Bari	03	then, afterward	PART
85 Chepang	38	just now	SUF
94 Tok Pisin	01	soon	PART

In the table, Expression Type gives the formal characteristics of all the elements of a form, including multi-element forms.

Table 7.1 reveals that the lexical sources of future grams are remarkably few and remarkably consistent cross-linguistically. The most frequent sources are movement verb constructions, with ten futures having their sources in constructions with 'come' and similar verbs and ten in constructions with 'go'. Next most frequent are constructions with 'be, become' and related meanings constituting the verbal core, which are more amply attested than the agent-oriented sources of desire, obligation, and others combined. In fact, were we to rely solely on the information available to us concerning lexical sources, it would appear that 'be, become' constructions are more deserving of treatment as a pathway than either desire, obligation, or ability. Fortunately, we are not entirely at the mercy of either time, which can easily obscure or erase evidence for the lexical sources of grammatical material, or the varying priorities of the authors of the grammars in our sample. The examination of patterns of use to identify retentions from earlier meanings can be a powerful additional diagnostic for the partial reconstruction of earlier history. In the following section, we illustrate how, taken together, evidence of lexical sources and retention of uses from earlier stages of a gram's life history allow us to trace the principal developmental pathways for future.

7.3. Pathways to future

As we saw in previous chapters, distinct lexical sources tend to converge in grammaticization paths. This convergence is apparent in the future paths long before the meaning of simple future or prediction is reached. While our evidence is not always of even quality, we hypothesize that all futures go through a stage of functioning to express the intention, first of the speaker, and later of the agent of the main verb (Bybee and Pagliuca 1987; Bybee 1988a). The meanings that can feed the future path must be meanings that appropriately function in statements that imply an intention on the part of the speaker. This implication of intention later becomes part of the meaning of the gram. A second inference leads to the meaning of prediction: the attribution of an intention to a third person can, in context, imply a prediction on the part of the speaker. In the following sections we argue for this hypothesized sequence of events.

7.3.1. Agent-oriented modalities

7.3.1.1 DESIRE

A common agent-oriented pathway to future begins with desire. In our database, there are eight grams that we classify as 'desire'-futures, five because they have desire (or willingness, see below) as another use along with future, and three because they come from lexical sources with earlier meanings of 'desire' (see Tables 7.2 and 7.3). Historical attestation of the origins of Danish *ville* (cognate with English *will*, earlier meaning 'need or want') and Tok Pisin *lajk* (< English *like*) are available, making it easy to establish clearly the sequence of developments. The Inuit suffix-*jumaar* appears to be related to another existing form in the language, -*juma*, meaning 'want to', giving less direct evidence about the ordering of developments (Fortescue 1984: 275).

Nimboran and Bongu have futures that have desire as another use,

Table 7.2.   Desire Futures

Language	Form No.	Future Use(s)	Other Uses
01 Inuit	18	indefinite future	
37 Buli	15	future	Desire, strong obligation
51 Danish	05	future	Willingness, imperative
58 Nimboran	06	future	Desire, intention, present inceptive, polite imperative
59 Bongu	09	non-immediate future	Desire, promise
	10	immediate future	Desire, promise
90 Dakota	03	future	Willingness, complements to 'want', complements to obligation, subsequent, purpose, imperative
94 Tok Pisin	07	immediate future	Desire

Table 7.3.   Desire Futures: Related Strings and Expression Types

Language	Form No.	Related String	Expression Type
01 Inuit	18	'want to'	SUF
37 Buli	15	('to be/be located')	PRE
51 Danish	05	'want to'	AUX-I
58 Nimboran	06		SUF
59 Bongu	09		SUF
	10		SUF SUF
90 Dakota	03		PART
94 Tok Pisin	07	'like, want'	PART

attesting to the relation among these functions, but not telling us anything about the order of developments. In Tok Pisin, the lexical
source as well as a desire use are found in grammatical descriptions,
with the desire meaning attested in earlier references (Hall 1943a: 32)
and other uses cited in more recent descriptions (Mühlhäusler 1985:
375, 378).

(38)   ju laik kılım pıg
       'You want to kill a pig.'
(39)   mi laik wokabaut
       'I shall walk'.
(40)   em i laik wokabaut
       'He is about to walk.'

We have assigned Dakota *kte* to the group of desire futures because
of the sense of willingness that Buechel 1939: 294 indicates can be
expressed by this form. The willingness sense makes it similar to English *will*, which conveys willingness in certain contexts, such as *I'm
sure he'll help you if you ask.* We argued in Bybee and Pagliuca 1987 that
the willingness nuance was a retention from the desire meaning of
will, since it is related to the agent's desire and since other futures,
such as *shall* and *be going to*, don't express this particular shade of
meaning. The Danish form *ville* appears to be similar to its English
cognate in conveying a sense of willingness in certain contexts.[3]
   In fact, for all desire futures, we hypothesize the pathway in (41)
below, even though we are unable to confirm willingness as a use separate and distinct from desire for most of the languages on the basis of
the information available in published descriptions. We predict the
futures from desire will have nuances of willingness at some stage in
their development. In addition, we predict that futures from desire
(and other types as well) will go through a stage in which the form is

3. Furthermore, the form *kte* is used in complements to 'want' and 'order', which
would be harmonic with an original meaning of desire (see §6.9).

used for the statement of intentions, initially in first person and later in other persons. We have documented this process for English, where we found a large proportion of tokens of *will* in Middle English and Early Modern English used for the statement of first-person intention or functions classifiable as promises or resolutions, often with nuances of willingness (Bybee and Pagliuca 1987). Even in Present-Day English, the use of *will* for intention and willingness comprises a major portion of its uses (Coates 1983: 170–77).

The sense of intention is inferrable from the use of a desire modal, especially in the first person. If someone says *I want to go now*, in most contexts, it is reasonable to infer that s/he in fact intends to leave soon and is communicating this. With a high frequency of usage, this inference can become part of the meaning of the modal. We hypothesize further that the prediction function arises from the intention function. Once intention is attributable to a third person using the form, the inference of speaker's prediction is available. Thus the statement *When Sally gets a raise, she's going to buy a new house* may be interpreted as a statement of the subject's intentions or as a prediction about what is going to happen. We hypothesize that sentences such as these with a desire modal give rise to the prediction (and hence simple future) sense (Bybee 1988a).

It is true that most of our reference material on futures did not mention intention, although often enough example sentences have this reading. However, all detailed studies of future that we have examined (such as Coates 1983; Dahl 1985; Fleischman 1982a; Ultan 1978; Moreno de Alba 1977) highlight intention as an important aspect of the meaning of future. We consider the intention stage essential to the understanding of the development of the prediction function. In (41) we have placed willingness before intention, when in fact one and the same token may express both; similarly the same token may express intention and imply prediction.

(41)   DESIRE > WILLINGNESS > INTENTION > PREDICTION

Our hypotheses concerning the descent of grams from lexical material along developmental pathways make strong predictions about what can and cannot happen in the evolution of a gram from a given source. We predict that lexical-like or rich meanings, such as those associated with earlier stages along the pathways to future from agent-oriented precursors, are found at later stages as alternate uses or as flavors only by virtue of being retentions, and cannot arise as later developments of futures from other sources (Bybee and Pagliuca 1987). For this reason we do not expect to find uses associated with more than one agent-oriented modality in a single gram. One of the seven desire futures violates these expectations and thus needs further consideration.

The form is a prefixed inflected auxiliary *bo-*, in the South Halma-hera–West New Guinea Austronesian language Buli, described in Maan 1951. Maan identifies *bo-* as directly related to an auxiliary verb meaning 'be' or 'be located', for which he provides Dutch glosses with *zitten* ('sit'), *staan* ('stand', 'be'), and *zijn* ('be') (pp. 84f.). For the readings of its grammaticized form, Maan provides translations of text sentences using *zullen* (the Dutch future auxiliary) and *willen* ('want to'), and once, when he introduces the form (p. 84), with a triple gloss, using *zullen*, *willen*, and *moeten* ('must') (42). However, no examples with the last modal are provided.

(42)   ja-bo-i-fān
       1.s.FUT:1.s:go
       'Ik zal/moet/wil gaan.'
       'I shall/must/want to go.'

The reason this form is troublesome is that the translation suggests that it can have both 'must' and 'want to' readings, whereas our hypothesis predicts that no gram should display obligation and desire as alternate uses. Obligation > future and desire > future are separate pathways, and agent-oriented uses proper to one pathway should not be found at any stage along the other. Thus, we might expect to see glosses using either *moeten* or *willen* as alternate readings for *zullen*, but not both. In this instance, as in many others, the problem is probably that we are at the mercy of translations. If we take frequency as a criterion, then the suspect translation here would be *moeten*, occurring as it does only once, in the citation example (42), whereas *zullen* and, somewhat less often, *willen* occur in translations of the texts. On the other hand, the gram's source in a 'be/be located' verb suggests that the path to future was not through desire at all. That, however, would leaves us with the burden of explaining text sentences glossed with *willen*. To do this, we would have to assume that the uses of *bo-* so glossed reflect those uses of *willen* which are closer to future than they are to 'want to'. These uses of *willen* (which, like the cognate forms in English and Danish, also has a willingness reading), are translated with 'intend' and 'be going to', suggesting that it may have intention readings under certain circumstances (Gerritsen and Osselton (1978/1983: 996). Given the difficulty of distinguishing between intention and future when the subject of a sentence is an animate agent, it is possible that the intention–future overlap, rather than genuine differences in modal flavors, is responsible for variation in the glosses. Unfortunately, although this seems to be a reasonable approach to explaining some of the variation in the glosses of sentences in the texts provided by Maan, it is not obviously applicable in all cases. We must therefore leave this as an unresolved anomaly.

7.3.1.2. OBLIGATION

The other common agent-oriented pathway to future is that of **obligation**, the raw material for which is more varied than that which feeds the other agent-oriented pathways. In addition to the relatively familiar 'owe' (Danish, Cantonese) and other verbs referring to possession—'have' (Danish, Slave, Temne); 'get, obtain, catch' (Lahu)—we also find as sources 'be, become' (Kui, Baluchi, Slave), 'need' (Basque), 'fall, befall' (Baluchi), and 'to be good' (Palaung). That the apparent diversity here is not a peculiarity of the particular sample we have drawn is clear from the fact that virtually all these sources are attested as precursors of obligation constructions in Indo-European languages. Impersonal obligation constructions with sources in 'need' appear in Greek (*dei* [< *deō* 'lack, miss, need']) and Latin (*opus est*); Palaung 'be good' resembles Latin impersonal *oportet* ('is proper, ought') and Greek *prepei* 'is fitting' (> Byzantine and later Greek also 'ought, must') (Buck 1949: 641). The 'be, become' source for Baluchi has parallels elsewhere in Indo-European, including Old Norse, with obligation readings of *verda* 'become, happen' in the sagas (Gordon 1957: 395); and the cognate of Baluchi 'befall' (which also occurs as a reading of *verda* in the sagas) has developed an obligation reading in Nepali and perhaps elsewhere in Indic.

A large number of grams in the database have obligation as a use (see Table 6.1), but only seven of these are also used as futures. Six of these are plain futures, the seventh is an immediate future; cf. Table 7.4. Only about half of the obligation grams are further designated as strong or weak, and of these about half are labeled strong and half, weak. Despite this parity, however, all but one of the obligation-derived futures in our sample—the first Basque form indicated in Table 7.4—descend from grams marking strong obligation. Following our general discussion, we will return to a consideration of why strong obligation and weak obligation do not appear to be equally fruitful sources of future markers.

Table 7.4.   Obligation Futures

Language	Form No.	Future Use(s)	Other Uses
01 Inuit	16	future	Strong obligation
02 Basque	05	future	Weak obligation, probability
	19	immediate future	Strong obligation
37 Buli	15	future	Strong obligation, desire
51 Danish	04	future	Strong obligation, intention, imperative
68 Slave	50	future	Strong obligation
86 Haka	10	future	Strong obligation, future probability

Table 7.5. Obligation Futures: Related Strings and Expression Types

Language	Form No.	Related String	Expression Type
01 Inuit	16		SUF
02 Basque	05	genitive suffix + Aux 'have' or 'be'	SUF SUF AUX
	19	to need' + Aux 'have' or 'be'	SUF AUX-U AUX-I
37 Buli	15	'be/be located'	PRE
51 Danish	04	'to owe' (Present)	AUX-I
68 Slave	50	'object is located'	AUX-I
86 Haka	10		PART

We have information concerning the likely lexical sources of five of the seven forms in Table 7.5. These are the Basque constructions, the first of which is built up from the affix -ko on the verb stem followed by an inflected auxiliary ('have' in the case of transitive verbs, 'be' in the case of intransitives), the second from the uninflected verb *bear* 'to need' followed by the same inflected auxiliary; Buli *bo-*, which as we saw earlier is a now-bound inflected auxiliary which as an independent auxiliary means 'be' or 'be located'; the Present of the Danish auxiliary *skal*, cognate with English *shall*, which earlier meant 'owe'; and the Slave inflected auxiliary *gó?o*, which is built up from the 'areal prefix' *gó* and *?o*, a verbal core meaning 'be', and is translated as 'object is located'; cf. Table 7.5.

The obligation and future uses of the Basque constructions are illustrated in (43) and (44), of Danish *skal* in (45) and (46) (Koefoed 1958: 184, 192), and of Slave *gó?o* in (47) and (48) (Rice 1990: 356).

(43)   ikusi-ko   dut
       see:PERF-GEN   3.S.ABS:have:l.S.ERG
       'I will see'/'I ought to see.'

(44)   ikusi   bear   dut
       see:PERF   need   3.S.ABS.have:l.S.ERG
       'I have to see'/'I am about to see.'

(45)   Du skal   gå   nu.
       2.S.FAM.AUX   go   now
       'You must go now.'

(46)   Jeg   skal   (nok)   komme   i morgen.
       l.s   AUX   (certainly)   come   tomorrow
       'I will come tomorrow.'

(47)   kie ráyehdi gò?o
       'I must buy shoes.'

(48)   wohje gó?o
       'I will sing.'

Most of the examples in (43)–(48) are straightforward and show obligation and future uses of the forms in Table 7.4 to be alternate readings of identical structures. The Basque construction in (43), however, merits discussion.

The point of interest concerning Basque is the apparent role of a non-verbal source as an indicator of possession leading to obligation and future in the -*ko* construction. The suffix -*ko* here is identical to the genitive suffix used on nominals, both of which have a phonologically conditioned allomorph -*en*. This suggests that the construction with -*ko* may have evolved in a manner similar to the way in which a 'have + infinitive' construction might develop obligation or future readings.[4]

The behavior of the Buriat suffix -*xa*, which forms the verbal noun of the future, also suggests that possession as a source of obligation does not require a verbal source such as 'have', 'take, obtain' (Poppe 1960: 61ff.). When followed by the predicative person-number suffixes, -*xa* forms a finite-like construction with simple future as its reading, as in (49). When followed by possessive person-number suffixes, however, the reading is strong obligation, as in (50). The possessive suffixes here appear to function much as does 'have to' in obligation constructions in English or Romance. The difference is that in Buriat -*xa* places the event in the future; a clumsy paraphrase of (50) might be 'of me is a future going/I possess a future going'.

(49)   jaba-xa-b
       go-FUT-1.s
       'I will go.'
(50)   bi jaba-xa-mni
       I go-FUT-1.s-POSS
       'I must go.'

Note that even though the same future gram is found in both (49) and (50), it would not be legitimate to include it in Table 7.5, since it is not -*xa* as a future which has the obligation reading, but rather -*xa* in construction with the possessive affixes.

A similar though more complex case arises with the Chepang constructions with -*khe?* ('be, have'), which, as described in §7.1.2, is used to form an immediate future (cf. [8], repeated here).

(8)   kim-taŋ   dah-khe?-na?
      house-ALL   arrive-IMM-NPAST
      'He is about to arrive at the house.'

The suffix -*khe?* also figures in weak and strong obligation constructions ([51] and [52] respectively), but each reading appears to

4. Some Basque specialists suggest that the use of -*ko* reflects what amounts to a calque on the *de* of Spanish *haber de* (cf. Michelena 1981). We are grateful to Jose-Ignacio Hualde for this reference and for much of the information on Basque in this discussion.

be associated with particular sorts of nominal and verbal marking
(cf. Caughley 1982: 94 and passim). Thus although in (51), as in (8),
-*khe*ʔ and the 'Non-past' -*na(*ʔ*)* are serially suffixed to the main verb,
in (51) (the weak obligation form), but not (8), they are preceded by
what Caughley identifies as an Irrealis marker; (51) also indicates
the optional presence of a final person marker—here, First Person
Exclusive.

(51) ŋa waŋ-sa   kheŋ-na(-ŋ)ʔ
      1.s come-IRR.NM   be-NONPAST(-1E)
      'I ought to come.'

In (52), the strong obligation construction, like (51), the Irrealis
marker is used, but not the Non-past marker.

(52) ŋa waŋ-sa   kheʔ-(ŋo)-to
      1.s come-IRR.NM   be-(1E)-SECONDARY LINK
      'I must come.'

Thus, although we can assume the source meaning of -*khe*ʔ ('be,
have') to be essential to the development of both future and obligation
readings, the relative richness of nominal and verbal marking in Chepang insures that 'is about to/is on the point of', 'ought to', and 'must',
which we might expect to be alternate readings of a single construction, are each formally distinct.

It is nevertheless troublesome that we do not appear to have solid
evidence for obligation and future arising as alternative readings of a
single construction built up from a verb of possession. The question
thus arises: is the relation between possession and obligation and future which we see in Buriat and Chepang ascribable to the relatively
robust morphological resources these languages enjoy, or is the pathway possession > obligation often separate from that of possession >
future?

Benveniste 1968 has argued that the evolution of the post–Classical
Latin *habēre* + infinitive construction into the periphrastic future of
Romance languages was more complex than earlier scholars had assumed. In particular, he insisted that it is erroneous to assume that
obligation played a role in the development of the construction into
the Romance future:

> The overwhelming majority of examples show that: (1) the
> periphrasis began with *habēre* and the PASSIVE infinitive; (2) it
> was initially used with the IMPERFECT tense of *habēre;* and (3) it
> was restricted to SUBORDINATE, chiefly relative, clauses. (Ben-
> veniste 1968: 89–90)

He goes on to argue that the infinitive + *habēre* construction func-
tioned like a future passive participle and did not indicate obligation,

that is, was not equivalent to English *have to* or French *j'ai à travailler.*
He believes that the construction conveyed a sense of predestination
or what 'will be done' rather than a sense of personal obligation. It
would thus resemble the English phrase *be to* more than English *have
to* (but see Fleischman 1983: 56–59). It is interesting that English *shall*
and especially its past tense *should* had a sense of predestination
throughout Old, Middle, and Early Modern English.

We are suggesting, then, that constructions with 'be' or 'have' auxiliaries may have a sense of predestination which can evolve directly
into prediction, without necessarily going through a stage in which
they express obligation. If this is so, then 'obligation path' falls short
of an accurate characterization—in the case of possession (for Romance, Buriat, and Chepang) and, probably, for at least some futures
with sources in constructions with 'be'. Languages in which 'be' and
'have' are alternate readings of a single lexical verb (as they are in
Chepang *-kheʔ*) are candidates here, as are futures for which 'be, become' are identifiable as sources but which appear not to have had
obligation readings. In this group we might include the Latin future in
-b, from 'be, become' (which is in the database), and German *werden.*[5]

In the database are five future grams which appear to descend
from 'be' verbs but which do not display obligation uses; compare
Tables 7.6 and 7.7. This by itself is not evidence that their evolution
into futures was via predestination rather than obligation, since we
expect agent-oriented uses to be lost as forms age. Moreover, four of
the five display semantic and formal hallmarks of older future grams:
late-developing uses, such as imperative, purpose, and appearance in
complement clauses, and affixal form. These four—among which is
the Latin *-b* future, which we cited above as a potential candidate—may then simply represent older obligation-derived futures.
However, two of the forms would appear to be not quite so old—the
Tigre immediate future construction and the Yagaria suffix, which
has intention, an early agent-oriented use, as an alternate reading.
Furthermore, time typically erases not only earlier uses but also evidence of lexical source, making it somewhat odd that we should find
five grams with still-robust synchronic lexical antecedents but no trace
of obligation uses. The presence of lexical sources and the lack of

5. To such a list might also be added Danish *blive* 'become', which according to Koefoed 1958: 183 "contains futuric sense"; cf.(i).

(i) *Det **bliver**   nodvendigt   at   standse   maskinen.*
     It   become:PRES   necessary   to   stop   the.engine.
     'It will be necessary to stop the engine.'

Also note that Old Norse *verda* 'become' developed an obligation reading but not a
future use, while its descendent, Modern Icelandic *verda*, has future uses; Abraham
(1989: 377–79) calls it a 'conditional future' and classifies it as an aspectual future.

Table 7.6. Candidates for Futures from 'be, become' Sources
Not on the Obligation > Future Pathway

Language	Form No.	Future Use(s)	Other Uses
08 Tigre	41	immediate future	
47 Latin	09	future	Probability, request
52 Yagaria	23	future	Intention, imperative, hortative, sequence first
60 Yessan-Mayo	14	future	Purpose, almost, complements to clauses of admonition
82 Maidu	42	future	Polite imperative

Table 7.7. Related Strings and Expression Types for the Futures in Table 7.6

Language	Form No.	Related String	Expression Type
08 Tigre	41	be 3s + in order to	PART STCH AUX-U
47 Latin	09	be, become	SUF
52 Yagaria	23	be, do, make, speak	SUF
60 Yessan-Mayo	14	be	SUF
82 Maidu	42	be	SUF SUF

obligation uses would not, however, be at all odd for futures derived via predestination.

The possibility remains that for some 'be, become' futures, obligation is an intermediate stage. Further, since the conceptual distance between obligation and scheduled future and predestination is minimal, it may be possible for a single structure to branch into future and obligation uses. In fact, some constructions built on markers of possession may have branched in just this way, as in Spanish *haber de* + infinitive, with both (weak) obligation and future as readings in some dialects (note, however, that here two markers of possession, and not simply 'have' + infinitive, are involved). We thus are suggesting that for 'be' and 'have' constructions, two pathways to future may exist: a direct path with no intermediate obligation stage, and a path through obligation. Thus, to the more general path from obligation to future, from sources such as 'need', 'be proper', 'ought', and the like, we posit two alternative paths for constructions involving 'be', 'become', 'have', and perhaps other markers of possession.

(53) 'be', 'become', 'have'/POSSESSION > OBLIGATION

(54) 'be', become', 'have'/POSSESSION > PREDESTINATION

(55) PREDESTINATION ⎫
                      ⎬ > INTENTION > FUTURE
      OBLIGATION   ⎭

Both the paths (53) and (54) feed (55).

It will be noted that we have postulated that the path in (55) also involves a stage in which the gram signals intention, just as we proposed for desire futures. The inferential mechanism that we are positing for this stage is very similar to that we described for desire. Especially in first person, a statement of obligation such as *I have to go now* or predestination as in *I am to go now* strongly implies that the speaker intends to leave soon. For example, this implication had become part of the meaning of *shall* by the Middle English stage and is amply represented in texts. Similarly, Old Spanish uses of the future from infinitive plus *haber* frequently express intention of a first person subject, for example in *El Cantar del Mio Cid*. Just as with desire futures, it is from the intention sense that the prediction use can develop. Especially with regard to a third person, a statement of intention implies a prediction.

The inferential mechanism and postulation of an intention stage are consistent with the fact that most obligation markers that become futures express strong rather than weak obligation. The difference between the two, as we explained in §6.3.2, is that strong obligation compels one to follow the social or moral course set by a belief system or social norms, whereas weak obligation merely counsels or recommends following the course. Thus intention may be inferred from statements of strong obligation, but not from statements of weak obligation; thus, (56) but not (57) is a sensible utterance.

(56)   I should go now, but I'm gonna stay.
(57)   *I have to go now, but I'm gonna stay.

The statement of a strong obligation in most contexts leads to the implication of an intention, which can become part of the meaning of the obligation marker and can eventually become the basic meaning of that marker.

7.3.1.3. OTHER AGENT-ORIENTED MODALITIES

One language in our sample, Inuit, has a gram with uses labeled as attempt, intention, and future. While there are eleven forms in our database with attempt as their meaning, only this one has future as another use. The form in question is the suffix -*niar*, which Fortescue describes as a 'verb-extending affix' meaning 'try to', as illustrated in (58), but which also has an intention use, as in (59), and a future use (60) (Fortescue 1984: 275).

(58)   qitinniarpunga
        dance-try-1.s:IND(INTR)
        'I tried to dance.'

(59)   atuarniarpara
       read-try-ls.SBJ-3s.OBJ.IND
       'I'm going to read it'/'I will try reading it.'
(60)   siallirniarpuq
       rain-try-3.s.IND(INTR)
       'It's going to rain.'

The last example is a particularly good one for illustrating the prediction sense, since the subject is not human and thus not capable of either attempting or intending.

We propose the path shown in (61), despite the fact that we have only a single case, because of what we know about the relation of intention to future.

(61)   ATTEMPT > INTENTION > FUTURE

We suggest that from an utterance such as *I'll try to read it,* one can infer an intention on the part of the speaker. Once the gram can state an intention of persons other than the speaker, the inference of a prediction is also possible, as in the other cases we have discussed.

Another agent-oriented modality that gives rise to future in one language of the database is ability. Cantonese has two particles expressing future that descend from verbs meaning 'be able to'. According to Kwok 1971: 77, *hó nàng* and *wǔi* express both possibility and future. Both *hó* and *nàng* derive from verbs meaning 'be able to', as does *wǔi*. Example (62) expresses future possibility, while (63) expresses ability.

(62)   háà sing gèi   ngǒ   waāk jé   wǔi   hēui   yât bún
       next week   I   perhaps   will go   Japan
       'I may be going to Japan next week.'
(63)   kēui   hóu   wǔi jýu   sūng gāā
       he   very can cook food SP
       'He can cook very well.'

While Kwok states that these markers can be used for simple future, all the examples illustrating future also contain other markers with the meaning of epistemic possibility, such as (62). However, the Mandarin form cognate with *wǔi*, which is *hui*, is discussed in Tsang 1981, where it is argued that *hui* has simple future or prediction uses along with uses for epistemic possibility, cf. (64) and (65) (Tsang 1981: 167).

(64)   Yueliang   hai   shi hui   chulai   de
       moon   still cop.FUT   come.out   EMP
       'The moon will still come out.'

(65) Daxue   jin   bu   qu,   bu   hui   you   chutou
      University enter   NEG   go   NEG   FUT   have   make it
      de   rizi
      MOD   days
      'Not entering university means there will be no chance for
      achieving something in life.'

In the last chapter we established the path of development for
ability as shown in (66).

(66) MENTAL ABILITY ⎫
                       ⎬ > ABILITY > ROOT POSSIBILITY > EPISTEMIC POSSIBILITY
      PHYSICAL ABILITY ⎭

Our task now is to consider where along this developmental pathway future emerges, and why this pathway is not a more fruitful
source of future grams. As we saw in the last chapter, grams marking
one or more of the meanings ability, root possibility, permission, and
epistemic possibility are quite common, but their development into
future markers is apparently not common.

On the basis of what we have seen, it would appear that for grams
on the ability path, both epistemic possibility and future develop out
of root possibility, but do so independently. That is, the epistemic
uses of possibility and prediction are each evolutionary developments
from the root possibility stage, but neither is a necessary precursor of
the other. This interpretation receives strong confirmation from the
fact that none of the primary futures from sources other than ability
have epistemic possibility as an alternate use. This suggests that epistemic possibility is not a necessary precursor to future, and that,
among future precursors, only ability grams can develop epistemic
possibility readings.

(67) ROOT POSSIBILITY > ⎰ INTENTION > FUTURE
                          ⎱ EPISTEMIC POSSIBILITY

Again we propose an intention stage, on the basis of the fact that a
statement of root possibility, especially in the first person, can be interpreted as an intention: for example, *I can get that door for you* implies that the speaker intends to do just that. However, we suspect
that intention is not a very frequent implication from root possibility,
which would explain the scarcity of futures derived from ability.

7.3.2. *Futures from movement verbs*

As we saw earlier, and as we reported in 1991 on the data from an
almost-complete version of the database, for those future grams for

Table 7.8. Related Strings and Mode of Expression for Movement-derived Futures

Language	Form No.	Future Use(s)	Related String	Expression Type
		'come'		
03 Margi	42	immediate future	approach, come near to	AUX-I
14 Tucano	28	immediate future certainty	come + do	SUF SUF SUF AUX-I
	32	future certainty	come	SUF SUF
	34	probable future	come	SUF AUX-I
	35	immediate future	come	SUF SUF
40 Guaymí	18	immediate future inceptive	come to	AUX-I
51 Danish	18	future	come + to	AUX-I PART PART
69 Krongo	12	immediate future	come	AUX-I
72 Mwera	36	future	come	PRE
73 Tem	14	immediate future	come	AUX-I
75 Mano	03	future	come + progressive to/towards	AUX-U PART
80 Tojolabal	04	immediate future	return	AUX-I
89 Cantonese	20	immediate future	be near to, reach	PART
		'go'		
03 Margi	37	future	go	AUX-I
11 Cocama	06	future	go	AUX-I
18 Maung	03	future	going to	PRE
27 Atchin	03	future	go	AUX-I
43 Abipon	07	future	go	SUF
69 Krongo	08	future	go to	AUX-I
75 Mano	05	future	go	AUX-U
76 Bari	05	future intention	go	PART
81 Zuni	03	future	go	SUF
88 Nung	08	future	go	AUX-I

which we can identify lexical sources, movement verbs figure more prominently as sources than verbs or other lexical material of any other type. The final version of the database contains ten languages with futures which descend from 'come' and similar verbs, and ten with futures whose lexical source is 'go'; cf. Table 7.8.[6] In thirteen of these twenty separate cases, the future from a movement verb is expressed as an auxiliary; in only three cases is the future a suffix, in only two is it a prefix, and in two it is a particle. As can be seen from Table 7.9, relative to futures from other sources, movement-verb futures also typically have only one other use or no other uses. Not surprisingly, the two forms with the late-developing

6. Because all four of the Tucano futures in Table 7.8 are based on a suffixal form descended from 'come', we only count Tucano once for purposes of tallying up 'come'-derived futures; the distinct future uses of these four constructions are given in Table 7.9.

Table 7.9.   Movement Verb Futures: Other Uses

Language	Form No.	Future Use(s)	Other Uses
03 Margi	37	future	andative
	42	immediate future	
11 Cocama	06	future	andative, intention
14 Tucano	28	immediate future certainty	
	32	future certainty	
	34	probable future	
	35	immediate future	
18 Maung	03	future	protasis hypothetical
27 Atchin	03	future	imperative, purpose
40 Guaymí	18	immediate future inceptive	venitive
43 Abipon	07	future	
51 Danish	18	future	imperative
69 Krongo	08	future	
	12	immediate future	
72 Mwera	36	future	
73 Tem	14	immediate future	
75 Mano	03	future progressive venitive	
	05	future	
76 Bari	05	future intention	
80 Tojolabal	04	immediate future	
81 Zuni	03	future	apodosis hypothetical
88 Nung	08	future	
89 Cantonese	20	immediate future	

lower-clause uses, protasis hypothetical and apodosis hypothetical, are also formally the most reduced—these are the Maung prefix and the Zuni suffix.

The evolution of movement constructions into futures is somewhat more direct than the evolution of agent-oriented modalities into futures, producing fewer other uses along the way. The semantics of 'movement toward' constructions implies movement in time as well as space, making the transition to future easier. However straightforward this change appears, we must still examine it in detail for what it teaches us about grammaticization.

First, it is important to note that simple movement does not evolve into future. To derive future there must be an allative component, 'movement toward', either inherent in the semantics of the verb or explicit in the construction. As we have argued elsewhere (Bybee and Pagliuca 1987; Bybee, Pagliuca, and Perkins 1991), the source meaning for movement futures is that 'the agent is on a path moving toward a goal'. Another important part of the meaning is that the agent is already on the path and the movement is in progress; thus the overt or inherent aspect of the construction is progressive, present, or imperfective.

While some have argued that a metaphorical transfer is involved in deriving future meaning from a movement construction (Sweetser 1988; Emanation 1992), we do not see the need for invoking a metaphorical mechanism in this case. The temporal meaning that comes to dominate the semantics of the construction is already present as an inference from the spatial meaning. When one moves along a path toward a goal in space, one also moves in time. The major change that takes place is the loss of the spatial meaning. Here again the function of expressing intention comes into play. When the speaker announces that s/he is going somewhere to do something, s/he is also announcing the intention to do that thing. Thus intention is part of the meaning from the beginning, and the only change necessary is the generalization to contexts in which an intention is expressed, but the subject is not moving spatially to fulfill that intention.

Emanation 1992 details the difference in temporal deixis between *go to* and *come to.* For *go to,* the speaker's vantage point is approximately simultaneous with the moment of speech, and the point in time when the event or situation occurs is in the future. The subject is thus moving away from the speaker's vantage point toward the event. With *come to,* the speaker's vantage point is in the future, very close to the time at which the event is anticipated to occur. Thus (68) is appropriate if the addressee is in Dallas and the speaker is taking the vantage point of the addressee.

(68)   I'm coming to Dallas next week.

With the temporal interpretation, the speaker and the addressee are located at the same point in time, but the speaker hypothetically takes a vantage point at a future time, the time at which the event will occur.

It is probably not accidental that seven of the eleven 'come'-futures in our database are actually immediate futures, while none of the 'go'-futures are.[7] A 'come'-future requires that the speaker's point of view be some time in the future, and it is only reasonable to suppose that this dislocation of perspective would not usually involve a projection into the distant future but would more often be a point in time near at hand, yielding an immediate future.

Fleischman 1982b proposes a distinction between 'come'- and 'go'-futures derived from two different metaphors concerning time. She suggests that 'go'-futures involve the "moving ego" metaphor, in which the subject is moving away from the present moment, and that 'come'-futures involve the "moving time" metaphor, in which the subject is stationary and time moves toward him or her (as in the phrase *the coming weeks,* etc.) As Emanation points out (1992: 17), this analysis

7. One obligation future and two desire futures also have immediate future readings; see §7.5.

cannot be correct, because in both cases it is the subject who moves. We can add that "moving time" cannot lead to grammatical future or prediction because an animate agent is necessary to give rise to the intention reading, which is the source of the prediction sense. We claim that all modal and movement future sources begin with human agents and move from the expression of the intentions of that agent to the expression of prediction. There is even some evidence that futures from temporal adverbs follow a similar route (Romaine 1992).

7.3.3. Futures from temporal adverbs

The final source of future grams which we can document from the languages of the sample is temporal adverbial expressions. The database contains four cases of futures which are candidates for descent from temporal adverbs, each occurring in a language with other primary futures; cf. Tables 7.10 and 7.11. Thus, no language has a temporal adverb supply its only future.

The status of futures from temporal adverbs is not always clear, although clear cases have been discussed by Marchese 1986; Heine and Reh 1984; and, for Tok Pisin, a sample language, by Romaine 1992. In two of the four cases in our data, the evidence for temporal adverbials as lexical ancestors of future markers appears to be somewhat problematic. As we saw earlier (§7.1.2), Chepang -dhan is marginal, in two respects: it signals immediacy but may not by itself signal future, since it apparently requires the future suffix -ca? to co-occur with it; second, Caughley suggests its ancestry in deni ('just now') as a possibility rather than a certainty. Perhaps similar is the Karok adver-

Table 7.10. Futures from Temporal Adverbs: Related Strings and Expression Types

Language	Form No.	Source	Expression Type
33 Trukese	03	then, thereafter	PART
76 Bari	03	then, afterwards	PART
85 Chepang	38	just now	SUF
94 Tok Pisin	01	soon	PART

Table 7.11. Futures from Temporal Adverbs: Uses

Language	Form No.	Future Use(s)	Other Uses
33 Trukese	03	future	Possibility, complements to 'think', subsequent, complements to 'want'
76 Bari	03	future	
85 Chepang	38	immediate future	Inceptive
94 Tok Pisin	01	future intention	Imperative

bial *cími*, which co-occurs with the future suffix *aviš* to lend an immediate future or intention reading (Bright 1957: 134f.), but it is not clear whether by itself it can mark future. The second case is that of the Trukese particle *qaaq* 'then', 'thereafter'. The analytic difficulty here is that it is not clear whether sentences with this form are better viewed as essentially tenseless.

Romaine's (1992) detailed study of the development of *bai* (from *by and by*) in Tok Pisin shows that futures from adverbs can develop many of the same uses as futures from modal or movement sources. *Bai* can be used in clause-initial position as a clausal connective, but in preverbal position it occurs primarily in main clauses and is used to express intentions, suggestions, imperatives, and predictions. Again, it may be that the statement of the speaker's intention plays a crucial role in the development of future meaning. Although it would not seem that the meaning of *by and by* needs to change much to express future time reference, it still appears as though a first person statement with this temporal phrase can be taken to be a statement of intention, and that further developments may result from this use. If this is the case, then the temporal adverb path may converge with the other paths of development for future.

7.4. Immediate futures

Twenty-six primary future grams have immediate future of some kind as a use; in nineteen of the cases, this is the sole use. Immediate future is also the sole future reading of two imperfectives and two perfectives. In an earlier work (Bybee, Pagliuca, and Perkins 1991) we interpreted primary future grams with immediate future as a use as younger than grams whose future use was simple future; that is, we were in effect suggesting that, for primary futures, the use immediate future is diagnostic of a simple future at an earlier stage of its development. Although we are not aware of strong historical evidence attesting the generalization of an immediate future to a general future gram (but see Fleischman 1983 for a claim that this occurs), there are both formal and semantic indications of the youth of immediate futures. When all primary futures are considered, we find about half of them have periphrastic expression and half affixal expression (which corroborates Dahl's 1985 findings), but only four of the twenty-six immediate futures are simple affixal forms (all are suffixes), and ten are expressed via two or more elements. More important, although five immediate futures have agent-oriented uses as alternate uses, no primary immediate future displays truly late-developing uses, such as occurrence in subordinate clauses; imperative appears as an alternate use only twice.

Table 7.12.
Distribution of Sources for Primary Immediate Futures

Source type	Number of Grams from Each Source	Number of Immediate Futures
Attempt	1	0
Ability	4	0
Desire	8	2
Obligation	6	1
Come	11	7
Go	10	0
Temporal adverbs	6	1

If we cannot actually verify the evolution of immediate futures into simple futures, we can approach the problem from the other direction and ask, in effect, where immediate futures come from. We have already seen that 'come' futures often have immediate future as a meaning. Table 7.12 shows the relation between sources and immediate future for the eleven immediate futures for which information is available.

Heine, Claudi, and Hünnemeyer, aware of our earlier results (Bybee, Pagliuca, and Perkins 1991), remark that some futures derived from 'go to' also seem to have immediate future rather than simple future as a use, and suggest that immediate future may be a developmental stage to (simple) future for all movement-verb derived futures (1991b: 174). But their cautiousness, along with our failure to establish immediate future as a use for any of our 'go' futures, makes us somewhat hesitant to agree. It is not that we would be surprised to find cases of 'go'-derived immediate futures, but rather that the imbalance reflected in Table 7.12 suggests that the special meaning of 'come' futures gives rise to the immediateness meaning, while other sources do not do so as readily.

Of the other sources in Table 7.12, the problematic status of one—Chepang -dhan, which may or may not descend from the temporal adverbial expression for 'just now'—was discussed in §7.3.3, but the contribution of such an adverb to the immediacy sense would be obvious. Of the two desire sources in Table 7.12, one from Bongu, one in Tok Pisin, we can eliminate the former from consideration, since this immediate future is built up from the simple future plus another element, and it is this element which signals immediacy. But neither the immediate future reading nor the provenience of Tok Pisin *lajk* are in doubt, as we saw in §7.3.1.3 (cf. [40], repeated here).

(40)   em i laik wokabaut
       'He is about to walk.'

But both *lajk* and the sole obligation-derived immediate future—
the Basque construction with *bear* 'need', which is also clearly an
immediate rather than a simple future—are also arguably young
grams. In addition to the obvious youth suggested by the presence
of agent-oriented uses in the first place, the Basque construction remains, in most dialects, a marker of obligation, which suggests that its
use as a future is a relatively recent development.

Even with some hints of immediate future as a sort of way station
for the occasional recently derived future from desire or obligation,
however, we are still left with the dominance of descendants of constructions with 'come' and similar verbs and the apparent absence, in
our data, of 'go'.

One final point about immediate futures seems worthy of discussion. The prototypical glosses for such grams are 'be about to do
something' and 'be on the point of doing something'. Although this is
obviously very much like the notion 'entering on a path to do something' (especially, of course, in the case of such grams descending
from 'come'), it is in a sense also not at all like a prediction.

If immediate futures cannot be said to involve prediction, they may
be regarded in either of two ways: as necessarily young futures, somewhere between proto-futures and a mature future with prediction as
its core function; or if not young, but rather established and stable,
not strictly speaking futures at all, at least not in epistemic terms,
amounting more to assertions announcing the imminence of an event
rather than a prediction that it will take place.

7.5. Futures used as imperatives

As mentioned in §6.8, there are thirteen languages in our database
which have primary futures that can be used as imperatives. We mentioned there that future was the most commonly occurring other use
of imperatives. It is also true that imperative is the most commonly
occurring other use for futures. We propose that the imperative use
develops out of the future use, rather than vice versa, because the
futures that are used as imperatives in all other respects have the
properties of primary futures. In particular, they seem to develop
from the same lexical sources as futures (movement, copulas, adverbs,
and auxiliaries expressing desire), while there are no imperatives
from these sources that do not also signal future. In §6.8 we explained
that this imperative use can develop from an indirect speech act in
second person that can be reinterpreted as a command.

In Bybee and Pagliuca 1987 and Bybee, Pagliuca, and Perkins 1991
we proposed that the imperative use of futures was a late-developing
use, since futures from all lexical sources are capable of developing

274 Chapter Seven

this use. However, some doubt is cast on this proposal by the fact that futures with imperative uses tend to have periphrastic expression. Of the seventeen futures with imperative in the thirteen languages, only six have bound (suffixal) expression; the other eleven are periphrastic. Since the overall ratio of bound to periphrastic expression of futures is about fifty-fifty, it would appear that futures with imperative uses are younger than average.

7.6. Subordinate clause uses of futures

Since the focal use of futures is to make predictions—that is, to make an assertion about future time, futures tend to occur in main clauses. In fact, the inference necessary for the creation of prediction as a sense of future—the inference from the statement of a third person's intentions to a prediction about that third person—can only take place in main clauses. Thus we do not find futures commonly used in subordinate clauses with future time reference, such as hypothetical *if* and *when* clauses, because these clauses do not make assertions about future time. In our database we found only two instances of futures that could be used in hypothetical protases (Maung and Nakanai). Of course, futures would be harmonic with such contexts (see §6.9), but we predict that they would not move into such non-assertive environments until they have lost much of their original force and meaning.

On the other hand, apodoses are prime environments for future grams. Apodoses are main clauses where predictions are made that are contingent on the conditions stated in the protasis. Our reference material contained many explicit statements about futures in apodoses, and we suppose that even where not explicitly stated, futures would be appropriate in this environment.

Other common subordinate clause contexts for futures are purpose clauses and the complements to main verbs meaning 'want' or 'order', as discussed in §§6.9–10. Table 7.13 shows the futures in our database with these uses. We argued in §6.10 that both the purpose clause and the complements of 'want' and 'order' are compatible or harmonic with the intention or goal-orientation of future grams. The fact that no aspectual futures have this use gives evidence that the substance of the future meaning is what makes these grams appropriate in these contexts.

As these are not assertive contexts, we would argue that uses in these contexts should develop late; however, only three of these nine forms are affixes, while the others are auxiliaries or particles, making it difficult to argue on the basis of form for an advanced stage of grammaticization. On the other hand, most of the particles and auxi-

Table 7.13. Purpose and Complement Clause Uses of Future Grams

Language	Form No.	Purpose	Complement
01 Inuit	16	x	
06 Touareg	15	x	'want' and 'order'
26 Motu	07		'want' and 'order'
27 Atchin	03	x	'want'
32 Nakanai	13	x	'want'
33 Trukese	03		'want' and 'think'
52 Yagaria	23	x	'order'
60 Yessan-Mayo	14	x	'want'
90 Dakota	03	x	'want' and 'order'

liaries used here are extremely reduced in form. The fact that they are not very early uses is shown by the fact that grams from any of the usual sources for futures can move into these clause types. The Atchin form is related to the verb 'go'; the Yagaria and Yessan-Mayo forms are from auxiliaries meaning 'do' or 'be'; and the Trukese form is possibly related to the conjunction or adverb 'then'.

Clearly, more research is necessary on the exact stages of diachronic development for futures in these types of subordinate clauses.

7.7. Aspectual futures

For grams marking perfective and imperfective aspect, future arises as a contextually determined use, and not, as is the case with primary futures, as an evolutionary endpoint in the unfolding development of originally lexical material. Since we have already explored the development of aspectual forms in some detail, we will rely heavily on the analyses presented in chapters 3 and 5. What we will see in this section is that presents tend to have future uses much more commonly than either general imperfectives or perfectives, and that since the future use is contextually determined, it more commonly arises in more generalized, more grammaticized, forms, which have less meaning of their own (cf. §6.11). Our report here differs considerably from the report on aspectual futures found in Bybee, Pagliuca, and Perkins 1991, since that report was written before an in-depth treatment of aspect and tenses other than future was accomplished.

The most usual case is the one in which a general present imperfective (cf. §5.6) can also be used for future time reference in a future context. The presence of the future context is essential, since the form would be interpreted as indicating present if no temporal reference is established by the context. Table 7.14 lists the languages in our sample which were described as having a future use for the general present. These eleven languages represent only one third of the

Table 7.14. Presents with Future Uses

Language	Form No.	Future Use	Other Uses
05 Agau	07	future	Present
15 Gugada	03	expected future	Present
17 Alyawarra	04	immediate future	Present
	05	immediate future	Present
47 Latin	07	expected future	Present
48 Maithili	15	future	Present
49 Baluchi	01	future	Present
	09	expected future	Progressive
50 Mod. Greek	07	expected future	Present
51 Danish	01	future	Present
71 Temne	10	future	Present
73 Tem	13	remote future	Imperfective
91 Udmurt	01	immediate future	Present
	02	negative immediate future	Present negative

languages analyzed as having a general present (see Table 5.4), and interestingly include all the Indo-European languages in our sample. It could be that the Indo-European descriptive tradition calls for the mention of this (usually minor) use of presents, while in other traditions it is simply not noted, though it may exist.

Of the languages in Table 7.14, all but one (Baluchi) have other, more direct means of signaling future, which justifies our claim that this use, although widespread, is a minor use of presents. Further, it can be noted that the future use is often specialized as being either immediate or expected future. In fact, as explained in §7.1.5, expected futures tend to occur only as other uses of presents. Even the progressive in Baluchi gives a sense of future progressive, suggesting that it is really the Baluchi present that is being used as a future here.

As mentioned before, the presents used as futures tend to be highly generalized, having progressive, habitual, gnomic, and often narrative uses. This suggests that the more specific meaning they once might have possessed has given way to a meaning so highly generalized as to be heavily influenced by the context. We can cite here the Tahitian form, classifiable either as a present or imperfective (see Table 7.16 and discussion below), with many diverse uses, including future, which is formed with the copula. This well-developed form can be compared to the obviously younger progressive in Tahitian, formed with a periphrasis meaning 'be here', which does not have a future use. The few cases we can find of younger grams, especially progressives, that can be used for future time reference are nonetheless relatively generalized. The English Progressive comes to mind: it can be used in future contexts, but then, the English progressive is so well developed as to be used even in habitual contexts (*I'm playing tennis every day now*). Similarly, the Alyawarra form *-iyla*, discussed in §5.6, is commonly used as a progressive, but it also has other uses that led us to classify it as an incipient present; thus it is not surprising that it can be used for future as well.

The fact that the future use of a present is a late development may help to explain why in some cases future is coupled with uses that are just a subset of the general present uses. In such cases it may be that a newly developed present has taken over the early core uses of the present and left the old present to serve a miscellaneous set of functions. A clear case of this sort of development may be found in the Dravidian language Kui, where a synthetic paradigm is used for future and present habitual, while a periphrastic one is used for present progressive. The synthetic form is the old present, which now survives in the two uses that the new progressive has not subsumed. Other, possibly similar, cases are listed in Table 7.15.

The Margi form consists of a prefix *a-*, which has a range of use so general as to appear to be a default form. It appears that it can be used in almost any temporal context, and is furthermore used in cases where it lacks a subject and is used after another finite verb (Hoffman 1963: 190–96). It could certainly be an old present, or even a nonfinite form, which now absorbs all its meaning from context. As we would predict, Margi also has a periphrastic imperfective for progres-

Table 7.15. Possible Old Presents Used for Future

Language	Form No.	Future Use	Other Uses
03 Margi	32	future	Present, past, habitual, root possibility, subjunctive
08 Tigre	21	future	Present habitual, narrative time
34 Pangasinan	05	future	Progressive (with reduplication)
42 Kui	02	future	Habitual, intention

Table 7.16. Imperfectives with Future Uses

Language	Form No.	Future Use	Other Uses
10 Isl. Carib	16	future	Subordinate imperfective
25 Tahitian	04	future	Present, past imperfective negative, polite imperative, hypothetical and counterfactual apodoses
35 Rukai	04	future	Imperfective, iterative
78 Kanuri	01	future	Subordinate imperfective

sive and habitual meaning, as well as a periphrastic future. The Tigre form used for future is formed by stem change, while the more specific progressive is formed with an auxiliary. The Pangasinan prefix used for future also appears on the progressive, which is a reduplicated form. A possible hypothesis about how this same prefix can occur on the progressive and future is that it is an old present, now augmented by reduplication to mean progressive, but surviving in its future use.

Many fewer imperfectives are used for future, and even some of these do not exactly qualify as general imperfectives (which explains why they do not appear in Table 5.2). For instance, the Island Carib and Kanuri forms have present and future uses but are used for past imperfective only in subordinate clauses in past contexts. The Tahitian form, classified as a present in chapter 5, is used in the negative where the distinction between present and past imperfective is neutralized. Only the Rukai form, which is a reduplicated form used for progressive, iterative, habitual, and future, appears to be a true imperfective in that it meets the criterion of being used in both present and past for imperfective.

Perfectives with future uses are even less common than imperfectives, as we would expect, given the widespread restriction of perfectives to the past (§3.11). The only cases we were able to verify in the sample are listed in Table 7.17. It can be seen that these perfectives all have other uses, and that in the case of the Tahitian form, the result of using the perfective in a future environment is a future anterior (*When you return, I will already be dead*). The other two perfectives give only an immediate future reading. It is possible to combine perfective and future morphemes in Touareg to give a future perfective sense, but here the perfective is not signaling future, it is merely compatible with it.

To summarize, then, it is most commonly presents that can be used to refer to future time, given the appropriate context. Much more rarely, imperfectives and perfectives can have future interpretations. The development of a new present (via a progressive) can have the effect of limiting an old present to future uses (and at times some other uses).

Table 7.17. Perfectives with Future Uses

Language	Form No.	Future Use	Other Uses
25 Tahitian	03	future anterior	Perfective, present state, resulting state
39 Abkhaz	44	Immediate future	Perfective, resultative, concessive
63 Baining	05	Immediate future	Perfective, imperative

7.8. Form–meaning covariation in futures

Dahl 1985 reported that in his survey of sixty-four languages, futures tended to have inflectional expression and periphrastic expression in approximately equal numbers. The same is true of the present survey. Since futures cover a wide range of expression types, it is possible to use grams expressing future meaning to test the form–meaning covariation hypothesis. In "Back to the Future" (Bybee, Pagliuca, and Perkins 1991) we reported on statistical findings that form and meaning covary in the grammaticization of future grams in sixty-seven of the languages of our database. The method used there is the same one illustrated in chapter 4 above.

We established four semantic ages for futures as in (69).

(69)   Futage 1: Futures with the agent-oriented uses of obligation, desire and ability
       Futage 2: Futures with the later agent-oriented uses of intention, root possibility, and the specific use of immediate future
       Futage 3: Grams with simple future as their only use
       Futage 4: Futures with epistemic, speaker-oriented, and subordinate uses

Using the same formal measures of shortness, dependence, and fusion as described in chapter 4, we sought statistical support for the hypothesis that formal change proceeds in parallel with semantic change in grammaticization. As with the perf grams discussed in chapter 4, we found highly significant relationships between the four semantic ages and the measures of formal grammaticization. We also found significant relationships between the overall degrees of formal grammaticization in a language and the extent to which its future gram(s) had undergone semantic development. Finally, even controlling for the effects of typology, we found significant relationships between form and meaning due to grammaticization. In sum, all the relations that were found to hold for perf grams in chapter 4 also hold for future grams.

As we mentioned earlier, another specific relationship that holds in our data is that immediate futures (with their more specific meaning) tend very strongly to be periphrastic rather than affixal: eight are affixal while twenty-two are periphrastic.

7.9. Conclusion

In this chapter we have reconsidered the paths of development for future grams from various sources. We have argued that despite a range of sources, from agent-oriented modalities to movement verbs to temporal adverbs, the paths converge early in the function of expressing the speaker's intentions. We also suggest that intention is the crucial bridge to prediction and that the change from intention to prediction occurs via the inferences that hearers make on the basis of the speaker's utterance. The more common sources for futures are those that yield the intention inference most easily—desire, strong obligation, and movement toward a goal. Weak obligation, ability, attempt, and temporal adverbs are not as susceptible to the intention inference and thus do not yield futures as readily. In re-examining futures derived with auxiliaries meaning 'be' or 'have', we have explored the possibility that such futures may develop without a stage in which they indicate obligation. Evidence suggests, however, that such futures do go through a stage of signaling intention.

Whereas earlier we claimed that the imperative use of futures was a development that took place late on the grammaticization path (Bybee and Pagliuca 1987; Bybee, Pagliuca, and Perkins 1991), the evidence examined here shows that futures that have not undergone a lot of formal grammaticization can have an imperative function.

Our data contain a large number of futures restricted to a time immediately after the moment of speech, but very few futures designated as referring to remote future time. A comparison with past grams shows more remote pasts than immediate pasts. Thus, future grams that divide future time according to the daily cycle are much rarer than past grams that refer to the daily cycle.

The most common sources of immediate futures in our database are verbs meaning 'come to'; 'go to' sources do not yield immediate futures in our data. Emanation's 1992 analysis of movement-derived futures helps to explain this distribution. 'Come to' futures require that the speaker's vantage point be displaced into the future. We suggest that such displacement is constrained to time relatively close to the present.

We have argued here and earlier, as has Dahl 1985, that the central functions in future grams are intention and prediction. It follows from this that future is less a temporal category and more a category resembling agent-oriented and epistemic modality, with important temporal implications. It follows also that both the expression of intentions (usually by the speaker) and the offering of predictions are commonly occurring interactional functions which are inferred from what is said, if not explicitly stated. It is these inferences which create the meaning of future grams.

• CHAPTER EIGHT •

Mechanisms of Semantic Change

8.1. Mechanisms

The foregoing chapters have demonstrated that the diachronic patterns created by grammaticization provide a useful framework for the cross-linguistic comparison of the form and meaning of grammatical morphemes. Synchronic universals have been elusive in the area of grammatical meaning because at any given time a gram's uses stretch over a sequence of links in the grammaticization chain. Only the diachronic perspective can reveal how these uses are related and how a given gram compares to similar grams in other languages.

The discovery that grammaticization paths are universal raises a whole new set of questions. We can now ask why languages have grammar and what processes lead to thē creation of grammar. Structuralist approaches to grammatical meaning sought to identify the one abstract meaning that all uses of a grammatical morpheme had in common. Facts about grammaticization suggest that grammatical meaning is constituted from a set of diachronically related uses with meanings that are contextually determined to a large extent. Meaning is substance, and the data suggest that the erosion of that substance in one environment does not necessarily entail the loss of meaning in all contexts. Thus we cannot always identify one abstract meaning that will be appropriate in all contexts. English *will* indicates willingness in *if*-clauses and certain other contexts, but prediction in other cases, especially with an inanimate subject. The fact that it occurs with a more abstract meaning in some contexts does not mean that we have to deny its more specific meaning in other contexts.[1]

Rather than searching for a single abstract sense of each gram, our

1. In such cases distinct but homophonous morphemes might have partially autonomous representations, which may undergo independent development.

research program asks us to identify diachronic relations between the uses of grams and to ask by what processes language users move a gram from one use to another. Thus despite the diachronic perspective of grammaticization, the ultimate question is a synchronic psycholinguistic question—how does meaning change in grammaticization take place in the minds of speakers while they are using language? Our understanding of the psychological and cognitive processes underlying language will be enhanced by the discovery of the mechanisms of change that create grammar.

Some of the questions that grammaticization theory asks have been examined here and in other recent work: Why are certain lexical sources commonly chosen for grammaticization? Why do particular changes occur along the way? Why is there convergence into a small number of universal gram-types? Underlying these questions is a still more basic one, which concerns mechanisms of change: How does grammaticization proceed? What are the mechanisms of change that propel a gram along a path of change?

Broad cross-linguistic data such as those examined in our reference grammar survey cannot always lead directly to the answer to this question. The question of mechanisms of change is most profitably studied by a close examination of texts which show a change in progress. Thus in various places in this work we have cited text-based studies such as Coates 1983, Bybee 1988b, and Faltz 1989, where the distribution and relative frequency of different uses of the same gram give evidence for the mechanism of change. While we do not have access to text-based studies for all the changes we have examined here, the very nature of the steps in the grammaticization chain often gives evidence for the mechanisms of change.

In the following sections we discuss five mechanisms of semantic change that we have found evidence for in the foregoing study of the development of tense, aspect, and modality. We will attempt to classify the changes we have discussed in the preceding chapters into one of these five mechanisms. We will also argue that certain of these mechanisms, such as metaphor, are characteristic of early stages of paths of change, while others, such as harmony, are found only in the later stages of grammaticization. The five mechanisms we discuss are **metaphorical extension**, **inference** or the conventionalization of implicature, **generalization**, **harmony**, and **absorption** of contextual meaning. In addition, we discuss briefly the mechanism by which zero grams are created. It should be emphasized, however, that grammaticization changes are complex and comprise many small steps. Close analysis of changes in progress may reveal a complex network of mechanisms applying together or in sequence.

8.2. Metaphor

When one compares a lexical source with the resulting grammatical meaning, or two grammatical meanings along a grammaticization path, one often finds a metaphorical relation between the two meanings. That is, one often finds a shift from a more concrete to a more abstract domain, with preservation of some of the relational structure originally expressed. This relation has led some researchers to propose that the major mechanism of change in grammaticization is metaphorical extension (Sweetser 1990; Heine, Claudi and Hünnemeyer 1991b; Lichtenberk 1991).

A comprehensive treatment of this position is found in Heine, Claudi, and Hünnemeyer 1991b, who discuss grammaticization in terms of 'problem solving' and the 'need' for the expression of certain grammatical functions in discourse:

> We try to demonstrate that metaphorical transfer forms one of the main driving forces in the development of grammatical categories; that is, in order to express more "abstract" functions, concrete entities are recruited. (p. 48)

Heine et al. recognize that metaphorical transfer entails an abrupt shift from one domain to another, while grammaticization is a gradual process. To account for the gradual shift of meaning in grammaticization, they recognize a second process, which is pragmatically motivated. This process "involves context-induced reinterpretation and metonymy and leads to the emergence of overlapping senses" (p. 113). According to this second process, a gram in a certain context acquires a sense in addition to its original sense, and this second sense then gradually becomes the conventionalized meaning of the gram (pp. 70ff.). This process is what we have referred to as change by inference or the conventionalization of implicature.

Heine et al. seem to be arguing that both metaphor and inference or context-induced reinterpretation are involved in all grammaticization changes. We, on the other hand, will argue that these are different mechanisms of change that occur under different circumstances. In our study of the grammaticization of tense, aspect, and modality, we have found very few examples of changes that can be accommodated in the metaphorical model. Those that we have found occur very early on the grammaticization paths and are perhaps best understood as similar to lexical changes. We proceed now to discuss some semantic changes that we regard as metaphorical in nature. In the following sections we discuss some changes that Heine et al. claim are metaphorical but which we regard as due to inference or simple generalization.

Perhaps the best-documented metaphorical changes that lead to the development of grammatical categories are the changes that allow body-part terms to be used to express spatial concepts (Svorou 1986, 1993; Heine, Claudi, and Hünnemeyer 1991a and b). Thus 'head', 'back', 'face', and 'stomach' are commonly used to express 'on', 'back', 'front', and 'in'. There is no reason to question the claim that metaphor is the mechanism of change that produces these spatial terms. We do question, however, whether these changes occur during grammaticization; it appears rather that these metaphors precede grammaticization and occur on the more lexical end of the continuum. Notice that English uses body-part terms for spatial relations in restricted contexts such as *the foot of the bed*, *the face of the cliff*, and *the face of the clock*. However, none of these phrases is grammaticized or grammaticizing in English at the moment. Such expressions may be the basis from which grammaticization of spatial terms proceeds, but the metaphor that produces them occurs before the generalization that is necessary for grammatical status is achieved.

Another change in which metaphor appears to be operative as the mechanism is the development of an epistemic sense for the English modal *must*. As we observed in §6.6.3, the obligation and probability senses of *must* occur in mutually exclusive environments. The obligation sense occurs in future contexts such as (1) and (2), while the probability reading occurs in past and present environments (3)–(6).

(1)   The letter must arrive sometime next week.
(2)   He must call Edith right now.
(3)   The letter must be in the mail.
(4)   The letter must have been in the mail.
(5)   He must have called three times while you were gone.
(6)   He must be trying to call me right now.

Since the two readings are not possible in the same context, the change to epistemic from the historically prior obligation sense cannot have occurred by inference. Metaphor is suspected because in the two readings *must* has a very similar meaning, but it is applied in two different domains. In the agent-oriented domain the speaker asserts that the subject is obliged to do something, while in the epistemic domain the speaker asserts that the proposition is obliged to be true and thus probably is true.

In chapter 6 we compared the distribution of agent-oriented and epistemic meanings for *must* with the distribution of the very similar agent-oriented and epistemic readings of *should* and found these distributions to be significantly different. *Should* can have obligation and probability readings in the same contexts, as shown by examples (7)–(9), which are all ambiguous.

(7) The letter should arrive sometime next week.
(8) The letter should be in the mail.
(9) The letter should have come last week.

We argued that the obligation reading of *should* implies the probability reading so that both readings can be obtained from the same sentence, suggesting that inference is the mechanism of change in this case.

The comparison of *must* and *should* is important for several reasons: (i) it shows that metaphor and inference do not necessarily always act together, but rather that the different mechanisms of change are operative in different cases; (ii) it shows that two very similar changes can be brought about in two distinct ways; and (iii) it shows that the stronger, more lexical meaning of *must* changes by metaphorical extension, while the more grammaticized *should* changes by the conventionalization of implicature or inference.

The evidence at hand, then, suggests that metaphor is a mechanism of semantic change for lexical meaning and for grammatical meaning closer to the lexical end of the scale, while inference is one of the mechanisms applicable to more grammaticized or more abstract meaning (cf. a similar claim made by Traugott 1989: 50). The reason is that metaphor requires a clear image-schematic structure that crosses cognitive domains. Such structures are more available near the lexical pole of the grammaticization continuum. As grammatical meaning becomes more abstract and more eroded, it is less suitable for metaphor and more subject to the contextual pressures that produce change by inference. We will continue to argue for the application of different mechanisms at earlier versus later stages of grammaticization. Our examples will also make it clear that metaphor is not involved in all grammaticization changes, as Heine et al. have argued.

8.3. Inference

Semantic change by inference was introduced in §6.6, but examples of inferential change occur in various sections of the book and we gather them together here to examine their common properties and attempt to distinguish metaphor from other mechanisms of semantic change. Note first that inference and implicature are two sides of the same coin: the speaker IMPLIES more than s/he asserts, and the hearer INFERS more than is asserted. We refer to the relevant mechanism of change as inference because it appears to be the hearer-based strategy and the speaker's sensitivity to the hearer's needs that conditions the semantic changes in question.

Inferencing is ongoing in verbal exchange. Recent treatments of inference identify a role for both the speaker and the hearer (Horn 1985; König 1988; García and van Putte 1989). Horn relates these roles to a principle of least effort. From the speaker's perspective this principle requires that the speaker say no more than s/he must, while from the hearer's perspective the principle requires that the speaker say as much as s/he can. There is a certain tension in these two requirements, a tension that both parties are aware of. One of the results of this delicate balance is that the hearer is obliged to extract all the meaning possible from the message, which includes all the implications that are not controversial. A semantic change can take place when a certain implication commonly arises with a certain linguistic form. That implication can be taken as part of the inherent meaning of the form, and can even go so far as to replace the original meaning of the form.

In comparing metaphor to inference it is important to remember that Heine et al. argue that metaphor is involved in a semantic change (i) if it moves from a more concrete to a more abstract domain and (ii) if the relational structure or image schema of the meaning is preserved in the transfer (1991b: 46–47). We argue first that there are changes which meet these criteria but which are not accomplished through the mechanism of metaphorical extension, and second that there are many changes in grammaticization that do not meet criterion (ii).

First consider two changes from agent-oriented to epistemic modality presented in §6.6, the changes of *should* and *may*. We have just reviewed the evidence that *should* does not acquire epistemic meaning by metaphorical extension, although it appears that *must* does. We have not examined texts which show the onset of epistemic meaning for *should*, although this should be possible as it must be a very recent change.[2] On the other hand, Bybee 1988b analyzes texts which show the onset of epistemic meaning for English *may* and comes to two very surprising conclusions. The image schema is precisely transferred from the agent-oriented to epistemic domains, as described by Sweetser 1990: 59).

> *May* is an absent potential barrier in the sociophysical world, and the epistemic *may* is the force-dynamically parallel case in the world of reasoning. The meaning of epistemic *may* would thus be that there is no barrier to the speaker's process of reasoning from the available premises to the conclusion expressed in the sentence qualified by *may*.

2. The epistemic use of *should* was not yet possible in Shakespeare's time; however, some past evidential uses of *should* occur in the Old English period (Traugott 1989: 41–43).

The first surprise is that despite the perfect transfer of the image schema, the texts show that inference was the process of change. As we showed in chapter 6, examples such as (10) (from *Sir Gawain and the Green Knight*) show *may* with a root possibility sense implying the epistemic sense.

(10)   ȝe ar a sleper ynslyȝe, that mon **may** slyde hider;
        'You are so unwary a sleeper that someone can sneak in here;'

The second surprise is that the scope change from verb phrase scope to propositional scope that is necessary for epistemic meaning and which one would surmise would have to be abrupt (indicating a metaphorical shift) is actually gradual. The examples of *may* that imply epistemic meaning are just those in which the agent is an indefinite pronoun, as in (10), or not present, as in a passive or stative sentence. In just such cases, verb phrase scope is nearly equivalent to propositional scope, since the only element that lies outside the verb phrase is the agent, and in these cases the agent is practically devoid of semantic content. Notice that the properties of inference are compatible with these intermediate examples, but that metaphor as the mechanism would predict that the change could occur in any type of sentence, and that it would be an abrupt change.

As we have pointed out in a number of publications (Bybee and Pagliuca 1987; Bybee, Pagliuca, and Perkins 1991; Bybee 1988a), the future meaning of *will* and *shall* arises through a stage in which these grams are used for intention with first person subjects. In *Sir Gawain and the Green Knight,* almost one half of the uses of *shall* and almost one half of the uses of *will* are with first person subjects. In both cases the sense is one of intention, with the further nuance of a promise or threat for *shall* and willingness or resolution for *will*. We suggest that the intention use arises through inference from the use of the obligation and desire senses in first person. This mechanism can be illustrated by considering some Modern English counterparts of *shall* and *will*—*hafta* and *wanna*. If someone says *I hafta go now,* the speaker is invited to infer that the speaker intends to go now unless otherwise advised. (In fact, *I hafta go now, but I'm not going to* sounds contradictory, suggesting that the intention meaning is already conventionalized with *hafta*). That is, the hearer looks for "an enriched interpretation" (König 1988: 160) that will explain why the speaker is mentioning his obligations. The hearer asks, Why would s/he say 'I hafta go now' unless s/he indeed were going now? Similarly, if someone says *I wanna go now,* the hearer is expected to infer that the speaker is on his/her way out unless otherwise informed. (In this case *I wanna go now, but I can't* does not sound contradictory.) These normal inferences can become so associated with the verbal expressions that they in fact become part of the meaning of the expressions, leading to the process that Traugott 1989 calls "pragmatic strengthening."

From intention we can also arrive at prediction through inference. This step can be illustrated with the Modern English phrase *be going to*, which is used both for intention and prediction. If someone says *When he gets a pay raise, Jack's gonna start looking for a house*, we could actually interpret that as a statement about the subject's intentions or a prediction made by the speaker. If the speaker asserts that someone intends to do something, the hearer can safely infer (unless otherwise advised) that the speaker also predicts that the subject will do that thing. The hearer's reasoning is that the speaker would not report someone's intentions (without further comment) unless the speaker expects the intentions to be carried out.

Now the change from obligation and desire to intention cannot very well be interpreted as metaphorical in nature. First, the change does not entail moving from one domain to another, since intention is in the realm of human goal-oriented activity just as obligation and desire are (Heine, Claudi, and Hünnemeyer 1991b: 174). On the other hand, the shift from intention to prediction is a clear change in domain and scope—from what an agent intends to what the speaker asserts. Yet here it does not seem possible to locate the image schema that is transferred from one domain to the other. It appears that inference provides a more accurate account of these changes than metaphor does.

Another clear case of the operation of inference in semantic change is the case of the development of present state uses for anterior and perfective grams with stative predicates, as discussed in §3.9. There we presented examples from a number of languages showing that anteriors and perfectives can develop a present state reading with process or change of state predicates. Consider these examples from Kanuri, which uses the Perfect suffix *nà* (Hutchison 1981: 121–22) in the two cases in (11).

(11)   With dynamic predicates:
          Módù ísɔ́nà. 'Modu has arrived.'
          Shíà rúkɔ́nà.'I have seen him.'
       With 'completive stative' meaning:
          Nòngɔ́nà.   'I know.'
          Ríngɔ́nà.   'I am afraid.'
          Gɔ́rgázɔ́nà. 'S/he is angry.'

This stative sense derives from the implications inherent in the use of the anterior with a change of state predicate. Thus 'the fruit has ripened' or 'the fruit has gotten ripe' implies that the fruit is now ripe.

The hearer is entitled to infer from such statements in most contexts that the important message the speaker is conveying does not concern the process of ripening, but rather the fact that the fruit is now ripe and perhaps ready for eating. With certain types of verbs, the presence of this implication is so reliable that it becomes first part of the meaning of the construction and later the only meaning of the construction.

This inferential change is an interesting one because it does not resemble change by metaphor in the least. It is not even clear that it represents a change from a more concrete domain to a more abstract domain, unless a process is more concrete than a state (cf. Heine et al.'s ranking of 'process' and 'quality,' with the latter represented as more abstract [1991b:55]). More importantly, there appears to be no way in which this semantic change can be regarded as a change that transfers an image-schema structure from one domain to another. The image-schema structures of entering a state and being in a state do not resemble one another. If anything, the link between them is chronological and/or causal.

Another change by inference in which the context plays a decisive role is the change of an anterior to a hodiernal past. This infrequent change is attested in seventeenth-century French and Modern Spanish, as we reported in §3.16 (see Comrie 1985b:85). Schwenter 1993 has argued that such a change takes place by the frequent reporting of situations as anterior (past with current relevance) which have occurred on the same day as the speech event. Such frequent use of a gram in a particular context, as we have seen, can lead to the inference that that context is actually part of the meaning of the gram.

What makes inference interesting as a mechanism of change is the fact that inference allows the incorporation of new meaning into a gram. Meaning from the context that was not originally present can inhere in a gram as the result of inference. Yet the orderliness of semantic change in grammaticization and the universality of paths of change demonstrate that the process of infusion of new meaning into a gram is quite constrained. The constrained set of inferential changes that can be discovered in grammaticization are interesting in their own right, as they will reveal to us the nature of the commonly made inferences that guide speakers and hearers in conversation.

8.4. Generalization

Generalization is the loss of specific features of meaning with the consequent expansion of appropriate contexts of use for a gram. Generalization can be seen as a description of what happens in some cases of grammaticization, but what is not clear is whether generalization is itself a mechanism of change or whether generalization is just the outcome of a change caused by some other mechanism. An elegant example of generalization can be found in the development of verbs signaling mental or physical ability into markers of general ability and root possibility. The meaning changes at each stage can be described as the loss of one feature of meaning (Bybee 1988b).

(12)   *can*
        mental ability
                (i)   mental enabling conditions exist in
                        an agent for the completion of the
                        predicate situation
        general ability
                (ii)   enabling conditions exist in an agent
                        for the completion of the predicate
                        situation
        root possibility
                (iii)   enabling conditions exist for the
                        completion of the predicate situation

The same series of events follows from physical ability (as with *may*); each step in the process can be seen as the loss of one of the components of the meaning.

The question concerns the mechanism that causes the loss of meaning; Is generalization itself a mechanism, or is some other mechanism such as metaphor or inference involved? The answer to this question can be gained only through textual evidence, but the alternate scenarios can be sketched in anticipation of textual evidence.

If metaphor were involved, the first uses of *can* for general or physical ability would be anomalous, for as Heine et al. point out (1991b: 47), the standard definitions of metaphor observe that metaphors violate the rules for putting words together. Thus the jump to use with non-mental activities would be abrupt (perhaps analogous to *I know how to bench press 200 pounds*).

Another route to generalized ability (Bybee 1988b) takes into account the fact that many activities have both a mental and a physical component. While *can* would have originally been used with complement verbs such as *read*, *spell*, and *paint*, it might have gradually generalized to verbs that involve both mental and physical skills, such as *sew*, *cook*, *build*, or *plant*. Once it is used with these activities, its meaning would appear to refer to general ability, and it could further be extended to use with verbs that suggest more physical than mental prowess, such as *swim* or *lift*.

A similar generalization can be envisioned for the development of the root possibility uses, which are appropriate when the enabling conditions exist both in the subject and in the general physical or social environment. That is, what one is able to do often depends on the external conditions; whether or not someone can ride a particular horse or play a particular sonata depends in some measure on the horse and the sonata. Similarly, social conditions impinge on one's ability to complete certain activities, so that the move to root possibility could proceed by the physical and social routes simultaneously.

Thus generalization might be viewed as a slow and gradual movement through the catalogue of possible activities, starting in this case with those involving mental skills and expanding gradually to those that involve both the mental and physical, to those that involve only physical, and finally to those that involve external conditions. This gradual lexical expansion could be viewed as segmentable into numerous tiny metaphors or even multiple and equally tiny changes by inference, but until the textual evidence has been uncovered and analyzed, it appears that generalization can be regarded as a mechanism of change.

The development of progressives and *go*-futures might also be described as generalization, but here the claim is more controversial since both of these constructions involve a change from the spatial to the temporal domain, and such changes resemble metaphorical change. The most commonly used construction for the expression of progressive meaning is a phrase meaning 'to be at doing', which originally has locative meaning. In many languages such a construction has a purely temporal sense, expressing the progressive. Does this change involve a metaphorical jump from the spatial to the temporal domain?

As pointed out in Bybee and Dahl 1989 and here in §5.3, there is no reason to invoke a metaphorical extension to explain the temporal meaning of progressive constructions. An expression that means that an agent is located spatially in an activity also implies in every instance that that agent is temporally located in that activity.[3] That is, from the beginning that construction had both a spatial and a temporal dimension. Of course, at first the spatial is explicitly expressed and the temporal just follows from it. So what needs explaining is how the spatial sense is lost and only the temporal remains. A reasonable account

3. Since the implication is always present, the hearer does not have to supply the inference, which makes this case of inference different from those discussed in §8.3.

Chapter Eight

might postulate that at first the progressive is used where both spatial and temporal readings are reasonable, but gradually the construction is expanded to use with activities for which spatial location is less important and temporal involvement is more important—that is, from activities that take place at special locations such as 'he is fishing' or 'he is bathing', to activities that might take place at various locations such as 'he is working' or 'he is helping someone', finally to activities that imply no location, such as 'he is talking' or 'he is singing'. Of course, what is important here also is the main message being conveyed in the context: while both spatial and temporal meaning is conveyed, the temporal may be more important more often, leading to the interpretation that the progressive basically signals temporal meaning.[4]

One might ask of such cases why the shift in meaning is from spatial to temporal if no metaphor is involved, since there is no disputing the validity of spatial to temporal metaphors in lexical change. The answer to this is that shifting to the purely temporal meaning is the only direction of change that would lead to an increase in frequency and thus to the grammaticization of the construction.

The same reasoning applies to futures such as the English *be going to* future. While it is certainly the case (as pointed out by Sweetser 1988) that the same image schema structure for spatial 'be going to' is preserved in temporal 'be going to', it does not follow that metaphorical extension is the operative mechanism of change. Once again, the temporal meaning was present in the construction from the beginning. *We're going to Windsor to meet the King* emphasizes the spatial but certainly makes a temporal statement as well. Again, the construction can spread gradually from cases where the spatial is important to cases where both temporal and spatial are important and finally to cases where only the temporal is relevant.

The cases of the generalization of ability on the one hand, and the emergence of the temporal components of progressive and 'go'-futures are not exactly parallel and may eventually be shown to be controlled by different mechanisms. However, these cases resemble one another more than any of them resembles change by metaphor or by inference. Unlike change by inference, in generalization the context is important not because meaning from the context is transferred to the developing gram, but because use in more contexts causes a shift in the primary message being conveyed, which contributes eventually to the loss of specific features of meaning.

4. An anonymous reader of this manuscript pointed out that the metaphor necessary for this type of progressive occurs very early, at the point at which a verb denoting an activity comes to be used in the locative phrase rather than an actual locative term. E.g., *He is at the swimming hole* and the later development *He is (at) swimming*.

Other cases where generalization might be the mechanism have been discussed in the preceding chapters and in the literature on grammaticization. One interesting set of cases is those in which an emphatic morpheme loses its emphatic value. We suspect that has happened where a completive with a stative verb signals simple present state. Other well-known cases are the loss of emphatic value for pronouns and for markers of negation, e.g. English *nought* > *not* and French *ne . . . pas*, both of which were formerly used for emphasis and are now the normal non-emphatic methods of negation.

Another change that is probably attributable to generalization is the change from progressive to imperfective, which involves an extension of the progressive to habitual contexts. Similarly, the change of an anterior (past action with current relevance) to a simple past or perfective involves the loss of the current relevance component of meaning, and generalization to more and more contexts. The latter change might occur in discourse when the speaker wants to present his/her narrative as though it were currently relevant, which would lead to the use of the anterior in narrative environments and the erosion of the current relevance aspect of the meaning. These aspectual changes cannot be attributable to metaphorical transfer because the meaning does not change domains—it is in the temporal domain both before and after the change. Nor is the image schema maintained; in fact, the image schema loses a feature.

Perhaps more than the other mechanisms we have reviewed, generalization needs more careful study. The cases we have mentioned in this section are not all completely parallel and may reveal more than one mechanism at work. However, it is important to recognize that inference and metaphor are not sufficient to account for all cases of grammaticization and that cases describable as generalization give evidence for other mechanisms.

8.5. Harmony

In our discussion of the development of subordinating moods (in §6.9), we argued that the use of modal elements in subordinate clauses could be explained as cases of modal harmony. That is, modal elements such as British *should* are used in subordinate clauses where their modal force agrees with or harmonizes with the modal force of the main clause. In such circumstances, the modal element does not contribute additional meaning to the sentence. From uses in such cases, we argued, the modal element can be generalized to other subordinate clauses, even those in which it is not modally harmonic.

As a mechanism of change, harmony would be restricted to cases in which the grammaticizing element had already lost most of its semantic content, because it must be interpreted as not contributing its own meaning to the clause. This mechanism, then, applies only to the later stages of grammaticization. It is not necessarily restricted to modal meanings, however. Sequence of tense phenomena may be attributable to harmony, and other types of agreement, such as negative agreement, or even number and gender agreement, may result from the harmonic occurrence of grams in context.

8.6. The development of zero grams

Our study of grammaticization has focused on the inherent semantic content of grams and how use and context change this content in the process of grammaticization. Cases also exist, however, in which the development of one gram has the effect of endowing certain meaning in another paradigmatically contrasting gram or even in the absence of a gram, a zero morpheme. Again, context plays a very important role in this process. We will review two types of cases here—the development of zeroes in tense/aspect systems in this section, and the restriction of old indicatives to "subjunctive" contexts in the next.

Since we have claimed that grams have semantic substance that erodes or is modified in grammaticization, the development of morphemes with zero expression is of special interest to us. Bybee 1990b addresses the question of the source of the meaning that is assigned to zero grams, arguing that this meaning arises from the context. The particular mechanism that allows the absence of a gram to be interpreted as meaningful is inferential: as a developing overt gram (such as a past) is used with greater frequency, the inference is eventually made that if the speaker does not use the past gram, then s/he means to contrast with past. By this inference, tense becomes obligatory and the absence of a tense marker signals present tense (see also García and van Putte 1989).

The use of zero grams for certain meanings but not for others is a consequence of which meanings tend to be overtly grammaticized. We observed in chapter 3 that when an anterior gram generalizes, it will become a past if there is no existing imperfective past. The result of this generalization will be a zero present, if no overt present already exists or is developing. A progressive will generalize to an imperfective in a language lacking tense, and the result can be a zero perfective (see also Bybee 1990b). What is remarkable is that the senses conveyed by zero grams is similar in content and structure to that carried by overt grams. The reason for this similarity is the important role played by context in the development of both zero and overt grams.

The evidence from grammaticization and the existence of universal gram types (Dahl 1985) suggests that the conceptual domain of tense and aspect is universal, as is the way in which it is actualized in discourse. The way human discourse is framed relies on certain ever-present discourse or conceptual functions. One of these occurs in narrative as the main sequence of events and is grammaticized as perfective or simple past. Another is the descriptive or background function, grammaticized in imperfective aspect. For present tense descriptions there is the generic function stating the way things are and grammaticized as habitual (which is almost always zero; Bybee 1990b), as well as the ongoing, temporary situations, expressed in the progressive.

The scheme of temporal space that is outlined by grammatical categories is very broad, as these categories are very general and make very little semantic contribution in context. The meaning they explicitly express cuts out certain large areas of the conceptual space that is present in the speech context. These same areas can be evoked by other linguistic elements or by the non-linguistic context, making the explicit meaning of the gram redundant in many cases. Since the functional context is ever-present and portions of it can be evoked in various ways, every language does not have to have explicit grammatical markers for all functions. In fact, three options are available: these major functions can be marked overtly; they can be marked with zero; or they can be without grammatical exponence. As Bybee (1990b: 6) puts it:

> This view explains why such obviously important grammatical distinctions as between present and past time reference, or perfective and imperfective aspect are so similar across languages, and yet can be completely lacking in grammatical systems without impeding communication in the least: they are ever present in the context and thus can be inferred if a marker is lacking, but if one should be developing, it naturally extends to cover these focal portions of the conceptual space.

8.7. Older grams with restricted domains

Since grammaticization is a continuous process and new grams are always developing along the major grammaticization paths, it is often the case that certain functions of older grams are being replaced by newly developed ones. Many examples are at hand: *can* is replacing *may* as the expression of root possibility; the English Progressive is replacing the simple present; *will* is replacing *shall* and *be going to* is replacing *will*. In German and Dutch the Perfect is replacing the older simple past; in French and Spanish the 'go'-future is replacing the older synthetic future. What effect does this replacement process have on the meaning of the older grams?

In some cases the older grams are completely replaced and thereby lost from the language. In other cases they are restricted to special contexts, but their meaning remains unchanged. Such is the case with the Passé Simple of French, which now occurs only in written texts but is semantically equivalent to the newer Passé Composé.

More interesting from our perspective, however, are the cases discussed in §6.11 of grams whose meaning appears to change due to the linguistic contexts to which they are restricted by newer developing grams. In these cases, modal meaning seems to arise in forms that were previously indicatives. As we pointed out there, since new grammaticizations of tense and aspect tend to arise in main, asserted clauses, pre-existing tense and aspect forms tend to be preserved longer in subordinate clauses, especially those that are not asserted but rather have some other modality, such as the expression of conditions or purposes or complements to verbs of wanting or ordering. Since these old forms have so little semantic content of their own, if they survive, they are available to absorb the modal content of their context. After being excluded from indicative functions for a time and associated only with subordinate modal functions, when these forms move back into main clauses uses, they are reported to express a weak kind of hortative or obligation sense. Our claim is that these elderly forms have picked up some modal flavor from their subordinate clause environment. Note that such cases differ from the more usual change by inference in that the meaning they are absorbing comes from the LINGUISTIC context, the context of the clause and its function in the sentence, more than from the general pragmatic context.

Even changes of this sort are highly constrained and in principle predictable. One constraint is that such radical meaning shifts will occur only in the very late stages of grammaticization, when the original meaning of the gram has so weakened as to be unable to resist infusion from the outside.

8.8. The mechanisms of change at different stages of development

The claim we have been developing in this chapter is that different mechanisms of change are operative at different stages in the grammaticization process. In particular, metaphor is only possible in the very early stages, when the semantic content is very specific.

(13)

Early	Middle	Late

—— metaphor —— - - -

———————————————— inference ——————————————————▶

———————————————— generalization ———————- - - - - - - -

———————— harmony ————————▶

—— absorption of context ——————▶

Inference and generalization appear to be possible mechanisms at various stages; inference in particular may be a part of change of all types. Generalization would seem to grow less likely as the meaning of the gram fades more and more and becomes more dependent on context.

The most important point that can be made from the discussion of mechanisms of change is that context is all-important. Everything that happens to the meaning of a gram happens because of the contexts in which it is used. It is the use of language in context that shapes the meaning of grammatical morphemes. Thus a true understanding of the mechanisms of change that create grammatical meaning must proceed from analyses of the use of grams as these changes are taking place.

8.9. Explanation

Of course, the ultimate question concerning grammaticization is why it occurs at all. Why do languages develop grammatical morphemes and grammatical structures? Our approach to explanation differs from that of some other researchers examining grammaticization in that we do not appeal to motivations or to functional teleology. That is, we do not subscribe to the notion that languages develop grammatical categories because they NEED them. A recent statement of this view can be found in Heine, Claudi and Hünnemeyer 1991b: 29, who say, "Grammaticalization can be interpreted as the result of a process that has problem solving as its main goal, whereby one object is expressed in terms of another." Their model explicitly maintains that "the need for presenting a certain grammatical function . . . in discourse leads to the recruitment of a lexical form for the expression of this function" (ibid).

Arguments against this position (which has often been expressed earlier, see Givón 1982: 117) are presented in Bybee (1985: 203–5) and repeated here.

(i) We cannot claim that a language NEEDS a particular gram-type because no gram-type is universal. For example, while future is a very common gram-type, it is not universal, and we cannot claim that a language which lacks a future gram is dysfunctional. Apparently the speakers of such languages find it completely adequate for communication.

(ii) Two or more markers can arise to fulfill very similar communicative needs. This would apparently not occur if only communicative need were motivating grammaticization.

(iii) Inflectional markers are often redundant in context, suggesting that speakers do not really NEED them to be there.

(iv) Finally, a case is presented in Bybee 1985 from Silva-Corvalán 1985 which shows that the spread of the Conditional marker in Spanish at the expense of the Imperfect Subjunctive actually CREATES ambiguity rather than increasing expressiveness.

To add to these arguments, we refer back to our discussion of mechanisms of change. The minute semantic changes that constitute a grammaticization chain are not each one directed toward creating a grammatical morpheme. When a verb 'want' is first used with a verb phrase complement, it is not because the language has the ultimate goal of creating a future tense several centuries later. Even when a hearer infers intention from a statement expressing desire (*I wanna*), it is not with the goal of creating a future tense. When prediction is inferred from a statement of intention, it is not because the language NEEDS a future tense. All these events would occur whether or not the language already has a future tense.

Thus our view of grammaticization is much more mechanistic than functional: the relation between grammar and function is indirect and mediated by diachronic process. The processes that lead to grammaticization occur in language use for their own sakes; it just happens that their cumulative effect is the development of grammar. The very systematic nature of the development of grammar is attributable to the very systematic nature of the mental and communicative processes that govern language use. Thus grammaticization presents us with one of the most valuable tools for investigating speaker/hearer interaction in language use, as well as strong evidence that such processes are universal.

Further evidence against the functionalist teleology is the ironical fact that efforts to be more concrete and specific lead to the loss of specific concrete components of meaning in grammaticization (Lehmann 1985; García 1987). For instance, if a verb formerly meaning 'want' is now used for intention or prediction, then speakers must choose another verb with a more specific meaning of 'want' if that is what they mean to express. However, the increased use of the new verb 'want' starts it down the grammaticization path toward losing its specific meaning and traveling toward the expression of intention and prediction. Thus the need to be more specific increases the frequency of more specific items, which in the end has the effect of reducing their specificity. The attempt to be more specific leads in the long run to generalization.

In a paper circulated since 1971 and published in 1990, Labov asks the question of why languages have grammar, in particular why languages have tense. His examination of discourse by pidgin speakers convinced him that languages do not really need tense; speakers can communicate their thoughts without recourse to grammar. Even so, studies of creole grammar show a clear and inexorable grammaticization of tense and aspect markers. Labov says:

> It is clear that grammatical innovations are usually conceived as responses to conceptual needs. Yet here in the elaboration of creole auxiliaries we see a grammatical process with the same compulsive, automatic character as we recognize in sound change. (p. 32)

Labov goes on to point out that almost as soon as an auxiliary develops in a creole system, phonological erosion and coalescence begin to destroy its perceptibility, leaving us wondering once again how such grams could be fulfilling communicative needs.

What, then, is the reason for grammar to exist? Labov's observation is the following:

> On the whole grammar is not a tool of logical analysis; grammar is busy with emphasis, focus, down-shifting and upgrading; it is a way of organizing information and taking alternative points of view. (p. 45)

According to this view, tense and aspect grams allow speakers to present temporal information without necessarily foregrounding it by framing it in lexical terms. Being grammatical information, temporal reference can be incorporated into a sentence without interfering with other dimensions of the message, as lexical expression of time might.

To this observation we would like to add that the grammatical framework, consisting of both word order regularities and grammatical morphemes, provides a means of facilitating production through automation. The obligatory grams and the rule-like nature of word order patterns are automatically supplied so that the speaker's attention may be directed to the propositional content of the utterance. The advantages of automation can explain why categories or structures become obligatory despite the fact that they are not always strictly necessary for communication.[5] Automation thus leads to the semantic reduction that propels the inexorable cycling of grammatical material.

Our view, then, is that grammaticization is not goal-directed; grams cannot "see" where they are going, nor are they pulled into abstract functions. The push for grammaticization comes from below—it originates in the need to be more specific, in the tendency to infer as much as possible from the input, and in the necessity of interpreting items in context. This means of course that the grammaticization process has the potential for revealing a great deal about the psychology of language use, but it also means that the method for studying grammaticization must at once be cross-linguistic and context-oriented.

8.10. Implications for synchronic analysis and cross-language comparison

Here we summarize our conclusions with regard to synchronic analysis and typological comparisons. First, the view of grams as ever-developing along universal pathways has implications for language-specific synchronic analysis; in particular, we do not expect each language to have a unique system of contrasts that display economy and symmetry. Rather we expect to find that language-specific grams have inherent semantic content (derived from their original lexical content), and that grams are polysemous in predictable ways, that is, that they span contiguous areas of a grammaticization path. Since the development of individual grams is independent, we are not surprised to find some overlap in the function of grams and the continuous introduction of new grams into the grammatical system despite the prior existence of functional grams.

Second, our theory has implications for language universals: following Dahl 1985 and Bybee and Dahl 1989, we claim that the substantive universals are the gram-types, the focal areas of semantic domains that come to have grammatical expression. Under this view, focal gram-types such as perfective or present can be the vehicle for cross-language comparison. Of course, there are many language-specific differences in the manifestation of these gram-types, but still they offer a useful level of cross-language comparison. As noted in §5.6.2, gram-types can be viewed as analogous to phonetic descriptions of the type "voiceless bilabial stop." All linguists are familiar with

---

5. In support of this notion, we refer to Labov's (1990: 14) observation that pidgins are spoken in a slow and deliberate manner, but "when pidgins become creoles, and acquire native speakers, they are spoken with much greater speed and fluency." Of course it is precisely this speed and fluency that leads to the continual phonological reduction of grammatical morphemes.

the prototype of this category, phonetic transcription systems offer a simple symbol for representing this category, and general statements can be made about such an entity, such as that voiceless bilabial stops tend to spirantize and eventually delete. At the same time, it is true that voiceless bilabial stops differ from one language to another, in terms of their physical properties such as voice-onset timing and in terms of their contextual variants or morphophonemic alternants. This particular level of comparison, then, affords us a means of pointing both to similarities and differences among languages.

In the discussions in this book we have pointed to similarities among grams, which we attribute to the existence of universal paths of semantic development, and we have pointed to differences among grams of the same gram-type. The differences have three sources: (i) grams can differ in their meaning because they may develop from different sources and retain traces of their source meanings; (ii) grams may be at different stages on the same path, and thus cover different ranges of meaning; and (iii) grams necessarily interact with other grams in the same semantic domain, either because they contrast with them (as perfective contrasts with imperfective) or because they compete for some of the same uses (as *will*, *shall*, and *be going to* compete for future functions in English).

8.11. Tense, aspect, and modality

In this book we have identified the most commonly occurring gram-types in the temporal and modal semantic domains:

> those that express the completion of an action (completive), or a past action with resulting current state (resultative) or current relevance (anterior);
> the more general expression of a situation as bounded (perfective) or as having occurred before the moment of speech (past), grams whose function in discourse is to foreground and sequence events;
> those that view a situation as ongoing (progressive) or characteristic of a period of time (habitual), or in other ways continuing or repeated;
> the more general view of a situation from within (imperfective);
> those that describe human desires, obligations, abilities, and intentions (agent-oriented modalities);
> those that express the degree of assertion of the speaker (epistemic modalities);
> those with which the speaker performs an act (speaker-oriented modalities);
> those that indicate the speaker's prediction (future);

those that occur regularly in certain types of subordinate clauses.

This catalogue reflects the most frequently occurring discourse and interactional functions in these semantic domains. As we said above, these particular functions do not grammaticize because speakers need markers for them; rather, they are simply available, as very frequent functions, for developing grams with appropriate meanings to encompass. Thus our study has revealed some basic substantive categories of human discourse and interaction.

As striking as these generalizations are, they are not as strong as the generalizations we can make concerning paths of change. The proposed paths of change developed in the preceding chapters have greater potential for validity as absolute universals (of the sort "given a source construction x, a set sequence of changes will be followed"). Moreover, as we have shown, the view that grammatical categories span points along a continuous path, trailing some past traits and pushing forward into new uses, offers a greater potential for making grammatical meaning across languages comparable.

However, the search for explanation takes us to yet another level: underlying these cross-linguistic patterns are the true universals, which are the mechanisms of change that propel grams along these paths of development. The changes we have studied reflect what is commonly used in conversation, they reflect the metaphorical processes that are based on human cognitive make-up, and they reflect the inferences that humans commonly make when they communicate. The cross-linguistic similarity of these paths of change, then, attests to universal mechanisms of metaphor, inference, and contextual influence in the use of language in the cultures of the world.

• • •

Appendix A
GRAMCATS Sampling Procedure

I. Sampling Objectives

A. Sample between seventy-five and one hundred languages to test linguistic hypotheses concerning relationships between form and meaning in verbs.

B. Minimize the relationships between sampled languages so that reasonable inferences can be made as to relationships across linguistic TYPES as opposed to across languages. Care should be taken in the sampling design to insure that the languages are maximally unrelated.

C. Language isolates and pidgin/creoles should be represented in the sample by a number roughly proportional to their numbers in the universe of all languages. This restriction with regard to language isolates is necessary to insure against the results being due to a large number of language isolates appearing in the sample (as they would if the preceding requirement was not qualified by this one). There is a chance that language isolates are significantly different from other language types; alternatively, additional data may reveal genetic relations between isolates and other languages. Establishing this is not the purpose of this research, and in order to have a more "representative" sample of languages and fewer than one hundred languages in the sample, this restriction is imposed. Pidgins/creoles are usually listed as related to the language from which their vocabulary is derived. This is clearly unacceptable for the present work, since grammar and not vocabulary is the focus of research. Therefore, the pidgins/creoles in the universe to be sampled are put into a separate list and sampled separately.

D. Use Voegelin and Voegelin 1978, *Classification and index of the world's languages,* as the universe of languages on which to base a sample. It provides the most complete and uniformly applied listing of the world's languages to date. This is with clear recognition that there are problems with the list, such as the treatment of pidgins/ creoles mentioned above. Other obvious problems are the unevenness of the criteria used in grouping languages and the terminology used to refer to these groups. In some cases the grouping criteria are due to extensive historical reconstruction, in others they emerge from lexicostatistic studies, and in others it is admittedly only the languages of a geographic region that are identified as a group. Nevertheless, Voegelin and Voegelin's listing is useful because it provides an objective basis for sampling that has been established without regard to the current hypotheses.

E. In order to derive a bona fide probability sample, every language in the universe must have a specifiable chance of being in the sample, so that statistical techniques may be legitimately applied. If all languages do not have the same chance of being sampled, the sample is still a probability sample since the results from such a sample can be adjusted mathematically, if desired, to be identical to that obtained by simple random sampling where each language has an equal chance of being selected. The results obtained by a stratified sample where languages do not have equal chances of being selected are more conservative than those obtained by pure random sampling, since there will presumably be more variation in the data introduced by the stratification techniques. Therefore, the mathematical techniques to produce the results obtained by strictly random sampling need not be applied as long as it is understood that the results obtained are a conservative test of the hypothesis with regard to the languages in the universe.

II. Descriptive background on the universe of languages

Table A.1.   Group Size

Number of Languages	Number of Groups	Group Type
1	47	Minimal
2	4	
4	1	
5	1	
6	2	
22	1	Small
23	1	
25	1	
26	1	
30	2	
32	1	
33	2	
36	1	
50	1	Medium
60	1	
78	1	
89	1	
109	1	
122	1	
155	1	Large
209	1	
249	1	
275	1	
289	1	
323	1	
747	1	Macro
792	1	
1046	1	

III. Sampling definitions

Due to the lack of standard terminology for the various sorts of linguistic groupings, the following are used here for the purpose of sampling.

A. Language: An entity identified as such by Voegelin and Voegelin that does not have members that are also languages. Dialects and alternate names are often listed for a language. A language is the lowest level of grouping for languages. They are not printed in all capitals by Voegelin and Voegelin.

B. Linguistic group: A set of languages named by Voegelin and Voegelin, perhaps containing only a single language. These are printed in all capital letters by Voegelin and Voegelin.

C. Maximal group: A linguistic group that does not belong to any larger linguistic group. There is no restriction here on the number of languages in a group, so that language isolates are also maximal groups.

Note that the pidgins and creoles are considered a maximal group for sampling purposes although they are not grouped in that way by Voegelin and Voegelin.

D. Primary subgroup: A linguistic group that is a member along with others of a maximal group with no intervening level of grouping. Again, this says nothing about the number of languages contained in a primary group.

E. Secondary subgroup: A linguistic group that is a member along with others of a primary subgroup with no intervening level of grouping. Again, this says nothing about the number of languages contained in a secondary group.

F. Primary-residue subgroup: The set of all languages in a maximal group that do not belong to a primary subgroup of twenty or more languages.

G. Secondary-residue subgroup: The set of all languages in a primary subgroup that do not belong to a secondary subgroup of twenty or more languages.

Table A.2.   Grouping of Languages from Which the Sample Was Selected

UNAFFILIATED			AUSTRALIAN		(323)
(i.e., <7 in group)		(76)	*Pama-Nyungan*		(241)
AFROASIATIC		(209)	PAMA-MARIC	(36)	
Chadic		(108)	SW PAMA-NYUNGAN	(46)	
EAST CHADIC	(32)		Other	(159)	
WEST CHADIC	(76)		*Other*		(82)
Berber		(24)	AUSTROASIATIC		(109)
Cushitic		(29)	*Mon-Khmer*		(82)
Omotic		(23)	BAHNARIC	(32)	
Semitic		(24)	KATUIC	(24)	
Egyptian/Coptic		(1)	Other	(26)	
MACRO-ALGONQUIAN		(30)	*Other*		(27)
ANDEAN-EQUATORIAL		(249)	AUSTRONESIAN		(792)
Andean		(24)	*Oceanic*		(391)
Equatorial		(183)	EASTERN OCEANIC	(116)	
ARAWAKAN	(119)		PAPUA AUSTRONESIAN	(52)	
TUPI	(39)		NW NEW HEBRIDES	(26)	
Other	(25)		NW & CENTRAL		
Jivaroan		(5)	SOLOMONS	(26)	
Macro-Tucanoan		(37)	ADMIRALITY-WESTERN	(24)	

Note. **MAXIMAL GROUP,** *Primary subgroup,* SECONDARY SUBGROUP, *Primary residue* (Single language), Secondary residue.

BISMARCK ARCHIPELAGO	(34)	
NEW CALEDONIA	(23)	
NE NEW GUINEA	(64)	
Other	(26)	
Malayo-Polynesian		(378)
FORMOSAN	(20)	
HESPERONESIAN	(218)	
EAST INDONESIAN	(101)	
MOLUCCAN	(24)	
Other	(15)	
South Halmahera-		
W. New Guinea		(23)
AZTEC-TANOAN		(30)
CAUCASIAN		(33)
MACRO-CHIBCHAN		(60)
Chibchan		(22)
Other		(38)
DRAVIDIAN		(22)
GE-PANO-CARIB		(275)
Macro-Carib		(98)
Macro-Ge-Bororo		(97)
Macro-Panoan		(71)
Other		(9)
HOKAN		(36)
INDO-EUROPEAN		(155)
Indo-Iranian		(71)
Other	(6)	
INDIC	(37)	
IRANIAN	(28)	
Italic		(21)
Other		(63)
INDO-PACIFIC		(747)
Central New Guinea		(123)
E NEW GUINEA		
HIGHLANDS	(50)	
HUON-FINISTERRE	(62)	
W NEW GUINEA		
HIGHLANDS	(11)	
Eastern = Southeast New Guinea		(103)
KOIARI	(32)	
Other	(71)	
North New Guinea		(230)
NORTH PAPUAN	(41)	
SEPIK	(39)	
BOGIA	(88)	
TORRICELLI	(38)	
Other	(24)	

Northeastern New Guinea		(28)
Western New Guinea		(34)
Central and South New Guinea		(124)
Other		(105)
KHOISAN		(50)
South African Khoisan		(48)
<u>Hatsa</u>		(1)
<u>Sandawe</u>		(1)
NA-DENE		(32)
NIGER-KORDOFANIAN		(1046)
Kordofanian		(29)
Niger-Congo		(1017)
ADAMAWA-EASTERN	(87)	
WEST ATLANTIC	(47)	
BENUE-CONGO	(700)	
GUR-VOLTAIC	(76)	
KWA	(84)	
MANDE	(23)	
NILO-SAHARAN		(122)
Chari-Nile		(104)
CENTRAL SUDANIC	(34)	
EASTERN SUDANIC	(67)	
Other	(3)	
Other		(18)
OTO-MANGUEAN		(25)
PENUTIAN		(78)
Mayan		(25)
Other		(53)
SALISH		(23)
SINO-TIBETAN		(289)
Kam-Tai		(54)
Tibeto-Burman		(217)
GYARUNG-MISHMI	(47)	
NAGA-KUKI-CHIN	(88)	
BURMESE-LOLO	(51)	
BODO-NAGA-KUCHIN	(21)	
Other	(10)	
Other		(18)
MACRO-SIOUAN		(26)
URAL-ALTAIC		(89)
Uralic		(28)
Altaic		(61)
TURKIC	(30)	
Other	(31)	
PIDGINS/CREOLES		(33)

Note. MAXIMAL GROUP, *Primary subgroup*, SECONDARY SUBGROUP, *Primary residue* (<u>*Single language*</u>), Secondary residue.

IV. Procedures

Case I. Maximal groups consisting of fewer than 21 languages:
Procedure:
  A. Include all languages from such groups in a set.
  B. Randomly choose the first two from the set subject to the conditions that:
    1. The languages do not belong to the same maximal linguistic groups.
    2. There are sufficient sources.

Discussion:

The third sampling objective is that language isolates be represented in rough proportion to their representation in the universe of languages. There are 76 languages belonging to minimal linguistic groups, 47 of which are singletons. 76 divided by the total of 4959 languages in the universe yields 1.53. Without isolates the sample contains 92 languages; the proportion of isolates should thus be 1.4. Given a choice between one or two isolates in the sample, we chose to include two.

Case II. Maximal groups consisting of more than 20 but fewer than 41 languages:

Procedure:

Randomly choose one language from each such maximal group subject to the condition that there are sufficient sources.

Discussion:

There are 9 maximal linguistic groupings that fit this criterion, containing from 22 to 38 languages each. Within groups of this size there is a fairly close, well-established relationship.

Case III. Maximal groups consisting of more than 40 languages:

Case III A. No primary subgroup includes a secondary subgroup of 20 or more languages with more than 20 other languages in that primary subgroup.

Procedure:

  A. Randomly choose n languages from the maximal group so that n equals the number of primary subgroups with 20 or more languages plus the number of languages in the primary residue subgroup divided by 30 rounded to the nearest integer.
  B. Use the first languages chosen subject to the constraints that at most one language from any subgroup is chosen and that there are sufficient sources.
  C. If there are primary subgroups of 20 or more languages and more than 20 languages in the primary residue, sample the primary subgroups independently.

Discussion:

Cases that fit this criterion (but not that of III B) include Macro-Chibchan, Ge-Pano-Carib, Khoisan, and Penutian. These are groups that are still fairly well defined and accepted. The relationships between languages not in the same primary subgroups are, however, presumably more distant, and thus when there are several primary subgroups, more than one language from the maximal group can probably be safely included. In order to keep the representation somewhat proportional but not include similar languages, the cut-off point for primary subgroup size is set at 20, roughly the lower boundary for small group sizes. In order to insure against including related languages that happen to be from small subgroups, the divisor for the primary residue is set at 30. The mean for small groups is roughly 30 and serves as the basis for the divisor here.

Case III B. At least one primary subgroup can be subdivided into at least one secondary subgroup consisting of 20 or more languages with more than 20 other languages in that primary subgroup.

Procedure:

A. Randomly choose m languages from each primary subgroup containing at least one secondary subgroup with 20 or more languages and more than 20 others. m is equal to the number of such secondary subgroups, plus one if the languages in the primary subgroup that do not belong to such a secondary subgroup together comprise a set of more than 20 languages.

B. Use the first languages chosen subject to the constraints that at most one language per secondary subgroup or secondary residue is chosen and that there are sufficient sources.

C. Randomly choose r languages from the set of all languages from primary subgroups from which no language has been chosen by A and B above so that r equals the number of primary subgroups with 20 or more languages that have not yet been sampled plus the number of languages in the primary residue subgroup divided by 30 rounded to the nearest integer.

D. Use the first languages chosen subject to the constraints that at most one language per primary subgroup is used and that there are sufficient sources.

Discussion:

Many of the groups included here are comprised of subgroups that have only been suggested or hypothesized to belong together (e.g., Indo-Pacific) and/or that have relationships based only on lexicostatistic relationships or geographical proximity. In order to include only languages that can be presumed to be substantially unrelated, no more than three levels of relationship are permitted. This means that groups that are only geographically defined will not have more than a single representative in the sample. This almost completely precludes the necessity of later discarding any languages after bibliographic and analytic work because they turn out to be closely related to a language already in the sample. 20 is again used as the size for determining groups and 30 is the divisor for the residue to determine the number of languages from the primary residue.

Table A.3.   Sampling Procedure Summary

CONDITION (number of languages per group)				
<21	21–40	>40	Secondary subgroup >20	PROCEDURE
Y	N	N	N	I
N	Y	N	N	II
N	N	Y	N	III A
N	N	Y	Y	III B

Table A.4. GRAMCATS Sample

1. Grouping	2	3	4	5. Language
I. Unaffiliated languages [76]	(2)	01	4.	Inuit
		02	6.	Basque
II. Afroasiatic [209]				
A. Chadic [108]				
1. East Chadic [32]	(1)	03	29.	Margi
2. West Chadic [76]	(1)	04	9.	Kanakuru
		05	1.	Awiya (Agau) [Cushitic]
B. Other Afroasiatic [101]	(4)	06	14.	Tuareg [Berber]
		07		
		08	6.	Tigre [Semitic]
III. Macro-Algonquian [30]	(1)	09	4.	Cheyenne
IV. Andean-Equatorial [249]				
A. Equatorial [183]				
1. Arawakan [119]	(1)	10	5.	Island Carib
2. Tupi [39]	(1)	11	2.	Cocama
3. Other Equatorial [25]	(1)	12	5.	Chacobo
		13	1.	Jivaro [Jivaroan]
B. Other Andean-Equatorial [42]	(2)	14	3.	Tucano [Tucanoan]
V. Australian [323]				
A. Pama-Nyugan [241]				
1. Southwest P-N [46]	(1)	15	17.	Gugada
2. Pama-Maric P-N [36]	(1)	16	29.	Gugu-Yalanji
3. Other Pama-Nuyngan [159]	(1)	17	11.	Alyawara
		18	2.	Maung [Iwaidjan]
B. Other Australian [82]	(3)	19	4.	Worora [Wororan]
		20	5.	Alawa [Maran]

Table A.4. (continued)

1. Grouping	2	3	4	5. Language
VI. Austroasiatic [109]				
A. Mon-Khmer [82]				
1. Katuic [24]	(1)	21	3.	Koho
2. Bahnaric [32]	(1)	22	3.	Palaung
3. Other Mon-Khmer [26]	(1)	23	3.	
B. Other Austroasiatic [27]	(1)	24	2.	Car [Nicobarese]
VII. Austronesian [792]				
A. Oceanic [391]				
1. Eastern Oceanic [116]	(1)	25	1.	Tahitian [Polynesian]
2. Papua Austronesian [52]	(1)	26	4.	Motu
3. NW New Hebrides [26]	(1)	27	3.	Atchin
4. NW & Central Solomons [26]	(1)	28	24.	Halia
5. Admiralty-Western [24]	(1)	29		
6. Bismarck Archipelago [34]	(1)	30	33.	Tanga
7. New Caledonia [23]	(1)	31		
8. NE New Guinea [64]	(1)	32	8.	Nakanai
9. Other Oceanic [26]	(1)	33	1.	Trukese
B. Malayo-Polynesian [378]	(3)	34	7.	Pangasinan [Hesperonesian]
		35	121.	Rukai [Formosan AN]
		36		(1 from either Moluccan or Northern Celebes)
C. S Halmahera–W New Guinea [23]	(1)	37	18.	Buli
VIII. Aztec-Tanoan [30]	(1)	38	1.	Tohono O'odham
IX. Caucasian [33]	(1)	39	3.	Abkhaz
X. Macro-Chibchan [60]				
A. Chibchan [22]	(1)	40	16.	Guaymi
B. Other Macro-Chibchan [38]	(1)	41		
XI. Dravidian [22]	(1)	42	1.	Kui

XII. Ge-Pano-Carib [275]	(3)	43 44 45	8.	Abipon [Macro-Panoan] (2 from Macro-Carib, Macro-Ge-Bororo, Huarpe, Nambicuara, Taruma)
XIII. Hokan [36]	(1)	46	2.	Karok
XIV. Indo-European [155]				
A. Italic [21]	(1)	47	13.	Latin
B. Indo-Iranian [71]	(2)	48	1.	Bihari (Maithili) [Indic]
		49	5.	Balochi [Iranian]
C. Other Indo-European [63]	(2)	50	3.	Modern Greek [Hellenic]
		51	4.	Danish[a] [Germanic]
XV. Indo-Pacific [747]				
A. Central New Guinea [123]	(2)	52	23.	Yagaria[b] [E NG Highlands]
		56	18.	Ono [Huon-Finisterre]
B. Eastern = SE New Guinea [103]	(2)	53 57		
C. North New Guinea [230]	(4)	58	3.	Nimboran [North Papuan]
		60	38.	Yessan-Mayo [Sepik]
		61 55		(2 from Bogia, Torricelli, and Other North New Guinea)
D. Northeastern New Guinea [28]	(1)	59	5.	Bongu [Northeastern New Guinea]
E. Western New Guinea [34]	(1)	62		
F. Central + South NG [124]	(1)	54		
G. Other Indo-Pacific [105]	(4)	63 64 65 66	2.	Baining [New Britain]
XVI. Khoisan [50]	(1)	67	22.	!Kung
XVII. Na-dene [32]	(1)	68	6.	Slave

[a] Dialect of Continental Scandinavian.
[b] Dialect of Keigana.

Table A.4. (*continued*)

1. Grouping	2	3	4	5. Language
XVIII. Niger-Kordofanian [1046]				
A. Kordofanian [29]	(1)	69	8.	Krongo
B. Niger Congo [1017]				
1. Adamawa-Eastern [87]	(1)	70	3.	Temne
2. West Atlantic [47]	(1)	71	11.	Mwera
3. Benue-Congo [700]	(1)	72	1.	Tem
4. Gur [76]	(1)	73	12.	Engenni
5. Kwa [84]	(1)	74	1.	Mano
6. Mande [23]	(1)	75		
XIX. Nilo-Saharan [122]		76	8.	Bari [Eastern Sudanic]
A. Chari-Nile [104]	(2)	77	11.	Ngambay [Central Sudanic]
	(1)	78	3.	Kanuri
B. Other Nilo Saharan [18]	(1)	79	4.	Palantla Chinantec
XX. Oto-Manguean [25]	(2)			
XXI. Penutian [78]		80	3.	Tojolabal
A. Mayan [25]	(1)	81	1.	Zuni [Penutian isolate]
B. Other Penutian [53]	(2)	82	2.	Maidu [Maidu]
		83	2.	Shuswap
XII. Salish [23]	(1)			
XXIII. Sino-Tibetan [289]		84	9.	Laotian
A. Kam-Tai [54]	(1)	85	8.	Chepang [Gyarung-Mishmi]
B. Tibeto-Burman [217]	(4)	86	15.	Haka [Naga-Kuki-Chin]
		87	17.	Lahu [Burmese-Lolo]
		88	34.	Nung [Bodo-Naga-Kachin]
C. Other Sino-Tibetan [18]	(1)	89	1.	Cantonese

XXIV. Macro-Siouan [26]	(1)	90	2.	Dakota
XXV. Ural-Altaic [89]				
A. Uralic [28]	(1)	91	1.	Votyak-Udmurt
B. Altaic [61]				
1. Turkic [30]	(1)	92	1.	Uighur
2. Other Altaic [31]	(1)	93	1.	Buriat
XXVI. Creoles [33]	(1)	94	1.	Tok Pisin

Note. Col. 1: The numbers in brackets indicate the number of languages in the sampling group. Col. 2: The number in parentheses indicate the number of languages to be chosen from the sampling group. Col. 3: The two–digit number is the identification number assigned the language. Col. 4: The number followed by a period is the number of random choices made before a language with sufficient documentation could be found. Col. 5: A name in brackets indicates the subgroup to which the language belongs.

• • •

Appendix B
Meaning Labels

The following are excerpts from the GRAMCATS Coding Manual, defining and explaining the coding of the meanings of grams used in this book.

Meaning labels, which are primes in our theory, are written in lower-case letters. Language-specific labels for morphemes given by authors of grammars are cited with an initial capital letter. When we use such terms to refer informally to classes of morphemes, we put quotation marks around them. "Present Tenses," then, should be read "Things that people refer to as Present Tense."

The following is a list of meaning labels and their definitions. Notes and examples are added in cases where it will help to identify the sense of morphemes.

I. Aspects and tenses: meanings having to do with the temporal setting and constituency of situations. The term "situation" is a cover term for event, activity, and state, in other words, those notions covered by verbs.

    A. Temporal deixis: those terms establishing the temporal setting of the situation with regard to the moment of speech. Usually called "Tenses."

    present: the situation occurs simultaneously with the moment of speech.

    past: the situation occurred before the moment of speech.

    future: the situation takes place after the moment of speech; the speaker predicts that the situation in the proposition will hold.

    crastinal: tomorrow.

    hesternal: yesterday.

    hodiernal: today, normally with past.

    pre-hodiernal: before today.

    post-crastinal: after tomorrow.

    ancient past: used for narrating events in ancient or mythical time.

remote: combines with other tense labels to indicate a situation occurring temporally distant from the moment of speech.

immediate: a meaning label that may be combined with other tense labels to indicate a situation not simultaneous with the moment of speech, but very close to it:

immediate future: what is about to occur.

immediate past: occurring immediately before the moment of speech. Also called the Recent Past. Do not use this label if there is any sense of current relevance—use anterior for that.

Immediate may also be combined with **anterior** or **imperative**.

B. Aspect

1. Dynamic Verbs: The following meanings describe the temporal contours of a situation. They are usually called "Aspects." They may be combined with any of the meanings that signal deictic time, either in the same morpheme or in combinations of morphemes.

   habitual: the situation is customary or usual, repeated on different occasions over a period of time. English *used to* is past habitual; English *Nancy sings* is present habitual.

   continuous: a single situation is viewed as in progress, as maintained over a period of time; also called "durative." The English Progressive is a continuous restricted to dynamic verbs. English *I am reading; *I am knowing the number.*

   continuative: keep on doing what is being done. Restricted to dynamic verbs.

   progressive: the action takes place simultaneously with the moment of reference, 'to be in the process of . . .'. This is more restricted than the English Progressive, which may be used for events that are not actually in progress at reference time: *I am writing a book* may be used even if the speaker is not at that moment writing.

   excessive duration: action is extended over a long period of time, longer than normal for that action.

   limited duration: action performed for a relatively short or bounded period of time.

   iterative: the action is repeated on one occasion; usually restricted to dynamic verbs, often further restricted to semelfactive verbs.

   frequentative: action occurs frequently, not necessarily habitually, nor necessarily on one occasion, as is the iterative.

   imperfective: the situation is viewed as unbounded in the sense that it is habitual, continuous, progressive, or iterative.

   perfective: the situation is viewed as bounded temporally. It cannot be simultaneous with the moment of speech; in the non-past it is sometimes interpreted as future.

completive: to do something thoroughly and to completion, e.g. *to shoot someone dead, to eat up.*

inceptive: the action or event begins. We are distinguishing this from the beginning of a state.

delimited: action is performed only a little.

The preceding terms or "Aspects" are not usually relevant to stative verbs. Therefore, the following set of terms can be used for coding the meanings possible with statives. They may all be combined with meanings that signal deictic time.

2. Stative Verbs

state exists: the state is begun before reference time and continues after reference time.

state commences: beginning of a state of "becoming." Often called Inceptive or Inchoative. If there is a morpheme specifically for this meaning, it is usually derivational and restricted to stative verbs. However, it is also possible for "Perfects" or "Perfectives" to have this as their use with stative verbs.

state ends: state existed in the past, but no longer exists. Also a possible meaning of "Perfects" or "Perfectives" in combination with stative verbs.

state continues: state is continuing at reference time.

state changes: (self-explanatory).

C. Relational tenses: where the reference time is not the same as the moment of speech.

resulting state (resultative): action in the past produces a state that persists into the present.

anterior continuing: past action continues into the present: *I have waited over an hour* (= and I'm still waiting).

anterior: the situation occurs prior to reference time, and is relevant to the situation at reference time. This is different from a simple past or perfective, where the situation is reported for its own sake and independent of its relevance to any other situation.

Note that the Perfect in English signals a non-specific event. Thus the Perfect is incompatible with a temporal adverb that refers to a specific point in time: **I have been to Japan in 1963.*

Sometimes an anterior has a present reading when used with stative verbs. So in order to say 'He has five children' one says literally "He has had five children. "He has been/become tall" means 'he is tall'. This should be coded as state exists, and if it is restricted to the moment of speech, it should also be coded as present.

A form that signals a situation that is prior to and relevant to a past reference time will be coded with two meaning labels, past and anterior.

Notes on the Uses of "Present Tenses"

A situation that is ongoing at the moment of speech could be either a situation that is in progress or a situation that is habitual. Furthermore, it could be a current state. Therefore, it would be indistinguishable from a present imperfective, since imperfective covers continuous, habitual, and is appropriate with stative verbs.

Often, what is called a Present Tense only covers part of this imperfective domain. For instance, the English simple Present, as in *They walk to school,* is only a habitual. In order to express the continuous, English uses the *be + ing* construction: *They are walking to school.* But the English simple Present is also used with stative verbs: *She knows the answer, She is smart.* So we would code English simple Present as habitual. Since the continuous/habitual distinction does not seem relevant to stative verbs, we should code English simple Present as also indicating state exists.

Often a Present Tense can be used to refer to future time, as in English *I see the President tomorrow at 3 p.m.* This use in English is necessarily accompanied by some contextual indication of future; otherwise a habitual reading is preferred. Note further that this use occurs with events that are scheduled to occur or expected to occur in the near future. This use is expected future:

> **expected**: the situation is to occur in the near future; what is scheduled to happen; qualifies future.

A Present Tense is also used in some languages as an optional narrative tense, what is called the "historical present." In this case, the past time reference is established and the entire sequence of narrative events is expressed in the present tense. I suggest we code this use as narrative time.

> **narrative time**: the use of a form with no other past uses for reporting a past narrative.

Another use that "Present Tenses" sometimes have is a use in timeless or generic statements, such as *Elephants have trunks.* Such statements are true in the past, present, and future—as long as elephants exist. The usual term for this meaning is gnomic present.

> **gnomic**: the situation described in the proposition is generic; the predicate has held, holds, and will hold for the class of entities named by the subject.

II. Agent-oriented modalities: internal or external conditions on a willful agent with respect to the completion of the predicate situation.

> **ability**: the agent of the verb has the mental or physical ability to complete the action of the main verb.
>
> **ability, mental**: English: *Melissa can speak Dutch.*
>
> **ability, physical**: English: *Hortense can swim the English Channel.*

attempt: the agent attempts to complete the action specified by the predicate. Note: this has a sense of incompleteness, and I have seen authors call this "Incomplete" and gloss the examples with 'try'.

desire: the agent of the verb desires or wants to complete the action of the main verb: *I want to go to the movies.*

obligation: the agent is obliged to perform the action of the verb.

obligation, strong: it is absolutely incumbent upon the agent to complete the action of the main verb: *I have to mail this letter today.*

obligation, weak: it is recommended that the agent complete the action of the main verb: *Harry ought to get a haircut before meeting Sue's mother.*

permission: the agent is allowed to complete the action of the main verb: *The students may check books out for two weeks.*

root possibility: it is possible for the agent to carry out the action of the main verb; i.e. s/he is able and external conditions allow it: *You can get that kind of paper at Ulbrich's.*

intention: the agent intends to carry out the action of the main verb: *Sam's gonna take Sanskrit next semester.*

andative: agent moves away from the deictic center in order to do something, literally 'be going to do something'. Of course, such forms are often related to the verb 'to go' and also may have uses of intention and future.

venitive: the agent moves toward the deictic center in order to do something, literally 'be coming to do something'. This may be related to the verb 'to come' and may have future uses as well.

III. Moods

A. Epistemic moods: these markers have the whole proposition in their scope and indicate the degree of commitment of the speaker to the truth or future truth of the proposition.

possibility: the speaker is indicating that the situation described in the proposition is possibly true. Some markers with this meaning also indicate future time: *He may arrive late because of the weather; It may snow again tomorrow; She could have already taken it.*

probability: the speaker is indicating that the situation described in the proposition is probably true. Some markers with this meaning also indicate future time. This is sometimes called the "Dubitative" in grammars: *Paula should be home by now.*

inferred certainty: the speaker infers from evidence that the proposition is true: *They must have killed a bear here (I can see blood on the snow).*

certainty: the speaker is emphasizing that the proposition is true.

uncertainty: the speaker is emphasizing that s/he doesn't know that the proposition is true.

indicative: main clause mood that also appears in questions. Contrasts with subjunctive, conditional, and imperative.

B. Imperatives

imperative: the verb form used for direct commands in the 2nd person. If there are also 1st and 3rd person forms, the meaning can still be that of imperative, with the 1st and 3rd persons being interpreted as 'Let us, let him . . .', etc.

optative: the proposition represents the speaker's will. Translated into English as 'May you prosper', 'May we all meet again.' with counterfactual: 'If only he had . . .', etc.

hortative: The speaker is encouraging or inciting someone to action.

prohibitive: the mood for expressing negative commands. The English is *Don't.*

admonitive: the command constitutes a warning; 'you had better not . . .'.

Meanings co-occurring with imperative:

polite: a mild or polite form of command.

delayed: the action of the command is to be carried out in the future rather than immediately.

immediate: the action of the command is to be carried out immediately.

strong: (self-explanatory).

C. Subordinating: Often there are special verb forms or morphemes associated with the verb that occur obligatorily in subordinate clauses of certain types. The extent to which such morphemes can be said to have "meaning" varies, since they often co-occur with other markers of subordination. Their function is primarily to signal the type of subordinate clause.

There are two situations we will encounter. In one, the special subordinate verb form occurs obligatorily with some other marker of subordination—a proposition-scope morpheme (a conjunction) giving the meaning of the subordinate clause: 'if', 'in order that', 'when'. In the other case the verb-associated morpheme is the only signal of the subordinate meaning: it might itself mean 'if', 'in order that', or 'when'. Meaning labels for subordinating morphemes name the type of clause they occur in, and co-occurring grams or lexical items will be recorded under 'Co-occurrence restrictions'.

Subordinate clauses often take non-finite verb forms, i.e. infinitives and participles. Since we have decided (somewhat arbitrarily) not to code infinitives and participles, we will ignore these.

The following types of subordinate clauses often take special verb forms or verb-associated morphemes:

Complement clauses: A main verb may take as its direct object a clause. These are often referred to as "Noun clauses" or "Noun complements". The verb form of the subordinate clause is usually determined by the semantics of the main verb, so in this case, our meaning labels will just refer to the context. If a verb form occurs in the complements to verbs of thinking and believing, the meaning label will be complement to verbs of thinking and believing.

complement to verbs of thinking

complement to verbs of believing

complements to verbs of saying

complement to verbs of ordering (in English we use an infinitive with these verbs)

complement to verbs of wanting (again, in English these are done with infinitives)

complement to verbs of emotion (surprise, regret, happiness, sadness, etc.; the complement proposition is presupposed to be true)

complement to verbs of obligation

complement to clauses of admonition

subsequent: following a reference time in the past.

subordinator: marker indicates that the verb is in a subordinate clause.

D. Conditional sentences: Conditional sentences consist of two clauses, the 'if'-clause or protasis (which is a subordinate clause) and the 'then'-clause or apodosis (which is the main clause). Both of these clauses may take special verb forms. (Interestingly enough, they sometimes both take the same special verb forms.)

There are at least three types of conditional sentences. (Labels, explanations, and examples from Li and Thompson 1981):

reality condition: a conditional relation between two propositions referring to the so-called real world: *If you see my sister, you will know that she is pregnant.*

hypothetical: the situation is unreal or imagined, but one that could be true: *If we moved, we could have a garden.*

counterfactual: the proposition describes an unreal or imagined situation that could have been true but was not: *If you had taken algebra, you would know this formula* (but you did not).

The verb forms that occur in these sentences will be coded according to the type of sentence, and according to which clause of the sentence they occur in.

Example: the English *had* + past participle would be coded as:

    meaning label: protasis

    meaning label: counterfactual

Since the conjunction *if* obligatorily occurs in the protasis, there will also be the following:

    Co-occurrence restriction: 'if'

This indicates that a morpheme meaning 'if' obligatorily occurs in the protasis. If no such morpheme is necessary, then there will be no co-occurrence restriction.

E. Other clauses: There are a variety of adverbial clauses (other than conditional clauses) that sometimes require a special verb form. The meaning labels for these uses are coded according to the type of clause (purpose, concessive, etc.), whether any particular temporal deixis is part of the meaning, and under "co-occurrence restrictions," whether a particular conjunction is present. The types of clauses we might run into are:

    purpose: the clause states the purpose for which the main clause action is taking place. Often called a "final" clause: *He was saving his money so that his son could go to college.*

    concessive: translated in English as 'although, even though, despite the fact that': *She was saving her money, even though she was a wealthy woman.*

IV. Evidentials: the speaker indicates the source of the information on which an assertion about a situation is based (Willett 1988).

    direct evidence: the speaker claims to have witnessed the situation, but does not specify the type of sensory evidence.

    visual evidence: the speaker claims to have seen the situation described.

    auditory evidence: the speaker claims to have heard the situation described.

    sensory evidence: the speaker claims to have physically sensed the situation described. This can be in opposition to one or both of the above senses (i.e. any other sense), or it can indicate sensory evidence that is not further specified (i.e. any sensory evidence).

    indirect evidence: the speaker claims not to have witnessed the situation, but does not specify further whether the evidence is reported or simply inferred.

    reported evidence: the speaker claims to know of the situation described via verbal means, but does not specify whether it is second-hand, hearsay, or via folklore.

    second-hand evidence: the speaker claims to have heard of the situation described from someone who was a direct witness.

evidence from hearsay: the speaker claims to have heard about the situation described, but not from a direct witness.

evidence from folklore: the speaker claims that the situation described is part of established oral history (e.g., mythology).

inferred evidence: the speaker infers the event/action, but does not specify whether the inference is based on observable results or on a purely mental process.

inference from results: the speaker infers the situation described from the evidence at hand (i.e. from the observable results of the causing event/action.)

inference from reasoning: the speaker infers the situation described on the basis of intuition, logic, a dream, previous experience, or some other mental construct.

Appendix C
Sources of Language Data

Table 3.1: Grams Having Two or More of the Meaning Labels Completive, Anterior, Resultative, Perfective, or Past

Language no.	Form no.	Source	Author's Name for Gram	Orthographic Shape
01	05	Fortescue 1980: 265–66	Perfective State	sima
03	34	Hoffman 1963: 196–200	Past	a..ɔri
05	08	Hetzron 1969: 13f.	Perfect Indefinite	-a
10	18	Taylor 1956a: 6, 20, 24, 30	Perfective	ha
10	41	Taylor 1956b: 144f.	Past	buga
25	03	Jaussen 1861: 62–63		ua
32	02	Johnston 1980: 129–30	Perfective	ti
33	01	Dyen 1965: 24	Perfective Particle	ja
42	25	Subrahmanyam 1971: 86–87	Perfective Tense	a ma-n
46	16	Bright 1957: 67	Past	at
47	10	Lane 1898: 149–52, 270–73	Perfectum	v
48	35	Jha 1958: 527–28	Past Perfect	ach ane
49	13	Barker & Mengal 1969: 336ff.	Past Perfect	yt + əg + ət
52	21	Renck 1975: 92f., 114f.	Past	d

Language no.	Form no.	Source	Author's Name for Gram	Orthographic Shape
68	54	Rice 1986: 360	Past	*yïlé*
78	06	Lukas 1967: 43–44	Perfect	*na*
93	38	Poppe 1960: 101	Perfective	*šxa*

Table 3.2: Lexical Sources for Completives

Language no.	Form no.	Source	Author's Name for Gram	Orthographic Shape
06	17	Cortade 1969: 57–59	Reciprocal	*nam*
11	23	Faust 1971: 113	All Inclusive	*pa*
14	22	Sorensen 1969: 171–76	Completive	*dü*
14	23	Sorensen 1969: 173–76, 90	Completive	*péò*
14	33	Sorensen 1969: 271–72	Complete Action	*a + waʔa*
23	15	Milne 1921: 77	Completed Action	*pɛt*
24	06	Braine 1970: 176–77	Perfective	*ŋ*
27	18	Capell & Layard 1980: 73f.	Completeness	*tsile*
28	45	Allen & Allen 1965: 32	—	*hakapa*
32	02	Johnston 1980: 129–30	Perfective	*ti*
33	20	Dyen 1965: 49ff.	Away, Completely	*nöò*
33	21	Dyen 1965: 49ff.	Up, East, Completely	*tää*
37	25	Maan 1951: 85	—	*tòtò*
37	26	Maan 1951: 85	—	*fonla*
42	21	Subrahmanyam 1971: 153	Emphatic Particle	*de*
46	24	Bright 1957: 106	Completely	*fĩp*
48	44	Jha 1958: 535–36	Completion	*ja*
48	55	Jha 1958: 540	Completion	*cuk*
48	61	Jha 1958: 535–36	Completion	*ga*
52	22	Renck 1975: 94	Completed Action	*bolo*
60	07	Foreman 1974: 38	Completive	*keyp*

60	26	Foreman 1974: 99	Completive	*yuwa*
69	47	Reh 1985: 226	—	*kúbú*
72	09	Harries 1950: 76	Perfective/Repetitive	*itila*
73	19	Der-Houssikian 1980a: 68–69	Finished Perfective	*tɛ*
74	06	Thomas 1978: 170f.	Finished, completely	*padhe*
78	07	Lukas 1937: 45–47	Predicative	*i*
82	25	Shipley 1964: 44	Completive	*bos*
84	39	Yates & Sayasithsena 1970: 318ff.	Aspect Particle	*lɛ̀ɛw*
85	29	Caughley 1982:	Emotive	*je?*
86	09	Newland 1897: 34	Past Perfect	*di*
87	29	Matisoff 1973: 237	Completive, Exhaustive	*pɔ̀*
89	22	Kwok 1971: 116–19	Aspect Marker	*yùn*
89	24	Kwok 1971: 117	Aspect Marker	*màai*
93	38	Poppe 1960: 101	Perfective	*šxa*
94	19	Mühlhäusler 1985: 380–81	Completion	*pinis*

Table 3.4: Grams with Anterior as Their Only Use (Young Anteriors)

01	20	Fortescue 1980: 278	Action Completed	*riir*
02	04	N'Diaye 1970: 202	Prétérit de l'actuel	*-tu da*
03	40	Hoffman 1963: 220–21	Before, Formerly	*era*
03	44	Hoffman 1963: 223–24	Just; Just Now	*maka*
03	45	Hoffman 1963: 224	(To Have Done) Before	*çivar*
03	46	Hoffman 1963: 224–25	To Have Done Before	*savar*
03	48	Hoffman 1963: 221–22	Quickly, Already	*kwia*
08	27	Raz 1983: 6, 199	Concomitance	*ʔɔndo*
08	38	Raz 1983: 73–74	Complex Perfect	*ka + halla*
08	39	Raz 1983: 73–74	Complex Perfect	*ka + ʔala*
08	40	Raz 1983: 75	Complex Perfect	*ka + sanha*
11	14	Faust 1971: 72	Perfective Particle	*utsu*
11	15	Faust 1971: 72	Perfective Particle	*awe*
13	25	Turner 1958: 64, 93	Present Completive	ZERO

Table 3.4: (*continued*)

Language no.	Form no.	Source	Author's Name for Gram	Orthographic Shape
14	03	Sorensen 1969: 29	Emphatic	*s*
14	21	Sorensen 1969: 171–73	Completive	*thóà*
17	03	Yallop 1977:51	Past Perfect	*ikala*
23	15	Milne 1921: 67	Past Tense Prefix	*huǫ-i*
24	14	Braine 1970: 194–95	Sequential	*hε:*
25	07	Jaussen 1861: 64, 72	Past	*i...na*
26	11	Lister-Turner & Clark n.d.: 14, 16, 17	Perfect	*vada*
35	01	Li 1973: 81, 150, 156, 160, 265	Completive	*ɲa*
37	17	Maan 1951: 85	Completed Action	*tò*
38	10	Mathiot 1973: 58	Completive	*ok*
40	08	Kopesec 1975: 24	Perfecto	*ni*
40	10	Kopesec 1975: 45	Completed Action	*ra*
46	40	Bright 1957: 125	Anterior Tense	*ahe:n*
46	42	Bright 1957: 138–89	Perfective	*tah*
48	21	Jha 1958: 511f.	Past Perfect	*ra*
48	24	Jha 1958: 526	Pres Perfect Instantaneous	*ach* + PST
48	35	Jha 1958: 427–28	Past Perfect	*ach ane*
49	12	Barker & Mengal 1969: 333ff.	Present Perfect	*yt əg*
49	14	Barker & Mengal 1969: 338–39	Past Completive	*yt ət*
50	12	Householder et al. 1964: 132	Perfect Tense	*exo*
50	17	Householder et al. 1964: 105–6	Modal Particle	*θa*
51	12	Koefoed 1958: 189f.	"have" Aux, Perfect/Pluperf	*have...et*
51	13	Koefoed 1958: 189f.	["være" Aux Perfect/Pluperf	*være...et*
52	33	Renck: 133f.	Aspectual Continuative	*-mo...o-*

59	25	Hanke 1909: 53; 67	Plusquamperfectum	*ǵurat*
69	06	Reh 1985: 188f.	Perfective	LOW TONE
71	19	Wilson 1961: 26	Finish	*p̣o*
72	44	Harries 1950: 110	To Have Already Done	*mala*
73	17	Der-Houssikian 1980a: 68–69	Perfective	REDUP
73	18	Der-Houssikian 1980a: 68–69	Perfective (just)	*ngbedi*
75	07	Becker-Donner 1965: 41ff.	'be, do, make' Aux	*kè*
76	07	Spagnolo 1933: 105	Pluperfect	*ado*
80	08	Furbee-Losee 1976: 129, 133–34	Perfective	*uneh*
84	39	Yates & Sayasithsena 1970: 318f.	Aspect particle	*lèɛw*
85	39	Caughley 1982: 108–9	Near Relative Past	*ʔataʔ*
85	40	Caughley 1982: 109	Non-Perf. Relative Past	*ʔak*
86	07	Newland 1897: 34	Present Perfect	*ai*
87	48	Matisoff 1973: 322ff	Perfective Permanence	*tà*
88	11	Barnard 1934: 20–22, 27–28	Past Perfect	*ngut*
89	18	Kwok 1971: 108–9	Aspect Marker	*gwo*
90	22	Buechel 1939: 279–80	Past perfect	*kʼuŋ*
92	19	Nadzhip 1971: 117–18	Past Indefinite	*gan*
93	45	Poppe 1960: 103	VN of Imperf w/han	*aa han*

Tables 3.5 & 3.6: Resultatives

01	05	Fortescue 1984: 265–66	Perfective state	*sima*
03	34	Hoffman 1963: 196–200	Past	*a...əri*
05	46	Hetzron 1969: 23f.	Terminative	*-amba*
10	18	Taylor 1956: 6, 20, 24, 30	Perfective	*ha*
14	17	Sorensen 1969: 165–67	Perfective	*ka*
14	29	Sorensen 1969: 75–76	Proof of Action	*kɨ + ni*
32	02	Johnston 1980: 129–30	Perfective	*ti*
33	01	Dyen 1965: 24	Perfectic Particle	*ja*
33	39	Dyen 1965: 43f, 41f	(Causativizer +)	*jA*
42	06	Subrahmanyam 1971: 157–60	Past	*it*

Table 3.5 & 3.6: (continued)

Language no.	Form no.	Source	Author's Name for Gram	Orthographic Shape
42	25	Subrahmanyam 1971: 86–87	Perfective Tense	a ma-n
42	26	Subrahmanyam 1971: 86–87	Pluperfect	a ma-s
48	34	Jha 1958: 526	Present Perfect Indefinit	-ame ach
51	11	Koefoed 1958: 190f.	være Aux Passive	være...et
68	10	Rice 1986:	Perfective Mode	ɲ
75	06	Becker-Donner 1965: 41	Longer Duration of Action	to
78	06	Lukas 1937: 43–44	Perfect	nà
79	10	Merrifield 1968: 22f.	Stativizing Prefix	ri:²-
86	09	Newland 1897: 34	Past Perfect	di
93	23	Poppe 1960: 64	VN of the Passive	aatai
93	24	Poppe 1960: 64	VN of Distant Past	nxai
93	38	Poppe 1960: 101	Perfective	šxa

Tables 3.7 & 3.8: Old Anteriors

Language no.	Form no.	Source	Author's Name for Gram	Orthographic Shape
01	05	Fortescue 1980: 265–56	Perfective State	sima
03	34	Hoffman 1963: 196–200	Past	a..əri
05	08	Hetzron 1969: 13f.	Perfect Indefinite	-a
05	29	Hetzron 1969: 27f.	Anteriority	ðasaŋ
10	18	Taylor 1956a: 6, 20, 24, 30	Perfective	ha
10	41	Taylor 1956b: 144f.	Past	buga
23	05	Milne 1921: 67	Past Tense Prefix	hwɣ-i
25	03	Jaussen 1861: 62–63	Perfective	ua
32	02	Johnston 1980: 129–30	Perfective	ti
39	47	Hewitt 1979a: 175, 180–81	Perfect	x'a
42	06	Subrahmanyam 1971: 60–85, 157–60	Past	it

42	25	Subrahmanyam 1971: 86–87	Perfective Tense	*a ma-n*
46	16	Bright 1957: 67	Past	*at*
47	10	Lane 1898: 149–52, 270–73	Perfectum	*v*
48	34	Jha 1958: 526	Present Perfect Indefinite	*-ane ach*
49	13	Barker & Mengal 1969: 336ff.	Past Perfect	*yt ag ət*
49	15	Barker & Mengal 1969: 340–1	Past Perfect Completive	*yt atət*
52	21	Renck 1975: 92f., 114f.	Past	*d*
63	05	Rascher 1904: 62ff.	Perfect Particle	*sa*
68	54	Rice 1986: 360	Past	*yilé*
72	31	Harries 1950: 94–97	Immediate Past	*ci*
74	09	Thomas 1978: 73, 170, 174–75	Completive aspect	*ni*
75	04	Becker-Donner 1965: 38ff.	Completed Action (A-form)	*-á*
78	06	Lukas 1937: 43–44	Perfect	*na*
79	03	Merrifield 1968: 25	Perfect	*ma²-*
82	41	Shipley 1964: 46–47	Present-Past Tense	*k*
86	09	Newland 1897: 34	Past Perfect	*di*
87	56	Matisoff 1973: 335, 341f.	Completed Action	*ò*
91	05	Perevoshikov et al. 1962: 202–4	First Past Affirmative	*-i-*
91	07	Perevoshikov et al. 1962: 204–6	Second Past Tense	*-em*

Table 3.10: Mode of Expression and Related Strings for Simple Past

05	10	Hetzron 1969: 13f.	Perfect Definite	*-ɣʷà*
08	20	Raz 1983: 5–6	Past Tense	STCH
09	64	Leman 1980a: 191	Past	*s*
09	67	Leman 1980a:191	Past	*hta*
13	27	Turner 1958: 64, 93	Past Tense	*ma*
15	04	Platt 1972: 29	Past	*nutj*
16	01	Patz 1982: 153–54	Past	*ny*
18	05	Capell & Hinch 1970: 67ff., 73ff., 78ff.	Past Simple or Complete	*tj*
19	13	Love 1932: 13	past	*na*
27	01	Capell & Layard 1980: 75ff., & passim	Root of Past Tense Part.	*m-*

Table 3.10: (continued)

Language no.	Form no.	Source	Author's Name for Gram	Orthographic Shape
30	08	Bell 1977: xvi, xvii	Past	gi
35	05	Li 1973: 156, 193	Past	wa
48	20	Jha 1958: 502ff.	Past	h
49	11	Barker & Mengal 1969: 282ff.	Past Tense	yt
50	08	Householder et al. 1964: 116ff.	Past Tense	ε STRESS
51	02	Koefoed 1958: 181ff., 189f.	Preterite	-ede
71	09	Wilson 1961: 25	Past	TNCH
76	06	Spagnolo 1933: 105	Past	a
78	03	Lukas 1937: 40–41	Past	go
81	01	Newman 1965: 37	Past Tense	ka
88	07	Barnard 1934: 19	Past	bü
91	06	Perevoshikov et al. 1962: 202–4	First Past Negative	ŏ-...-y
93	02	Poppe 1960: 56ff.	Past Tense Suffix	ba
93	22	Poppe 1960: 62f.	(Verbal N of) Imperfect	aa
93	46	Poppe 1960: 103	VN of Perfect w/han	han han
94	23	Mühlhäusler 1985: 388–89	General Past	bin

Tables 3.11 & 3.12: Perfectives

Language no.	Form no.	Source	Author's Name for Gram	Orthographic Shape
02	07	N'Diaye 1970: 204	Prétérit du Passé	tu zen
04	09	Newman 1974: 45ff.	Perfective	TNCH
04	10	Newman 1974: 45ff.	Second Perfective	á
06	02	Cortade 1969: 29–30, 189–90	Prétérite	STCH
10	21	Taylor 1956a: 7, 9, 19, 22–25	Aorist	ti
12	41	Prost 1967b: 118, 339	Completive	ki
17	01	Yallop 1977: 49–52	Past	ika

17	17	Yallop 1977: 62–63	Punctiliar	*alh*
18	05	Capell & Hinch 1970: 67ff., 73ff., 78ff.	Punctiliar	ZERO
19	33	Foley n.d.: 22	Punctiliar	ZERO
20	29	Sharpe 1972: 79, 87–90	Past Punctiliar Indicativ	*wun*
25	03	Jaussen 1861: 62–63		*ua*
32	01	Johnston 1980: 129–30	Aorist	ZERO
33	01	Dyen 1965: 24	Perfectic Particle	*ja*
34	06	Benton 1971: 125, 123, 128	Complete	*in*
38	39	Mathiot 1973: 92	Contemporaneous	*t*
39	44	Hewitt 1979a: 173	Aorist	ZERO
39	46	Hewitt 1979a: 173	Past	*n*
40	01	Kopesec 1975: 22		*-ri*
40	02	Kopesec 1975: 22	Remote	*-ba*
50	10	Householder et al. 1964: 116	Perfective	*s*
50	13	Householder et al. 1964: 120–23	Passive Aorist	*ik*
52	31	Renck 1975: 110f.	Perfective	*du*
63	05	Rascher 1904: 62ff.	Perfect Particle	*sa*
68	10	Rice 1986:	Perfective Mode	STCH
69	07	Reh 1985: 188f.	Präteritum	*Á(k)-*
72	13	Harries 1950: 79–83	Perfect	*ile*
72	32	Harries 1950: 95f.	Remote Past	*aci*
72	55	Harries 1950: 96–97	Remote Past, Indefinite	*á*
73	15	Der-Houssikian 1980a: 64f.	Past	ZERO
74	14	Thomas 1978: 70–71	Aorist	TNCH
77	01	Vandame 1963: 94ff.	Aoriste	ZERO
80	03	Furbee-Losee 1976: 129, 134	Completive	ZERO
83	45	Kuipers 1974: 74, 80	Aorist	*m*
85	13	Caughley 1983: 49, 104–11	Past	*ʔaka*
89	13	Kwok 1971: 105–8	Aspect Marker	*jǒ*
92	18	Nadzhip 1971: 117	Past Definite	*di*
93	25	Poppe 1960: 65	VN of the Perfect	*han*

Table 3.13: Degrees of Remoteness with Hodiernal and Hesternal

Language no.	Form no.	Source	Author's Name for Gram	Orthographic Shape
11	01	Faust 1971: 12	Immediate Past	*ui*
11	04	Faust 1971: 42	Remote Past	*tsuri*
11	03	Faust 1971: 42	Recent Past	*icuá*
12	35	Prost 1967b: 117	Just now (past)	*ya*
12	36	Prost 1967b: 117	Yesterday	*ʔita*
12	37	Prost 1967b: 118	Short time ago	*yami*
12	38	Prost 1967b: 118	Long time ago	*ni*
28	21	Allen & Allen 1965: 20	Past Locative	*la*
28	23	Allen & Allen 1965: 18, 34	Dist Past Pers Markers	*tu*
58	07	Anceaux 1965: 59f.	Past	*k*
58	08	Anceaux 1965: 60f., 79	Recent Past	*p*
60	12	Foreman 1974: 39–40	Near Past	*ye*
60	13	Foreman 1974: 40	Far Past	*im*
72	13	Harries 1950: 79–83	Perfect	*ile*
72	31	Harries 1950: 94–95	Immediate Past	*ci*
72	32	Harries 1950: 95f	Remote Past	*aci*
72	55	Harries 1950: 96–97	Remote past, indefinite	*ā*
79	06	Merrifield 1968: 25	Early same day	*na²-*
79	07	Merrifield 1968: 25	Previous day	*ka¹*

Table 3.14: Degrees of Remoteness Not Referring to the Daily Cycle

Language no.	Form no.	Source	Author's Name for Gram	Orthographic Shape
01	13	Fortescue 1980: 273	Recent Past	*qqammir*
01	14	Fortescue 1980: 273	Distant Past	*riirkatag*
09	65	Leman 1980a: 191	Far Past	*neh*
14	01	Sorensen 1969: 28	Remote Past	*w*

		Source	Meaning	Form
14	02	Sorensen 1969: 27	Supposed Past	*p*
38	38	Mathiot 1973: 92	Remote	*d*
40	01	Kopesec 1975: 22	—	*-ri*
40	04	Kopesec 1975: 23	Remote potential	*-i*
49	13	Barker & Mengal 1969: 336ff.	Past Perfect	*yɩ əg ət*
56	02	Wacke 1930: 165	Preterite I (near past)	ZERO
56	03	Wacke 1930: 165	Preterite II (dist. past)	*ko*
59	08	Hanke 1909: 52, 57, 86f.	Aorist I	*e*
59	18	Hanke 1909: 52, 66, 86f.	Aorist II	*r*
68	48	Rice 1986:	Recent Past	*ʔégúh*
82	62	Shipley 1964: 53		*ky?ym + ka + ?*
82	63	Shipley 1964: 52	Long ago	*wono*
82	64	Shipley 1964: 52	Ancient Times	*pa?áje*
91	25	Perevoshikov et al. 1962: 206–8		*val + Past*
92	22	Nadzhip 1971: 118–19	Pluperfect	*ǧan e*
92	34	Nadzhip 1971: 120	Recent Past	*ivid*
93	24	Poppe 1960: 64	VN of Distant Past	*nxai*

Table 5.1: Lexical Sources and Mode of Expression of Progressives

		Source	Meaning	Form
01	21	Fortescue 1980: 279	Imperfective	*riar*
02	02	N'Diaye 1970: 209		*ai*
02	04	Saltarelli 1988: 229		*ihardun*
04	11	Newman 1974: 50f	Continuous	*à*
10	17	Taylor 1956a: 6f., 23f.	Progressive	*ia*
11	08	Faust 1971: 55	Aspect Aux	*yuti*
12	19	Prost 1967b: 116	Now (w/tr)	*ca*
12	20	Prost 1967b: 116	Now (w/Intrans)	*ci*
13	68	Turner 1958: 66, 80, 111	In the Process of	*sa*
14	24	Sorensen 1969: 267–69	Continuative	*gi + we*
16	08	Patz 1964: 39–43	Continuative	REDUP
17	19	Yallop 1977: 64–65	Continuous, Durative	*an*

Table 5.1: (*continued*)

Language no.	Form no.	Source	Author's Name for Gram	Orthographic Shape
17	20	Yallop 1977: 62–65	Continuous, Durative	*aynt*
25	01	Iorss 1963: 62	Présent	*te...nei*
26	20	Lister-Turner & Clark n.d.: 24	"come to speaker"	*me*
26	32	Lister-Turner & Clark n.d.: 14	Immediate Present	*ina*
32	04	Johnston 1980: 131–32	Imperfective	REDUP+ti
34	02	Benton 1971: 126–27	Continuous Action	CV-REDUP
38	12	Mathiot 1973: 59	Durative	*da*
39	53	Hewitt 1979a: 181–82, 128	Progressive	*c'a*
40	15	Kopesec 1975: 25f.	Aux of Movement	*rig*
40	16	Kopesec 1975: 25	Aux of Movement	*kit*
40	23	Kopesec 1975: 27	Aux of State	*tä*
42	23	Subrahmanyam 1971: 85–87	Present tense	*ai ma-n*
49	09	Barker & Mengal 1969: 233–34	Continuative	*əga*
56	17	Wacke 1930: 168–69	Continuative	*ge*
58	32	Anceaux 1965: 107ff.	Durative	*tiem*
59	17	Hanke 1909: 51, 62ff., 86	Durativ	*s*
68	12	Rice 1986:	Progressive	*y*
69	05	Reh 1985: 188–90	Imperfectiv	HIGH TONE
69	09	Reh 1985: 190f.	Kontinuativ	*áalá*
72	47	Harries 1950: 110	Progressive	*li*
73	16	Der-Houssikian 1980a:68	Progressive	*bamaa*
75	02	Becker-Donner 1965: 36f.	Progressive	*pèá*
75	08	Becker-Donner 1965: 37; 42	Past Progressive	*kè...pèá*
77	02	Vandame 1963: 95	Duratif	*isi*
77	03	Vandame 1963: 95	Duratif	*isi mba k*

		Reference	Meaning	Form
77	04	Vandame 1963: 95	Duratif	*ar*
77	05	Vandame 1963: 95	Duratif	*ar mba k- wa*
80	01	Furbee-Losee 1976: 129, 135	Present Progressive	*ye:*
81	20	Newman 1965: 52–3	Continuative	*dom + ka*
82	70	Shipley 1964: 53	—	*w'ex*
83	08	Kuipers 1974: 44–45, 79–80	= English Progressive	*ko*
86	36	Newland 1897: 36, 439	Able, Can	*che*
87	24	Matisoff 1973: 237, 240, 255	Continuative	*der al*
88	10	Barnard 1934: 20	Present Continuous	*gán*
89	14	Kwok 1971: 104–5	Aspect marker	*jyū*
89	28	Kwok 1971: 104	Aspect marker	*haŋ*
90	23	Buechel 1939: 281	Progressive	*yaŋká*
90	24	Buechel 1939: 281	Progressive	*uŋ*
90	25	Buechel 1939: 282	Progressive	*ža bai*
93	40	Poppe 1960: 102	Compound Imperf Gerund	*stap*
94	16	Mühlhäusler 1985: 379–80	Progressive	*nau*
94	17	Mühlhäusler 1985: 380	Progressive	*wok long*
94	18	Mühlhäusler 1985: 380	Progressive	

Table 5.2: Imperfectives

		Reference	Meaning	Form
03	27	Hoffman 1963: 175–77	Progressive	*ɔ̌vɔ̌r*
06	03	Cortade 1969: 29–30	Aoriste intensif	*t*
32	03	Johnston 1980: 131	Continuative/Habituative	REDUP
35	04	Li 1973: 156f., 267f., 177f., 208	Continuative	REDUP
50	07	Householder et al. 1964: 115ff.	Imperfect	STCH
68	09	Rice 1986:	Imperfective Mode	ZERO
72	15	Harries 1950: 87–109	Continuous	*ga*
74	15	Thomas 1978: 71–72	Descriptive tense	TNCH
78	01	Lukas 1967: 35, 36, 48, 50ff	Continuous	*in*
83	27	Kuipers 1974: 51, 53, 71	Customary	*c*

Table 5.3: Past Imperfectives

Language no.	Form no.	Source	Author's Name for Gram	Orthographic Shape
02	06	N'Diaye 1970: 203–4	Présent du passé	-tzen zen
04	13	Newman 1974: 55	Past Continuous	ji
05	30	Hetzron 1969: 28f.	Durative	šiŋ
08	42	Raz 1983: 71–72	Imperfect + ʔala	ʔala
17	02	Yallop 1977: 50–53	Past Continuous	ina
18	06	Capell & Hinch 1970: 67ff., 78	Past Imperfect/Continuous	niŋ
20	33	Sharpe 1972: 87ff.	Past Continuous Indicative	na
25	02	Jaussen 1861: 62	Imparfait	te...ra
39	46	Hewitt 1979a: 173	Past	n
42	24	Subrahmanyam 1971: 85–87	Imperfective Tense	i ma-s
47	08	Lane 1898: 148, 153, 269–70, 272	Imperfect Indicative	-ba-

Table 5.4: Presents

Language no.	Form no.	Source	Author's Name for Gram	Orthographic Shape
02	01	N'Diaye 1970: 201–2	Présent de l'actuel	-tzen da
05	07	Hetzron 1969: 13	Imperfect Indefinite	é
08	17	Raz 1983: 7	Present	halla
08	21	Raz 1983: 6–7	Imperfect	STCH
12	42	Prost 1962: 118	Incomplete	ki
13	24	Turner 1958: 64	Present	a
15	03	Platt 1972: 29	Non-past Tense	ninj
16	02	Patz 1982: 153	Non-past	l
17	04	Yallop 1977: 49, 52–53	Present Continuous	ima
17	05	Yallop 1977: 51–52	Present Indicative	iyla
18	04	Capell & Hinch 1970: 73ff., 67ff.	Present Continuous Indic.	g
20	34	Sharpe 1972: 87ff.	Present Continuous Indic.	n
25	01	Jaussen 1861: 62	Présent de L'indicatif	te...mei

			Root of Indefinite tense	
27	02	Capell & Layard 1980: 75ff., & passim	Present	e-
35	08	Li 1973:	Present	ZERO
39	01	Hewitt 1979a: 167, 172, 181	Present	-w + p'
40	05	Kopesec 1975: 23, 72;	—	en
47	07	Lane 1898: 145–49, 268–69	Present Indicative	ZERO
48	15	Jha 1958: 482f., 522f., 602f.	—	acha -a
49	01	Barker & Mengal 1969: 129–30	Present-Future	ZERO
50	07	Householder et al. 1964: 115ff.	Present	ZERO
51	01	Koefoed 1958:[1] 180f., 85	Present tense	-r
52	19	Renck 1975: 86f.	Present	STCH
52	20	Renck 1975: 90ff.	Present Progressive	no
56	01	Wacke 1930: 164	Present	mai
58	05	Anceaux 1965: 58f., 61, 79f.	Present	t
59	36	Hanke 1909: 51, 6, 4, 6	Present	m
60	11	Foreman 1974: 39	Praesens	bwa
71	08	Wilson 1961: 23, 25	Present Continuous	TNCH
73	13	Der-Houssikian 1980a: 64	General present tense	n
76	08	Spagnolo 1933: 104, 106	Present & remote future	ZERO
81	02	Newman 1965: 37	Present	ʔa
85	11	Caughley 1982: 49, 104–11	Present, Imperative	naʔ
86	38	Newland 1897: 33f.	Non-past	ZERO
88	06	Barnard 1934: 19, 26	Present	e
91	01	Perevoshikov et al. 1962: 197–200	Present Tense Affirmative	-içk-o-
92	35	Nadzhip 1971: 122	Present	ivati
93	01	Poppe 1960: 56ff.	Present Tense Suffix	na

Table 5.5: Habituals without Tense Restrictions

01	10	Fortescue 1980: 268, 279, 283	Get to/(Try To)Cause to	sari
01	29	Fortescue 1980: 281f.	Continuous	juaar
01	50	Fortescue 1980: 279–80	Habitually Early	jaallu
01	91	Fortescue 1980: 120–26, 297	Contemporative	llu

Table 5.5: (continued)

Language no.	Form no.	Source	Author's Name for Gram	Orthographic Shape
04	36	Newman 1974: 55–56	Habitual Sequential	ɓuwo
19	31	Love 1932: 32	Custom	da
27	17	Capell & Layard 1980: 81, 83	Part of Continued Action	mʼok
28	41	Allen & Allen 1965: 16	Habitual, Repeated Action	hi
33	41	Goodenough & Sugita 1980: xxiii–xxv	—	REDUP
40	21	Kopesec 1975: 25–29	—	nän
43	12	Najlis 1966: 38	Habitual	aage
46	29	Bright 1957: 109	Habitually	o:
52	46	Renck 1975: 134	Habitual Continuative	-go + REDUP + h
56	16	Wacke 1930: 169f	Durative	okan
60	10	Foreman 1974: 39	Repetitive	bi
68	02	Rice 1986:	d- Classifier	d
68	38	Rice 1986:	Customary	n -
80	02	Furbee-Losee 1976: 129, 134	Incomplete	š
90	26	Boas and Deloria 1941: 106	Regularly, Habitually	sʼa
94	10	Mühlhäusler 1985: 339, 381	'Know how to'	sævi

Table 5.6.: Past Habituals

Language no.	Form no.	Source	Author's Name for Gram	Orthographic Shape
08	16	Raz 1983: 72	—	nabra
12	34	Prost 1967b: 117	What a situation was	pao
20	02	Sharpe 1972: 77–78	Habitual	kay
71	17	Wilson 1961: 26	Used to	la
73	20	Der-Houssikian 1980a: 71	Past Habitual	gbizzi
82	43	Shipley 1964: 48	Habitual Aspect	ʔus
91	27	Perevoshikov 1962: 207–8	—	val + Future
92	26	Nadzhip 1971: 121	Past Habitual	digan

			1st VN of Present Frequentative VN w/han	*gša han* *dag han*
93	43	Poppe 1960: 103		*gša han*
93	44	Poppe 1960: 103		*dag han*

Table 5.7: Iteratives

		Reference	Description	Form
01	10	Fortescue 1980: 268, 279, 283	—	*sari*
01	37	Fortescue 1980: 283–84	Indefinite Iterative	*qattaar*
10	26	Taylor 1956a: 13	Inclusive	*-buri*
12	09	Prost 1967b: 116	Twice or Repeatedly	*rabi*
17	16	Yallop 1977: 61–62	Iterative	*iyna*
20	36	Sharpe 1972: 37, 58, 77	Repeated action	REDUP
27	17	Capell & Layard 1980: 81, 83	Part of Continued Action	*m'ok*
28	41	Allen et al 1982: 16	Habitual or Repeated	*hi*
30	01	Bell 1977: xiii	Intensity, Repetition	REDUP
33	42	Goodenough & Sugita 1980: xxiii–xxv		REDUP
34	20	Benton 1971: 133	Frequentative	*man*
35	04	Li 1973: 156ff., 267f., 177, 208	Continuative	REDUP
42	20	Subrahmanyam 1971: 142–45	Plural Action Form	*k*
46	17	Bright 1957: 88–89	Iterative	*ip*
46	19	Bright 1957: 89–91	Reduplication	REDUP
46	20	Bright 1957: 92–93	Plural Action	*va*
49	19	Barker & Mengal 1969: 237	Iterative	*an bu*
52	34	Renck 1975: 120	Prolonged Action	*gogo*
52	35	Renck 1975: 119f., 135	Habitual	*go*
58	28	Anceaux 1965: 97–103	Iterative	*ka*
59	05	Hanke 1909: 20	Continuative or Iterative	*er*
68	16	Rice 1986:	Seriative	*i*
69	18	Reh 1985: 201–9	Frequentativ	*i*
71	29	Wilson 1961: 48, 27	Iterative or Intensive	*s*
72	12	Harries 1950: 77	Frequentative	REDUP
74	12	Thomas 1978: 143	More than once	*ru*
82	03	Shipley 1964: 41	Repetitive Action	*jo*

Table 5.7: (continued)

Language no.	Form no.	Source	Author's Name for Gram	Orthographic Shape
91	22	Perevoshikov et al. 1962: 219–20, 224	Aspectual Suffix -l-	-yl-
92	36	Nadzhip 1971: 108	Frequentative	REDUP
94	13	Mühlhäusler 1985: 383	Repetition	REDUP

Table 5.8: Continuatives

Language no.	Form no.	Source	Author's Name for Gram	Orthographic Shape
01	30	Fortescue 1980: 282	Keep on -ing	usaar
01	31	Fortescue 1980: 282	Progressive	giartur
01	32	Fortescue 1980: 282	Protracted Progressive	giartuaar
04	36	Newman 1974:55–56	Habitual sequential	ôuvo
10	28	Taylor 1956a: 13, 1956b: 148	Continuative	meme
27	17	Capell & Layard 1980: 81, 83	Continued action	m'ok
48	32	Jha 1958: 525	Past imperfect conditional	rah + Past
49	19	Barker & Mengal 1969: 237	Iterative	an bu
59	33	Hanke 1909: 15	—	REDUP
60	24	Foreman 1974: 95ff.	Continuation of Action	REDUP
60	31	Foreman 1974: 136–37	Continuous Action	yi
82	28	Shipley 1964: 44	Durative	nu
86	14	Newland 1897: 36	Continuation of Action	len ko
87	24	Matisoff 1973: 237, 240, 255	Continuative	che
89	17	Kwok 1971: 110–11	Aspect marker	lôk hēui
94	13	Mühlhäusler 1985: 383	Repetition	REDUP

Table 5.9: Frequentatives

Language no.	Form no.	Source	Author's Name for Gram	Orthographic Shape
18	09	Capell and Hinch 1970: 81f	Frequentative	CV# REDUP
19	32	Love 1934: 31, (Foley n.d.: 23)	Frequentative	ba

39	55	Hewitt 1979a: 183, 212	'Several Times'	*ka*
42	30	Subrahmanyam 1971: 125	Subjunctive	*duh*
56	14	Wacke 1930: 167ff.	Frequentative	*ma*
59	05	Hanke 1909: 20	Continuative or Iterative	*er*
59	33	Hanke 1909: 15	—	REDUP
68	38	Rice 1986:	Customary	*n -*
69	18	Reh 1985: 201–209	Frequentative	*I-*
69	45	Reh 1985: 201, 205–7	Frequentative	LOW TONE
69	46	Reh 1985: 201, 207–8	Frequentative	REDUP
76	30	Spagnolo 1933: 140–41	Frequentative	REDUP
83	29	Kuipers 1974: 62	Do Something All the Time	*amie*
85	43	Caughley 1982: 110	Repetitive	*jhug*

Table 6.1: Related Strings and Mode of Expression for Grams Expressing Obligation

01	06	Fortescue 1980: 265	Must	*sariaqar*
02	19	N'Diaye 1970: 211–12	Obligation	*-tu bear*
09	39	Leman 1980a: 110	Obligative	*áh*
14	31	West 1980: 78	Obligatory Action	*ro + ia*
16	20	R. Hershberger 1964b: 37	Should	*nyaku*
16	21	Patz 1982: 273–82	Purposive	*nkV*
19	18	Love 1932: 14f.	Obligatory	*p...nya*
22	07	Manley 1972: 192f.	Necessity	*pal*
23	10	Milne 1921: 77	To Be Good	*la*
23	13	Milne 1921: 71	Ought	*taik*
28	03	Allen & Allen 1965: 14	Auxiliary Verb 'can'	*tale*
28	22	Allen & Allen 1965: 21, 29, 33, 42, 44–45		*go/gïy*
33	04	Dyen 1965: 24	Negative of Future/Prob.	*saq*
33	14	Dyen 1965: 25	'By rights'	*wiisen*
34	22	Benton 1971: 136	Actor Responsible	*nai*
37	15	Maan 1951: 84ff.	Future Aux	*bo-*

Table 6.1: (continued)

Language no.	Form no.	Source	Author's Name for Gram	Orthographic Shape
39	56	Hewitt 1979a: 27, 184, 192, 195	Protasis	*r*
40	07	Kopesec 1975: 24, 79, 80	Potential	*re*
42	31	Subrahmanyam 1971: 124–125	Necessity	*ba ane*
48	43	Jha 1958: 534	Ought	*cah*
48	50	Jha 1958: 539	Ought	*bujh*
49	03	Barker & Mengal 1969: 179–90	Subjunctive	*bə̀*
49	08	Barker & Mengal 1969: 197–98	Compulsion	*əg kap*
49	10	Barker & Mengal 1969: 239	Obligation	*əgɨ bu*
49	21	Barker & Mengal 1969: 459–60	Past Subjunctive	*bə̀ yɨ*
50	14	Householder et al. 1964: 107	Modal Particle	*na*
50	16	Householder et al. 1964: 106–7	Modal Particle	*as*
51	04	Koefoed 1958: 192	'shall' Future Auxiliary	*skulle*
51	09	Koefoed 1958: 192, 185	Aux 'may, must'	*mätte*
51	16	Koefoed 1958: 116, 181f.	'ought to' Aux	*burde*
60	21	Foreman 1974: 24, 94	Should Not	*kap*
68	45	Rice 1986:	Prohibitive	*sáná*
68	47	Rice 1986:	Unrealized Action in Past	*álô*
68	50	Rice 1986:	Future	*gó'o*
68	53	Rice 1986: 359	Future Intentionality	*woleani*
71	34	Wilson 1961: 29	N/A	*ba kə*
72	42	Harries 1950: 109	Be Fitting	*wandicila*
76	04	Spagnolo 1933: 105	Obligation Future	*kɔ*
81	04	Newman 1965: 38	Past Conditional	*nka*
84	33	Yates & Sayasithsena 1970: 390	Must, Have to	*tcɔ̀ɔ̀*
84	34	Yates & Sayasithsena 1970: 390	Should, Ought	*khuan*
85	26	Caughley 1982: 94–95	Irrealis Nominal	*sa*

85	44	Caughley 1982: 112	Indefinite Necessative	*haŋ*
86	40	Reichle 1981: 58–60, 67–70, 79	Compulsion	*ding*
87	04	Matisoff 1973: 211ff.	Obligative	*ya*
87	20	Matisoff 1973: 234f.	Ought to/Should/By chance	*cɔ*
88	13	Barnard 1934: 21f., 32	Necessity	*ra*
89	05	Kwok 1971: 77	Obligation	*ying goi*
93	21	Poppe 1960: 61f.	Future Suffix	*xa*
93	47	Poppe 1960: 103	VN of Future w/han	*xa han*
94	09	Mühlhäusler 1985: 386	Must, Have To	*mas*

Tables 6.2. & 6.3: Ability, Root Possibility and Permission

01	66	Fortescue 1980: 293	"can"	*sinnaa*
01	69	Fortescue 1980: 293	"be good at"	*llaqqig*
02	12	N'Diaye 1970: 206–7	Potential	*ke*
02	17	N'Diaye 1970: 211	—	*tzen al*
03	49	Hoffman 1963: 222–23	Ability	*baitka*
03	50	Hoffman 1963: 222–23	Ability	*mbagà*
18	07	Capell & Hinch 1970: 67–68, 78ff.	Potential	*ji*
19	19	Love 1932: 16	Potential mood, can	*golleh*
20	35	Sharpe 1972: 87ff., 51	Present Punctiliar Subjun	*ripa*
22	06	Manley 1972: 192f.	Ability	*ragay*
22	08	Manley 1972: 192f.	Permission	*di*
26	17	Lister-Turner & Clark n.d. 23–24	Can, able to	*diba*
28	03	Allen & Allen 1965: 14	Auxiliary Verb 'can'	*tate*
28	22	Allen & Allen 1965: 21, 29, 33, 43, 44–45	—	*goˡg/ɿy*
34	07	Benton 1971: 126–41	Potential Complete Active	*maka*
39	61	Hewitt 1979a: 194–95	Potential	*a-l-sa-ra*
40	19	Kopesec 1975: 25f.	Aux of state	*reb*
42	30	Subrahmanyam 1971: 125	Subjunctive	*duh*

Table 6.2 & 6.3: (*continued*)

Language no.	Form no.	Source	Author's Name for Gram	Orthographic Shape
48	51	Jha 1958: 539	To be able	*par*
48	52	Jha 1958: 539	To be able	*sak*
49	06	Barker & Mengal 1969: 197	Know How To	*əga zan*
49	10	Barker & Mengal 1969: 239	Obligation	*əgi bu*
49	16	Barker & Mengal 1969: 343	Present Potential	*yi kan*
51	08	Koefoed 1958: 192, 185	Aux 'can, may'	*kunne*
51	09	Koefoed 1958: 192, 185	Aux 'may, must'	*mätte*
59	11	Hanke 1909: 53, 87	Modus Potentialis	*era*
71	16	Wilson 1961: 26	Able	*gbali*
72	46	Harries 1950: 110	To Know How To Do	*manya*
76	24	Spagnolo 1933: 186f	Be Able to	*bulö*
84	12	Yates & Sayasithsena 1970: 70, 16, 186	"have the opportunity to"	*daj*
84	35	Yates & Sayasithsena 1970: 390	May, might	*àat*
84	41	Hoshino & Marcus 1973: 153	Skill, learned activity	*bpe:n*
86	21	Newland 1897: 37, 647	Able, Can	*tium*
86	36	Newland 1897: 36, 439	Able, Can	*ko*
87	16	Matisoff 1973: 231ff., 221	Potentiality	*phe*
87	17	Matisoff 1973: 232, 247f.	Have the ability	*pi*
87	18	Matisoff 1973: 233	Able to	*ɣa*
87	19	Matisoff 1973: 233.f.	Able to	*gà*
87	25	Matisoff 1973: 237, 244, 240	Causative	*ci*
88	11	Barnard 1934: 20–22, 27–28	Past Perfect	*ngut*
88	22	Barnard 1934: 16, 22	Know	*shang*
89	01	Kwok 1971: 77–78	Possibility	*nàng gau*
89	02	Kwok 1971: 77–78	Possibility	*hó yǐ*
89	03	Kwok 1971: 77–78	Possibility	*hó nàng*

		Description	Reference	Gram
89	04	Possibility, Future	Kwok 1971: 77	*wŭü*
89	25	Aspect marker	Kwok 1971: 119	*dóu*
92	31	Potentialis	Nadzhip 1971: 107, 117	*al*
94	02	Can	Mühlhäusler 1985: 385	*kæn*
94	10	'Know how to'	Mühlhäusler 1985: 387	*sævi*
94	22	Physical ability	Mühlhäusler 1985: 386–87	*inap*

Table 6.4: Other Uses of Grams Expressing Epistemic Possibility

		Description	Reference	Gram
02	12	Potential	N'Diaye 1970: 206–7	*ke*
02	13	Potential, Non-Actuel	N'Diaye 1970: 207	*izhe*
10	42	Future	Taylor 1956: 144–45	*me*
11	13	Potential	Faust 1971: 58	*mia*
12	48	'might'	Prost 1967b: 336	*mica*
17	11	Potential/Conditional	Yallop 1977: 56	*imira*
19	20	Potential and might	Love 1932: 16	*ŋunna*
20	31	Future Continuous Subjunc	Sharpe 1972: 87ff.	*yar*
32	13	Non-imminent irrealis	Johnston 1980: 63–65	*ge*
33	03	'Future, Probable' Part.	Dyen 1965: 24	*qe*
38	37	Potential	Mathiot 1973: 90–91	*p*
39	65	Contingent	Hewitt 1979a: 197	*a-q'a-la-*
39	66	Impersonal Contingent	Hewitt 1979a: 197	*a-l-sa-ra*
42	30	Subjunctive	Winfield 1928: 125	*duh*
47	11	Potential	Lane 1898: 147–48, 152–53, 259–65	*-a-*
48	29	Present subjunctive	Jha 1958: 523	*aitᵃ hoe*
48	36	Present presumptive	Jha 1958: 528	*ane ho*
48	49	Past presumptive	Jha 1958: 538–39	*par*
59	23	can, could	Hanke 1909: 54, 68, 88	*bo*
68	43	Modus Dubitativus	Rice 1986:	*ʔesih*
82	45	Uncertainty, Possibility, Periphrastic subjunctive	Shipley 1964: 48–9, 54	*jak+k'e*
84	35	May, Might	Yates & Sayasithsena 1970: 390	*aat*
84	36	May, Might	Yates & Sayasithsena 1970: 390	*khyy*

Language no.	Form no.	Source	Author's Name for Gram	Orthographic Shape
85	12	Caughley 1982: 49, 104–111, 92–3	Future (Indefinite)	*ca?*
88	09	Barnard 1934: 19	Conjectural	*tangi*
89	03	Kwok 1971: 77–78	Possibility	*hó nǎng*
92	23	Nadzhip 1971: 119	Past Uncertain	*du*
93	41	Poppe 1960: 103	Compound of Imperf Gerund	*ža bol*

Table 6.5: Other Uses of Grams Expressing Probability

Language no.	Form no.	Source	Author's Name for Gram	Orthographic Shape
01	74	Fortescue 1980: 293–94	'probably, presumably'	*jumnarsi*
02	05	N'Diaye 1970: 203	Futur de l'actuel	*-ko da*
02	08	N'Diaye 1970: 204	Futur du Passé	*ko zen*
08	15	Raz 1983: 6	Perhaps, Probability	*man gäbbǝ'*
12	23	Prost 1967b:116	Potential	*tiǝri*
13	30	Turner 1958: 64, 72, 89	Indefinite	*aint*
14	16	Sorensen 1969: 156–61	Probable	*sa*
14	34	Sorensen 1969: 34	—	*gǝ̀ + sa*
39	50	Hewitt 1979a: 176–77	Future II	*s+t'*
40	04	Kopesec 1975:23; 7	Remote potential	*-i*
47	09	Lane 1898: 149, 273–75	Future	*bi*
49	03	Barker & Mengal 1969: 179–90	Subjunctive	*by*
49	15	Barker & Mengal 1969: 340–41	Past Perfect Completive	*yǝ + ǝtǝt*
82	46	Shipley 1964: 48–49, 54	Periphrastic subjunctive	*na+k'e*
84	37	Yates & Sayasithsena 1970: 390	Probability	*khǒŋ*
86	10	Newland 1897: 34f., 40, 468	Future	*lai*
86	40	Reichle 1981: 58–60, 67–70, 79	Compulsion	*ding*

349

Reference			Use	Form
Matisoff 1973: 331ff.	87	51	Desiderative	ga
Nadzhip 1971: 117	92	21	Past Suppositional	gandi

Table 6.11: Purpose Markers with Other Uses

Reference			Use	Form
Fortescue 1980: 274–75, 64–67	01	16	Future	ssa
Saltarelli 1988: 237	02	14	Subjunctive	ie
Newman 1974: 48–49	04	33	Subjunctive	bàlà
Cortade 1969: 38–40	06	15	Future	ed
Leslau 1945: 7–8	08	22	Jussive	STCH
Platt 1972: 32	15	08	Desiderative/Purposive	ngunjdjagu
Patz 1982: 273–81	16	21	Purposive	nka
Capell & Layard 1980: 75ff. & passim	27	03	Root of future tense	p-
Johnston 1980: 63–5	32	13	Non-imminent irrealis	ge
Hewitt 1979a: 191–92, 199–201	39	59	Purposive	na
Kopesec 1975: 24, 79, 80	40	07	Potential	re
Lane 1898: 147–48, 152–53, 259–65	47	11	Present subjunctive	-a-
Householder et al. 1964: 107	50	14	Modal particle	na
Renck 1975: 94, 118	52	23	in order to	s
Foreman 1974: 40–41	60	14	Future	iti
Rice 1986:	68	08	Optative mode	ghu-
Buechel 1939: 31, 275–78	90	03	Future	kte

Table 7.1: Sources and Expression Types for Primary Future Grams

Reference			Use	Form
Hoffman 1963: 222	03	42	Be About to, Soon	làgɔ̀ri
West 1980: 36	14	32	Definite Future	gɨ + tɨ
Sorensen 1969: 74–75	14	28	Anticipated action	gɨ + tɨ + gɨ + wé
Kopesec 1975: 25ff.	40	18	Aux of movement	jat
Koefoed 1958: 18, 183, 185	51	18	Future Phrase	komme til at
Reh 1985: 191	69	12	Nahes Futur	àdìyà
Harries 1950: 99	72	36	Remote Future	jìya

Table 7.1: *(continued)*

Language no.	Form no.	Source	Author's Name for Gram	Orthographic Shape
73	14	Der-Houssikian 1980a: 64f.	Near Future	*ngɔni*
75	03	Becker-Donner 1965: 37f.	Future Progressive	*nà pèá*
80	04	Furbee-Losee 1976: 129, 135	Future progressive	*ʔoh*
89	20	Kwok 1971: 114	Aspect marker	*jau*
03	37	Hoffman 1963: 212–17	Auxiliary 'Go'	*rà*
11	06	Faust 1971: 55	Aux of Aspect	*utsu*
18	03	Capell and Hinch 1970: 74, 67ff.	Future Indicative	*wana*
27	03	Capell & Layard 1980: 75ff & passim	Root of Future Tense	*p̪-*
43	07	Najlis 1966: 37	Future	*am*
69	08	Reh 1985: 188–89	Futur	*ákkà*
75	05	Becker-Donner 1965: 40f.	Future	*lò*
76	05	Spagnolo 1933: 105	Determinative Future	*tu*
81	03	Newman 1965: 37	Future	*ʔanna*
88	08	Barnard 1934: 19, 21, 28–29	Future	*di*
01	18	Fortescue 1984: 275, 325	Indefinite Future	*jumaar*
51	05	Koefoed 1958: 192	'vil' Future Aux	*ville*
94	07	Hall 1943a.: 32–33	Want/Wish; Be About to	*lajk*
89	03	Kwok 1971: 77–78	Possibility	*hà nóng*
89	04	Kwok 1971: 77	Possibility, Future	*wui*
02	05	N'Diaye 1970: 203	Futur de l'actuel	*-ko da*
08	41	Raz 1983: 68–69	Futurity	*ʔəgəl...tu*
37	15	Maan 1951	Future aux	*bo-*
47	09	Lane 1898: 149, 273–75	Future	*bi*
52	23	Renck 1975: 94	Intentional Future	*s*
60	14	Foreman 1974: 40–41	Future	*iti*
68	50	Rice 1986:	Future	*gòʔo*
82	42	Shipley 1964: 47	Future tense	*mak*

85	41	Caughley 1982: 199	Imminence	*khe?*
01	17	Fortescue 1980: 274–75, 325	Future	*niar*
02	19	N'Diaye 1970: 211–12	Obligation	*-tu bear*
51	04	Koefoed 1958: 192	'shall' Future Auxiliary	*skulle*
51	06	Koefoed 1958: 192	Future Aux	*fä*
60	32	Foreman 1974: 144–45	Immediacy	*nin*
76	04	Spagnolo 1933: 105	Obligation Future	*kɔ́*
76	23	Spagnolo 1933: 186	—	*dɔ'ya*
33	03	Dyen 1965: 24	Future, Probable Part.	*ɟe*
76	03	Spagnolo 1933: 105	Future	*dé*
85	38	Caughley 1982: 108, 101, 124	Near Future	*dhaŋ*
94	01	Mühlhäusler 1985: 388	Future	*bajmbaj*

Tables 7.2 & 7.3: Desire Futures

01	18	Fortescue 1984: 275, 325	Indefinite Future	*jumaar*
37	15	Maan 1951: 84ff.	Future aux	*bo-*
51	05	Koefoed 1958: 192	'will' Future Aux	*ville*
58	06	Anceaux 1965: 58f., 71, 79, 112	Future.	*d*
59	09	Hanke 1909: 52f., 66, 87	Futurum Indefinitum	*aʁ*
59	10	Hanke 1909: 53; 87	Futurum Instans	*aʁ...m*
90	03	Boas and Deloria 1941: 31, 275–78	Future	*kte*
94	07	Hall 1943a: 32–33	Want/Wish; Be About to	*lajk*

Tables 7.4. & 7.5: Obligation Futures

01	16	Fortescue 1980: 274–75, 64–67	Future	*ssa*
02	19	N'Diaye 1970: 211–12	Obligation	*-tu bear*
02	05	N'Diaye 1970: 203	Futur de l'actuel	*-ko da*
37	15	Maan 1951: 84ff.	Future aux	*bo-*
51	04	Koefoed 1958: 192	'shall' Future Auxiliary	*skulle*
68	50	Rice 1986:	Future	*gó'o*
86	10	Newland 1897: 34f., 40, 468	Future	*lai*

Language no.	Form no.	Source	Author's Name for Gram	Orthographic Shape
		Tables 7.6. & 7.7: Candidates for Futures from 'be, become' Sources Not on the Obligation > Future Pathway		
08	41	Raz 1983: 68–69	Futurity	*ʔəgəl...tu*
47	09	Lane 1898: 149, 273–75	Future	*bi*
52	23	Renck 1975: 94	Intentional Future	*s*
60	14	Foreman 1974: 40–41	Future	*iti*
82	42	Shipley 1964: 47	Future tense	*mak*
		Table 7.8: Related Strings and Mode of Expression for Movement-derived Futures		
03	42	Hoffman 1963: 222	Be About to, Soon	*làgàrì*
14	28	Sorensen 1969: 74–75	Anticipated action	*gɨ + tɨ + gɨ + wé*
14	32	West 1980: 36	Definite Future	*gɨ + tɨ*
14	34	West 1980: 34	—	*gɨ + sa*
14	35	Sorensen 1969: 270	Periphrasis	*gɨ + súa*
40	18	Kopesec 1975: 25ff.	Aux of movement	*jat*
51	18	Koefoed 1958: 18, 183, 185	Future Phrase	*komme til at*
69	12	Reh 1985: 191	Nahes Futur	*àdiyà*
72	36	Harries 1950: 99	Remote Future	*jíya*
73	14	Der-Houssikian 1980a: 64f.	Near Future	*ngɔni*
75	03	Becker-Donner 1965: 37f.	Future Progressive	*nì pɛ́à*
80	04	Furbee-Losee 1976: 129, 135	Future progressive	*ʔoh*
89	20	Kwok 1971: 114	Aspect marker	*jau*
03	37	Hoffman 1963: 212–17	Auxiliary 'Go'	*ra*
11	06	Faust 1971: 55	Aux of Aspect	*utsu*
18	03	Capell & Hinch 1970: 74, 67ff.	Future Indicative	*uana*
27	03	Capell & Layard 1980: 75ff. & passim	Root of Future Tense	*p-*
43	07	Najlis 1966: 37	Future	*am*
69	08	Reh 1985: 188–89	Futur	*àkkà*

75	05	Becker-Donner 1965: 40f.	Future	lò
76	05	Spagnolo 1933: 105	Determinative Future	tu
81	03	Newman 1965: 37	Future	ʔanna
88	08	Barnard 1934: 19, 21, 28–29	Future	di

Table 7.9: Movement Verb Futures: Other Uses

03	37	Hoffman 1963: 212–17	Auxiliary 'Go'	rà
03	42	Hoffman 1963: 222	Be About to, Soon	làgàrì
11	06	Faust 1971: 55	Aux of Aspect	utsu
14	28	Sorensen 1969: 74–75	Anticipated action	$gɨ + tɨ + gɨ + wé$
14	32	West 1980: 36	Definite Future	$gɨ + tɨ$
14	34	West 1980: 34	—	$gɨ + sa$
14	35	Sorensen 1969: 270	Periphrasis	$gɨ + súa$
18	03	Capell & Hinch 1970: 74, 67ff.	Future Indicative	wana
27	03	Capell & Layard 1980: 75ff. & passim	Root of Future Tense	p-
40	18	Kopesec 1975: 25ff.	Aux of movement	jat
43	07	Najlis 1966: 37	Future	am
51	18	Koefoed 1958: 18, 183, 185	Future Phrase	komme til at
69	08	Reh 1985: 188–89	Futur	àkká
69	12	Reh 1985: 191	Nahes Futur	àdìyà
72	36	Harries 1950: 99	Remote Future	jìya
73	14	Der-Houssikian 1980a: 64f.	Near Future	ngɔmi
75	03	Becker-Donner 1965: 37f.	Future Progressive	nù pèá
75	05	Becker-Donner 1965: 40f.	Future	lò
76	05	Spagnolo 1933: 105	Determinative Future	tu
80	04	Furbee-Losee 1976: 129, 135	Future progressive	ʔoh
81	03	Newman 1965: 37	Future	ʔanna
88	08	Barnard 1934: 19, 21, 28–29	Future	di
89	20	Kwok 1971: 114	Aspect Marker	jaìi

Tables 7.10. & 7.11: Futures from Temporal Adverbs

Language no.	Form no.	Source	Author's Name for Gram	Orthographic Shape
33	03	Dyen 1965: 24	'Future, Probable' Part.	*qe*
76	03	Spagnolo 1933: 105	Future	*dé*
85	38	Caughley 1982: 108, 101, 124	Near Future	*dhaŋ*
94	01	Hall 1943a: 90, 27	Future	*bajmbaj*

Table 7.13: Purpose and Complement Clause Uses of Future Grams

Language no.	Form no.	Source	Author's Name for Gram	Orthographic Shape
01	16	Fortescue 1980: 274–75, 64–67	Future	*ssa*
06	15	Cortade 1969: 38–40	Future	*ed*
26	07	Lister-Turner and Clark n.d.: 11, 18	Future	*bain*
27	03	Capell & Layard 1980: 75ff. & passim	Root of Future Tense	*p-*
32	13	Johnston 1980: 63–65	Non-imminent irrealis	*ge*
33	03	Dyen 1965: 24	'Future, Probable' Part.	*qe*
52	23	Renck 1975: 94	Intentional Future	*s*
60	14	Foreman 1974: 40–41	Future	*iti*
90	03	Buechel 1939: 31, 275–78	Future	*kte*

Table 7.14: Presents with Future Uses

Language no.	Form no.	Source	Author's Name for Gram	Orthographic Shape
05	07	Hetzron 1969: 13	Imperfect Indefinite	*é*
15	03	Platt 1972: 29	Non-past Tense	*ninj*
17	04	Yallop 1977: 49, 52–53	Present	*ima*
17	05	Yallop 1977: 51–52	Present Continuous	*iyla*
47	07	Lane 1898: 145–49, 268–69	Present Indicative	ZERO
48	15	Jha 1958: 482f, 522f, 602f	-0-	*acha-aita*
49	09	Barker & Mengal 1969: 233–34	Continuative	*əga bu*
49	01	Barker & Mengal 1969: 129–30	Present-Future	ZERO

			Present tense	ZERO
50	07	Householder et al 1964: 115ff.	Future	-r
51	01	Koefoed 1958: 180f., 185		tə
71	10	Wilson 1961: 25	Present & Remote Future	n
73	13	Der-Houssikian 1980a: 64	Present Tense Affirmative	-içk-o-
91	01	Perevoshikov 1962: 197–200	Present Tense Negative	u-...-içk-y
91	02	Perevoshikov 1962: 197–200		

Table 7.15: Possible Old Presents Used for Future

			Present	a
03	32	Hoffman 1963: 190–96	Imperfect	STCH
08	21	Leslau 1945: 6–7	Incomplete	on
34	05	Benton 1971: 133ff., 196–97	Future	in
42	02	Winfield 1928: 60–85		

Table 7.16: Imperfectives with Future Uses

			Imperfective	-ba
10	16	Taylor 1956a: 6, 23–24, 20, 42f, xxiv	Future	e
25	04	Iorss 1963: 63	Continuative	REDUP
35	04	Li 1973: 156ff., 267f., 177, 208	Continuous Suffix	in
78	01	Lukas 1937: 35–36, 48, 50ff.		

Table 7.17: Perfectives with Future Uses

			Aorist	ua
25	03	Iorss 1963: 62–63	Perfect Particle	ZERO
39	44	Hewitt 1979a: 173		sa
63	05	Rascher 1904: 62ff.		

Bibliography for GRAMCATS Sample

01 Fortescue, Michael. 1980. Affix ordering in West Greenlandic derivational processes. *International Journal of American Linguistics* 25: 259–78.

01 ———. 1984. *West Greenlandic*. London: Croom Helm.

01 Schultz-Lorentzen. 1945. *A grammar of the West Greenland language.* Copenhagen: Reitzel.

01 ———. 1927. *Dictionary of the West Greenland Eskimo language.* Copenhagen: Reitzel.

02 Bakker, Peter. 1984. The order of affixes in the Basque synthetic verb. *Seminario de Filología Vasca 'Julio de Urquijo'*, Anuario 18, no. 2: 65–87.

02 Houghton, Herbert Pierrepont. 1961. *An introduction to the Basque language: Labourdin dialect.* Leiden: Brill.

02 N'Diaye, Genevieve. 1970. *Structure du dialecte Basque de Maya.* The Hague: Mouton.

02 Saltarelli, Mario, Miren Azkarate, David Farwell, John Ortiz de Urbina, and Lourdes Oñederra. 1988. *Basque.* New York: Croom Helm.

02 Trask, Robert L. 1977. Historical syntax and Basque verbal morphology: Two hypotheses. In *Anglo-American contributions to Basque Studies. Essays in honour of Jon Bilbao*, ed. W. A. Douglass, R. W. Etulain, and W. H. Jacobsen, Jr., 203–17. Reno, Nevada.

03 Hoffman, Carl. 1963. *A grammar of the Margi language.* London: Oxford University Press.

04 Newman, Paul. 1974. *The Kanakuru language.* Leeds: Institute of Modern English Language Studies, University of Leeds, in association with The West African Linguistic Society.

05 Hetzron, Robert. 1969. *The verbal system of Southern Agaw.* Berkeley: University of California Press.

06 Cortade, Jean-Marie. 1969. *Essai de grammaire Touareg (dialecte de l'Ahaggar).* Algiers: Université d'Alger, Institut de Recherches Sahariennes.

06 Prasse, Karl-G. 1972. *Manuel de grammaire Touaregue (tahaggart)*, parts 1–3: *Phonétique, Ecriture, Pronom.* Copenhagen: Editions de l'Université de Copenhague.

08 Leslau, Wolf. 1945. *Short grammar of Tigré (Publications of the American*

Oriental Society, offprint series no. 18). New Haven: American Oriental
Society.

08 Raz, Shlomo. 1983. *Tigre grammar and texts* (Afroasiatic dialects, 4) Malibu: Undena.

09 Leman, Wayne. 1980a. *A reference grammar of the Cheyenne language* (Occasional Publications in Anthropology, Linguistic series no. 5). Greeley: University of Northern Colorado Museum of Anthropology.

09 Leman, Wayne, ed. 1980b. Cheyenne texts: An introduction to Cheyenne literature (Occasional Publications in Anthropology, linguistic
series no. 6). Greeley: University of Northern Colorado Museum of
Anthropology.

10 Taylor, Douglas. 1955. Phonemes of the Hopkins (British Honduras)
dialect of Island Carib (= Island Carib I). *International Journal of American
Linguistics* 21: 233–41.

10 ———. 1956a. Island Carib II: Word-classes, affixes, nouns and verbs.
International Journal of American Linguistics 22: 1–44.

10 ———. 1956b. Island-Carib morphology III: Locators and particles. *International Journal of American Linguistics* 22: 138–50.

10 ———. 1958. Island Carib IV: Syntactic notes, texts. *International Journal
of American Linguistics* 24: 36–60.

10 ———. 1959. Errata in Island Carib IV. *International Journal of American
Linguistics* 25: 137.

11 Faust, Norma. 1971. Cocama clause types. In *Tupi Studies I*, ed. D Bendor-
Samuel, 73–105. (= SIL Publications in Linguistics and Related Fields
no. 29). Norman, Okla.: Summer Institute of Linguistics.

11 ———. 1978. *Gramática Cocama: Lecciones para el aprendizaje del idioma
Cocama* (Serie Lingüística Peruana No. 6). Lima: Ministerio de Educación,
Instituto Lingüístico de Verano.

12 Prost, Gibert R. 1962. Signalling of transitive and intransitive in Chacobo
(Pano). *International Journal of American Linguistics* 28: 108–18.

12 ———. 1965. Chacabo. In *Gramáticas estructurales de lenguas Bolivianas II*,
1–130. Riberalta, Beni, Bolivia: Instituto Lingüístico de Verano en colla-
boración con el Ministerio de Asuntos Campesinos.

12 ———. 1967a. Phonemes of the Chacobo language. *Linguistics* 35: 61–65.

12 ———. 1967b. Chacobo. In *Bolivian Indian Grammars I*, ed. Esther Matte-
son, 286–359. (SIL Publication in Linguistics and Related Fields no. 16).
Norman, Okla.: Summer Institute of Linguistics.

13 Turner, Glen D. 1958. Jivaro: Phonology and morphology. Ph.D. diss.,
Indiana University, Bloomington.

14 Sorensen, Arthur P., Jr. 1969. The morphology of Tucano. Ph.D. diss.,
Columbia University, New York.

14 West, Birdie. 1980. *Gramatica popular del Tucano*. Bogotá: Ministerio de
Gobierno, Instituto Lingüístico de Verano.

15 Platt, J. T. 1972. *An outline grammar of the Gugada dialect, South Australia*.
Canberra: Australian Institute of Aboriginal Studies.

16 Hershberger, Henry. 1964. Gugu-Yalanji noun phrases. In 16 Pittman
and Kerr 1964: 83–90.

16 Hershberger, Ruth. 1964a. -KU 'then' and -DA 'now' in Gugu-Yalanji. In 16 Pittman and Kerr 1964: 69–72.

16 ———. 1964b. Notes on Gugu-Yalanji verbs. In 16 Pittman and Kerr 1964: 35–54.

16 Patz, Elizabeth. 1982. A grammar of the Kuku Yalanji language of North Queensland. Ph.D. diss., Australian National University, Canberra.

16 Pittman, Richard, and Harland Kerr, eds. 1964. *Papers on the languages of the Australian Aborigines* (Occasional Paper in Aboriginal Studies no. 3). Canberra: Australian Institute of Aboriginal Studies.

17 Yallop, Colin. 1977. *Alyawarra: an aboriginal language of central Australia.* Canberra: Australian Institute of Aboriginal Studies.

18 Capell, A., and H. E. Hinch. 1970. *Maung grammar: Texts and vocabulary.* The Hague: Mouton.

19 Foley, J. S. n.d. A grammar of the Worora language. ms.

19 Love, J. R. B. 1931. An introduction to the Worrora language, Part I. *Journal of the Royal Society of Western Australia* 17: 53–69.

19 ———. 1932. An introduction to the Worrora language, Part II. *Journal of the Royal Society of Western Australia* 18: 13–22.

19 ———. n.d. An outline of Worrora grammar. In *Studies in Australian Linguistics,* ed. A. P. Elkin, 112–24. Sydney: The Australian National Research Council.

19 Love, J. R. B. n.d. The grammatical structure of the Worrora language of North-Western Australia. ms.

20 Sharpe, Margaret C. 1972. *Alawa phonology and grammar* (Australian Aboriginal Studies no. 37). Canberra: Australian Institute of Aboriginal Studies.

22 Manley, Timothy M. 1972. *Outline of Sre structure.* Honolulu: University of Hawaii Press.

22 Nguyen van Hoan. 1973. Ko'ho Sre affixation. Master's Thesis, Faculty of Letters, University of Saigon.

23 Milne, Mrs. Leslie. 1921. *An elementary Palaung grammar.* Oxford: Clarendon.

23 Shorto, H. L. 1960. Word and syllable patterns in Palaung. *Bulletin of the School of Oriental and African Studies* 23: 544–57.

24 Braine, Jean Critchfield. 1970. Nicobarese grammar (Car dialect). Ph.D. diss., University of California, Berkeley.

25 Iorss, Martial T. 1963. *Grammaire tahitienne.* Papeete, Tahiti: Imprimerie Officielle.

25 Jaussen, Tepano. 1861. *Grammaire et dictionnaire de la langue tahitienne.* Repr. Paris: Musée de l'Homme, 1969 (Publications de la Société des Océanistes no. 22).

26 Lawes, W. G. 1896. *Grammar and vocabulary of langauge spoken by Motu tribe.* 3d ed. Sydney: Charles Potter, Government Printer, Phillip-Street.

26 Lister-Turner, R., and J. B. Clark. n.d. *A grammar of the Motu language of Papua.* 2d ed. by Percy Chatterton. Sydney, N.S.W.: A. H. Pettifer, Government Printer.

27 Capell, A., and J. Layard. 1980. *Materials in Atchin, Malekula: Grammar,*

vocabulary and texts (Pacific Linguistics Series D no. 20). Canberra: Australian National University.

28 Allen, Jerry, and Janice Allen. 1965. *Halia language course*. Port Moresby, Papua New Guinea: Department of Information & Extension Services.

28 Allen, Jerry, Marcello Latu, Maurice Koesana, and Maurice Tsirumits. 1982. *Halia dictionary* (Dictionaries of PNG, Vol. 6). Dallas: Summer Institute of Linguistics.

30 Bell, F. L. S. 1977. *Tanga-English, English-Tanga dictionary* (Oceania Linguistic Monographs no. 21). Sydney: University of Sydney.

30 Burgmann, Arnold. 1966. [Review of 30 Maurer 1966]. *Anthropos* 61: 294–97.

30 Maurer, H. 1966. *Grammatik der Tangga-Sprache (Melanesien)* (Micro-Bibliotheca Anthropos, vol. 40). St. Augustin bei Bonn: Anthropos-Institut.

32 Johnston, Raymond Leslie. 1980. *Nakanai of New Britain* (Pacific Linguistics B 70). Canberra: Australian National University.

33 Dyen, Isidore. 1965. *A sketch of Trukese grammar* (American Oriental Essay No. 4). New Haven: American Oriental Society.

33 Goodenough, W. H., and H. Sugita. 1980. *Trukese-English Dictionary*. Philadelphia: American Philosophical Society.

34 Benton, Richard A. 1971. *Pangasinan reference grammar*. Honolulu: University of Hawaii Press.

35 Li, Paul Jen-Kuei. 1973. Rukai Structure. Ph.D. diss., The University of Hawaii, Honolulu.

37 Maan, G. 1951. *Proeve van een bulische spraakkunst* (Verhandelingen van het Koninklijk Instituut voor Taal-, Land- en Volkenkunde 10). The Hague: Nijhoff.

38 Hale, Kenneth L. 1959. A Papago grammar. Ph.D. diss., Indiana University, Bloomington.

38 Mason, J. Alden. 1950. *The language of the Papago of Arizona*. Philadelphia: University of Pennsylvania, The University Museum.

38 Mathiot, Madeleine. 1973–78. *A dictionary of Papago usage*, 2 vols. (Indiana University Publications Language Science Monographs). Bloomington: Indiana University.

38 Zepeda, Ofelia. 1983. *A Papago grammar*. Tucson: University of Arizona Press.

39. Allen, W. Sidney. 1956. Structure and system in the Abaza verbal complex. *Transactions of the Philological Society* 127–76.

39 Hewitt, B. G. 1979a. *Abkhaz* (Lingua Descriptive Studies, vol. 2). Amsterdam: North-Holland.

39 ————. 1979b. Aspects of verbal affixation in Abkhaz (Abžui dialect). Transactions of the Philological Society 211–38.

40 Alphonse, Ephraim S. 1956. *Guaymí grammar and dictionary with some ethnological notes* (Bureau of American Ethnology Bulletin 1962). Washington, D.C.: Government Printing Office.

40 Kopesec, M. F. 1975. Los elementos verbales y sustantivos y la oración en Guaymí. In *Lenguas de Panama*, vol. 2: *Observaciones gramaticales*, ed.

S. Levinsohn. República de Panamá: Instituto Nacional de Cultura, Dirección del Patrimonio Histórico (y) Instituto Lingüístico de Verano.

40 Young, P.D. 1987. Ergativity in Ngabere: From ergative to active? Paper
read at American Anthropological Association meeting, Chicago.

40 Young, P. D. n.d. Ngawbere numeral classifiers. ms.

42 Subrahmanyam, P. S. 1971. *Dravidian verb morphology.* Tamilnadu: Annamalai University.

42 Winfield, W. W. 1928. *A grammar of the Kui language* (Biblioteca Indica,
work no. 245). Calcutta: The Asiatic Society of Bengal.

43 Najlis, Elena Lidia. 1966. *Lengua Abipona,* vol. 1 (Archivo de Lenguas
Precolombinas, vol. 1). Buenos Aires: Universidad de Buenos Aires, Cen-
tro de Estudios Lingüísticos.

46 Bright, William. 1957. *The Karok language* (University of California Publications in Linguistics, vol. 13). Berkeley: University of California.

47 Lane, George M. 1898. *A Latin grammar for schools and colleges.* New York:
Glenwood.

48 Grierson, George A. 1909. *An introduction to the Maithili dialect of the
Bihari language as spoken in North Bihar,* part 1: *Grammar.* Calcutta: The
Asiatic Society.

48 Jha, Subhadra. 1958. *The formation of the Maithili language.* London:
Luzac.

49 Barker, Muhammad Abd-al-Rahman, and Aqil Khan Mengal. 1969. *A
course in Baluchi,* 2 vols. Montreal: McGill University, Institute of Islamic
Studies.

49 Elfenbein, J. H. 1966. *The Baluchi Language* (Royal Asiatic Society Monographs, vol. 27). London: Royal Asiatic Society of Great Britain and Ireland.

50 Householder, Fred W., Kostas Kazasis, and Andreas Koutsoudas. 1964.
Reference grammar of Literary Dhimotiki (*International Journal of American Linguistics* 30, no. 2, part 2).

50 Svorou, Soteria. Personal communication.

51 Berulfsen, Bjarne. 1963. *Norwegian grammar.* Oslo: Aschehoug.

51 Haugen, Einar, and Kenneth G. Chapman. 1964. *Spoken Norwegian.*
Revised ed. New York: Holt, Rinehart and Winston

51 Koefoed, H. A. 1958. *Teach Yourself Danish.* London: The English Universities Press.

52 Renck, G. L. 1975. *A grammar of Yagaria.* (Pacific Linguistics B 40) Canberra: Australian National University.

52 ———. 1977. *Yagaria Dictionary* (Pacific Linguistics C 37). Canberra:
Australian National University.

56 Wacke, K. 1930. Formenlehre der Ono-Sprache (Neuguinea). *Zeitschrift
für Eingeborenen-Sprachen* 21: 161–208.

58 Anceaux, J. C. 1965. *The Nimboran language: Phonology and morphology*
(Verhandelingen van het Koninklijk Instituut voor Taal-, Land- en Volkenkunde 44). The Hague: Nijhoff.

59 Hanke, A. 1909. *Grammatik und Vokabularium der Bongu-Sprache (Astrola-
beai, Kaiser-Wilhelmsland)* (Archiv für das Studium deutscher Kolonial-
sprachen, vol. 8). Berlin: Reimer.

60 Foreman, Velma M. 1974. *Grammar of Yessan-Mayo* (Language Data Asian-Pacific Series no. 4). Santa Ana: Summer Institute of Linguistics.

63 Rascher, Matthäus. 1904. Grundregeln der Bainingsprache. *Mitteilungen des Seminars für Orientalische Sprachen* 7 part 1: 31–85.

67 Snyman, J. W. 1970. *An introduction to the !Xũ (!Kung) language* (University of Cape Town School of African Studies Communication no. 34). Cape Town: Balkema.

68 Rice, Keren. 1986. Personal communication.

68 ———. 1989. *A Grammar of Slave.* New York: Mouton de Gruyter.

69 Reh, Mechthild. 1985. *Die Krongo-Sprache.* Berlin: Reimer.

71 Wilson, W. A. A. 1961. *An outline of the Temne language.* London: University of London, School of Oriental and African Studies.

72 Harries, Lyndon. 1950. *A grammar of Mwera.* Johannesburg: Witwatersrand University.

73 Der-Houssikian, Haig. 1980a. *Tem grammar handbook* (Peace Corps language handbook series). Brattleboro, Vt.: The Experiment in International Living.

73 ———. 1980b. *Tem special skills handbook* (Peace Corps language handbook series). Brattleboro, Vt.: The Experiment in International Living.

74 Thomas, Elaine. 1978. *A grammatical description of the Engenni language.* Arlington, Texas: Summer Institute of Linguistics.

75 Becker-Donner, Etta. 1965. *Die Sprache der Mano* (Österreichische Akademie der Wissenschaften, Philosophisch-Historisch Klasse, Sitzungsberichte 245, Band 5). Vienna: Böhlaus.

76 Spagnolo, L. M. 1933. *Bari grammar.* Verona: Missioni Africane.

77 Vandame, R. P. Charles. 1963. *Le Ngambay-Moundou: Phonologie, grammaire et textes* (Mémoires de l'Institut Français d'Afrique Noire no. 69). Dakar: Ifan.

78 Hutchison, John. 1981. *The Kanuri language: A reference grammar.* Madison: The University of Wisconsin, African Studies Program.

78 Lukas, Johannes. 1937. *A study of the Kanuri language: Grammar and vocabulary.* London: Oxford University Press. Repr. London: Dawsons of Pall Mall for the International African Institute, 1967.

79 Merrifield, William R. 1963. Palantla Chinantec syllable types. *Anthropological Linguistics* 5, no. 5: 1–16.

79 ———. 1968. *Palantla Chinantec grammar.* Mexico City: Instituto Nacional de Antropología e Historia de México.

80 Furbee-Losee, Louanna. 1976. *The correct language: Tojolabal: A grammar with ethnographic notes.* New York: Garland.

81 Newman, Stanley. 1965. *Zuni grammar* (University of New Mexico Publication in Anthropology no. 14). Albuquerque: University of New Mexico Press.

81 ———. 1958. *Zuni dictionary* (Indiana University Research Center in Anthropology, Folklore, and Linguistics, publ. 6).

82 Shipley, William F. 1964. *Maidu grammar* (University of California Publications in Linguistics, vol. 41). Berkeley: University of California Press.

83 Kuipers, Aert H. 1974. *The Shuswap language: Grammar, texts, dictionary.* The Hague: Mouton.

84 Hoshino, Tatsuo, and Russell Marcus. 1973. *Lao for beginners*. Tokyo: Charles E. Tuttle Co.

84 Yates, Warren G., and Souksomboun Sayasithsena. 1970. *Lao basic course*, vol. 1. Washington, D.C.: Foreign Service Institute.

84 Morev, L. N., A. A. Moskalyov, and Y. Y. Plam. 1979. *The Lao language*. Moscow: Nauka.

85 Caughley, Ross Charles. 1969. *Chepang Phonemic Summary* (Tibeto-Burman Phonemic Summaries no. 4). Dallas: Summer Institute of Linguistics.

85 ———. 1982. *The syntax and morphology of the verb in Chepang* (Pacific Linguistics Series B no. 84). Canberra: Australian National University.

86 MacNabb, Donald John Campbell. 1891. *Hand book of the Haka or Baungshe dialect of the Chin language*. Rangoon: Government Printing.

86 Newland, A. G. E. 1897. *A practical hand-book of the language of the Lais as spoken by the Hakas and other allied tribes of the Chin hills (commonly the Baungshè dialect)*. Rangoon: Government Printing.

86 Reichle, Verena. 1981. *Bawm language and lore*. Bern: Peter Lang.

87 Matisoff, James A. 1973. *The grammar of Lahu* (University of California Publications in Linguistics, vol. 75). Berkeley: University of California Press.

88 Barnard, Joseph Terence Owen. 1934. *A handbook of the Răwang Dialect of the Nung Language*. Rangoon: Government Printing.

89 Kwok, Helen. 1971. *A linguistic study of the Cantonese verb* (Center of Asian Studies Occasional Papers and Monographs no. 3). Hong Kong: Center of Asian Studies, University of Hong Kong.

89 Leung, Peter C. Y. 1973. *Essential Cantonese grammar*. Davis: University of California, Department of Applied Behavioral Sciences, Asian American Studies Division.

90 Boas, Franz, and Ella Deloria. 1941. *Dakota grammar*. Memoirs of the *National Academy of Sciences*, vol. 23, no. 2: 1–183.

90 Buechel, Eugene. 1939. *A grammar of Lakota: The language of the Teton Sioux Indians*. Saint Francis, S. Dak.: Rosebud Educational Society.

90 ———. 1983. *A dictionary/oie wowapi wan of Teton Sioux: Lakota-English: English-Lakota/Lakota-Ieska: Ieska-Lakota*, ed. Paul Manhart. Pine Ridge, S. Dak.: Red Cloud Indian School, Holy Rosary Mission.

90 University of Colorado Lakhota Project. 1974. Lakhota sketch ms. Boulder: University of Colorado, Department of Linguistics.

90 ———. 1976a. *Beginning Lakhota*. 2 vols. Boulder: University of Colorado, Department of Linguistics.

90 ———. 1976b. *Elementary bilingual dictionary: English-Lakhóta, Lakhóta-English*. Boulder: University of Colorado, Department of Linguistics.

90 ———. 1976c. *Lakhóta wayawapi/Lakhóta readings*. Boulder: University of Colorado, Department of Linguistics.

91 Perevoshikov, P. N. 1956a. *Russko-udmurtskij slovar*. Moscow: Gosudarsstvennoe yedatelstvo inostrannix i natsionalinix slovarei.

91 ———. 1956b. *Kratkij očerk grammatiki udmurtskogo jazyka* (Supplement to Perevoshikov 1956a).

91 ———. 1962. *Grammatika sovremennogo udmurtskogo jazyka: Fonetika i morfologija.* Izhevsk: Udmurtskoe Knizhnoe Izdatelstvo.
92 Nadzhip, E. N. 1971. *Modern Uigur,* trans. D. M. Segal. Moscow: Nauka.
93 Poppe, Nicholas N. 1960. *Buriat grammar* (Indiana University Publications Uralic and Altaic Series, vol. 2). Bloomington: Indiana University; The Hague: Mouton.
94 Hall, Robert A., Jr. 1943a. *Melanesian Pidgin English: grammar, texts, vocabulary.* Baltimore: The Linguistic Society of America.
94 ———. 1943b. *Melanesian Pidgin phrase-book and vocabulary with grammatical introduction.* Baltimore: The Linguistic Society of America.
94 Mühlhäusler, Peter. 1985. Inflectional morphology of Tok Pisin; Syntax of Tok Pisin. In *Handbook of Tok Pisin (New Guinea Pidgin),* ed. S. A. Wurm and P. Mühlhäusler, 335–40; 341–421. (Pacific Linguistics C 70). Canberra: Research School of Pacific Studies.
94 Woolford, Ellen B. 1979. *Aspects of Tok Pisin grammar* (Pacific Linguistics B 66). Canberra: Australian National University.

• • •

References

Abraham, Werner. 1989. Futur-Typologie in den germanischen Sprachen. In *Tempus-Aspekt-Modus: Die lexikalischen und grammatischen Formen in den germanischen Sprachen,* ed. Werner Abraham and Theo Janssen, 345–89. Tübingen: Max Niemeyer.

Aksu-Koç, Ayhan and Dan I. Slobin. 1986. A psychological account of the development and use of evidentials in Turkish. In Chafe and Nichols 1986: 159–67.

Alphonse, Ephraim S. 1956. *Guaymí grammar and dictionary with some ethnological notes* (Bureau of American Ethnology Bulletin 162). Washington, D.C.: Government Printing Office.

Anderson, John M. 1973. *An essay concerning aspect: some considerations of a general character arising from the Abbé Darrigol's analysis of the Basque verb.* The Hague: Mouton.

Anderson, Lloyd B. 1982. The 'Perfect' as a universal and as a language-particular category. In Hopper 1982: 227–64.

Bach, Emmon, and Robert T. Harms, eds. 1968. *Universals in linguistic theory.* New York: Holt.

Barker, Muhammad Abd-al-Rahman, and Aqil Khan Mengal. 1969. *A course in Baluchi.* 2 vols. Montreal: McGill University, Institute of Islamic Studies.

Barnard, Joseph Terence Owen. 1934. *A handbook of the Rāwang dialect of the Nung language.* Rangoon: Government Printing.

Bennett, M., and Partee, Barbara. 1978. Toward the logic of tense and aspect in English. Reproduced by the Indiana University Linguistics Club, Bloomington.

Benton, Richard A. 1971. *Pangasinan reference grammar.* Honolulu: University of Hawaii Press.

Benveniste, Emile. 1968. Mutations of linguistic categories. In Lehmann and Malkiel 1968: 83–94.

Bickerton, Derek. 1975. *Dynamics of a creole system.* Cambridge: Cambridge University Press.

———. 1977. Pidginization and creolization: language acquisition and language universals. In *Pidgin and creole linguistics,* ed. Albert Valdman, 49–69. Bloomington: Indiana University Press.

365

Blansitt, Edward L. 1975. Progressive aspect. *Working Papers on Language Universals* 18: 1–34.

Bolinger, Dwight L. 1947. More on the present tense in English. *Language* 23: 434–36.

Bouquiaux, L., ed. 1980. *L'Expansion bantoue*. Paris: Centre National de la Recherche Scientifique.

Bright, William. 1957. *The Karok language* (University of California Publications in Linguistics, vol. 13). Berkeley: University of California.

Buck, Carl Darling. 1949. *A dictionary of selected synonyms in the principal Indo-European languages: A contribution to the history of ideas.* Chicago: University of Chicago Press.

Buechel, Eugene. 1939. *A grammar of Lakota: The language of the Teton Sioux Indians.* Saint Francis, S. Dak.: Rosebud Educational Society.

Bull, William E. 1971. *Time, tense and the verb: A study in theoretical and applied linguistics, with particular attention to Spanish.* Berkeley: University of California Press.

[Bybee: see also Hooper]

Bybee, Joan L. 1985. *Morphology: A study of the relation between meaning and form.* Amsterdam: Benjamins.

———. 1986. On the nature of grammatical categories: a diachronic perspective. *Eastern States Conference on Linguistics* 2: 17–34.

———. 1988a. Semantic substance vs. contrast in the development of grammatical meaning. *Berkeley Linguistic Society* 14: 247–64.

———. 1988b. The diachronic dimension in explanations. In Hawkins 1988: 350–79.

———. 1990a. The semantic development of past tense modals in English and other languages. *Buffalo Working Papers in Linguistics 90-01: A Special Issue for Paul Garvin,* 13–30.

———. 1990b. The grammaticization of zero: asymmetries in tense and aspect systems. *La Trobe Working Papers in Linguistics* 3: 1–14. To appear in Pagliuca 1994.

Bybee, Joan L., and Östen Dahl. 1989. The creation of tense and aspect systems in the languages of the world. *Studies in Language* 13: 51–103.

Bybee, Joan L., and William Pagliuca. 1985. Cross-linguistic comparison and the development of grammatical meaning. In Fisiak 1985: 59–83.

———. 1987. The evolution of future meaning. In Ramat, Carruba, and Bernini 1987: 109–22.

Bybee, Joan L., William Pagliuca, and Revere Perkins. 1990. On the asymmetries in the affixation of grammatical material. In Croft, Denning and Kemmer 1990, 1–42.

———. 1991. Back to the future. In Traugott and Heine 1991, 2: 17–58.

Calver, E. 1946. The uses of the present tense in English. *Language* 22: 317–25.

Capell, A., and H. E. Hinch. 1970. *Maung grammar: texts and vocabulary.* The Hague: Mouton.

Capell, A., and J. Layard. 1980. *Materials in Atchin, Malekula: Grammar, vocabulary and texts* (Pacific Linguistics Series D no. 20). Canberra: Australian National University.

Caughley, Ross Charles. 1982. *The syntax and morphology of the verb in Chepang* (Pacific Linguistics Series B no. 84). Canberra: Australian National University.

Chafe, Wallace, and Johanna Nichols, eds. 1986. *Evidentiality: The coding of epistemology in language.* Norwood, N.J.: Ablex.

Chung, Sandra, and Alan Timberlake. 1985. Tense, aspect and mood. In *Language typology and syntactic description,* ed. Tim Shopen, 3: 202–58. Cambridge: Cambridge University Press.

Clark, Herbert H., and Barbara C. Malt. 1984. Psychological constraints on language: a commentary on Bresnan and Kaplan and on Givón. In Kintsch, Miller, and Polson 1984: 191–214.

Coates, Jennifer. 1983. *The semantics of the modal auxiliaries.* London: Croom Helm.

Colombo, L., and Flores D'Arcais, G. 1984. The meaning of Dutch prepositions: A psycholinguistic study of polysemy. *Linguistics* 22: 51–98.

Comrie, Bernard. 1976. *Aspect.* Cambridge: Cambridge University Press.

———. 1985a. Derivation, inflection and semantic change in the development of the Chukchi verb paradigm. In Fisiak 1985: 83–96.

———. 1985b. *Tense.* Cambridge: Cambridge University Press.

Coseriu, Eugenio, ed. 1975. *Esquisses Linguistiques II.* Munich: Fink.

Croft, William, Keith Denning, and Suzanne Kemmer, eds. 1990. *Studies in Diachronic Typology.* Amsterdam: Benjamins.

Curme, G. O. 1913. The development of the progressiv [sic] form in Germanic. *Proceedings of the Modern Language Association* 28: 159–87.

Dahl, Östen. 1985. *Tense and aspect systems.* Oxford: Blackwell.

Dixon, R. M. W. 1980. *The languages of Australia.* Cambridge: Cambridge University Press.

Dowty, David R. 1979. *Word meaning and Montague grammar: The semantics of verbs and times in generative semantics and in Montague's PTQ.* Dordrecht: Reidel.

Dryer, Matthew P. 1989. Large linguistic areas and language sampling. *Studies in Language* 13: 257–92.

Dyen, Isidore. 1965. *A sketch of Trukese grammar* (American Oriental Essay no. 4). New Haven: American Oriental Society.

Emanation, Michele. 1992. Chagga 'come' and 'go'. metaphor and the development of tense-aspect. *Studies in Language* 16: 1–33.

Emeneau, Murray B., and T. Burrow. 1961. *A Dravidian Etymological Dictionary.* Oxford: Clarendon.

Ernout, A., and F. Thomas. 1951. *Syntax latine.* Paris: Klincksieck.

Erwin, Wallace M. 1963. *A short reference grammar of Iraqi Arabic.* Washington, D.C.: Georgetown University Press.

Fairbanks, G. H., and Stevick, E. W. 1958. *Spoken East Armenian.* New York: American Council of Learned Societies.

Faltz, Leonard M. 1989. A role for inference in meaning change. *Studies in Language* 13: 317–31.

Faust, Norma. 1978. *Gramática Cocama: Lecciones para el aprendizaje del idioma Cocama* (Serie Lingüística Peruana No. 6). Lima: Ministerio de Educación, Instituto Lingüístico de Verano.

Fillmore, Charles, and D. Terence Langendoen, eds. 1971. *Studies in linguistic semantics*. New York: Holt, Rinehart, and Winston.

Fisiak, Jacek, ed. 1985. *Historical semantics, historical word formation*. Berlin: Mouton.

Fleischman, Suzanne. 1982a. *The future in thought and language*. Cambridge: Cambridge University Press.

———. 1982b. The past and the future: are they coming or going? *Berkeley Linguistic Society* 8: 322–34.

———. 1983. From pragmatics to grammar: Diachronic reflections on complex pasts and futures in Romance. *Lingua* 60: 183–214.

Fleischman, Suzanne, and Linda R. Waugh, eds. 1990. *Discourse-pragmatics and the verb: Evidence from Romance*. London: Routledge.

Foley, William A. 1986. *The Papuan languages of New Guinea*. Cambridge: Cambridge University Press.

Foreman, Velma M. 1974. *Grammar of Yessan-Mayo* (Language Data Asian-Pacific Series no. 4). Santa Ana: Summer Institute of Linguistics.

Forsyth, J. 1970. *A grammar of aspect: Usage and meaning in the Russian verb*. Cambridge: Cambridge University Press.

Fortescue, Michael. 1980. Affix ordering in West Greenlandic derivational processes. *International Journal of American Linguistics* 25: 259–78.

———. 1984. *West Greenlandic*. London: Croom Helm.

Friedman, Victor A. 1986. Evidentiality in the Balkans: Bulgarian, Macedonian and Albanian. In Chafe and Nichols 1986: 168–87.

Friedrich, Paul. 1974. *On aspect theory and Homeric aspect. International Journal of American Linguistics* Memoir 28.

García, Erica. 1987. Reanalysing actualization, and actualizing reanalysis. Paper presented at the 8th International Conference on Historical Linguistics, Lille.

García, Erica, and E. van Putte. 1989. Forms are silver, nothing is gold. *Folia Linguistica Historica* 8/1–2: 365–84.

Genetti, Carol. 1986. The grammaticalization of the Newari verb tɔl. *Linguistics of the Tibeto-Burman Area* 9.2: 53–70.

Gerhardt, Julie, and Iskender Savasir. 1986. The use of the simple present in the speech of two three-year-olds: Normativity and subjectivity. *Language in Society* 15: 501–36.

Gerritsen, J., and N. E. Osselton. 1978/1983. *K. Ten Bruggencate Engels Woordenboek*, vol. II: *Nederlands/Engels* 18th ed. Groningen: Wolters-Noordhoff.

Gili y Gaya, S. 1964. *Curso superior de sintaxis española*. Barcelona: Bibliograf.

Givón, Talmy. 1973. The time-axis phenomenon. *Language* 49: 890–925.

———. 1975. Serial verbs and syntactic change: Niger-Congo. In Li 1975: 47–112.

———. 1979a. *On understanding grammar*. New York: Academic Press.

———, ed. 1979b. *Syntax and semantics 12*. New York: Academic Press.

———. 1982. Tense-Aspect-Modality: the creole proto-type and beyond. In Hopper 1982: 115–63.

Goldsmith, John, and E. Woisetschlaeger. 1982. The logic of the English progressive. *Linguistic Inquiry* 13: 79–89.

Goodenough, W. H., and H. Sugita. 1980. *Trukese-English Dictionary*. Philadelphia: American Philosophical Society.

Gordon, E. V. 1957. *An introduction to Old Norse*. Second revised edition, 1974. Oxford: Clarendon.

Greenberg, Joseph H. 1963. Some universals of grammar with particular reference to the order of meaningful elements. In *Universals of language*, ed. J. H. Greenberg, 73–113. Cambridge: MIT Press.

———. 1966. *Language universals*. The Hague: Mouton.

———. 1987. *Language in the Americas*. Stanford, Calif.: Stanford University Press.

Greenberg, Joseph, Charles Ferguson, and Edith Moravcsik, eds. 1978. *Universals of human language*. Stanford, Calif.: Stanford University Press.

Haiman, John. 1983. Iconic and economic motivation. *Language* 59: 781–819.

Hall, Robert A., Jr. 1943a. *Melanesian Pidgin English: Grammar, texts, vocabulary*. Baltimore: The Linguistic Society of America.

Hammond, Michael, and Michael Noonan, eds. 1988. *Theoretical morphology*. New York: Academic Press.

Harries, Lyndon. 1950. *A grammar of Mwera*. Johannesburg: Witwatersrand University.

Harris, Martin. 1982. The 'Past Simple' and 'Present Perfect' in Romance. In Vincent and Harris 1982: 42–70.

Haspelmath, Martin. 1989. From purposive to infinitive: a universal path of grammaticization. *Folia Linguistica Historica* 10, no. 1/2: 287–310.

Hatcher, Anna Granville. 1951. The use of the Progressive form in English. *Language* 27: 254–80.

Hawkins, John, ed. 1988. *Explaining language universals*. Oxford: Blackwell.

Heine, Bernd. 1990. Grammaticalization as an explanatory parameter. Paper presented at the Symposium on Explanation in Historical Linguistics, Milwaukee, April. To appear in Pagliuca 1994.

Heine, Bernd, and Ulrike Claudi. 1986. *On the rise of grammatical categories: Some examples from Maa*. Berlin: Reimer.

Heine, Bernd, Ulrike Claudi, and Friederike Hünnemeyer 1991a. From cognition to grammar: evidence from African languages. In Traugott and Heine 1991, 1: 149–87.

———. 1991b. *Grammaticalization: A conceptual framework*. Chicago: University of Chicago Press.

Heine, Bernd, and Mechthild Reh. 1984. *Grammaticalization and reanalysis in African languages*. Hamburg: Buske.

Hetzron, Robert. 1969. *The verbal system of Southern Agaw*. Berkeley: University of California Press.

Hewitt, B. G. 1979a. *Abkhaz* (Lingua Descriptive Studies, vol. 2). Amsterdam: North-Holland.

Hoffman, Carl. 1963. *A grammar of the Margi language*. London: Oxford University Press.

Hooper, Joan B. 1975. On assertive predicates. In Kimball 1975: 91–124.

Hooper, Joan B., and Sandra A. Thompson. 1973. On the applicability of root transformations. *Linguistic Inquiry* 4: 465–97.

Hopper, Paul J. 1979. Aspect and foregrounding in discourse. In Givón 1979b: 213–41.

———. 1982a. Aspect between discourse and grammar: An introductory essay for the volume. In Hopper 1982b: 3–18.

———, ed. 1982b. *Tense-Aspect: Between semantics and pragmatics.* Amsterdam: Benjamins.

———. 1991. On some properties of grammaticization. In Traugott and Heine 1991, 1: 17–35.

Hopper, Paul J., and Sandra Thompson. 1980. Transitivity in grammar and discourse. *Language* 56: 251–99.

Horn, Laurence. 1972. On the semantic properties of logical operators in English. Ph.D. diss., University of California, Los Angeles.

———. 1985. Towards a new taxonomy for pragmatic inference: Q-based and R-based implicature. In *Meaning, form and use in context,* ed. D. Schiffrin, 11–42. Washington, D.C.: Georgetown University Press.

Huffman, Franklin E. 1967. An outline of Cambodian grammar. Ph.D. diss., Cornell University, Ithaca, N.Y.

Hutchison, John. 1981. *The Kanuri language: A reference grammar.* Madison: The University of Wisconsin, African Studies Program.

Hyman, Larry M., and J. R. Watters. 1984. Auxiliary focus. *Studies in African Linguistics* 15: 233–73.

Hymes, Dell. 1975. From space to time in tenses in Kiksht. *International Journal of American Linguistics* 41: 313–29.

Jeffers, Robert J., and Arnold M. Zwicky. 1980. The evolution of clitics. In *Papers from the 4th International Conference on Historical Linguistics,* ed. E. C. Traugott, R. Labrum, and S. Shepherd, 221–31. Amsterdam: Benjamins.

Jespersen, Otto. 1949. *A Modern Grammar of English on Historical Principles,* vol. 4, *Syntax,* part 3, *Time and tense.* London: Allen and Unwin.

Jha, Subhadra. 1958. *The formation of the Maithili language.* London: Luzac.

Johnston, Raymond Leslie. 1980. *Nakanai of New Britain* (Pacific Linguistics Series B no. 70). Canberra: Australian National University.

Jorgensen, Joseph G., ed. 1974. *Comparative studies by Harold E. Driver and essays in his honor.* New Haven, Conn.: HRAF Press.

Keenan, Edward L., and Bernard Comrie. 1977. Noun phrase accessibility and universal grammar. *Linguistic Inquiry* 8: 63–100.

Kimball, John, ed. 1975. *Syntax and semantics 4.* New York: Academic Press.

Kintsch, W., J. R. Miller, and P. G. Polson, eds. 1984. *Method and tactics in cognitive science.* Hillsdale, N.J.: Erlbaum.

Kiparsky, Paul. 1968. Linguistic universals and linguistic change. In Bach and Harms 1968: 171–202.

Kirsner, Robert S. 1969. The role of ZULLEN in the grammar of Modern Standard Dutch. *Lingua* 24: 101–54.

Klein, Flora. 1975. Pragmatic constraints in distribution: the Spanish subjunctive. Chicago Linguistic Society 11: 353–65.

Klein-Andreu, Flora. 1990. Losing ground: a discourse-pragmatic solution to the history of *-ra* in Spanish. In Fleischman and Waugh 1990: 164–78.

Koefoed, H. A. 1958. *Teach Yourself Danish.* London: English Universities Press.

König, Ekkehard. 1988. Concessive connectives and concessive sentences: Cross-linguistic regularities and pragmatic principles. In Hawkins 1988: 145–66.

Kopesec, M. F. 1975. Los elementos verbales y sustantivos y la oración en Guaymí. In *Lenguas de Panama*, vol. 2: *Observaciones gramaticales*, ed. S. Levinsohn. República de Panamá: Instituto Nacional de Cultura, Dirección del Patrimonio Histórico (y) Instituto Lingüístico de Verano.

Kuryłowicz, Jerzy. 1965. The evolution of grammatical categories. In Coseriu 1975: 38–54.

Kwok, Helen. 1971. *A linguistic study of the Cantonese verb* (Center of Asian Studies Occasional Papers and Monographs no. 3). Hong Kong: Center of Asian Studies, University of Hong Kong.

Labov, William. 1990. On the adequacy of natural languages: I. The development of tense. In Singler 1990, 1–58.

Lakoff, George, and Mark Johnson. 1980. *Metaphors we live by*. Chicago: University of Chicago Press.

Lancelot, C., and Arnauld, A. 1660. *Grammaire général et raisonnée*. Paris: Pierre le Petit.

Lehmann, Christian. 1982. *Thoughts on grammaticalization: A programmatic sketch*, vol. I (Arbeiten des Kölner Universalien-Projekts Nr. 48). University of Cologne.

———. 1985. Grammaticalization: Synchronic variation and diachronic change. *Lingua e Stile* 20, no. 3: 303–18.

Lehmann, W. P., and Malkiel, Yakov, eds., 1968. *Directions for historical linguistics: A symposium*. Austin: University of Texas Press.

Leman, Wayne. 1980a. *A reference grammar of the Cheyenne language* (Occasional Publications in Anthropology, Linguistic series no. 5). Greeley: University of Northern Colorado Museum of Anthropology.

Li, Charles N., ed. 1975. *Word order and word order change*. Austin: University of Texas Press.

Li, Charles N., and Sandra A. Thompson. 1981. *Mandarin Chinese: A functional reference grammar*. Berkeley and Los Angeles: University of California Press.

Li, Charles N., Sandra A. Thompson, and R. M. Thompson. 1982. The discourse motivation for the perfect aspect: the Mandarin particle LE. In Hopper 1982: 19–44.

Lichtenberk, Frantisek. 1991. Semantic change and heterosemy in grammaticalization. *Language* 67, 475–509.

———. 1992. Apprehensional epistemics. Paper presented at the Symposium on Mood and Modality, University of New Mexico, May. To appear in Joan Bybee and Suzanne Fleischman (eds.), *Modality in grammar and discourse*, Amsterdam: Benjamins.

Lin, Zi-yu. 1991. The development of grammatical markers in Archaic Chinese and Han Chinese. Ph.D. diss., State University of New York, Buffalo.

Lukas, Johannes. 1937. *A study of the Kanuri language: Grammar and vocabulary*. London: Oxford University Press. Repr. London: Dawsons of Pall Mall for the International African Institute, 1967.

Lyons, John. 1977. *Semantics*. Cambridge: Cambridge University Press.

Maan, G. 1951. *Proeve van een bulische spraakkunst* (Verhandelingen van het

Koninklijk Instituut voor Taal-, Land- en Volkenkunde 10). The Hague: Nijhoff.

MacNamara, John, ed. 1977. *Language learning and thought.* New York: Academic Press.

Marchese, Lynell. 1986. *Tense/aspect and the development of auxiliaries in Kru languages.* Arlington, Texas: Summer Institute of Linguistics.

Matisoff, James A. 1973. *The grammar of Lahu* (University of California Publications in Linguistics, vol. 75). Berkeley: University of California Press.

Matsumoto, Yo. 1988. From bound grammatical markers to free discourse markers: history of some Japanese connectives.Berkeley Linguistic Society 14: 340–51.

McCawley, James D. 1971. Tense and time reference in English. In Fillmore and Langendoen 1971: 96–113.

McCoard, R. W. 1976. *The English perfect.* Amsterdam: North Holland.

Meillet, Antoine. 1912. L'evolution des formes grammaticales. *Scientia* 12.26: 6. Repr. in A. Meillet, *Linguistique historique et linguistique général,* 1: 130–48. Paris: Champion, 1948.

Merrifield, William R. 1968. *Palantla Chinantec grammar.* Mexico City: Instituto Nacional de Anthropología e Historia de México.

Michelena, Luis. 1981. Lingua commun y dialectos Vascos. *Anuario del Seminario del Filologia Vasca Julio de Urquijo* 15: 291–313. Repr. in L. Michelena, *Palabras y textos.* Leioa: Universidad del Pais Vasco.

Milne, Mrs. Leslie. 1921. *An elementary Palaung grammar.* Oxford: Clarendon.

Mitchell, T. F. 1956. *An introduction to Egyptian Colloquial Arabic.* Oxford: Oxford University Press.

Mithun, Marianne. 1988. Lexical categories and the evolution of number marking. In Hammond and Noonan 1988: 211–34.

Moore, S., and T. A. Knott. 1955. *The elements of Old English.* Ann Arbor: Wahr.

Moreno de Alba, J. G. 1977. Vitalidad del futuro del indicativo en la norma culta del español hablada en México. *Anuario de Letras* 8: 81–102.

Morev, L. N., A. A. Moskalyov, and Y. Y. Plam. 1979. *The Lao language.* Moscow: Nauka.

Mühlhäusler, Peter. 1985. Inflectional morphology of Tok Pisin; Syntax of Tok Pisin. In *Handbook of Tok Pisin (New Guinea Pidgin),* ed. S. A. Wurm and P. Mühlhäusler, 335–40; 341–421. (Pacific Linguistics C 70). Canberra: Research School of Pacific Studies.

Murray, James A., et al., eds. 1889–1933. *The Oxford English Dictionary.* Compact ed., 1971. Oxford: Oxford University Press.

Naroll, R., and R. Cohen. 1973. *A handbook of method in cultural anthropology.* New York: Columbia University Press.

Naroll, R., G. L. Michik, and F. Naroll. 1974. Hologeistic theory testing. In Jorgensen 1974: 121–48.

Naroll, R., and F. Naroll. 1973. *Main currents in cultural anthropology.* New York: Appelton, Century, Crofts.

Nedyalkov, V. P., ed. 1988. *Typology of resultative constructions.* Amsterdam: Benjamins.

Nedyalkov, V. P., and S. J. Jaxontov. 1988. The typology of resultative constructions. In Nedyalkov 1988: 3–62.

Noonan, Michael. 1985. Complementation. In Shopen 1985: 42–140.

Pagliuca, William. 1982. Prolegomena to a theory of articulatory evolution. Ph.D. diss., State University of New York, Buffalo.

———, ed. 1994. *Perspectives on grammaticalization.* Amsterdam: Benjamins.

Pagliuca, William, and Richard Mowrey. 1987. Articulatory evolution. In Ramat, Carruba, and Bernini, 459–72.

Palmer, F. R. 1974. *The English verb.* London: Longman.

———. 1979. *Modality and the English modals.* London: Longman.

———. 1986. *Mood and modality.* Cambridge: Cambridge University Press.

Patz, Elizabeth. 1982. A grammar of the Kuku Yalanji language of North Queensland. Ph.D. diss., Australian National University, Canberra.

Perkins, Revere D. 1980. The evolution of culture and grammar. Ph.D. diss., State University of New York, Buffalo.

———. 1989. Statistical techniques for determining language sample size. *Studies in Language* 13: 293–315.

———. 1992. *Deixis, grammar and culture.* Amsterdam: Benjamins.

Phillips, Judith W. 1983. A partial grammar of the Haitian Creole verb system: Forms functions and syntax. Ph.D. diss., State University of New York, Buffalo.

Poppe, Nicholas N. 1960. *Buriat grammar* (Indiana University Publications Uralic and Altaic Series, vol. 2). Bloomington: Indiana University; The Hague: Mouton.

Prost, Gilbert R. 1962. Signalling of transitive and intransitive in Chacobo (Pano). *International Journal of American Linguistics* 28: 108–18.

Quirk, Randolph, Sidney Greenbaum, Geoffrey Leech, and Jan Svartvik. 1985. *A comprehensive grammar of the English language.* London: Longman.

Ransom, Evelyn. 1988. *Complementation: Its meanings and form.* Amsterdam: Benjamins.

Ramat, A. G., O. Carruba, and G. Bernini, eds. 1987. *Papers from the 7th International Conference on Historical Linguistics.* Amsterdam: Benjamins.

Rascher, Matthäus. 1904. Grundregeln der Bainingsprache. *Mitteilungen des Seminars für Orientalische Sprachen* 7 part 1: 31–85.

Raz, Shlomo. 1983. *Tigre grammar and texts* (Afroasiatic dialects, 4) Malibu: Undena.

Reichle, Verena. 1981. *Bawm language and lore.* Bern: Peter Lang.

Renck, G. L. 1975. *A grammar of Yagaria* (Pacific Linguistics B 40). Canberra: Australian National University.

———. 1977. *Yagaria Dictionary* (Pacific Linguistics C 37). Canberra: Australian National University.

Rice, Keren. 1989. *A grammar of Slave.* New York: Mouton de Gruyter.

Roberts, John R. 1990. Modality in Amele and other Papuan languages. *Journal of Linguistics* 26: 363–401.

Romaine, Suzanne. 1992. The grammaticalization of irrealis in Tok Pisin. ms. To appear in Joan Bybee and Suzanne Fleischman (eds.), *Modality in grammar and discourse*, Amsterdam: Benjamins.

Saltarelli, Mario, Miren Azkarate, David Farwell, Jon Ortiz de Urbina, and Lourdes Oñederra. 1988. *Basque.* New York: Croom Helm.

Samarin, William. 1967. *A grammar of Sango.* The Hague: Mouton.

Sankoff, Gillian. 1990. The grammaticalization of tense and aspect in Tok Pisin and Sranan. *Language Variation and Change* 2: 295–312.

Sapir, Edward. 1921. *Language.* New York: Harcourt, Brace and World.

Scheffer, J. 1975. *The progressive in English.* Amsterdam: North Holland.

Schwenter, Scott A. 1993. The grammaticalization of an anterior in progress: Evidence from a peninsular Spanish dialect. *Studies in Language.*

Shepherd, Susan. 1981. Modals in Antiguan Creole, child language and history. Ph.D. diss., Stanford University, Stanford, Calif.

Shipley, William F. 1964. *Maidu grammar* (University of California Publications in Linguistics, vol. 41). Berkeley: University of California Press.

Shopen, Tim., ed. 1985. *Language typology and syntactic description, II.* Cambridge: Cambridge University Press.

Silva-Corvalán, Carmen. 1985. Modality and semantic change. In Fisiak 1985: 547–72. The Hague: Mouton.

Singler, John Victor. 1990. *Pidgin and creole tense-mood-aspect systems.* Amsterdam: John Benjamins.

Slobin, Dan I. 1977. Language change in childhood and history. In MacNamara 1977: 185–214.

Slobin, Dan I., and A. A. Aksu. 1982. Tense, aspect and modality in the use of the Turkish evidential. In Hopper 1982: 185–200.

Sorensen, Arthur P., Jr. 1969. The morphology of Tucano. Ph.D. diss., Columbia University, New York.

Spagnolo, L. M. 1933. *Bari grammar.* Verona: Missioni Africane.

Steele, Susan. 1975. Is it possible? *Stanford Working Papers in Language Universals* 18: 35–58.

Subrahmanyam, P. S. 1971. *Dravidian verb morphology.* Tamilnadu: Annamalai University.

Svorou, Soteria. 1986. On the evolutionary paths of locative expressions. *Berkeley Linguistic Society* 12: 515–27.

———. 1993. *The grammar of space.* Amsterdam: Benjamins.

Sweetser, Eve E. 1984. Semantic structure and semantic change: A cognitive linguistic study of modality, perception, speech acts and logical relations. Ph.D. diss., University of California, Berkeley.

———. 1988. Grammaticalization and semantic bleaching. *Berkeley Linguistic Society* 14: 389–405.

———. 1990. *From etymology to pragmatics* (Cambridge Studies in Linguistics 54). Cambridge: Cambridge University Press.

Taylor, Douglas. 1956a. Island Carib II: Word-classes, affixes, nouns and verbs. *International Journal of American Linguistics* 22: 1–44.

———. 1956b. Island-Carib morphology III: Locators and particles. *International Journal of American Linguistics* 22: 138–50.

Thomas, Elaine. 1978. *A grammatical description of the Engenni language.* Arlington, Texas: Summer Institute of Linguistics.

Thomson, R. W. 1975. *An introduction to Classical Armenian.* Delmar, N.Y.: Caravan Books.

Traugott, Elizabeth Closs. 1972. *A history of English syntax.* New York: Holt, Rinehart and Winston.

———. 1978. On the expression of spatio-temporal relations in language. In Greenberg, Ferguson, and Moravcsik 1978, 3: 369–400.

———. 1982. From propositional to textual to expressive meanings: some semantic-pragmatic aspects of grammaticalization. In *Perspectives in histori-*

cal linguistics, ed. W. P. Lehmann and Yakov Malkiel. 245–71. Amsterdam: John Benjamins.

———. 1989. On the rise of epistemic meaning: An example of subjectification in semantic change. *Language* 65: 31–55.

Traugott, Elizabeth Closs, and Bernd Heine, eds. 1991. *Approaches to grammaticalization.* 2 vols. Amsterdam: Benjamins.

Traugott, Elizabeth Closs, and Ekkehard König. 1991. The semantics-pragmatics of grammaticalization revisited. In Traugott and Heine 1991, 1: 189–218.

Tsang, Chui Lim. 1981. A semantic study of modal auxiliary verbs in Chinese. Ph.D. diss., Stanford University, Stanford, Calif.

Uhlenbeck, C. C. 1938. *A concise Blackfoot Grammar.* Amsterdam: North Holland.

Ultan, Russell. 1978. The nature of future tenses. In Greenberg, Ferguson, and Moravcsik 1978, 3: 83–123.

Underhill, Robert. 1976. *Turkish grammar.* Cambridge: MIT Press.

Urdiales, J. M. 1966. *El hablo de Villacidayo (León).* (Anejos del Boletín de la Real Academia Española 13). Madrid.

Vermant, S. 1983. *The English present perfect: A dynamic-synchronic approach* (Antwerp Papers in Linguistics no. 32).

Vincent, Nigel. 1982. The development of the auxiliaries HABERE and ESSE in Romance. In Vincent and Harris 1982: 71–96.

Vincent, Nigel, and Martin Harris, eds. 1982. *Studies in the Romance verb.* London: Croom Helm.

Voegelin, C. F., and F. M. Voegelin. 1978. *Classification and index of the world's languages.* New York: Elsevier.

Voeltz, F. K. E. 1980. The etymology of the Bantu perfect. In Bouquiaux 1980: 487–92.

Waugh, Linda. 1976. A semantic analysis of the French tense system. *Orbis* 24: 436–85.

West, Birdie. 1980. *Gramatica popular del Tucano.* Bogotá: Ministerio de Gobierno, Instituto Lingüístico de Verano.

Westermann, D. 1907. *Grammatik der Ewe-Sprache.* Berlin: Reimer.

Wierzbicka, Anna. 1972. *Semantic primitives,* trans. Anna Wierzbicka and John Besemeres. Frankfurt am Main: Athenäum.

Willett, Thomas. 1988. A cross-linguistic survey of the grammaticalization of evidentiality. *Studies in Language* 12, no. 1: 51–97.

Winfield, W. W. 1928. *A grammar of the Kui language* (Biblioteca Indica, work no. 245). Calcutta: The Asiatic Society of Bengal.

Woodworth, Nancy L. 1991. From noun to verb and verb to noun: A cross-linguistic study. Ph.D. diss., State University of New York, Buffalo.

Yallop, Colin. 1977. *Alyawarra: an aboriginal language of central Australia.* Canberra: Australian Institute of Aboriginal Studies.

Yates, Warren G., and Souksomboun Sayasithsena. 1970. *Lao basic course,* vol. 1. Washington, D.C.: Foreign Service Institute.

Zipf, George Kingsley. 1932. *Relative frequency, abbreviation, and semantic change: Selected studies of the principle of relative frequency in language.* Cambridge: Harvard University Press.

———. 1935. *The psycho-biology of language.* Boston: Houghton Mifflin.

Author Index

Languages Index

Languages Index

Spanish, 11, 12, 38, 68, 69, 81, 87, 90,
101, 102, 126, 130, 131, 132, 133,
136, 137, 181, 184, 190, 202, 207,
213, 222, 224, 227, 234, 235, 239,
263, 289, 296, 298. *See also* Old
Spanish
  Alicante, 102
  Castilian, 85
  León dialect, 225, 235
  Mexican, 235
Swedish, 70

Tahitian, 53, 55, 64, 79, 80, 84, 93, 95,
128, 142, 143, 212, 221, 276, 277,
278
Tanga, 82, 168
Tem, 58, 65, 84, 90, 93, 129, 143, 245,
252, 267, 268, 276
Temne, 64, 82, 143, 182, 183, 185, 188,
189, 258, 276
Thai, 204
Tibetan, 95
Tigre, 32, 56, 64, 82, 83, 142, 143, 144,
146–47, 148, 206, 207, 209, 220,
229, 230, 245, 252, 262, 263, 277,
278
Tojolabal, 65, 84, 90, 93, 128, 154, 252,
267, 268
Tok Pisin, 30, 58, 71, 74, 82, 118, 128,
129, 154, 164, 168, 169, 183, 188,

189, 190, 245, 252, 253, 254, 255,
270, 271, 272
Touareg, 58, 84, 93, 142, 220, 229, 275
Trukese, 53, 58, 66, 67, 75–76, 84, 93,
154, 159, 168, 172, 173, 182, 206,
208, 212, 220, 222, 245, 253, 270,
271, 275
Tucano, 57, 58, 65, 66, 67, 95, 96, 97, 98,
103, 129, 135, 153, 182, 186, 207,
248, 252, 267, 268
Turkic languages, 127
Turkish, 52, 59, 95, 96, 141

Udmurt, 56, 79, 80, 82, 95, 97, 102, 143,
158, 276
Uigur, xv, 65, 84, 93, 98, 143, 168, 188,
189, 191, 206, 207

Worora, 82, 84, 90, 93, 153, 154, 165,
182, 188, 189, 191, 206

Yagaria, 53, 58, 64, 79, 80, 84, 93, 94,
143, 144, 145, 148, 154, 211, 220,
228, 229, 245, 252, 262, 263, 275
Yessan-Mayo, 58, 60, 143, 153, 154, 159,
164, 168, 169, 182, 220, 221, 229,
245, 252, 253, 263, 275
Yoruba, 127, 141

Zuni, 82, 129, 143, 182, 252, 267, 268

Subject Index